5, 7, 8, 9, 11, (12)

MATHEMATICAL PROGRAMMING FOR ECONOMIC ANALYSIS IN AGRICULTURE

BIOLOGICAL RESOURCE MANAGEMENT

A Series of Primers on the Conservation and Exploitation of Natural and Cultivated Ecosystems

Wayne M. Getz, Series Editor
University of California, Berkeley

Adaptive Management of Renewable Resources, by Carl Walters
Building Models for Wildlife Management, by Anthony Starfield and
   A. L. Bleloch
Mathematical Programming for Economic Analysis in Agriculture, by Peter B. R.
   Hazell and Roger D. Norton
Range Economics, by John P. Workman

MATHEMATICAL PROGRAMMING FOR ECONOMIC ANALYSIS IN AGRICULTURE

PETER B. R. HAZELL

International Food Policy Research Institute

ROGER D. NORTON

University of New Mexico
Oklahoma State University

MACMILLAN PUBLISHING COMPANY
NEW YORK

Collier Macmillan Publishers
LONDON

Macmillan Publishing Company
866 Third Avenue, New York, NY 10022

Collier Macmillan Canada, Inc.

Printed in the United States of America

printing number   year
1 2 3 4 5 6 7 8 9 10   6 8 7 8 9 0 1 2 3 4 5

Library of Congress Cataloging-in-Publication Data

Hazell, P. B. R.
    Mathematical programming for economic analysis in
agriculture.

    Bibliography: p.
    Includes index.
    1. Agriculture—Econometric models—Linear pro-
gramming. 2. Agriculture—Developing countries—
Econometric models—Linear programming. I. Norton,
Roger D., 1942–   II. Title.
HD1433.H39 1986   338.1'0724   85-23085
ISBN 0-02-947930-4

Contents

Foreword

From the earliest days, quantitative methods have played a more crucial role in agricultural economics as a field of study than in any other area of applied economics. The scope of quantitative studies was understandably constrained when computations were made using pencil and paper, hand-powered calculators, or even electrically driven desk calculators. The advent of high-capacity electronic computers allowed researchers to conduct systematic analyses of vastly more complex empirical problems. With the very recent introduction and rapid spread of high-speed microcomputers, it is now entirely feasible for decision makers to conduct sophisticated analyses of their own rather than to rely wholly on the work of others.

The primary constraint on relevant and useful quantitative analysis has shifted from the mechanics of the solution process to the analyst's skill in design of appropriate structures for the question at hand. This book provides both traditional and innovative methods for approaching questions of interest to individual farmers and managers of agricultural marketing firms or to policy analysts who are charged with the responsibility of evaluating the impacts of alternative policy choices that may be under consideration. For each of these groups, the ability to select an appropriate frame for analysis and to mold the model in such a way that a large number of possible events can be considered is of great importance.

Linear programming has proven to be one of the most powerful tools for analysis of resource allocation choices at the firm and sector level. The introduction of nonlinear methods, multiple time period systems, and structures that make it possible to consider risk in the selection of enterprise combinations represent major contributions in programming analysis. The present volume is organized in a way that allows the reader to progress, in an understandable and logical fashion, from simple models to those of increasing complexity. It is equally suitable for advanced undergraduate and graduate students or for use by policy analysts who seek tools that will provide the fast turnaround time necessary for responding to day-to-day policy requests.

Widespread use of the analytical models developed in this book can serve to greatly enhance the quality of policy analysis available to ministries of agriculture in developing countries as well as in offices having access to the most powerful main-frame computers. The insights needed for decision making at the farm or regional level can be provided only by considering a variety of scenarios. This book offers guidelines to facilitate the construction of models that generate such insights at reasonable computer cost. Further, the presentation is sufficiently clear that noneconomists can readily discern the role and impact of technological information they may be invited to provide as team members and thus enhance their contributions to the model design process.

A unique feature of this book is the integration of farm-level decisions with regional aggregates and the art of making viable policy choices. Discussion of the basic structure of programming models and a review of computational methods are followed by an analysis of multiperiod structures that focus on potential conflicts among competing objectives. Consideration of risk in the analysis is shown to bring about important modifications of results generated under a risk-free environment.

Considerable attention is given to the problem of aggregating farms in a region. Consumption changes at the farm level in response to market price and interdependencies among products in the market and on the farm are examined. Methods for introducing market demand relationships and transportation and processing costs are developed and applied. The importance of model validation is explained, and the authors provide useful tests that they have found to be workable.

The range of policy issues that can be addressed using mathematical programming methods is illustrated through a variety of practical examples. Policy analysis is an art that must be practiced. The creative application of mathematical programming methods throughout this book is a reflection of the authors' technical competence and a demonstration of the potential contributions of quantitative agricultural policy analysis.

Richard A. King
Raleigh, North Carolina

Acknowledgments

Many individuals have worked with us over the years in applying the models presented in this book and in helping develop some of the concepts. We are grateful to them all. A special note of thanks is due to both Leopoldo Solís, Chairman of Mexico's Council of Economic Advisors, and Louis Goreux, now of the International Monetary Fund, who sponsored and encouraged the work on the Mexican model that was one of the points of departure for this odyssey. Dean Schreiner of Oklahoma State University encouraged us to write this book and helped to get the effort off the ground. Richard King of North Carolina State University, Rafael Celis of the International Food Policy Research Institute, and Vittorio Santaniello of the University of Rome read the manuscript and offered many valuable suggestions for improvements.

We wish to acknowledge with thanks the important contributions of our former colleagues in the Development Research Center of the World Bank who, as the text shows, participated in the development of some of the central ideas in this book: Wilfred Candler, Apostolos Condos, John Duloy, Gary Kutcher, and Pasquale Scandizzo.

Numerous other colleagues have shared with us the excitement and frustrations of developing the models mentioned in this book or have played key roles in seeing that the models were built and used. There are too many to mention all individually, but we would like to acknowledge especially the contributions of Bayoumi Attia, Nicole Ballenger, Luciano Barraza, Luz María Bassoco, Ronald Brousseau, Richard Burcroff, Carlo Cappi, Celso Cartas, Enrique Delgado, Julio Echevarría, Hasan Gencaga, Hunt Howell, Tariq Husain, Cassio Luiselli, Alan Manne, Carlos Pomareda, Henri Quaix, Teresa Rendón, Vittorio Santaniello, José Silos, Santiago Sindich, Javier Tellez, the late Hernán Tenorio, Rodney Vissia, and Donald Winkelmann. Also, critical assistance in making these models computable was provided by Roberto Cánovas, Richard Inman, Vinh Le-Si, Selchuk Marmara, Alexander Meeraus, and Malathi Parthasarathy. Marcella Dekker managed cheerfully and outstandingly well the laborious process of typing and revising the manuscript. In that process she was assisted ably by Sonia Regalado.

The applied models discussed most fully in the latter part of the book were sponsored by the Interamerican Development Bank, the International Food Policy Research Institute, the Mexican Government, the Secretariat for Economic Integration in Central America, the United Nations Development Program, the United Nations Food and Agriculture Organization, the United States Agency for International Development, and the World Bank.

We thank Oklahoma State University and the United States Agency for International Development for having sponsored part of the writing of this book and the University of New Mexico for having provided research facilities.

Parts of this book are adaptations of previously published material. Section 4.7 is taken from the Appendix to J. H. Duloy and P. B. R. Hazell, "Substitution and Nonlinearities in Planning Models" in *Economy-Wide Models and Development Planning* (C. R. Blitzer, P. B. Clark, and L. Taylor, eds.), Oxford University Press, 1975. Sections 8.5 and 12.8.3 are adapted from Chapters 3 and 16, respectively, of R. D. Norton and L. Solís, *The Book of CHAC: Programming Studies for Mexican Agriculture*, Johns Hopkins University Press for the World Bank, 1983. Permission from the publishers to use these materials is gratefully acknowledged.

Several tables and figures are also taken from other publications. The sources are cited at the appropriate places in the text, but we wish to express our gratitude to the *American Journal of Agricultural Economics*, the *Journal of Policy Modeling*, Johns Hopkins University Press, and the Macmillan Press, Ltd., of London and Basingstoke for permission to copy these materials.

Chapter 1

Introduction

1.1 THE PURPOSE AND SCOPE OF THE BOOK

Mathematical programming has been used in agricultural economics for more than 30 years. It has become such a useful tool of analysis that its basic principles are taught in all colleges of agricultural economics, and its applications have been spreading geographically, particularly in the last decade. Programming models for agriculture have been used in a large number of developed and developing countries.

In the last 10 to 15 years there also have been a number of methodological advances in this field. The improvements have been in the direction of incorporating more economic theory and observed institutional and economic reality into the models. The more noteworthy advances have occurred in the areas of modeling consumer demand, market equilibrium in both product and factor markets, risk and risk aversion, and the role of instruments of economic policy. The profession's ability to model decisions of the farming household has improved as well. The cumulative effect of these advances has been to provide a tool of analysis that is much more adaptable to different situations and a potentially more realistic portrayal of agricultural reality.

This book draws together many of the recent methodological contributions in the field, and it also provides a reasonably comprehensive review of the state of the art as regards agricultural programming models at the farm and the sector levels. Two principal aims have guided the writing of the book: to provide a textbook of the relevant theory and methodology, and to provide detailed guidelines for practitioners regarding the process of building and implementing these models. To be useful, a model has to be well grounded in theory, but it also has to fulfill many practical requirements. It has to be appropriate to the problem at hand and to the available data, it requires an appropriate institutional framework, and the economics must be expressed in the model in an appropriate and interpretable way.

Models provide the link between economic theory and data, on the one hand, and practical appreciations of problems and policy orientations, on the other. They are imperfect abstractions, but by virtue of their logical consistency frameworks they can provide the analyst and policy maker with a valuable economic representation of the sector and a laboratory for testing ideas and policy proposals. However, experience has shown that the construction of a model requires not only a grasp of the relevant economics and an understanding of the issues to be addressed, but also a familiarity with sound techniques of building and applying models. Yet these techniques are rarely stressed in university curricula, and for agricultural programming models there are very few workshops that the practitioner can attend. Given the frequency with which agricultural models are built, and the fact that they usually are fairly complex constructions, this gap is an important one. Hence a central focus of this book is on technique, both for building and for applying models. A subsidiary aim is to provide an appreciation of the range of possible applications that have been and can be made with these models.

The book is intended for students, practitioners, and researchers. It is suitable for individual reading and for use in university courses. The theory and techniques presented are usable in widely differing situations, in both industrialized and developing countries. Existing texts give little attention to developing countries, so we have used a number of illustrations from case studies in those countries.

The presentation is generally aimed at the level of the master's student who has some familiarity with quantitative techniques. A few sections are more accessible to the Ph.D. student. The mathematical proofs in those sections may be omitted without loss of understanding of either the economics or the model-building procedures. The level of economic and mathematical preparation required includes microeconomic theory, introductory calculus, and linear algebra, except for the above-mentioned proofs which require multivariate calculus. Chapters 5 and 10, which deal with risk, also require some knowledge of basic statistics. For the student interested in a concise presentation of the relevant mathematical theory, a self-contained appendix is provided which develops the mathematics of linear programming with emphasis on economic interpretations. On the other hand, the reader who is looking for an introduction to linear programming for farm models will find all the material in Chapters 2, 3, and 6 accessible without much mathematics. The same can be said for Chapters 11 and 12 which concern practical techniques for building and using sector models.

The book is organized in three parts. The first part (Chapters 2 to 6) lays the microeconomic foundations for most of the rest of the book, with emphasis on modeling farm-level production functions and farmers' objectives. It also introduces the ways of organizing information in a linear programming framework, and discusses the principles and procedures for obtaining and interpreting a model's solution. Part II provides the model framework at the sector level, along with some additional theory for modeling market equilibrium and practical procedures for model construction and validation. Part III discusses the principles underlying useful applications and gives many examples of applications.

In algorithmic terms, the material is written for use in the context of either linear or nonlinear programming algorithms. Common examples of the latter are quadratic programming and mixed integer programming. However, for the treatment of risk, consumer demand, and the objective function, emphasis is placed on linear programming, because it still is the most widely available algorithm and because it has some advantages in interpretability and it is amenable to extension to the general equilibrium case. As the material in this book shows, linear programming models are not necessarily linear in the economic behavior they represent.

1.2 THE AGRICULTURAL PROGRAMMING MODEL

Mathematical programming in agriculture had its origins in attempts to model the economics of agricultural production, including its spatial dimension. The mathematical programming format—sometimes known as process analysis or activity analysis—is a particularly suitable one for agriculture. Farmers, agronomists, and other agricultural specialists share a common way of thinking about agricultural inputs and outputs in terms of the annual crop cycle, and about input-output coefficients per acre or hectare or other unit of land. Yields are conceived of in tons or bushels per land unit, fertilizer applications in kilograms per hectare or like units, and so on. In farm-level cost-of-production studies, input costs are typically disaggregated into labor, machinery services, draft animal services, fertilizer costs, other chemical costs, credit costs, etc., per land unit. For this way of visualizing agriculture production in numbers, it is but a short step to forming the column vectors of inputs and outputs that constitute the backbone of the programming model.

Similarly, agriculturalists often pose their problems in terms of inequality constraints, such as upper bounds on seasonal resource availability. And they are accustomed to the existence of slack resources in some seasons while the same resources are fully utilized in other seasons. This kind of thinking fits naturally into an analysis via programming models. For these reasons, experience has shown that it is feasible to review the production coefficients of a model directly with field experts, and to either verify or revise them accordingly. While the model has a mathematical expression, much of its empirical content is accessible to experts in other professions.

Thus the programming model provides a rather natural framework for organizing quantitative information about the supply side of agriculture, whether at the farm level or the sector level. Indeed, one of the uses of a model is to help reconcile initially inconsistent data (as discussed in Chapter 11).

Other uses of the model often involve different kinds of sensitivity analysis. At the farm level, the model can be useful in calculating the implications of different resource endowments, different market conditions, improved or new technologies, etc. This kind of information is generated by the model via variations in parameter values, with a new solution obtained for each set of parameter values.

At the sector level, parametric variations can be used to generate response functions that are implicit in the model's structure. Examples are factor substitution surfaces, supply response functions, response functions associated with particular policy instruments, and so forth. When used in this way, the model becomes a device for translating micro-level (farm-level) information into macro-level (sector-level) functions that are more familiar to many economists. At both the farm level and sector level, the model's solution also assigns valuations to fixed resources, such as land and water supplies, whose prices may not reflect their economic values.

It may be asked why the supply response functions are not taken from econometric studies. At the sector level, a set of estimated supply and demand functions can indicate equilibrium levels of production and prices, toward which the sector would tend to move. Supply functions are estimated in agriculture, and of course they can be quite useful in understanding the sector's behavior. The main problem with relying only on econometrics is twofold: data difficulties and changes in underlying economic structure. The data problem arises because, in many cases, large numbers of crops compete for the available fixed resources, and, therefore, cross-supply effects are important components of the supply functions. Normally there are not enough degrees of freedom in a time series data set to estimate both own and cross-supply elasticities. This is especially true in developing countries. Also, aggregate time series on production are often quite unreliable, again especially in developing countries. The programming model relies on cross-sectional farm budget data, which usually are more reliable, and other micro-level information to generate supply functions.

The question of changes in economic structure applies especially to technologies of production, market opportunities, and prices. Public policies can influence all of these, and in the policy options analyzed with the model, policy instruments may need to take on values lying outside the range of values observed historically. This possibility can make it unwise to base policy analyses on extrapolations from historically estimated parameters. Also, programming models can be used to analyze the consequences of direct changes in economic structure, such as those that would arise from the introduction of new crop varieties or from land reform that changes the size distribution of farms. The consequences of these kinds of changes are difficult to capture in econometric models of supply, and yet failure to do so means that the estimated supply elasticities are not reliable if the structural changes are introduced.

In addition to these considerations, a programming model's supply functions provide information on associated responses of inputs, such as labor, agrochemicals, and the like. Seasonality of the responses also is taken into account. Thus the study of supply response by means of a programming model can answer many policy-oriented inquiries and not just provide supply elasticities. Other examples of policy applications can include evaluations of comparative advantage, assessment of the employment effects of different policies, generation of input demand functions, and joint evaluation of sets of investment projects. These and other applications of sector models in several countries are discussed in Chapters 12 and 13.

When the transition from farm model to sector model is made, an important shift occurs in the model's role, and that shift has not always been recognized by model builders. At the farm level, the programming model is explicitly a *normative* or *prescriptive* tool. The decision maker, who may be the farmer himself, specifies his decision rule (profit maximization, cash-flow improvement, profit maximization subject to risk aversion, etc.), and the model helps simulate the consequences of that decision rule and the associated constraints on the farmer's choices. On the other hand, in a decentralized economy there is no single decision maker at the sector level. There are basically two levels of decision makers, the policy makers and the farmers, whose interests do not necessarily coincide. A model's solution that is designed, say, to maximize agricultural export earnings will give an export-intensive cropping pattern but it will not indicate which, if any, policies exist that will induce farmers to adopt that cropping pattern. To deal adequately with maximization of a policy goal, the model would have to contain a specification of policy instruments and also a set of relationships that describe how producers will react to possible policy changes.

As discussed in Chapter 7, it is difficult to specify mathematically and solve this two-level policy problem, and so in many cases it is more productive to develop a model that will help explain producers' reactions to external changes. While the policy model alone is normative, this second kind of model is *descriptive* or *positive*. Among other things, the descriptive model can be solved under different assumptions about policy parameters, and the corresponding solutions provide some information about the consequences of policy changes. For these reasons, this book places most of its emphasis on developing the descriptive model, although parts of Chapters 7 and 12 discuss the policy model.

Since policy goals are not necessarily the farmers' goals, the descriptive model must be set up to maximize something other than a policy goal function. On the other hand, if, for example, all producers aimed to maximize profits, then a sector model that maximized aggregate profits would not be correct either, for it would give the monopolistic outcome. This is the well-known paradox of the competitive market. For the model a different kind of objective function is needed, one that drives its solution to a market-equilibrium outcome in the presence of downward-sloping demand curves. These matters are taken up in the last part of Chapter 7 and in Chapters 8 and 9. Extensions to the case of simulating market equilibrium under risk are given in Chapter 10, on the basis of the farm level risk analysis given in Chapter 5.

A common thread through all the chapters is the emphasis on ways of putting economics into agricultural models. Properly constructed, programming models can reflect a wide range of economic and institutional behavior, and they can be powerful tools of analysis. They provide an analytic and empirical link between economic theory and observed behavior. We hope this book helps stimulate others to continue with the challenging task of matching theory with the real world.

Part One

The Farm Model

Chapter 2

Mathematical Programming and the Farm Model

2.1 INTRODUCTION

Individual farmers must repeatedly make decisions about what commodities to produce, by what method, in which seasonal time periods, and in what quantities. Decisions are made subject to the prevailing farm physical and financial constraints, and often in the face of considerable uncertainty about the planning period ahead. Uncertainty may arise in forecasted yields, costs, and prices for the individual farm enterprises, in enterprise requirements for fixed resources, and in the total supplies of the fixed resources available.

Traditionally, farmers have relied on experience, intuition, and comparisons with their neighbors to make their decisions. Formal techniques of budgeting and comparative analysis have been developed by farm management specialists, and these can be useful aids for making decisions in less complex situations or for analyzing selected decisions when all the other farm decisions are taken as given. It is only with the more recent advances in computers and in mathematical programming software that satisfactory procedures have been developed for whole-farm planning in more complex situations.

Whole-farm planning can assist farmers in efficiently adapting to a changing economic and technological environment. There are many examples of this normative use of linear programming in the literature.[1] Surprisingly, though, optimization models which adequately articulate the goals and constraints of representative farmers also can often predict quite accurately what these farmers do. This is particularly true in more stationary situations where farmers have time to adapt to the economic and technological environment. It is this predictive possibility of representative farm models that makes them useful for inclusion in agricultural sector models intended for aggregate policy analysis.

In its simplest form, linear programming is a method of determining a profit maximizing combination of farm enterprises that is feasible with respect to a set of fixed farm constraints. Early applications of linear programming in farm planning assumed profit maximizing behavior, a single-period planning horizon (no growth), and a certain environment (no uncertainty about prices, yields, and so forth).[2] As we shall see, there have been many subsequent developments that permit the construction of more flexible and realistic models, but we defer these developments until following chapters. This chapter is devoted to a discussion of the structure and solution of single-period, deterministic linear programming models. Emphasis is placed on the linear programming aspect of the farm model, and the economics of the model are developed more fully in Chapters 3, 4, and 5.

2.2   A SIMPLE MODEL

For a given farm situation the linear programming model requires specification of:

1   The alternative farm activities, their unit of measurement, their resource requirements, and any specific constraints on their production
2   The fixed resource constraints of the farm
3   The forecast activity returns net of variable costs, hereafter called gross margins.

To formulate the problem mathematically we introduce the following notation:

X_j = the level of the jth farm activity, such as the acreage of corn grown. Let n denote the number of possible activities; then $j = 1$ to n.

c_j = the forecasted gross margin of a unit of the jth activity (e.g., dollars per acre).

a_{ij} = the quantity of the ith resource (e.g., acres of land or days of labor) required to produce one unit of the jth activity. Let m denote the number of resources; then $i = 1$ to m.

b_i = the amount of the ith resource available (e.g., acres of land or days of labor).

With this notation, the linear programming model can be written as follows:

$$\max Z = \sum_{j=1}^{n} c_j X_j \qquad (2.1)$$

such that

$$\sum_{j=1}^{n} a_{ij} X_j \le b_i, \qquad \text{all } i = 1 \text{ to } m \qquad (2.2)$$

and

$$X_j \ge 0, \qquad \text{all } j = 1 \text{ to } n \qquad (2.3)$$

In words, the problem is to find the farm plan (defined by a set of activity levels X_j, $j = 1$ to n) that has the largest possible total gross margin Z, but which does not violate any of the fixed resource constraints (2.2), or involve any negative activity levels (2.3). This problem is known as the primal linear programming problem.

The problem defined by (2.1) to (2.3) is portrayed in Table 2.1, a matrix showing all the coefficients of the algebraic statement of the model. By convention, this way of presenting a linear programming model is called a tableau. Several conventions have been introduced in Table 2.1. First, the equation to be maximized is called the objective function. In the current problem the objective function is total gross margin (2.1), but other objective functions are also possible. Second, the constraints are called rows and the activities are called columns. Third, the fixed resource supplies, the b_i coefficients, are called the right-hand side, or RHS, of the problem. They have all been stipulated as less than or equal ($\le$) constraints, though it is also possible to include equality constraints ($=$) or greater than or equal ($\ge$) constraints.

The nonnegativity requirements (2.3) are not included in Table 2.1. By convention they are taken for granted in such linear programming tableaux.

To fix ideas, Table 2.2 portrays a simple linear programming model for a small farm in a hypothetical country called Mayaland.

Table 2.1 A Linear Programming Tableau

Row name	Columns				RHS
	X_1	X_2	$\ldots$	X_n	
Objective function	c_1	c_2	$\ldots$	c_n	Maximize
Resource constraints:					
1	a_{11}	a_{12}	$\ldots$	a_{1n}	$\le b_1$
2	a_{21}	a_{22}	$\ldots$	a_{2n}	$\le b_2$
$\vdots$	$\vdots$	$\vdots$	$\ldots$	$\vdots$	$\vdots$
m	a_{m1}	a_{m2}	$\ldots$	a_{mn}	$\le b_m$

Table 2.2   The Mayaland Farm Model

Row name	Corn (ha)	Beans (ha)	Sorghum (ha)	Peanuts (ha)	RHS
Objective function (pesos)	1372	1219	1523	4874	Maximize
Land (ha)	1	1	1	1	≤ 5.0
Labor (months)	1.42	1.87	1.92	2.64	≤ 16.5
Mules (months)	1.45	1.27	1.16	1.45	≤ 10.0
Market constraint (tons)	—	—	—	0.983	≤ 0.5

Four crops can be grown each year—corn, beans, sorghum, and peanuts —each of which has specified per hectare requirements for labor and mules. For example, production of 1 hectare of corn requires 1.42 months of labor and 1.45 months of draft animal services (mules). A total of 16.5 months of labor is potentially available, being the amount provided by family workers during the year. The farm family owns a mule, and this is capable of providing 10 months of draftpower service during the year.

The activity gross margins in the objective function are similar for each unit (hectare) of corn, beans, and sorghum. Peanuts are much more profitable though, with a gross margin of 4874 pesos per hectare. Unfortunately, the farmer faces a limited market for peanuts and can sell no more than 0.5 tons each year. This constraint is portrayed in the last row of Table 2.2. Since a hectare of peanuts yields 0.983 tons of product per hectare, the constraint limits the farmer to growing at most $0.5/0.983 = 0.509$ hectares of peanuts.

The link between the tableau and algebraic formulations of the model can also be illustrated with the Mayaland example. Letting X_1 = corn, X_2 = beans, X_3 = sorghum, and X_4 = peanuts, then the algebraic version of the model becomes:

$$\max Z = 1372\, X_1 + 1219\, X_2 + 1523\, X_3 + 4874\, X_4$$

such that

$$1.0\, X_1 + 1.0\, X_2 + 1.0\, X_3 + 1.0\, X_4 \leq 5.0$$
$$1.42\, X_1 + 1.87\, X_2 + 1.92\, X_3 + 2.64\, X_4 \leq 16.5$$
$$1.45\, X_1 + 1.27\, X_2 + 1.16\, X_3 + 1.45\, X_4 \leq 10.0$$
$$0.983\, X_4 \leq 0.5$$

and

$$X_1, X_2, X_3, X_4 \geq 0$$

2.3 ASSUMPTIONS OF LINEAR PROGRAMMING

A number of assumptions about the nature of the production process, the resources, and activities are implicit in the linear programming model (2.1) to (2.3).

1 *Optimization.* It is assumed that an appropriate objective function is either maximized or minimized. In the Mayaland example total gross margin is maximized.

2 *Fixedness.* At least one constraint has a nonzero right hand side coefficient.

3 *Finiteness.* It is assumed that there are only a finite number of activities and constraints to be considered so that a solution may be sought.

4 *Determinism.* All c_j, a_{ij}, and b_i coefficients in the model are assumed to be known constants.

5 *Continuity.* It is assumed that resources can be used and activities produced in quantities that are fractional units.

6 *Homogeneity.* It is assumed that all units of the same resource or activity are identical.

7 *Additivity.* The activities are assumed to be additive in the sense that when two or more are used, their total product is the sum of their individual products. That is, no interaction effects between activities are permitted.

8 *Proportionality.* The gross margin and resource requirements per unit of activity are assumed to be constant regardless of the level of the activity used. A constant gross margin per unit of activity assumes a perfectly elastic demand curve for the product, and perfectly elastic supplies of any variable inputs that may be used. Constant resource requirements per unit of activity are equivalent to a Leontief production function (that is, a linear ray through the origin).

The assumptions of additivity and proportionality together define linearity in the activities, thereby giving rise to the name linear programming. They also define linear isoquants in factor use between pairs of activities. Perhaps most importantly, additivity and proportionality lead to an aggregate whole farm production function relating the value of the objective function Z and the fixed resources b that has constant returns to scale. We can write this aggregate relation as $Z = f(b)$, and constant returns to scale means that if all the fixed resources are increased by a factor of proportionality k, then the value of the objective function Z also increases by k. Specifically, $f(kb) = kf(b) = kZ$.

Since

$$Z = \sum_j c_j X_j$$

and the c_j coefficients are constants, it follows that

$$kZ = \sum_j c_j (kX_j)$$

Thus, if the supplies of the fixed factors are increased by a factor of proportionality k, then the optimal activity levels also increase by k. For example, if all the resource supplies are doubled, then all the activity levels in the optimal solution will also double, as well as the optimal value of the objective function Z. Constant returns to scale always apply in a linear programming model.

An important property of production functions exhibiting constant returns to scale is known as Euler's theorem. This states that if each factor is valued at its marginal product, then the sum of the factors multiplied by their marginal products is equal to total output. This theorem implies that in the optimal solution to a linear programming model, the sum of each b_i multiplied by its marginal value product exactly exhausts the value of the objective function Z.

The assumptions underlying the linear programming model are stringent. Fortunately, while these assumptions must hold for all the rows and columns of a model, they do not have to hold for the farm production processes themselves. Many ingenious methods of increasing the flexibility of the model are possible without violating the assumptions. For example, linearity between inputs and outputs can be relaxed in modeling the production of an individual crop or livestock product by incorporating several activities which, taken together, provide a piecewise linear approximation to observed nonlinear relations. Activities can also be defined to represent mixed enterprises (for example, intercropped corn and beans) to relax the additivity requirement and allow joint production and complementary or supplementary relationships between crops. The fixedness assumption can be relaxed through dynamic multiperiod specifications which allow for farm growth and changes in the resource constraints over time. Also, methods have been developed for modeling stochastic c_j, a_{ij}, and b_i coefficients and for incorporating less than perfectly elastic input supplies.

These and other modifications of the model will be taken up in Chapters 3, 4, and 5. Despite this flexibility though, it always remains true that the aggregate whole farm production function $Z = f(b)$ exhibits constant returns to scale. Euler's theorem is therefore always satisfied in an optimal linear programming solution, and this leads to the important topic of duality.

2.4 DUALITY

The primal problem defined by (2.1) to (2.3) can assist a farmer in deciding which farm enterprises to select, and how much of each to produce if he wishes to maximize his total gross margin. Further increases in total gross margin are only possible if the farmer can acquire additional units of the fixed resources. This raises an important question—how much should the farmer be willing to pay to rent an additional unit of each resource? Clearly he would wish to avoid paying too much since he would then lose money. On the other hand, if he undervalued the resources this might lead him to rent fewer resources than he can profitably use.[3] If additional units of the fixed resources are used in a profit-maximizing way, then there ought to be a unique rental value that can be assigned to each resource. From economic theory we know that this value is the marginal value product. In the linear programming literature these values are called shadow prices.

It is possible to specify a linear programming model to find the optimal shadow prices for the fixed resources. Let λ_i denote the shadow price of the ith fixed resource, then a related problem to (2.1) to (2.3) can be defined as:

$$\min W = \sum_{i=1}^{m} b_i \lambda_i \tag{2.4}$$

such that

$$\sum_{i=1}^{m} a_{ij} \lambda_i \geq c_j, \qquad \text{all } j = 1 \text{ to } n \tag{2.5}$$

and

$$\lambda_i \geq 0, \qquad \text{all } i = 1 \text{ to } m \tag{2.6}$$

In words, we seek to assign shadow prices to the farm resources b_i that yield the lowest possible value W for the total endowment of the fixed resources. This minimization avoids the problem of overvaluing the resources. In order not to assign too low a rental value to the farm resources, (2.5) requires that the total value of the resources used by one unit of each activity X_j, $j = 1$ to n, is not less than the gross margin c_j earned by that activity. The inequalties in (2.6) impose the self-evident requirement that the selected shadow prices are not negative.

Model (2.4) to (2.6) is mathematically closely related to the primal problem (2.1) to (2.3). In fact, (2.4) to (2.6) is called the dual problem to (2.1) to (2.3).

Table 2.3 portrays the dual problem for the Mayaland farm problem of Table 2.2. Note that the coefficients in Table 2.3 are the transpose of those in Table 2.2, in that the rows and columns of Table 2.2 become the columns and rows, respectively, of Table 2.3. There is therefore a symmetric relationship between the two problems. Also, both tables contain exactly the same data.

These relationships between the primal and dual problems are not mere curiosities, and in fact there is a rigorous connection between the two problems that is important in linear programming theory. These relationships are developed formally in the appendix to this book, but here a brief, somewhat intuitive discussion of them is given. Readers who already are comfortable with concepts of dual variables and shadow prices may wish to skip to the next section. (Note: the level of mathematics required in this section is a bit higher than that required in the rest of this chapter and the following two chapters.)

The primal linear programming problem always satisfies Euler's theorem, which says that the value of the output must equal the sum of values of all

Table 2.3   The Dual Model for the Mayaland Farm

	Marginal Values				
Row name	Land (pesos / hectare)	Labor (pesos / month)	Mules (pesos / month)	Market (pesos / ton)	RHS
Objective function (pesos)	5.0	16.5	10.0	0.5	Minimize
Corn (ha)	1	1.42	1.45	—	≥ 1372
Beans (ha)	1	1.87	1.27	—	≥ 1219
Sorghum (ha)	1	1.92	1.16	—	≥ 1523
Peanuts (ha)	1	2.64	1.45	0.983	≥ 4874

inputs, when those inputs are valued at their true opportunity costs. It follows that if the fixed resources are valued at their marginal value products (or shadow prices), the total rental value assigned to the inputs of the farm, $W = \Sigma_i b_i \lambda_i$, must exactly exhaust total output (gross margin) $Z = \Sigma c_j X_j$. Given optimal solutions to a pair of primal and dual problems, it is not surprising, therefore, that $Z^* = W^*$, where stars designate optimal values. Put another way, the maximum value of the objective function of the primal problem (2.1) is always equal to the minimum value of the objective function of the dual problem (2.4).

The shadow prices λ_i are also sometimes called Lagrangean multipliers. As discussed in the appendix, Lagrangean multipliers were introduced origi- nally in order to facilitate the solution of a maximization problem with constraints. If, for example, the problem is

$$\max Z = c_1 X_1 + c_2 X_2 + c_3 X_3$$

subject to

$$a_{11} X_1 + a_{12} X_2 + a_{13} X_3 = b_1$$
$$a_{21} X_1 + a_{22} X_2 + a_{23} X_3 = b_2$$

then Joseph-Louis Lagrange (1736–1813) showed that its optimal solution is the same as the solution to the following problem which has *no* constraints:

$$\max \mathscr{L} = \{ c_1 X_1 + c_2 X_2 + c_3 X_3 + \gamma_1 (b_1 - a_{11} X_1 - a_{12} X_2 - a_{13} X_3) + \gamma_2 (b_2 - a_{21} X_1 - a_{22} X_2 - a_{23} X_3) \}$$

In his honor, $\mathscr{L}$ is called the Lagrangean function and the variables γ_i are called Lagrangean multipliers. The numerical solution to Lagrange's refor- mulated problem can of course be found by methods of classical calculus, that is, by taking partial derivatives of the function $\mathscr{L}$ and setting them equal to zero:

$$\frac{\partial \mathscr{L}}{\partial X_1} = c_1 - a_{11}\gamma_1 - a_{21}\gamma_2 = 0 \tag{2.7a}$$

$$\frac{\partial \mathscr{L}}{\partial X_2} = c_2 - a_{12}\gamma_1 - a_{22}\gamma_2 = 0 \tag{2.7b}$$

$$\frac{\partial \mathscr{L}}{\partial X_3} = c_3 - a_{13}\gamma_1 - a_{23}\gamma_2 = 0 \tag{2.7c}$$

$$\frac{\partial \mathscr{L}}{\partial \gamma_1} = b_1 - a_{11}X_1 - a_{12}X_2 - a_{13}X_3 = 0 \tag{2.7d}$$

$$\frac{\partial \mathscr{L}}{\partial \gamma_2} = b_2 - a_{21}X_1 - a_{22}X_2 - a_{23}X_3 = 0 \tag{2.7e}$$

The solution in the five variables X_1, X_2, X_3; γ_1, γ_2 is given by simultaneous solution of the five linear equations (2.7a) to (2.7e). Thus a maximization problem has been reduced to a simultaneous equations problem.

Notice, however, that the five equations decompose into two subsets. The first subset, equations (2.7a) to (2.7c), is overdetermined, so one equation must be redundant. The second subset is underdetermined, and hence there will be no unique solution. In general, this outcome will occur with Lagrange's method *unless* the number of constraints is equal to the number of variables.

Equations (2.7a) to (2.7c) are equivalent to the dual constraints (2.5), when the latter hold as equalities. Similarly, equations (2.7d) and (2.7e) are equivalent to the primal constraints (2.2), when they hold exactly. Intuitively, these equivalences suggest that at optimality the γ_i in (2.7a) to (2.7c) are the dual variables, or shadow prices, which in fact they are.

A century and a half later, Harold Kuhn and A. W. Tucker generalized Lagrange's method so that it applied to problems with inequality constraints. Without going into the details of their mathematics, their main results can be stated briefly. They developed conditions that characterize the solution to the primal problem (2.1) to (2.3), which are as follows (see appendix):

$$\frac{\partial \mathscr{L}_P}{\partial X_j} = c_j - \sum_i a_{ij}\gamma_i \leq 0 \tag{2.8}$$

and

$$\frac{\partial \mathscr{L}_P}{\partial \gamma_i} = b_i - \sum_j a_{ij}X_j \geq 0 \tag{2.9}$$

where $\mathscr{L}_P$ is the Lagrangean of the primal problem:

$$\mathscr{L}_P = \sum_j c_j X_j + \sum_i \gamma_i \left(b_i - \sum_j a_{ij} X_j \right).$$

Similarly, the Lagrangean of the dual problem (2.4) to (2.6) is:

$$\mathscr{L}_D = \sum_i b_i \lambda_i + \sum_j \mu_j \left(c_j - \sum_i a_{ij} \lambda_i \right)$$

where μ_j, $j = 1$ to n, are new Lagrangean multipliers, and the relevant Kuhn-Tucker conditions for the dual are:

$$\frac{\partial \mathscr{L}_D}{\partial \mu_j} = c_j - \sum_i a_{ij} \lambda_i \leq 0, \qquad (2.10)$$

and

$$\frac{\partial \mathscr{L}_D}{\partial \lambda_i} = b_i - \sum_j a_{ij} \mu_j \geq 0. \qquad (2.11)$$

Clearly (2.8) and (2.10) are closely related, as are (2.9) and (2.11). In fact, if $\gamma_i = \lambda_i$, for all i, and $\mu_j = X_j$, for all j, then the Kuhn-Tucker conditions will be identical for the two problems. Given that the optimal values of the objective functions of the primal and dual problems are identical, it is not surprising that in fact the corresponding Kuhn-Tucker conditions can be shown to be identical. Also, the first set of Kuhn-Tucker conditions for the primal (equation 2.8) is in fact the dual constraint set (equation 2.5), and vice versa.

We arrive, therefore, at an important result: if after solving the primal problem the Lagrangean multipliers (the γ_i) can be extracted from the solution, these will be the shadow prices (the marginal value products or the λ_i) of the fixed resources of the farm. This information will then be available without having to solve the dual problem separately.

Similarly, if we solve the dual problem, then the Lagrangean multipliers (the μ_j), will be the optimal values of the activity levels (the X_j) of the primal problem. Again it is only necessary to solve a single problem to obtain the solutions to both the primal and the dual problems.

Apart from describing the primal–dual relationships, the Kuhn-Tucker conditions often are of great interest themselves, for they constitute a set of simultaneous equations that characterizes the optimal solution. In their complete form as equations rather than inequalities, they are nonlinear (see appendix), and they are more numerous than the constraints of the primal problem, so we normally do not try to use these conditions to *solve* the optimization problem numerically. If, however, we want to study the analytic properties of part or all of the model, the Kuhn-Tucker conditions can be helpful.

2.5 PRINCIPLES OF SOLVING LINEAR PROGRAMMING PROBLEMS

The solution to a linear programming problem is usually a unique farm plan in terms of the optimal activity levels chosen. However, the mathematics of finding this solution is not easy, because there are generally an infinite number of farm plans to choose from that satisfy the resource constraints. To develop ideas it is useful to resort to geometry.

Consider the following linear programming problem:

$$\max Z = 5X_1 + 6X_2$$

such that

$$2X_1 + 3X_2 \leq 12 \qquad \text{resource } b_1$$

and

$$6X_1 + 5X_2 \leq 30 \qquad \text{resource } b_2$$
$$X_1, X_2 \geq 0$$

If we plot the activity levels on the axes of a graph, then the constraints of this problem can be portrayed as in Figure 2.1.

Each constraint is represented by a straight line which intersects the axes at the maximum level of each activity that can be produced with the assumed supply of the associated resource. For the jth activity and the ith resource, the maximum activity level is b_i/a_{ij}. For example, the line for b_1 cuts the X_1 axis at $12/2 = 6$ units, and the X_2 axis at $12/3 = 4$ units. Intermediate points along a constraint depict linear combinations of the activities that also exactly

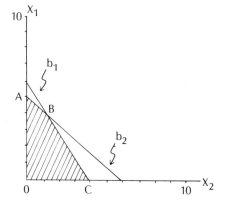

Figure 2.1 The feasible set.

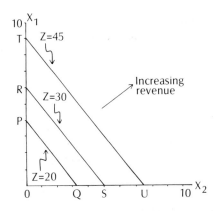

Figure 2.2 Isorevenue lines.

exhaust the resource. One permissible combination for b_1 is 3 units of X_1 and 2 units of X_2. The amount of b_1 used is then $(2)(3) + (3)(2) = 12$. Another possible combination is 5 units of X_1 and $((12) - (2)(5))/3 = 0.667$ units of X_2.

For a farm plan to be eligible for consideration as the optimal solution to the linear programming problem, it must be feasible (i.e., not use more of a resource than the available supply) for all of the resource constraints. In Figure 2.1 this limits consideration to those combinations of X_1 and X_2 contained in the shaded area $OABC$. ABC is known as the production possibility frontier; it defines the maximum amounts of X_1 and X_2 that can be produced for all possible ratios of the levels of these activities.

To identify the optimal farm plan in Figure 2.1 we need to introduce the objective function Z. This is done by drawing isorevenue lines which define the combinations of X_1 and X_2 that can be used to attain some fixed amount of total gross margin Z. In Figure 2.2, PQ is the isorevenue line corresponding to $Z = 20$. Since X_1 has a gross margin of 5, the isorevenue line intersects the X_1 axis at $X_1 = 4$. Similarly, since X_2 has a gross margin of 6, the isorevenue line cuts the X_2 axis at $X_2 = 3.33$. An isorevenue line can be drawn for any desired value of Z. For example, RS and TU in Figure 2.2 are isorevenue lines corresponding to $Z = 30$ and $Z = 45$, respectively. Isorevenue lines are always parallel, and the ones corresponding to larger values of Z always lie above and to the right of those corresponding to smaller values of Z.

As we want to maximize Z, the optimal farm plan is clearly the feasible plan that lies on the highest attainable isorevenue line. In Figure 2.3 isorevenue lines have been superimposed on the set of feasible farm plans from Figure 2.1. The highest isorevenue line touches the production possibility frontier at B. B is therefore the optimal solution to the linear programming problem. It calls for the production of 3.75 units of X_1 and 1.5 units of X_2, and yields a total gross margin of 27.75.

One approach to solving linear programming problems is to graph them carefully as in Figure 2.3, and then to read off the optimal solution. The

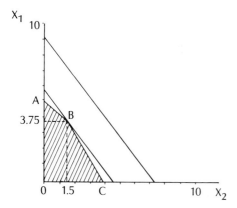

Figure 2.3 The optimal solution.

approach works well for two activities, but it quickly becomes unmanageable once three or more activities are introduced.

Another approach is to evaluate the total gross margin Z of each feasible farm plan, and to select the one with the largest value of Z. Since the number of feasible plans is infinite, this approach is not strictly possible. We could introduce some short cuts though. In the first place, it should be obvious from Figure 2.3 that the optimal farm plan will always lie on the production possibility frontier ABC. This means that we can limit consideration to those farm plans that use up all of one or more resources. This still leaves an infinite number of plans to consider, but we could further limit ourselves to a random sample of farm plans lying on the production possibility frontier, and hope that this sample would contain a plan that was close to the optimal plan. Solution procedures of this kind have been developed, and they are generally classified as simulation techniques in the literature [for example, Anderson (1974) and Thompson (1967)].

The difficulties with the approach are that (1) identification of the optimal plan is not assured, and (2) the cost of evaluating a large enough sample of farm plans to provide some assurance of getting close to the optimal plan can be prohibitive, particularly when solving large models. For these reasons, mathematical solution procedures have been developed which search for the optimal solution in a rigorous and efficient way.

Dantzig (1963) developed the simplex method for solving linear programming problems in 1947. Although this procedure has since been revised and extended to improve its computational efficiency for modern computers, the principles of the solution procedure remain unchanged. The mathematics and the computational procedures of the simplex method are extensively reviewed in such texts as Hadley (1962) and Heady and Candler (1958). In this chapter we limit ourselves to a brief and largely heuristic treatment of the simplex method.

The key to the simplex method is to reduce the feasible farm plans that need to be considered to a finite number. Suppose that in Figure 2.3 we were to rotate the isorevenue line to reflect alternative ratios of the activity gross margins. It should be clear that the optimal solution for each rotational shift must not only lie on the production possibility frontier ABC, but typically it will be either point A, B, or C. Some ambiguity arises if the isorevenue line is exactly parallel to either segment AB or BC. However, in each case any plan lying on the segment yields the same value of Z, so one can choose a plan lying at the end of the segment as the optimal solution. These end-point solutions are again A, B, and C.

Farm plans like A, B, and C are called basic solutions. Their number is always finite regardless of the size and complexity of the problem. Furthermore, if a unique optimal solution to the problem exists, it is always a basic solution. In the event that more than one optimal solution exists, there is always a basic solution that is as good as any other optimal solution. Given these properties, the search for an optimal farm plan can be restricted to the finite number of all possible basic solutions.

Basic solutions have some additional properties that are utilized by the simplex method. To understand these we need to introduce the notion of slack activities. An inequality constraint such as

$$\sum_j a_{ij} X_j \le b_i$$

can always be written as a strict equality by introducing a new (and nonnegative) activity S_i such that

$$\sum_j a_{ij} X_j + S_i = b_i$$

The activity S_i is known as a slack activity. It represents the amount of the ith resource not used in the farm plan.

Returning to Figure 2.1, note that at point A all of resource b_2 is used up, but some b_1 remains unused. In terms of the corresponding slack activities, this means that $S_1 > 0$ and $S_2 = 0$. Plan A also calls for complete specialization in the production of X_1, so that $X_1 > 0$ and $X_2 = 0$. Collecting the activities that are nonzero, we can characterize point A as a farm plan consisting of X_1 and S_1. We shall write this as (X_1, S_1).

In similar fashion point B corresponds to a farm plan (X_1, X_2). Both resources are fully used up in this plan, $(S_1 = S_2 = 0)$, while production is diversified to include both X_1 and X_2. Likewise point C is the farm plan (X_2, S_2). Note, too, that the zero solution is also basic, corresponding to the nonzero activities (S_1, S_2).

A pattern begins to emerge. Each basic solution consists of a unique combination of nonzero activities once the slack activities have been introduced.[4] Furthermore, there are always exactly as many activities in a basic solution as there are constraints to the original problem. We now have the necessary requirements for a solution procedure. They can be summarized as follows:

Step 1 Introduce slack activities to permit converting all inequality constraints to equalities.

Step 2 Choose an initial basic solution. The solution (S_1, S_2) will suffice.

Step 3 For each activity not in the initial basic solution, calculate the change in Z that would occur if one unit of that activity were brought into the solution. Since the number of activities in a basic solution is always the same, then the new activity can only be introduced into the solution if an activity previously in the basis is given up. The losses and gains involved in these substitutions must be fully accounted for in measuring the impact on Z. Call the resultant change in Z the opportunity cost of each activity.

Step 4 If all opportunity costs are zero or negative, then the starting solution is already optimal and the procedure can terminate. However, if at least one opportunity cost is positive, the solution can be improved. This is done by bringing into the solution the activity with the largest opportunity cost and removing an inferior activity. The level at which the new activity can be entered depends on additional calculations, but feasibility must always be observed. Once these calculations are performed return to Step 3.

Each pass through Step 4 is known as an iteration.

In the next section we consider the detailed calculations involved in the simplex method to obtain an optimal solution. In Chapter 6 we show how to set up a problem for solution on the computer.

2.6 SIMPLEX CALCULATIONS

The calculations performed with the simplex method can conveniently be organized in a table. Table 2.4 shows the steps for solving the Mayaland farm problem of Table 2.2.

The central columns of the table are the slack activities for the farm resources (the S_j) and the cropping activities (the X_j). The corresponding c_j coefficients (the objective function coefficients) are found in the top row of the table at the head of the activity columns. These coefficients are zero for the slack activities.

2.6.1 First Block

The calculations begin with the choice of an initial basic solution, which is entered in the first block of the table. The rows in this block correspond to the crop or slack activities included in the starting basis. We have chosen to start with the solution in which all the resources are idle, and all the crop activities

Table 2.4 The Simplex Calculations for Solving the Mayaland Farm Problem

c_j:			0	0	0	0	1372	1219	1523	4874	
			Slack activities				Crop activities				
c_i	Resource or activity at nonzero level	Activity level	S_1	S_2	S_3	S_4	X_1	X_2	X_3	X_4	R
0	S_1	5	1	0	0	0	1	1	1	1	5
0	S_2	16.5	0	1	0	0	1.42	1.87	1.92	2.64	6.250
0	S_3	10.0	0	0	1	0	1.45	1.27	1.16	1.45	6.897
0	S_4	0.5	0	0	0	1	0	0	0	0.983	0.5086
	Z	0	0	0	0	0					
	ΔZ						1372	1219	1523	4874	
0	S_1	4.4914	1	0	0	−1.0173	1	1	1	0	4.4914
0	S_2	15.1573	0	1	0	−2.6857	1.42	1.87	1.92	0	7.8944
0	S_3	9.2625	0	0	1	−1.4751	1.45	1.27	1.16	0	7.9849
4874	X_4	0.5086	0	0	0	1.0173	0	0	0	1	∞
	Z	2478.9									
	ΔZ		0	0	0	−4958.32	1372	1219	1523	0	
1523	X_3	4.4914	1	0	0	−1.0173	1	1	1	0	
0	S_2	6.5338	−1.92	1	0	−0.7325	−0.5	−0.05	0	0	
0	S_3	4.0525	−1.16	0	1	−0.2950	0.29	0.11	0	0	
4874	X_4	0.5086	0	0	0	1.0173	0	0	0	1	
	Z	9319.3									
	ΔZ		−1523	0	0	−3408.97	−151	−304	0	0	

24

are zero. The first four rows of Table 2.4, therefore, correspond to the slack activities S_1 to S_4, and these activities enter the farm plan at levels defined by the right-hand side coefficients. The levels are shown in the activity level column in the table.

The coefficients in the activity columns are the resource requirements for a unit of each activity. The coefficients for the crop activities are taken directly from Table 2.2. Those for the slack activities are simply zero or one; the latter occurring at the intersection of a slack column with its own row.

The solution in which all the resources are left idle has a total gross margin Z of zero. Since all the crop activities have positive gross margins (c_j) it must be possible to attain a higher value of Z. The next step is to select the crop activity which would add most to Z if one unit were introduced into the farm plan. To identify this activity we need to calculate the change in Z (denoted by ΔZ) that would result from adding one unit of each activity.

Consider the activity X_1. If one unit of this activity were brought into the farm plan then we would have to give up 1.0 unit of S_1, 1.42 units of S_2, and 1.45 units of S_3. Let c_i denote the gross margin of the ith slack activity, then the amount of Z foregone to grow one unit of X_1 is the sum 1.0 c_1 + 1.42 c_2 + 1.45 c_3. In return, a unit of X_1 would add 1372 to Z, so the net change in Z is

$$\Delta Z = 1372 - 1.0\, c_1 - 1.42\, c_2 - 1.45\, c_3$$

Since the gross margins of the slack activities are all zero, ΔZ reduces to the gross margin of X_1. Similarly, the ΔZ values for all the other crop activities in Table 2.4 are equal to their corresponding gross margins, and these values are entered in the last row of the first block in Table 2.4. Note that similar calculations performed for the slack activities lead to zero entries in the ΔZ row.

The activity with the largest ΔZ value is X_4, so this activity is chosen to enter the farm plan. Two questions now arise. How much X_4 should be brought into the farm plan, and which of the existing activities should it replace? As it happens, the answer to the first question automatically resolves the second.

Since a unit of X_4 requires 1 unit of S_1 and there are only 5 units of S_1 in the initial farm plan, then at most 5 units of X_4 can be introduced. This amount is entered in the column headed R in Table 2.4. Similarly, X_4 requires 2.64 units of S_2 and only 16.5 units are available. The second entry in the R column is therefore $16.5 \div 2.64 = 6.25$. Comparable calculations give R values of 6.897 and 0.5086 for S_3 and S_4, respectively.

The smallest R value is 0.5086 in the S_4 row. This is the maximum amount of X_4 that can be entered in the farm plan while still retaining feasibility. At this level of X_4, all of S_4 is displaced from the farm plan, so S_4 is the activity that is replaced.

2.6.2 Second Block

In the second block of Table 2.4 we first enter X_4 in place of S_4 in the fourth row at a level of 0.5086 units in the activity level column. How does this affect the level of the remaining activities S_1 to S_3 in the farm plan?

A unit of X_4 uses 1 unit of S_1, so 0.5086 units of X_4 use 0.5086 units of S_1. As S_1 entered the previous farm plan at 5 units, then $5 - 0.5086 = 4.4914$ units remain in the new plan. Similarly, $16.5 - (0.5086)(2.64) = 15.1573$ units of S_2 remain, and $10.0 - (0.5086)(1.45) = 9.2625$ units of S_3 remain. The new farm plan therefore consists of 4.4914 units of S_1, 15.1573 units of S_2, 9.2625 units of S_3, and 0.5086 units of X_4. The corresponding value of Z is 2478.9. All of this information is entered in the left-hand column of the second block in Table 2.4.

The next step is to update the coefficients in the main body of the table. These coefficients should indicate, for each column, the amounts of each activity in the new plan that would have to be foregone if a unit of the column activity were introduced into the plan.

Let us begin again with the column for X_1. In the first block of Table 2.4 we see that X_1 requires 1.0, 1.42, and 1.45 units of S_1, S_2 and S_3, respectively, but that it does not use any S_4. Since S_1, S_2, and S_3 are still in the farm plan then a unit of X_1 can be introduced into the new plan without displacing any X_4. The coefficients for X_1 in the second block are therefore the same as before. The same result applies for X_2 and X_3 because they do not use any S_4 either.

The new coefficients for X_4 are all zero except for a unit entry at the intersection of the X_4 column with its own row. This indicates that an extra unit of X_4 would have to displace an existing unit of X_4 because of the limitations of the market constraint. Similarly, the coefficients for S_1, S_2, and S_3 are also zero except for unit entries in their intersecting columns and rows. This is always true for an activity that is in the farm plan.

Turning now to S_4, this activity has been displaced from the plan and its coefficients are no longer simply 0 or 1. In order to reinstate a unit of S_4 in the farm plan it would be necessary to forego some X_4 in order to free up the required unit of b_4. Since a unit of X_4 uses 0.983 units of b_4 then a unit of S_4 would require the displacement of $1 \div 0.983 = 1.0173$ units of X_4. This amount becomes the entry in the second block of Table 2.4 for the intersection of the X_4 row with the S_4 column. Now S_4 does not use any other resources, but the displacement of 1.0173 units of X_4 would release $(1)(1.0173) = 1.0173$ units of S_1, $(2.64)(1.0173) = 2.6857$ units of S_2, and $(1.45)(1.0173) = 1.4751$ units of S_3. These numbers, preceded by a negative sign, become the relevant entries in the remaining rows of the S_4 column.

We are now in a position to ask again if the farm plan can be improved by bringing in a new activity. The calculation of the ΔZ values for a unit of each activity in the second block proceeds as before. The ΔZ values for X_1, X_2, and X_3 are again their unit gross margins, because the c_i values associated with their nonzero coefficients are all zero. The ΔZ values for all the activities in the current plan are also zero, since they displace exactly one unit of themselves.

The ΔZ value for S_4 turns out to be negative. It is calculated as

$$\Delta Z = 0 - (-1.0173)(0) - (-2.6857)(0) - (-1.4751)(0) \\ - (1.0173)(4874) = -4958.32$$

A negative ΔZ value implies that total gross margin Z would be reduced if the activity were entered into the solution.

X_3 has the largest ΔZ value so this activity should be brought into the solution. Computing the relevant R ratios, we see that S_1 is the limiting row, and that at most 4.4914 units of X_3 can be introduced into the plan.

2.6.3 Third Block

Activity X_3 is entered in the third section of Table 2.4 at the level of 4.4914 and S_1 is displaced from the plan. Activities S_2, S_3, and X_4 remain in the plan, but their levels have to be adjusted to reflect the resources used by X_3. These adjustments are calculated as before, but now using the coefficients in the second rather than the first block of Table 2.4.

Since X_3 had a coefficient of 1.92 in the S_2 row of the second block, the new level of S_2 in the farm plan is

$$15.1573 - (1.92)(4.4914) = 6.5338$$

This is the level of S_2 in the previous plan minus the unit requirements of X_3 for S_2 multiplied by the level of X_3 in the new farm plan.

Similarly, the new levels of S_3 and X_4 are, respectively,

$$9.2625 - (1.16)(4.4914) = 4.0525$$

and

$$0.5086 - (0)(4.4914) = 0.5086$$

These calculations can be generalized. The new level of an activity in the plan is always the previous level minus the unit requirements of the incoming activity for that activity or resource (as measured in the previous block of the table) multiplied by the level of the incoming activity.

Given these activity levels and their associated c_i values, the total gross margin Z for the new plan is 9319.3.

We can now proceed to update the coefficients under the activity columns in the third block of Table 2.4. We begin again with the column for X_1. In the second block of Table 2.4 we see that X_1 requires one unit of S_1, but this resource is now fully utilized in the farm plan. To introduce X_1 into the plan would therefore require that we give up some X_3. How much? Since X_3 also has a unit coefficient in this row, then the amount displaced would be exactly 1. This value becomes the entry in the X_3 row under column X_1 in the third block of Table 2.4. Then since X_3 required 1.92 units of S_2 in the previous block, displacing a unit of X_3 would release 1.92 units of S_2. But a unit of X_1 requires 1.42 units of S_2, so the difference -0.5 is the relevant entry for X_1 in the S_2 row in the third block. It is the amount of S_2 that would be released if a unit of X_1 were substituted for a unit of X_3 in the new plan. Similarly, the X_1 entries for the S_3 and X_4 rows are $1.45 - 1.16 = 0.29$ and $0 - 0 = 0$, respectively.

Similar calculations are performed for all the other activity columns in the table.

2.6.4 Generalizations

By now the reader may have noticed that a general pattern has emerged in these calculations. The procedure can be summarized as follows. First, the coefficients in the row of the incoming activity are always the coefficients of the outgoing row in the previous block divided by the coefficient that occurs at the intersection of the outgoing row and the incoming activity. This latter coefficient is known as the pivot.

In calculating the coefficients for the X_4 row in the second block of Table 2.4 the pivot was 0.983. This is the coefficient occurring at the intersection of the outgoing row S_4 and the incoming column X_4 in the first block of the table. Similarly, in computing the coefficients for the X_3 row in the third block, the relevant pivot is 1.0. This is the coefficient that occurs at the intersection of the outgoing row S_1 and the incoming column X_3 in the second block. Because the new pivot is 1.0, the coefficients in the X_3 row in the third block are the same as those in the S_1 row of the second block.

Second, the remaining coefficients in a new block also can be systematically derived. Consider the new entry for the ith row and the jth column. It is the i,jth coefficient in the previous block minus the product of the new coefficient in the incoming row for the jth column and the coefficient in the ith row under the incoming activity in the previous block. For example, the entry for X_1 in the S_3 row in the third block is calculated as the corresponding entry in the second block (1.45), minus the product of the new entry for X_1 in the X_3 row (1) and the previous requirement for S_3 by X_3 (the incoming activity) in the second block (1.16). This evaluates as $(1.45) - (1)(1.16) = 0.29$. Similarly, the coefficient for column S_4 in the S_3 row of the third block is calculated as

$$-1.4751 - (-1.0173)(1.16) = -0.2950$$

2.6.5 The Optimal Solution

Having calculated all the coefficients in the third block of Table 2.4, we again compute the ΔZ values for each activity. This time they are all either zero or negative, indicating that Z cannot be increased by bringing any other activity into the farm plan. Thus we have attained the optimal plan for the Mayaland farm. It consists of 4.4914 hectares of X_3 (sorghum), 0.5086 hectares of X_4 (peanuts), and it leaves 6.5338 months of S_2 (labor) and 4.0525 months of S_3 (mules) idle. The total gross margin is 9319.3 pesos. This optimal solution has been attained with only two iterations of simplex calculations.

In addition to indicating that an optimal solution has been reached, the ΔZ values provide further useful information. The ΔZ values on the slack activities are the shadow prices for the associated resources. They indicate how much Z would change if a unit of the resource were put into slack, or equivalently, if an additional unit of the resource could be procured. The ΔZ values on the crop activities indicate by how much the per hectare gross margin would have to be increased before the activity could be introduced into the farm plan without reducing Z.

2.7 COMPUTATIONAL DIFFICULTIES IN LINEAR PROGRAMMING

Linear programming problems cannot always be solved. In some cases an optimal solution may simply not exist. This may happen if the problem is infeasible or unbounded. In other cases, an optimal solution may exist, but the simplex procedure may converge only slowly, or not at all, because of degeneracy problems. We turn now to a discussion of each of these problems.

2.7.1 Infeasibility

A linear programming problem is said to be infeasible if there is no single solution that satisfies all the constraints. As a simple example of infeasibility, suppose that to the Mayaland farm problem of Table 2.2 we were to add an additional constraint requiring that the area of corn grown must exceed 5 hectares. In this case there would be an immediate conflict with the land constraint and there would not be a feasible solution to the problem.

Infeasibilities usually arise in practice because of mistakes in preparing the data for a linear programming problem. In large and complex problems they may also arise because the analyst fails to take adequate account of all the logical relations within the model.

2.7.2 Unboundedness

A linear programming problem is said to be unbounded if a feasible solution exists that has an infinite value for the objective function. A simple example would arise in the problem in Table 2.2 if the requirements by corn for land, labor, and mules were set to zero. In this case an infinite amount of corn could be grown without violating any of the constraints, and the objective function would be unbounded. Unboundedness is most commonly encountered because of errors in preparing the data for a linear programming problem.

2.7.3 Degeneracy

In Section 2.6, our description of the simplex procedure proceeded on the assumption that, at each iteration, there would always be a unique activity to bring into the basic solution which would add most to the value of the objective function. It was also assumed that the objective function would be increased at each iteration until an optimal solution is reached. These assumptions will not always hold.

Degeneracy exists in a problem if the value of the objective function does not change when moving from one iteration to the next. This happens when the best incoming activity can only enter the basis at zero level. Another problem associated with degeneracy is that of ties. A tie occurs when there are two or more possible incoming activities at a given iteration that are equally good in terms of the resultant increase in the objective function.

When degeneracy is present, one can no longer be sure that the simplex procedure will converge through a series of unique iterations to an optimal solution. Degeneracy does not affect the existence of an optimal solution,[5] but the number of iterations required to reach it may be so immense as to be impractical. In extreme cases, degeneracy may lead to cycling, whereby the simplex calculations will keep repeating the same sequence of iterations. When this happens the optimal solution will never be attained.

In practice, degeneracy is rarely a serious problem. Modern computer packages for solving linear programming problems include procedures for breaking ties and for ensuring that cycling does not occur. However, with large and highly interconnected linear programming models, it is possible to encounter problems with slow convergence.

2.8 POSTOPTIMALITY ANALYSIS

In solving a linear programming problem, all the c_j, a_{ij} and b_i coefficients are assumed to be known constants. However, the user may not always be sure of his data, particularly his forecasts of activity gross margins. Some coefficients, such as prices and yields, may also vary from year to year because of weather or economic changes beyond the farmer's control. One way of dealing with these uncertainties in the data is to solve the model for different but realistic sets of assumptions about the data to determine the stability or robustness of the optimal farm plan. Such postoptimality analysis is also useful for evaluating longer-term farm decisions, or changes in the economic and technological environment, which affect the fixed constraints of the farm.

One way to conduct postoptimality analysis is simply to solve the model separately for each set of data assumptions. However, this can be expensive and time consuming, especially when working with a large model. A more efficient approach is to use the special postoptimality procedures provided in modern computer software packages. These procedures, which can be used to provide additional information about the stability of the optimal farm plan, are illustrated in Chapter 6 for one particular computer software package.

Parametric programming is one of the most important methods of further analysis after an initial optimum solution is obtained. This procedure allows any of the model's a_{ij}, b_i, or c_j coefficients to be varied systematically to obtain a sequence of optimal solutions. For example, the amount of land available to the Mayaland farmer is 5 hectares. Parametric programming can be used to derive a series of optimal solutions that arises if the land constraint is systematically increased beyond 5 hectares. The attractiveness of the technique is that it identifies the critical values of available land that induce new activities to enter the optimal solution. That is, it derives a sequence of basic solutions. A particularly useful property of such parametrically derived solutions is that the solution corresponding to any noncritical value of the parameterized coefficient can always be derived by linear interpolation between adjacent basic solutions. Parametric programming is discussed more fully in Section 6.4.

NOTES

1 In addition to countless applications in journals and graduate theses, there are several examples of the development of computerized systems of representative farm models for use in extension work. The more advanced systems allow individual farm data to be fed into the model and the solution to be obtained by remote access.

2 The use of linear programming in farm planning was first reported by Heady (1954) and King (1953).

3 The discussion is presented in terms of the rental value of the resources. But given the optimal rental value λ for a resource, and the current interest rate r, then the optimal purchase price for an additional unit of the resource can be calculated as λ/r.

4 It is possible for an activity to enter a basic solution at zero level. This can happen when a linear programming problem is degenerate (see Section 2.7).

5 However, it can lead to the existence of more than one optimal solution, each having the same value of the objective function.

Chapter 3

Techniques of Modeling
the Farm

3.1 INTRODUCTION

Farm planning problems are much more complex than the simple Mayaland example given in Table 2.2. Farmers not only produce different crops and livestock products, but they usually also have to chose among a variety of ways of producing them. For example, crop production may involve choices about varieties, planting dates, fertilizer and pesticide treatments, and the type of mechanization, if any, used for different cultural operations.

Fixed resources such as land and labor may be of varying qualities. Some land might be irrigable while other land may only be rainfed and therefore less suitable or less productive for some crops. Some workers may be more skilled than others, and less restricted in the range of tasks they can perform. Because of the seasonality of most farming activities, supplies of land and labor may be much more critical at some times of the year than at others.

The farmer may have options for increasing his resource supplies. These might include renting land, hiring seasonal or day laborers, or investing in new machines, buildings, and the like. On the other hand, the production options open to a farmer may be restricted by the need to observe sound husbandry practices such as crop rotations, by the farmer's desire to be self-sufficient in feeding his family, or by his desire to avoid undue risks.

Linear programming has proved a very flexible tool for modeling these and similar kinds of complexities. However, the full power of the approach depends on knowledge of a range of modeling techniques. This chapter and the one that follows are devoted to a description of useful modeling techniques for specifying deterministic farm models. We defer the problem of incorporating risk in farm models until Chapter 5.

3.2 CHOICE OF PRODUCTION METHODS

A farm model can include a wide range of production activities representing not only the different crops or livestock products, but also different ways of producing them. Some of these choices involve different technologies, defined in the sense that the assumed input-output relations of the production function, for the crop or animal, are different for each method. Such choices might involve different crop varieties and animal breeds, or irrigated versus non-irrigated crops. These kinds of choices are incorporated in a linear programming model by treating each alternative technology as a different type of crop or animal. For example, if in the Mayaland farm problem of Table 2.2 we wanted to distinguish between irrigated and rainfed corn, then it would be necessary to have two corn activities, one with the returns and resource requirements appropriate for irrigated corn, and the other having data entries appropriate for rainfed corn.

Other choices in production relate to the amount of a variable input to use per hectare or animal (e.g., fertilizer or feed), or to the combination of factors to use (e.g., labor and machines) in producing a unit of a given crop or animal product. We shall refer to these as choices of technique. They differ from technology choices in that the assumed production function for the crop or animal is not changed. These concepts are illustrated in Figure 3.1, which shows how the yield response of corn to nitrogen might differ between irrigated and nonirrigated land in Mayaland. The response relations for irrigated and rainfed corn depict different production functions, or technologies, and they show how yield can be increased (e.g., from Y_0 to Y_2) even when the rate of nitrogen use is held constant (e.g., at N_0). Each response relation shows how the yield will change as the application of nitrogen is varied. Changing the nitrogen application represents a choice of technique, or a movement along a given production function. For example, increasing the nitrogen application from N_0 to N_1 on rainfed corn increases the yield from Y_0 to Y_1.

Many technique choices involve nonlinear relations, as in the example in Figure 3.1, and it is highly desirable to incorporate such relations in farm models. As we shall see, despite the apparently restrictive assumptions of

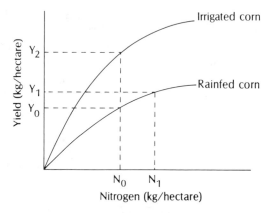

Figure 3.1 Illustration of techniques and technologies for corn.

linear programming, close approximations to nonlinear relations can easily be accommodated.

Two types of technique choices can usefully be distinguished. One type involves factor substitution relations, such as might occur when choosing between different levels of mechanization in undertaking individual cultural operations for a crop. In this case machines or work animals can be used to replace labor by choosing less labor intensive techniques. The other type of technique involves input/output response relations, such as portrayed by the choice of the rate of nitrogen use on a crop. Both types of choice of technique typically involve nonlinear relations.

3.3 FACTOR SUBSTITUTION

Suppose our Mayaland farmer of Table 2.2 can choose between weeding his corn by hand or with the aid of a mule-drawn hoe. If we define different activities to represent these alternative techniques, then the relevant part of the linear programming table might appear as follows.

	X_1 Corn weeded manually (ha)	X_2 Corn weeded by mule-hoe (ha)
Labor (months)	2.5	1.42
Mules (months)	1.0	1.45

The use of the mule-drawn hoe reduces the total labor requirement per hectare from 2.5 to 1.42 months, but increases the total mule requirement from 1.0 to 1.45 months.[1] Clearly mules and labor are partial substitutes in this formulation, and the choice of technique in an optimal solution will depend on the relative costs of mules and labor.

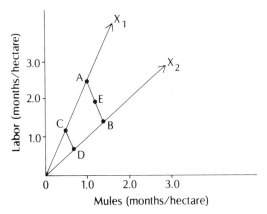

Figure 3.2 A vector diagram for corn weeding activities.

To explore more rigorously the nature of the economic assumptions underlying this formulation of the problem, we portray the problem in a vector diagram.

In Figure 3.2 the ray (or vector) OA represents the activity for manually weeded corn, X_1. The slope of this ray is the ratio of the per hectare requirements for labor to mules, i.e., $2.5 \div 1.0 = 2.5$. Any point on the ray gives the total hours of mules and labor required to produce the associated level of X_1. Point A, for example, corresponds to the production of 1.0 hectare of X_1, and requires 2.5 months of labor and 1.0 months of mules. If only 0.5 hectares of X_1 are grown then the total labor and mule requirements are exactly half, as depicted by point C where $OC = CA = \frac{1}{2}OA$.

Similarly, the ray OB represents the activity for corn weeded by a mule-drawn hoe, X_2. The slope of this ray is $1.42 \div 1.45 = 0.98$, and the ray is flatter than ray OA because X_2 is less labor intensive. Point B gives the total labor and mule requirements needed to produce one hectare of X_2. Point D gives the requirements for 0.5 hectares, where $OD = DB = \frac{1}{2}OB$.

Since points A and B both correspond to 1.0 hectare of corn then, assuming that the mechanization choice for weeding does not affect the corn yield, the output of corn will be the same at both points. Points A and B must therefore lie on the same isoquant. Any linear combination of X_1 and X_2 that also adds up to 1.0 hectare (e.g., 0.5 hectares each of X_1 and X_2) will produce an identical amount of corn. The total labor and mule requirements for such combinations of X_1 and X_2 can be represented by points that always lie on the line AB. For example point E, which is midway between A and B, corresponds to the production of 0.5 hectares each of X_1 and X_2. The total labor and mule requirements are $0.5(2.5 + 1.42) = 1.96$ and $0.5(1.0 + 1.45) = 1.225$, respectively.[2] The line AB therefore defines an isoquant for one hectare of corn. Any point on AB produces the same amount of corn, but uses a unique combination of labor and mules. The slope of AB is the marginal rate of technical substitution of mules for labor.[2]

Only two activities were included in the linear programming tableau, viz. X_1 and X_2, but since the simplex can choose either X_1 or X_2, or any linear combination of the two, then any point on the isoquant AB is clearly attainable in the model solution. Similar isoquants are attainable in the model for any other level of corn production. Line CD in Figure 3.2, for example, defines the isoquant corresponding to an output of 0.5 hectares of corn. It follows that the simple inclusion of two activities for manual and mule techniques is equivalent to incorporating a whole set of linear isoquants in the model.

What happens if additional techniques for corn weeding are introduced? Figure 3.3 is a vector diagram corresponding to four techniques, each involving different ratios of the per hectare requirements for labor and mules.

The isoquant $ABCD$ corresponds to an output of 1 hectare of corn. In this case there are three linear segments to the isoquant, each with its own marginal rate of technical substitution of mules for labor.[3] Taken together, these three segments provide a piecewise linear approximation to a curved isoquant, and it is not difficult to see that by adding more activities to the model, any desired degree of precision could be attained in approximating a given set of curved isoquants.

When activities for different techniques are included in a linear programming model in this way, at most two of the activities will be included in an optimal solution. Further, if two activities are selected, they must always be adjacent activities when ranked by their relevant factor ratios. For example, in Figure 3.3 an optimal solution may include any one of the vectors X_1, X_2, X_3, or X_4, or any one of the pairs X_1 and X_2, X_2 and X_3, or X_3 and X_4. To see why this is so consider a linear combination of activities X_1 and X_3. The resource requirements for any linear combination of these two activities can be depicted by a point, such as E, that lies on the dotted line AC. Any such point is always inferior to at least one point on the isoquant in that it requires more

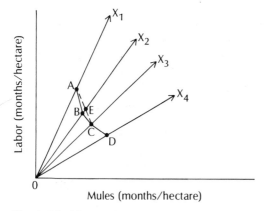

Figure 3.3 Linear approximation of curved isoquants.

of both labor and mules to produce the same amount of corn. Point B, for example, is clearly superior to point E.

In constructing Figures 3.2 and 3.3, we assumed that the choice of a weeding technique did not affect the corn yield. This type of assumption is not necessary in constructing linear programming models, and we made it only to simplify the economic interpretation of the factor substitution possibilities. If the assumption does not hold then the activities no longer approximate true isoquants, since different factor use ratios may then correspond to shifts in the underlying production function as well. That is, there is a compounding of choice of technique and choice of technology effects. This is not a problem in practical model building, and activities can be added at will to depict all realistic choices in technique, technologies or both.

Incorporating factor substitution possibilities into linear programming models usually renders the model much more flexible when solving for different prices or factor supplies. Factor substitution possibilities are commonly incorporated in models through alternative mechanization options. Other applications include choice among alternative fertilizers in meeting nutrient requirements for crops, and choice among different types of feeds required to meet the nutritional requirements of animals.

3.4 INPUT / OUTPUT RESPONSE RELATIONS

It is often necessary to model the relationship between the yield or productivity of a crop or animal and the rate of application of an input. We have already encountered an example of the response of corn yield to the rate of nitrogen application. Other examples are the yield response of a crop to weeding labor, pesticide application, or irrigation water, and the relationship between the milk yield of a cow and its consumption of concentrates. Information on such input/output relations is often available from agricultural experiment stations or from cross-sectional, farm management studies. By including these relationships in farm models, both the level of the production activity (e.g., hectares of corn) and the input (e.g., nitrogen per hectare) can be jointly determined. This considerably enhances the ability of a model to adjust realistically to changes in relative prices.

Figure 3.4 illustrates two types of input/output relations, using the yield response of corn to weeding labor as an example.

The line AB depicts a simple linear relationship between yield and weeding labor and, because the line has an intercept A, it is implied that some yield will be obtained (OA) even if no weeding is performed.

To incorporate a linear input/output relation like AB in a linear programming model requires exactly two activities. One of these should correspond to the use of zero weeding labor,[4] and the other to the use of the maximum amount of weeding labor that can realistically be used (depicted by

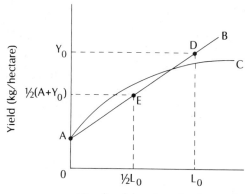

Figure 3.4 Illustrative yield response functions.

L_0 in Figure 3.4). The relevant data for the two activities are then as follows.

	X_1 Corn no weeding (ha)	X_2 Corn maximum weeding (ha)
Production (kg)	A	Y_0
Weeding labor (months)	—	L_0

If these two activities are included in a linear programming model, then an optimal solution may contain either of the two activities alone, or any linear combination of the two. Suppose a linear combination is chosen and, in particular, suppose equal amounts of X_1 and X_2 are chosen. In this case the average amount of weeding labor used per hectare will be 0.5 L_0, and the average yield will be 0.5 $(A + Y_0)$. This is exactly point E in Figure 3.4, which

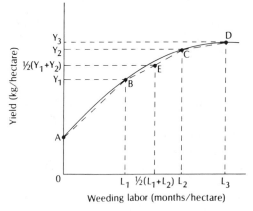

Figure 3.5 A linear approximation to a concave yield response function.

lies midway between A and D. Any other point on the line AD can also be attained in the model solution by taking appropriate linear combinations of the two activities.

The curve AC in Figure 3.4 depicts a concave input/output relation. Here the marginal productivity of weeding labor declines as more labor is used, until a point is reached beyond which additional weeding has no impact on yield.

A nonlinear relation of this kind can be incorporated in a linear programming model through a piecewise linear approximation. In Figure 3.5 we have defined three discrete levels of weeding labor use—L_1, L_2, and L_3—to each of which there is a corresponding corn yield—Y_1, Y_2, and Y_3. Four model activities can now be defined having relevant data entries as follows.

	X_1 Corn no weeding (ha)	X_2 Corn weeding option L_1 (ha)	X_3 Corn weeding option L_2 (ha)	X_4 Corn weeding option L_3 (ha)
Production (kgs)	A	Y_1	Y_2	Y_3
Weeding labor (months)	—	L_1	L_2	L_3

When included in a linear programming model, the optimal solution may contain any of the four activities alone, or any linear combination of them. If the model chooses a single activity, X_i, then for each hectare of corn produced the yield will be Y_i, and the weeding labor used per hectare will be L_i. These alternative solutions correspond to the points A, B, C, or D in Figure 3.5.

Suppose now that a linear combination of two activities is chosen, e.g., an equal mixture of X_2 and X_3. In this case the average weeding labor used per hectare will be $0.5 (L_1 + L_2)$ and the average yield will be $0.5 (Y_1 + Y_2)$. This corresponds to point E in Figure 3.5 which lies exactly midway between points B and C on the dotted line BC. Other points on the dotted line BC can also be attained in the optimal solution by taking appropriate linear combinations of X_2 and X_3. Since similar results hold for all adjacent pairs of activities, then any point on the sequence of dotted segments $ABCD$ is attainable in the model solution. In effect, this means that the original concave function AD has been approximated by a series of linear segments $ABCD$ through the use of four activities in the model. Clearly, additional activities could be defined to reduce the length of the segments, thereby providing a much higher degree of approximation to the original function.

The simplex method will never chose more than two linearizing activities, and if it chooses two, these will always be adjacent activities. In Figure 3.6, for example, a linear combination of X_2 and X_4 leading to point E will never be chosen because it is inferior to point F (obtained as a linear combination of the adjacent activities X_3 and X_4). This is because the yield at F is larger than at E, even though the same amount of weeding labor is used at both points. Similar results hold for any other combination of nonadjacent activities. This

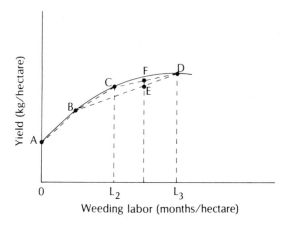

Figure 3.6 Superiority of linear combinations of adjacent activities.

result is important because it implies that the model will always seek solutions that lie on or close to the original function.

Not all nonlinear input/output relations can be linearized in this way. In particular, convex functions, such as portrayed in Figure 3.7, cannot be linearized in a linear programming model. In this case the marginal productivity of weeding labor increases as more is applied, and unlike the case of concave functions in Figure 3.6, combinations of nonadjacent activities are superior to single activities or to combinations of adjacent activities. Consider, for example, a linear combination of X_1 and X_4 leading to point E in Figure 3.7. This point is clearly superior to point B, which lies on the original function and which is obtained by choosing X_2 alone. The simplex will in fact always choose points lying on the dotted line AD, and no amount of additional segmentation will entice it to choose points lying on or close to the original function.

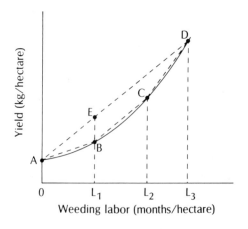

Figure 3.7 A linear approximation to a convex yield response function.

Special mixed integer programming algorithms are available which force the solution to choose either single activities or pairs of adjacent activities, and thereby to choose points lying on or near the original convex function. These algorithms are not nearly as efficient as the simplex though, particularly for large-dimensioned models. Fortunately, it is not usually necessary to include convex input/output relations in farm models. If a farmer seeks to maximize profits and the marginal productivity of an input is everywhere increasing, then it is always optimal to use as much of the input as possible.[5] This means that a single activity can be incorporated in the model representing the maximum permitted application rate of the input. The need to model convex input/output relations is more critical if the model's objective function is nonlinear, or if the supply of the required inputs is rationed.

3.5 QUALITY DIFFERENCES IN RESOURCES

Differences in the quality of resources can easily be incorporated into linear programming models by treating each resource quality as a different resource with its own set of activity requirements and right-hand side. For example, suppose the Mayaland farm of Table 2.2 has 1.0 hectare of irrigated land and 4.0 hectares of rainfed land. The land row would then be replaced by two rows as follows.

	Irrigated corn (ha)	Rainfed corn (ha)	RHS
Irrigated land (ha)	1	0	≤ 1.0
Dryland (ha)	0	1	≤ 4.0

Note that the crop activities also have to be differentiated according to whether they are irrigated or not, and this may lead to differences in yields and requirements for other resources. Some crops may only grow under irrigated conditions (e.g., paddy rice), in which case rainfed alternatives would not be included in the model.

Differences in labor skills are also commonly recognized in farm models because not all workers are equally capable of performing some tasks. For example, only some of the workers may have tractor driving skills. Another example arises in parts of Asia where tradition requires that some tasks must be performed by females (e.g., transplanting paddy). Again, children may be able to care for livestock, or to scare birds from the crops, but they may be of little help in undertaking basic field operations.

The procedure for incorporating labor skills in a model is the same as for land, though a new difficulty arises. To illustrate, suppose that local folklore requires that the weeding of corn and beans on our Mayaland farm must be undertaken by female labor, but that all other tasks can be accomplished by either male or female workers. The relevant part of the linear programming tableau may then appear as follows.

	Corn (ha)	Beans (ha)	RHS
Female labor (months)	0.3	0.2	≤ 4.0
Mixed labor (months)	1.12	1.67	≤ 12.5

Here we have assumed that the weeding of corn and beans requires 0.3 and 0.2 months of female labor, respectively, and that the total available supply of female labor is 4.0 months. The remaining tasks can be performed by either male or female labor (called mixed labor), but the available supply of mixed labor is now limited to male labor, of which there are 12.5 months. There is an obvious problem with this specification since female workers are no longer able to help with mixed labor tasks. In fact, a solution might easily be obtained in which some female labor is left idle even if the mixed labor constraint is binding.

To resolve this problem a transfer activity must be added; in this case a female labor transfer. This is done as follows.

	Corn (ha)	Beans (ha)	Female labor transfer (months)	RHS
Female labor (months)	0.3	0.2	1	≤ 4.0
Mixed labor (months)	0.12	1.67	−1	≤ 12.5

Each unit of the transfer activity takes one month of labor from the female labor row and releases it into the mixed labor row (the −1 entry effectively adds labor to the available supply of mixed labor). Note that the transfer works only in one direction; it cannot be used to transfer mixed labor to the female labor row.[6] The transfer activity may not enter the optimal solution, but its availability ensures that the mixed labor constraint will be binding only if all the female labor is also used up. Transfer activities of this type are very useful in constructing farm models, and we shall encounter them in a number of different contexts in this book.

3.6 SEASONALITY

Most cropping activities are seasonal and are confined to periods of the year when temperature and rainfall are conducive to plant growth. Within cropping seasons, cultural operations are also performed in set sequences, and most of these have to be performed within a relatively short period of time (e.g., sowing is usually performed in one or two days within a field so that the crop will grow and ripen evenly). These characteristics of farming lead to distinct seasonal patterns in resource use, and available supplies of land, labor, and other fixed factors may be fully utilized only during certain parts of the year. Table 3.1, for example, shows the monthly distribution of the labor require-

Table 3.1   Monthly Labor Requirement by Crop, Mayaland Farm

	Corn	Beans	Sorghum	Peanuts	Optimal farm plan*
			(months of labor / ha)		(total labor / month)
January	—	—	—	—	—
February	—	0.27	—	—	—
March	—	0.36	—	—	—
April	0.27	0.50	—	0.36	0.183
May	0.36	0.50	0.32	0.36	1.620
June	0.36	—	0.36	0.27	1.754
July	0.09	0.24	0.50	0.64	2.571
August	—	—	0.50	0.55	2.525
September	0.08	—	—	—	—
October	0.26	—	—	—	—
November	—	—	0.24	0.46	1.312
December	—	—	—	—	—
Total	1.42	1.87	1.92	2.64	9.965

*The optimal plan comprises 4.491 ha of sorghum and 0.509 ha of peanuts (see Table 2.4).

ments for corn, beans, sorghum, and peanuts in Mayaland. The last column of the table also shows the total labor required each month if the optimal farm plan derived in Chapter 2 were implemented by the farmer. The optimal plan only uses labor in 6 months, and these monthly requirements vary from a low of 0.183 months in April to 2.571 months in July.

If seasonal patterns of resource use are ignored in constructing a model, it is likely that the solution obtained will be unrealistic by requiring more resources in some periods than are available. The Mayaland farmer, for example, only has 16.5 months of labor available for the entire year. Since this labor is provided entirely by regular family workers, only 1.375 months of labor are available each month. Clearly the optimal plan we derived using an annual labor constraint is not realistic; it requires more than 1.5 months of labor in each of the months May, June, July, and August.

Seasonality in the use of resources is easily incorporated in a linear programming model by adding more rows; the problem is identical to the treatment of factor quality differences. In the Mayaland model, for example, the constraints on the use of land, labor, and mules could be defined monthly, and the activity requirements disaggregated as in Table 3.1.

Introducing seasonality in this way will further restrict the model solution and will likely lead to lower values of the objective function. It is therefore important to also include in the model any options the farmer has for reducing seasonal bottlenecks in resource use. One such option typically available to the farmer is to stagger the planting dates of his crops and/or fields to smooth out their total monthly labor requirements. In the Mayaland farm model we might introduce different activities for each crop to depict alternative months of planting. Corn, for example, can be planted in

Mayaland any time between March and May, so the relevant part of the revised tableau might appear as follows.

Labor (months)	Corn March planting (ha)	Corn April planting (ha)	Corn May planting (ha)	RHS
March	0.27	—	—	≤ 1.375
April	0.36	0.27	—	≤ 1.375
May	0.36	0.36	0.27	≤ 1.375
June	0.09	0.36	0.36	≤ 1.375
July	—	0.09	0.36	≤ 1.375
August	0.08	—	0.09	≤ 1.375
September	0.26	0.08	—	≤ 1.375
October	—	0.26	0.08	≤ 1.375
November	—	—	0.26	≤ 1.375

Similar monthly constraints could also be defined for land and mules.

Modeling seasonality quickly leads to much larger linear programming problems, so careful thought should always be given to the definition of the length, or number, of the periods included. The periods need not be of equal length. This means that long periods can be defined for the less busy times of year (e.g., a single period for the winter or dry season), and much shorter periods can be defined during parts of the year when resource bottlenecks are likely to occur (e.g., at planting and harvest times).

How long should the periods be? In theory, all the periods should be sufficiently short that any further disaggregation will not affect the optimal solution. Monthly constraints during the busiest times of the year are usually quite realistic, partly because farmers typically have some flexibility in scheduling the dates for each crop and operation, but also because a very temporary bottleneck can often be overcome by working harder or for longer hours. If daily or weekly constraints are defined in a model, then it is imperative to include all the options open to a farmer in meeting temporary bottlenecks, otherwise the model solution may be unrealistic because it is excessively constrained.

Sometimes, though, very short periods must be defined for some parts of the year. An example was encountered by one of the authors when modeling a small representative family farm in South India. The family farmed a single paddy field of about two acres, and for most of the year they relied entirely on family labor to undertake all of the work. However, female day labor was hired each season to assist with the transplanting of the paddy from the nursery. Calculations showed that if the transplanting was spread over a week or more, then the family female workers could perform the entire operation (only female workers are permitted to transplant paddy). Thus, if the labor constraints were defined as weekly or longer in the model, then the optimal solution would never include labor hiring. The practical problem confronting the family was the need to transplant the entire field in a single day so that the field could subsequently be irrigated and drained as a single unit. In this rather unusual case, daily labor constraints were required in the model at key times of the year in order to simulate the family's labor hiring decisions.

3.7 BUYING AND SELLING OPTIONS

Many of the resources available to a farmer are not strictly fixed because they can be supplemented through hiring or renting additional units. If the fixed supply of family labor is critical, for example, the farmer might hire additional workers. Similarly, the land area owned might be supplemented by renting additional land.

These kinds of options are incorporated in linear programming models through buying activities. Such activities typically have a negative entry in the model's objective function representing the wage or rent paid, and a -1 entry in the relevant resource row. The -1 entry indicates the supply of an additional unit of the resource; it is equivalent to adding one unit to the right-hand side of that row.

To illustrate the use of buying activities, suppose the Mayaland farmer of Table 2.2 has the options of renting additional land or hiring additional labor. The relevant part of the linear programming tableau might appear as follows.

	Corn (ha)	Renting land (ha)	Hire labor (months)	RHS
Objective function (pesos)	1372	-500	-50	
Land (ha)	1	-1		$\leq$ 5.0
Labor (months)	1.42		-1	$\leq$ 16.5

The annual land rent is assumed to be 500 pesos/hectare, and the monthly wage is 50 pesos.

If the land and labor rows were defined monthly, then the buying activities would also have to be defined appropriately. If the hired workers were available on a temporary basis then an activity would be included for hiring labor each month. However, if workers were available on a yearly basis, then a single hiring activity would be appropriate, but with a -1 entry in each of the monthly labor rows, and with the annual wage payment in the objective function. Similar principles apply for land, though in this case short term monthly leasing is hardly appropriate. Land would be rented for the entire crop season, and might appear in the tableau as follows.

	Corn (ha)	Renting land (ha)	RHS
Objective function (pesos)	1372	-500	
March land (ha)	1	-1	$\leq$ 5.0
April land (ha)	1	-1	$\leq$ 5.0
May land (ha)	1	-1	$\leq$ 5.0
June land (ha)	1	-1	$\leq$ 5.0

Buying activities are also used in farm models to provide for the purchase of direct inputs such as fertilizers or animal feeds. In the simplest models (e.g., Table 2.2) such inputs are charged to the enterprise gross margins, and they are not explicitly entered in the model. However, if the nutrient requirements of a crop or animal can be met from alternative types of fertilizers or feeds, then it may be appropriate to enter the nutrient requirements directly through new rows in the model, and to include buying activities for each type of fertilizer or feed. Expanding the model in this way then permits the nutrient requirements to be met in the least costly way.

To illustrate, suppose a hectare of corn grown by our Mayaland farmer requires 25 kg of nitrogen and 10 kg of potash. The available fertilizers are urea (46% nitrogen, 0% potash), a compound fertilizer (16% nitrogen, 10% potash), and muriate of potash (0% nitrogen, 30% potash). The appropriate part of the linear programming tableau might appear as follows, where P_u, P_c and P_m are the prices per kilogram of urea, compound, and muriate.

	Corn (ha)	Buy urea (kg)	Buy compound (kg)	Buy muriate (kg)	RHS
Objective function (pesos)	1700	$-P_u$	$-P_c$	$-P_m$	
Nitrogen (kg)	25	-0.46	-0.16	—	≤ 0
Potash (kg)	10	—	-0.10	-0.3	≤ 0

Note that the gross margin of corn has been increased since it is no longer appropriate to net out the cost of fertilizer; this is done directly through the buying activities.

An interesting feature in the above example is the introduction of rows whose right-hand side entries are zero, and whose entries include both positive and negative coefficients. Rows of this type are called balance rows, and their primary purpose is to require that the supply of an input or product must be at least as great as its demand in a model. Typically both the supply and demand are endogenous to the model, as in our fertilizer example. We shall encounter numerous applications of balance rows in the remainder of this book.

The counterpart to a buying activity is a selling activity. If a farmer has more land than he can profitably use, he may be able to rent or lease it out. Similarly, he may be prepared to work on other farms if there is insufficient work on his own farm, or to hire out his mule or tractor on a temporary basis. Selling activities can be included in a model to reflect these options. Typically they have a positive entry in the objective function representing the rent or wage received, and a $+1$ coefficient in the relevant resource row. Unlike buying activities, selling activities draw on the available resource in just the same way as a production activity.

3.8 CROP ROTATIONS

Crop rotations can be important for pest and disease control and for maintaining soil fertility. Typically they involve a definite sequence of crops. A traditional crop rotation in eastern parts of England, the Norfolk four-course rotation, involved planting land in sequence to wheat, roots, barley, and then grass for grazing by sheep or cattle. Each crop was grown for one, or at most, two years.

There are two possible ways of implementing a crop rotation of this type. One approach is to plant the entire farm to a single crop each year. In this case the same crop will only be grown again when its turn in the sequence arrives. This approach is not commonly practiced, particularly where special machines or equipment are required for individual crops, or where livestock are involved in the rotation. It is also a risky approach because the farmer is entirely dependent on the yield and price of a single crop each year.

The second approach is to divide the farm into roughly equal parts, and to rotate the crops within each part in such a way that the total acreage of each crop grown on the farm is about constant each year. This is the practice followed by most farmers who adopt a rotation.

Linear programming models are best suited to simulating the latter approach because the model solution provides the cropping pattern for a single year. However, it is always possible to interpret a solution as the average cropping pattern to be practiced over many years. This is less satisfactory, though, as it is necessary to assume that the solution will remain optimal for many years.

The technique for incorporating crop rotation requirements in linear programming models is relatively straightforward. To illustrate, suppose our Mayaland farmer wishes to adhere to a rotation in which peanuts, if grown, must be alternated with corn. The relevant part of the tableau would appear as follows.

	Corn (ha)	Peanuts (ha)	RHS
Rotation requirements (ha)	− 1	1	≤ 0

The rotation is enforced through the inclusion of a new balance row. If corn and peanuts had to be grown in equal amounts, then the constraint would be defined as a strict equality. By using an inequality constraint, the corn area can exceed the peanuts area if desired; the rotation only requires that peanuts be alternated with corn and not that all the corn has to be alternated with peanuts.

3.9 JOINT PRODUCTS AND INTERCROPPING

Many farm enterprises yield more than one product. For example, cereals provide straw as well as grains, which can be valuable for livestock feed or bedding. Dairy cows produce calves and manure in conjunction with milk, and upon their retirement, meat as well. In some cases, two or more crops may be grown together as an intercropped mixture, often with beneficial effects on yields and drought tolerance.

Joint relations of these kinds can be modeled in linear programming by incorporating single activities which, using a fixed bundle of resources, produce two or more outputs in fixed proportions. As a simple example, suppose our Mayaland farmer can grow an intercropped mixture of corn and beans. An appropriate activity for inclusion in the model might be as follows, where activities for sole stand crops are included for comparison.

	X_1	X_2	X_3
	Corn (ha)	Intercropped corn / beans (ha)	Beans (ha)
Corn (kg)	750	600	—
Beans (kg)	—	250	380
Land (ha)	1	1	1
Labor (months)	1.42	1.6	1.87
Mules (months)	1.45	1.3	1.27

Joint production activities of this type imply product/product relations which can be illustrated with the aid of vector diagrams. In Figure 3.8, the rays X_1 and X_3 represent the activities for sole-crop corn and beans, respectively. In both cases only a single product is produced, and points A and C denote the amount of corn and beans produced by one hectare of each activity (i.e., 750 and 380 kg of corn and beans, respectively). Ray X_2 represents the activity for intercropped corn and beans. In this case a single hectare leads to point B, with an output of 600 kgs of corn and 250 kgs of beans.

Since an optimal solution may include any one of the three activities, or any linear combination thereof, then a single hectare of land could produce any of the corn/bean output combinations portrayed along the linear segments ABC. Thus, ABC is the production frontier corresponding to one

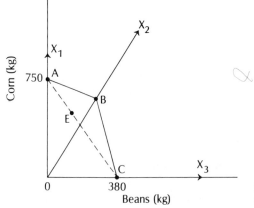

Figure 3.8 A vector diagram for pure stand and intercropped activities.

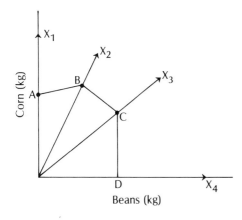

Figure 3.9 Activities to approximate different product / product relationships.

hectare of land. Points below ABC are also feasible and can be obtained by taking linear combinations of X_1 and X_3 (for example, point E). However, such points would never be chosen in an optimal solution because they are always dominated by those points on the frontier that offer more beans and/or corn without any sacrifice in either crop. Point E is dominated by point B, for example, since B yields more beans and corn from a single hectare of land.

By including a number of activities for alternative corn/bean mixtures, it should be apparent that a close approximation to a nonlinear frontier can readily be incorporated in a linear programming model. The activity yields may also be selected to provide supplementary, complementary, or substitution relations along the frontier. These kinds of relations are illustrated in Figure 3.9. Segment AB depicts a range of complementarity between corn and beans; a movement from A towards B adds to both beans and corn production. Such a relationship might exist if intercropping corn and beans leads to a positive interaction effect on the yield of each crop.

Segment BC depicts a more usual range of substitution between the two crops. Any increase in the yield of one leads to an offsetting reduction in the yield of the other. Finally, segment CD depicts a range of supplementarity along which more or less corn can be produced without any change in the yield of beans.

3.10 INTERMEDIATE PRODUCTS

Not all farm commodities are produced for sale or family consumption. Some, such as seeds, forage, and calves, are produced as intermediate products that are used in additional production activities on the farm. These products must be included in a farm model if a proper balance between their supply and demand is to be assured.

As a simple example, consider the supply of corn seed for our Mayaland farm. There are two potential sources; he may buy seed or retain some from the previous harvest. To ensure that adequate supplies are procured, it is necessary to introduce a balance row for corn seed as follows.

	Corn (ha)	Buy seed (kg)	Use own seed (kg)	Sell corn (kg)	RHS
Corn seed balance (kg)	10	−1	−1		≤ 0
Corn production (kg)	−750		1	1	≤ 0

The corn seed balance row requires that the total amount of seed purchased or retained from own production must be at least as large as the amount used. Own seed draws from a second balance row which requires that total corn production must at least exceed the total amount of corn sold or used for seed.

3.11 CREDIT AND CASH FLOW CONSTRAINTS

The available working capital required to finance purchases of seeds, feeds, fertilizers, hired labor, and other direct inputs can be an important constraint on the farm plan. Some working capital may be available from the farm family's own savings, but this can often be supplemented by borrowing.

The simplest way of introducing working capital in a farm model is to add an annual working capital constraint. In the case of our Mayaland example, the relevant part of the linear programming tableau might appear as follows.

	Crops (ha)	Borrow credit (pesos)	RHS
Objective function (pesos)	c_j	$-i$	
Credit row (pesos)	k_j	-1	≤ B

Here the k_j coefficients denote the direct cash costs of production of each crop, and B is the total amount of own funds that the farmer has available. Additional funds are available by borrowing credit at an annual interest rate i. The interest rate is charged as a cost to the model's objective function.

This formulation is quite flexible. The cash cost of any input for which there is a purchasing activity in the model can be entered directly in the credit row. Alternative sources of credit can be added as separate activities, e.g., credit from traditional money lenders, cooperatives, or banks. It is also possible to add constraints on the amount of each type of credit that can be borrowed. A bank, for example, might limit the amount of credit lent to a farmer by specifying that the ratio of the total credit to the farmer's own funds cannot exceed some given constant λ. Such a constraint would be added to the model in the following way.

	Borrow credit (pesos)	RHS
Objective function (pesos)	$-i$	
Credit row (pesos)	-1	$\leq \quad B$
Credit limit (pesos)	1	$\leq \lambda B$

A key presumption in specifying the working capital constraint on an annual basis is that all cash returns from the farm arise after all the cash inputs have been purchased. This can be a reasonable assumption if there is a single and well-defined cropping season during the year. It is a less tenable assumption if the growing seasons for different crops overlap, for then the cash proceeds from the harvest of one crop might be used to finance part or all of the cash costs of a later crop. Livestock enterprises such as milk cows and poultry can also provide a regular source of cash income, and their inclusion in the farm plan may ease the working capital constraint.

Incorporation of these concerns in a model requires tracking the seasonal, or perhaps monthly, cash flow of the farm. An example of how this is done is provided in Table 3.2.

In this example the agricultural year has been divided into three periods. Corn can be grown in any of these periods, so the corn production column should be interpreted as representing several different growing activities defined by planting date and, perhaps, by different methods of production as well. A hectare of each corn activity requires known amounts of cash inputs each period (the k_{jt} coefficients), and produces known amounts of corn (the y_{jt} coefficients). Some of these coefficients will of course be zero.

Corn production and selling activities have been separated to provide a disaggregated analysis of cash inflows and outflows. Since sales cannot exceed production, it has been necessary to incorporate a corn balance row for each period. It is implicitly assumed that all corn is sold at price p_j in the same period in which it is produced. This is not a necessary assumption. Storage activities could easily be added to transfer corn produced in one period for sale in the next. Since the revenue from selling corn is collected under the selling activities the c_j coefficients for the corn producing activities now represent the variable costs of production (hence their negative signs in the objective function row).

A cash balance row has been defined for each period. In period 1 the cash balance row requires that the initial amount of own funds available (B), plus any credit borrowed that period, must be at least as large as the working capital requirements for corn production during the period less any receipts from corn sales. However, if there is a surplus cash balance at the end of the period, this surplus can be transferred to period 2 through a cash transfer activity.

Table 3.2 Seasonal Cash Flow Constraints

	Corn production (ha)	Period 1			Period 2			Period 3			RHS
		Borrow credit (pesos)	Sell corn (kg)	Transfer cash surplus (pesos)	Borrow credit (pesos)	Sell corn (kg)	Transfer cash surplus (pesos)	Borrow credit (pesos)	Sell corn (kg)	Year-end cash balance (pesos)	
Objective function (pesos)	$-c_j$	$-i$	p_j		$-i$	p_j		$-i$	p_j		Maximize
Cash balance rows (pesos)											
Period 1	k_{j1}	-1	$-p_j$	1							$\leq B$
Period 2	k_{j2}			-1	-1	$-p_j$	1				≤ 0
Period 3	k_{j3}						-1	-1	$-p_j$	1	≥ 0
Own fund maintenance (pesos)		$-(1+i)$			$-(1+i)$			$-(1+i)$		1	$\geq B$
Corn balances (kg)											
Period 1	$-y_{j1}$		1								≤ 0
Period 2	$-y_{j2}$					1					≤ 0
Period 3	$-y_{j3}$								1		≤ 0

In period 2 the cash balance row requires that working capital requirements less the value of corn sales that period cannot exceed the opening cash balance (obtained from the first period transfer activity) plus any new credit that is borrowed. Again, any cash surplus at the end of the period can be transferred to the next period through a cash transfer activity.

The structure for period 3 is identical to that for period 2, and a cash balance transfer activity collects any year-end cash surplus. This balance must be adequate to repay, with interest, all the credit borrowed during the year and, if the farm is to survive over the years, to replenish the initial stock of own funds B. This requirement is captured in the specification of the own fund maintenance row.

Many variations on this basic model structure are possible. For example, alternative credit activities could be defined to represent loans of different duration. If any of these loans had to be repaid before the end of the year, then $1 + i$ would be entered in the cash balance row of the period in which repayment was due. In this case the corresponding $-(1 + i)$ entry would not also appear in the own fund maintenance row.

Another possible modification to the model would be to allow for the payment of farm overhead costs and the family's cash living expenses, since these may need to draw on the available cash balance in each period. If these expenses are predetermined each period, then they can simply be subtracted from the RHS coefficients of the cash balance rows. Only cash surpluses in excess of farm overhead and family living costs can then be transferred from one period to the next.

NOTES

1 Since weeding is only one of several operations involved in growing corn, the manually weeded corn still requires some mule time.
2 For those familiar with vector geometry, E is obtained as the sum of vectors OC and OD, which is equal to vector OE.
3 This concept of the marginal rate of substitution should not be confused with the more general Hicksian concept in which substitution is defined with respect to a change in the ratio of the factor prices.
4 This activity is required even if $A = 0$.
5 In production economics theory, the convex part of a production function is classified as falling in Stage I, and it is irrational to choose an input level lying in this stage.
6 A reverse transfer is possible if the transfer activity were to become negative, but this possibility is ruled out in linear programming.

Chapter 4

Advanced Techniques of Modeling the Farm

4.1 INVESTMENT ACTIVITIES

Farm investment decisions are inherently more difficult to model than the kinds of seasonal or annual cropping decisions that we considered in the previous chapter. This is because they have gestation periods extending beyond a single agricultural year, and their costs and returns are not uniformly distributed over their life. Typical investment decisions to be considered are the purchase of a machine or livestock shed, the rearing of cattle, breeding sows, or dairy cows, and the planting of tree crops such as rubber, coconuts, or coffee. In each case the largest part of the investment cost is incurred at an early stage, but the returns are spread over several (sometimes many) years. Some tree crops do not even begin to produce until after more than a decade of growth.

There are two basic approaches to modeling investment decisions in linear programming models. The first approach, which we shall call the stationary equilibrium approach, focuses on the optimal level of investments that should be attained in an equilibrium state. With this approach a model might provide information on the optimal size of a dairy herd, for example, as well as provide information on how to maintain the herd through appropriate culling and replacement policies. But the approach would offer no guidelines on how the optimal herd size should be achieved if the farmer initially has a different herd size.

The second approach, called multiperiod linear programming, takes the initial level of investments as given, and provides an optimal growth strategy for the farm which gives both the longer-term investment levels and the optimal adjustment path that should be pursued in achieving those goals. In this case a model could be used to advise a farmer in which year to buy, sell, or rear cows to adjust his herd size, as well as to define the optimal herd size he should aim for.

In both cases, linear programming solutions are only possible if investments can be treated as continuous variables. In some cases, e.g., hectares of tree crops, this condition is easily met. In other cases, such as the size of a dairy herd, the condition can be approximated by rounding off the optimal herd size to the nearest whole number. Where the condition is not reasonably met, then model solutions must be obtained through mixed integer programming algorithms.

4.2 STATIONARY EQUILIBRIUM MODELS OF INVESTMENT

To illustrate this approach to modeling investment decisions, suppose our Mayaland farmer wishes to consider investing in pigs. His intention is to obtain breeding sows and to fatten their offspring for pork using some of his corn production as feed. The problem for the model builder is to determine the optimal number of breeding sows he should carry, and whether he should rear or purchase replacements when needed. A simple linear programming tableau to address these issues is illustrated in Table 4.1.

Table 4.1   Livestock Investment Activities

	Breeding sow	Porker	Rear sow[a]	Buy sow	Corn (ha)	Sell Corn (kg)	RHS
Objective Function (pesos)	−150	2000	−180	−8000	−52	1.9	Maximize
Land (ha)	0.2		0.25		1		≤ 5.0
Labor (months)	1.1	0.5	0.9		1.42		≤ 16.5
Mules (months)					1.45		≤ 10.0
Replacement control	0.25		−1	−1			≤ 0
Litter balance	−8	1	1				≤ 0
Corn balance (kg)	300	500	350		−750	1	≤ 0

Note: All units are in numbers of animals unless otherwise indicated.
[a]A unit of replacement comprises two animals; one less than a year old, and one between 1 and 2 years old

Breeding sows are incorporated in the model through a single activity. Each sow is expected to produce eight healthy offspring per year and to require 0.25 replacements each year. That is, a breeding life of 4 years is assumed, implying that on average 25% of the sows must be replaced each year.

The replacement control row ensures that the necessary sows will be provided, either through purchase or by rearing replacements on the farm. Since a replacement sow takes up to 2 years to rear in Mayaland, it is assumed that a single unit of the replacement activity comprises two animals, one less than a year old and one between 1 and 2 years old. All the input coefficients must be calculated on this basis; that is, as the sum of the requirements of one animal in each age group.

The litter balance row requires that the number of porkers and replacements reared cannot exceed the number of piglets produced. Since the number of replacements required will be small relative to the total number of piglets produced, it is not necessary to include separate balance constraints for male and female piglets.

As corn is to be fed to the pigs, it is now necessary to include options for feeding or selling corn. To this end a corn balance row has been used which requires that the total amount of corn used or sold cannot exceed the amount produced. The coefficient for corn in the objective function does not include the value of the corn produced.

Since sows produce only intermediate products they are not credited with any revenue in the objective function. Their feed requirements are also largely met through the specified requirements for corn and land (for foraging). Consequently, the entry in the objective function is simply miscellaneous production costs (e.g., concentrates, medicines, and insemination services). Replacements also produce only intermediate products, and their entry in the objective function comprises miscellaneous production costs. The porkers are credited in the objective function with the full value of their output less all variable costs other than corn and the value of piglets.

An optimal solution to the model indicates the number of breeding sows that should be kept each year, as well as the number of replacements that must be reared or purchased to maintain the sow herd size. Since the gestation period for production is relatively short for breeding pigs, implementing the plan should not be difficult, even if the farmer initially has no pigs at all.

The situation is quite different with investments having much longer gestation periods, such as tree crops. Suppose our Mayaland farmer inherits 2.5 hectares of land on a nearby mountain and wishes to consider planting some coffee bushes on this land. He is concerned that he may not have enough labor to work his existing farm and a full 2.5 hectares of coffee.

The available coffee varieties require 5 years to mature. During this time they must be weeded and fertilized but they will not produce any revenue. In the stationary equilibrium approach, coffee would be added as another cropping activity in the model, but unlike crops such as corn, provision must be made to maintain the crop through appropriate replacement activities. The relevant columns and rows in the tableau might appear as follows.

	Productive coffee (ha)	Coffee replacement (ha)	Corn (ha)	RHS
Objective function (pesos)	5000	−100	1372	
Hill land (ha)	1	5		≤ 2.5
Low land (ha)			1	≤ 5.0
Labor (months)	3.5	0.8	1.42	≤ 16.5
Replacement control (ha)	0.1	−1		≤ 0

It is assumed that coffee bushes have a productive life of 10 years, after which they must be replaced. This constraint is entered in the model by requiring that 10% of the coffee area must be replaced each year. Note that this is not very realistic if the farmer can only plant up to 2.5 hectares, since he is likely to want to replace all the coffee bushes together at 10-year intervals. In this situation the model solution must be interpreted as the average cropping pattern that would be practiced over many years.

Unlike sows, coffee bushes do not produce a uniform stream of output over their productive years, nor do they have uniform input requirements. The coefficients in the model for productive coffee must therefore be calculated as the average coefficients for equal proportions of bushes ranging in age from 6 to 15 years. Similarly, the coefficients for coffee replacements must be calculated as the average coefficients for equal proportions of bushes ranging in age from 1 to 5 years.

The optimal solution to this problem gives the equilibrium stock of productive coffee bushes, the areas of young bushes of different ages that are necessary to maintain the productive bushes on an indefinite basis, and the optimal solution for the lowland farm. Such a solution might be useful in an agricultural sector model that purports to simulate the decisions of an aggregate of many farmers, but would it be useful for advising an individual farmer?

If our Mayaland farmer wishes to adopt the optimal solution he obviously could not hope to achieve it in less than 5 years. During that time he would not receive any income from the land allocated to coffee, and he would have to incur cash outlays for young seedlings, fertilizers, and the like, and divert labor from his lowland farm. Quite possibly, his cash flow situation would require considerable delay in adopting the optimal plan, during which time changes in the economic environment might make the plan redundant. There is also the problem that the optimal solution is derived in the model without any consideration of a time discount factor. By investing in coffee the farmer would tie up funds for many years that could be invested in annual crops or livestock on his lowland farm. If the returns from coffee were discounted to present day values, they might prove to be less attractive relative to annual crops. The timeless nature of stationary equilibrium models of investment decisions makes it difficult to introduce discount factors, consequently they may be misleading in guiding investment decisions involving long gestation periods (see, however, Section 12.8).

4.3 MULTIPERIOD LINEAR PROGRAMMING MODELS OF INVESTMENT

These models can overcome many of the limitations of the stationary equilibrium approach to modeling investment decisions. Unfortunately, they typically lead to much larger models and this greatly reduces their practical usefulness.

As their name implies, multiperiod models include two or more periods in which decisions must be made. Usually periods are defined as years, but they can also be based on longer intervals. It is not even necessary that all the periods be of equal length. Activities and constraints are included in each period for all the relevant decisions and many of these will be duplicated from one period to the next (e.g., activities for annual crops). A multiperiod model is more than a sequence of single period models though, because the investment decisions link the periods together. The objective function also provides a link between periods, and typically the discounted sum (or present-day value) of profits generated over the entire planning horizon is maximized.

Table 4.2 shows the structure of a simple multiperiod linear programming model for solving the Mayaland farmer's coffee problem. In this example, the planning horizon has been arbitrarily limited to 17 years, and only selected parts of the column and row entries are shown in the table.

A hectare of coffee has a sequence of annual gross margins and labor requirements over its 15 years of life. These are denoted by c_t and a_t respectively in Table 4.2, where t denotes the age of the bushes in years. Since coffee bushes take 5 years to mature, then c_1 to c_5 are negative and c_6 to c_{15} are positive. A hectare of coffee also ties up a hectare of land for 15 years.

In Table 4.2, provision has been made for planting coffee in each of the 17 years in the model. The relevant data coefficients for each activity enter the income and resource rows for every year of the coffee's 15-year life. Note that coffee planted in year 1 has no data entries for years 16 and 17 since the bushes would be uprooted at the end of the fifteenth year. Similarly, coffee planted in year 2 has no data entries for years 1 or 17.

Corn can be grown every year in the model, and since it is an annual crop, data coefficients only appear in the columns for the year in which the corn is grown.

The total gross margin is calculated each year through a series of counting activities and balance rows. The counting activities collect the annual gross margins into the objective function, but only after they are discounted to period 1 values. This is accomplished by multiplying all of the entries in the objective function (which would otherwise be unity) by r^{t-1}, where $r = 1/(1 + i)$, i is the discount rate, and t is the year number of the relevant activity. Thus the model's objective is the maximization of the discounted sum of the annual gross margins.

Unlike the stationary equilibrium model, there is no need to distinguish between mature trees and replacement trees in the multiperiod model to ensure that the two are in balance. The individual history of each coffee planting is now explicitly tracked over time in the model, and the decision to replace is made independently of decisions about earlier plantings. The solution to the model provides a complete decision strategy for the farmer, telling him how many hectares of coffee and corn to plant in each of the 17 years. Notice too that there is no presumption that the stock of trees will ever attain an equilibrium.

In building multiperiod models four key issues have to be resolved.

First, it is necessary to decide on the number of periods to include in the model—the length of the planning horizon. Longer planning horizons add to the size of the model, but they increase the likelihood that activity levels in the later periods of an optimal solution will converge to a set of equilibrium values. Not all multiperiod models converge to an equilibrium set of investments (see Throsby 1967). If only a few periods are included in the model then the solution to the entire planning horizon may be devoted to a series of dynamic adjustments, with little indication of the optimal long-term investment goals. In practice, the number of periods included should be larger than the longest gestation period of any of the investments.

Second, it is necessary to assign terminal values to investments that extend beyond the planning horizon. We did not do this in Table 4.2, and as a result the optimal solution would never include coffee planted in years 13 to 17. These activities only have establishment costs in the model, and the future value of their production is not captured in the objective function. An appropriate procedure to resolve this problem is to calculate, for each activity, the discounted value of all returns to be realized beyond year 17, and to include these values directly in the objective function row under the activity columns.

Third, a discount rate has to be selected. The larger the discount rate the smaller will be the present-day value of investments with long gestations, and hence the less likely it is that the optimal solution will include investments made late in the planning horizon. Because of this, the use of bank interest rates as discount factors can often lead to unrealistic model solutions. Few farmers, for example, would find it profitable to grow tree crops if they were to plan on this basis. The fact that many farmers do plant tree crops suggests that either their objectives are very different from those assumed here, or that they have low personal discount rates.

Fourth, the model should be initialized to reflect the farmer's starting investment position. In Table 4.2 we assumed that the hill land was fully available for coffee planting in year 1. Suppose though that the farmer had already planted some coffee in the previous year. In this case we would have to add another activity in each of the first 14 periods corresponding to coffee

Table 4.2 A Multiperiod Linear Programming Model

	Year 1 (Plant)		Year 2 (Plant)		⋯	Year 5 (Plant)		Year 6 (Plant)		Year 15 (Plant)		Year 16 (Plant)		Year 17 (Plant)		Activities to count total gross margin by year (pesos)									RHS
	coffee	corn	coffee	corn		coffee	corn	coffee	corn	coffee	corn	coffee	corn	coffee	corn	1	2	⋯	5	6	⋯	15	16	17	
Objective function (pesos)																1	r	⋯	r^5	r^6	⋯	r^{14}	r^{15}	r^{16}	Maximize
Year 1																									
Gross margin (pesos)	$-c_1$	1372														-1									$= 0$
Hill land (ha)	1	—																							≤ 2.5
Labor (months)	a_1	1.42																							≤ 16.5
Year 2																									
Gross margin (pesos)	$-c_2$		$-c_1$	1372													-1								$= 0$
Hill land (ha)	1		1	—																					≤ 2.5
Labor (months)	a_2		a_1	1.42	⋯																				≤ 16.5
Year 5																									
Gross margin (pesos)	c_5		$-c_4$		⋯	$-c_1$	1372												-1						$= 0$
Hill land (ha)	1		1		⋯	1	—																		≤ 2.5
Labor (months)	a_2		a_4		⋯	a_2	1.42																		≤ 16.5

Year 6									
Gross margin (pesos)	c_6	c_5	...	$-c_2$	$-c_1$ 1372		-1		$= 0$
Hill land (ha)	1	1	...	1	1 —				≤ 2.5
Labor (months)	a_6	a_5 ...		a_2	a_1 1.42				≤ 16.5 ...
Year 15									
Gross martin (pesos)	c_{15}	c_{14}	...	c_{11}	$-c_1$ 1372		-1		$= 0$
Hill land (ha)	1	1	...	1	1 —				≤ 2.5
Labor (months)	a_{15}	a_{14}	...	a_{11}	a_1 1.42				≤ 16.5
Year 16									
Gross margin (pesos)	c_{15}	c_{12}	...	c_{11}	$-c_2$	$-c_1$ 1372	-1		$= 0$
Hill land (ha)	1	1	...	1	1	1 —			≤ 2.5
Labor (months)	a_{15}	a_{12}	...	a_{11}	a_2	a_1 1.42			≤ 16.5
Year 17									
Gross margin (pesos)		c_{13}	...	c_{12}	$-c_3$	$-c_2$	$-c_1$ 1372	-1	$= 0$
Hill land (ha)		1		1	1	1	1 —		≤ 2.5
Labor (months)		a_{13}		a_{12}	a_3	a_2	a_1 1.42		≤ 16.5

Note: All crop activities are in hectare units.

planted in year 0, and this activity would have to be constrained to the area actually planted. Initializing a multiperiod model in this way is essential if the optimal solution is to provide guidance to the farmer on how he should adjust his investments over future years.

Our treatment of multiperiod models has been simplistic in that we have ignored capital constraints. The method of incorporating capital is very similar to the way seasonal cash flows were formulated in Section 3.11. Capital balance rows are added to the rows section for each period, and activity requirements for capital are entered. Capital can be supplied in each period from credit, or from family savings carried over from the previous period through transfer activities. A model of this type would determine the optimal growth path for a farm given an initial stock of capital and investment levels. For a full treatment of such growth models and of the problems involved see Boussard (1971), Dean and de Benedicitis (1964), Loftsgard and Heady (1959), and Rae (1970).

4.4   CONSUMPTION AND WORK / LEISURE PREFERENCES

4.4.1   Objectives of the Farm Household

So far we have been concerned with methods of modeling the technical and economic aspects of the farm, and have assumed throughout that the farmer simply seeks to maximize profits. In this section we begin the task of broaching more realistic formulations of a farmer's goals.

The maximization of farm income may represent a reasonable objective for commercial farmers, particularly in industrial countries.[1] However, for small-scale farmers in developing countries, a more primary objective is often to provide their families with adequate food. Such farmers face rural markets that are often incomplete, exploitative, or unreliable, and trading cash crops for food is rarely a sound strategy for ensuring survival. Under these circumstances, it is not surprising that farmers first allocate resources to assuring necessary food supplies, and only then are remaining resources used to generate cash income.

Another important consideration for small-scale farmers is often a desire to enjoy more leisure. As incomes rise above subsistence levels and the required drudgery to eke out a living is reduced, farmers typically display a strong preference to reduce their manual labor. This effect may be partly a consequence of the increased managerial and marketing time required to cope with improved technologies and additional output. It is also because the demand for leisure is income elastic.

If the consumption of foods and leisure by a farm household can be empirically related to income through estimated functions, then these behavioral functions can be incorporated into linear programming models with resultant effects on the optimal choice of the mix and level of crops and livestock products produced. We first review how such relations are included in linear programming models and then, in Section 4.5, turn to the more difficult task of analyzing the implications of such functions for household behavior when decisions about production, leisure, and consumption are interdependent.

4.4.2 Consumption Constraints

The simplest way of incorporating consumption behavior in a linear programming model is to add lower bound constraints on the production of the required food crops. Since production consumed is not then sold, cash income can only be measured in the model by separating the production and selling activities with the aid of balance rows.

To illustrate, suppose our Mayaland farmer wishes to assure his family of an annual food supply of 1000 kg of corn. The relevant part of the model tableau might appear as follows:

	Corn production (ha)	Sell corn (kg)	Consume corn (kg)	RHS
Objective function (pesos)	− 50	1.9		
Corn balance (kg)	− 750	1	1	≤ 0
Consumption requirement (kg)			1	≥ 1000

Since the consumption requirement must be met in any feasible solution, the selling activity can only dispose of surplus production after 1000 kgs of corn have been produced. The objective function in this formulation measures total gross margin net of the value of the corn consumed. If farm fixed costs K are deducted from the optimal value of the objective function, then the balance will be the required measure of cash income.

A limitation of this formulation is that the family's food consumption is assumed to be fixed, regardless of its level of income. More realistic formulations should allow the amount consumed to change with income in the model.

Suppose the Mayaland farm family behaves as if its consumption of corn were a linear function of income. That is,

$$C = \alpha + \beta Y \tag{4.1}$$

where C is the annual consumption of corn in kg

Y is annual income in pesos, defined as total gross margin including the value of corn consumed, but net of any farm fixed costs K

α is a subsistence corn requirement in kg

β is the marginal propensity to consume corn out of income (in kg per peso).

A linear programming model that maximizes cash income subject to the consumption constraint can be structured as follows.

	Corn production (ha)	Sell corn (kg)	Consume corn (kg)	Income (pesos)	RHS
Objective function (pesos)	− 50	1.9			
Income identity (pesos)	1372			− 1	= K
Corn balance (kg)	− 750	1	1		≤ 0
Consumption requirement (kg)			1	− β	≥ α

Income is measured through an identity row in this tableau and is defined as total gross margin less farm fixed costs K. The value of the income activity in an optimal solution to the model provides the required measure of income. The consumption requirement row requires that the level of the corn consumption activity must be at least as large as the right-hand side coefficient α plus β times the level of income.

Convex consumption functions can also be incorporated in a linear programming model using the linearization techniques described in Section 4.7. Such functions imply an increasing marginal propensity to consume the associated food, and are not likely to be realistic for most foods. A concave function is to be preferred, implying a declining marginal propensity to consume the associated food. However, if cash income is maximized, concave functions would present the same difficulties for linear programming as a convex input/output response function (see Section 3.4). The concave rather than the convex function presents problems in this case because the simplex will try to minimize consumption in seeking its objective of maximizing cash income. This means that for any given level of income, consumption will be smaller if combinations of non-adjacent linearization activities are used. Concave consumption functions can be included providing a mixed integer linear programming algorithm is used.

Incorporating consumption functions in a model is useful as a way of endogenizing the calculation of the marketed surplus of each crop in the optimal solution. However, the consumption constraints may also bear importantly on the choice of the optimal solution. If food buying activities are not included in the model, for example, or if they are included but there is a significant price wedge between the sale and purchase price of foods, then the consumption constraints may force an increased diversification of production over important food crops. Food consumption also affects cash income, and this in turn may affect the solution if cash flow constraints are included in the model as described in Section 3.11.

Price changes also affect the consumption of foods, but since prices are generally treated exogenously in farm models (i.e., the individual farmer is assumed to be a price taker) there is little point in modeling price responsive behavior. It should be noted though that the values of α and β in equation

(4.1) may well change if prices change, so when price experiments are conducted with a farm model that incorporates consumption behavior, the relevant coefficients may need to be adjusted before each price change is made.

4.4.3 Work / Leisure Choices

For modeling purposes the demand for leisure can be treated in much the same way as the demand for foods. Let l denote the month equivalents of leisure taken by the farm family during the year, then the relation between leisure and family income might be written as

$$l = \gamma + \phi Y \qquad (4.2)$$

where γ and ϕ, which are measured in months and months per peso respectively, are constants.

The amount of leisure taken is constrained by the amount of work to be done and the total time the farm family has available for allocation between work and leisure. Let $\bar{L}$ denote the total time available for the year in month equivalents after sufficient time has been deducted for sleeping, eating, non-farm activities, etc. Further, let L_F denote the amount of farm work performed by the family. The family time constraint is then

$$L_F + l = \bar{L} \qquad (4.3)$$

Equations (4.2) and (4.3) can be incorporated in a linear programming tableau as follows

	Corn production (ha)	Leisure (months)	Family labor (months)	Hired labor (months)	Income (pesos)	RHS
Income identity (pesos)	1372			$-w$	-1	$= K$
Labor (months)	1.42		-1	-1		≤ 0
Family time constraint (months)		1	1			$= \bar{L}$
Leisure requirement (months)		1			$-\phi$	$\geq \gamma$

As income increases in this model, less family labor becomes available to work on the farm and the optimal farm plan must become less labor intensive and/or more dependent on hired labor. The tableau has been simplified by assuming an annual labor constraint. It is a simple matter, though, to define similar relations seasonally or monthly.

An alternative approach for incorporating preferences for leisure in a model is to price family labor at a cost reflecting the marginal value of leisure to the farm family. In the Mexican agricultural model CHAC (see Chapter 12), for example, all family labor is charged at a reservation wage equal to 40% of the market wage. The structure of the tableau to achieve this is illustrated below for the Mayaland farm, where w denotes the wage rate.

	Corn production (ha)	Family labor (months)	Hired labor (months)	RHS
Objective function (pesos)	1372	$-0.4w$	$-w$	
Labor (months)	1.42	-1	-1	≤ 0
Family time constraint (months)		1		$\leq \bar{L}$

The essence of the approach is to treat family labor in the same way as hired labor, but with an upper bound constraint on the amount of family labor that can be used.

This approach assumes a constant reservation wage regardless of the amount of work performed by the farm family. However, the reservation wage could easily be allowed to increase as more work is performed.

The simplest way to do this is through a step-function approach. Suppose, for example, that three different reservation wages can be identified corresponding to three intervals of family labor use defined on the range zero to $\bar{L}$. Then three family labor-use activities would be included in the model, and each would be bounded by the end point of the labor-use interval over which its reservation wage applies. A tableau illustrating these ideas is shown below for reservation wages equal to 20%, 40%, and 60% of the market wage.

	Family labor use (months)			
	First level	Second level	Third level	RHS
Objective function (pesos)	$-0.2w$	$-0.4w$	$-0.6w$	
Labor (months)	-1	-1	-1	≤ 0
Family time constraints (months)				
First interval	1			$\leq \bar{L}_1$
Second interval		1		$\leq \bar{L}_2$
Third interval			1	$\leq \bar{L}$

4.5 INTERDEPENDENCIES IN PRODUCTION, LEISURE, AND CONSUMPTION[2]

Our discussion in the previous two sections takes for granted the existence of measured behavioral relations between consumption or leisure and income. Direct econometric measurement of such relations is relatively straightforward given farm survey data. A more worrisome problem that has emerged in the literature in recent years concerns possible inconsistencies between this treatment of leisure and consumption decisions in farm models and the theoretical ideal of a utility-maximizing farm household.

Problems arise if decisions about production, leisure, and consumption are interdependent, as will typically be the case with small-scale family farms. Static theories of the equilibrium of such farms assume the existence of a single period utility function for the household defined over the consumption of goods (including food) and leisure. It is assumed that the family maximizes this utility function subject to income and leisure constraints. Income depends on farm output, which in turn depends on the amount of work (and hence leisure) undertaken, as well as on the allocation of land and other farm inputs. Income may also be supplemented by off-farm wage earnings where opportunities exist.

In a pure subsistence situation without trade in goods or labor, application of this model leads to a firm-household equilibrium in which the levels of production, leisure, and consumption are all simultaneously determined (Nakajima 1970). Such models are inherently difficult to apply. The parameters of the utility function cannot be estimated in direct or indirect form, and it is difficult to estimate production and consumption systems simultaneously when these are nonlinear and inadequately identified.

Few family farms are isolated from all trading possibilities in goods and labor and most tend to specialize to increase production, trading surplus goods and labor for goods providing greater utility. If all goods and inputs, including labor, can be traded in competitive markets, then interdependencies between production, leisure, and consumption decisions break down completely (Lau et al. 1981; Barnum and Squire 1979, pp. 36–38). The firm-household equilibrium can then be derived from a two-stage decision process. First, the farm production problem is solved for maximum income given that all labor is valued at the market wage. Second, given income and the market wage, the household's consumption of goods and leisure is determined. This formulation has proved practical since indirect forms of the utility function can be derived in prices and income and can be estimated independently of the farm's production function. Work by Lau et al. (1981) has demonstrated the value of linear logarithmic expenditure systems and profit functions for these purposes. Barnum and Squire (1979) used a linear expenditure system and a Cobb-Douglas production function. As we now show, these results can be applied to mathematical programming models of the farm household.

Assume that the household maximizes a single-period utility function defined over n goods, Q_1 to Q_n, and leisure l. Let the function be written as

$$U = U(Q_1, \ldots, Q_n, l) \qquad (4.4)$$

and assume further that U is a differentiable and concave function.

Total expenditure on goods Q_1 to Q_n is restricted by the income identity

$$\sum_j P_j Q_j = \sum_j c_j X_j - wL_h - K \qquad (4.5)$$

where P_j denotes the market price of Q_j (we assume all Q_j are tradables)

$\quad$ X_j denotes the jth production activity of the farm; some production activities yield Q goods but others are traded for Q goods—to simplify notation we assume there are as many production activities as there are Q goods

$\quad$ c_j denotes the gross margin of X_j

$\quad$ L_h denotes the amount of labor hired

$\quad$ w denotes the market wage for hired labor

$\quad$ K denotes the fixed costs of the farm plus savings, less any exogenous source of nonfarm income

In words, the available income for consumption expenditure equals total gross margin less wage payments and fixed costs, including savings.

$\quad$ The consumption of leisure is also constrained by an identity equating the available supply of family labor to work performed by family labor (total work less hired labor) plus leisure.

$$l + \sum_j a_{jL} X_j - L_h = \overline{L} \tag{4.6}$$

Here a_{jL} denotes the labor requirements of the jth production activity, and $\overline{L}$ is the available supply of family labor.

$\quad$ Finally the household problem is constrained by a set of additional resource constraints.

$$\sum_j a_{ij} X_j \le b_i, \qquad \text{all } i, \tag{4.7}$$

where a_{ij} denotes the jth activity requirements for the ith resource, and b_i denotes the available supply of the ith resource.

$\quad$ Maximization of (4.4) subject to (4.5) through (4.7) defines the household model. To analyze the properties of an optimal solution to this problem, substitute (4.6) into (4.5) and form the Lagrangian function.

$$\mathcal{L}_1 = U(Q_1 \ldots Q_n, l) + \sum_i \mu_i \left(b_i - \sum_j a_{ij} X_j \right)$$
$$-\lambda \left[\sum_j P_j Q_j - \sum_j c_j X_j + w \left(l + \sum_j a_{jL} X_j - \overline{L} \right) + K \right]$$

where μ_i and λ are Lagrangean multipliers (shadow prices).

Apart from the feasibility requirements, the necessary Kuhn-Tucker conditions for an optimal solution are:

$$\frac{\partial \mathcal{L}_1}{\partial X_j} = \lambda(c_j - wa_{jL}) - \sum_i \mu_i a_{ij} \leq 0, \qquad \text{all } j \tag{4.8}$$

$$\frac{\partial \mathcal{L}_1}{\partial Y_j} = U_j - \lambda P_j \leq 0, \qquad \text{all } j \tag{4.9}$$

$$\frac{\partial \mathcal{L}_1}{\partial l} = U_l - \lambda w \leq 0 \tag{4.10}$$

For all $Q_j > 0$, (4.9) becomes the standard first-order condition of consumer demand theory, i.e., $U_j = \lambda P_j$ where U_j is the marginal utility of consumption of Q_j, and λ is the marginal utility of income. Similarly, if some leisure is taken, then (4.10) holds as the equality $U_l = \lambda w$, and the marginal utility of leisure equals the wage multiplied by the marginal utility of income.

Equation (4.8) is the condition for resource allocation. For each $X_j > 0$,

$$\lambda(c_j - wa_{jL}) = \sum_i \mu_i a_{ij} \tag{4.11}$$

That is, the net return from X_j (defined as the gross margin less the value of labor used) multiplied by the marginal utility of income is equal to the imputed value of the fixed resources used by that activity.

For the production decisions to be separable from the consumption and leisure choices, it is required that the conditions for resource allocation in (4.11) are identical to the conditions for resource allocation in a subsidiary mathematical programming problem in which income is maximized. This subsidiary problem is to maximize

$$Z = \sum_j c_j X_j - wL_h - K \tag{4.12}$$

such that

$$\sum_j a_{jL} X_j - L_h \leq \overline{L} \tag{4.13}$$

and

$$\sum_j a_{ij} X_j \leq b_i, \qquad \text{all } i \tag{4.14}$$

In this model, income is to be maximized independently of the consumption and leisure decisions.

The Lagrangean function for the subsidiary problem is:

$$\mathscr{L}_2 = \sum_j c_j X_j - wL_h - K + \theta\left[\bar{L} - \sum_j a_{jL} X_j + L_h\right] + \sum_i \gamma_i\left(b_i - \sum_j a_{ij} X_j\right)$$

where θ and γ_i are Lagrangean multipliers. The relevant Kuhn-Tucker conditions for an optimal solution are then:

$$\frac{\partial \mathscr{L}_2}{\partial X_j} = c_j - \theta a_{jL} - \sum_i \gamma_i a_{ij} \leq 0, \qquad \text{all } j \qquad (4.15)$$

and

$$\frac{\partial \mathscr{L}_2}{\partial L_h} = -w + \theta \leq 0 \qquad (4.16)$$

If hired labor is used, then (4.16) holds as an equality, implying that $\theta = w$. Then, for all $X_j > 0$, the conditions for resource allocation become

$$c_j - wa_{jL} = \sum_i \gamma_i a_{ij} \qquad (4.17)$$

Comparing (4.17) with (4.11), it can be seen that the production decisions are separable in the original utility maximizing problem only if $\mu_i = \gamma_i \lambda$, all i. This requirement is in fact met since, by definition of the Lagrangean multipliers,[3]

$$\mu_i = \frac{\partial U}{\partial b_i} = \frac{\partial U}{\partial Z} \cdot \frac{\partial Z}{\partial b_i} = \lambda \gamma_i$$

When separability results in this way, then it is permissible to set up an income maximizing problem, and to include consumption and leisure requirements as described in Section 4.4; see Ahn, Singh, and Squire (1981) for a recent application. Further, relations between consumption or leisure and income can be estimated econometrically without having to worry about biases in the estimated parameters because of simultaneity between production, consumption, and leisure decisions.

A key assumption in obtaining separability was the existence of a perfect labor market.[4] This ensured that $\theta = w$ in equation (4.16) whenever hired labor is used. Since L_h is not constrained to be nonnegative in this analysis, we have also implicitly assumed that family labor can be sold at wage w. This implies that the marginal utility of leisure U_l will also be equal to w.

Where a perfect labor market does not exist for hiring and selling labor, separability is no longer assured. Separability also breaks down when risk is introduced into the model and the farmer is assumed to maximize the expected value of his utility function. In these cases the only practical approach currently available for attaining separability is to assume that the household decisions are made sequentially rather than simultaneously. It might reasonably be argued that a household seeks to maximize farm income each year subject to minimum constraints on the production of certain food crops, and that once income is realized, the household then decides how to allocate income between savings and consumption, and between different items of consumption. This approach separates out the consumption decisions, but additional assumptions are required about leisure preferences to separate the production and work-leisure choices. An assumed reservation wage (or wage function) will perform the trick.

4.6 MULTIPLE GOALS

Given the inherent difficulties of formulating household models in which all the farmer's goals can be summarized as a single utility maximization problem, a more practical approach is to treat the farmer's goals as a series of separate objectives or constraints. This approach also opens up the possibility of including a variety of other goals that may be of interest to the farm family in addition to income, leisure, or consumption. Such goals might include family preferences not to become increasingly more indebted, to minimize dependence on certain kinds of hired labor (e.g., exchange labor), or to ensure the survival of the farm business in a risky environment.

The simplest way to handle multiple goals is to select one that will be maximized (or minimized) in the model, and to specify the remaining goals as inequality constraints. This is essentially what we did in Section 4.4 in setting up a model to maximize cash income subject to minimum constraints on food production. A limitation of this approach is that the goals included in the constraint set must be rigidly enforced; if they cannot be met then the problem will be infeasible.

An alternative approach, known as goal programming, establishes a target for each goal but rather than forcing compliance seeks instead to minimize the deviations between the achievement of the goals and their target levels.[5] Each goal has a set target $\overline{G}_g$, and the deviation from the target is calculated as

$$\sum_j a_{gj} X_j + G_g^- - G_g^+ = \overline{G}_g, \qquad \text{all } g = 1 \text{ to } t. \qquad (4.18)$$

Here $\sum_j a_{gj} X_j$ measures the achievement of the goal in the model (all goals must be specified as linear functions of the activities in a linear programming model), and G_g^- and G_g^+ are variables which measure, respectively, the amount by which the achievement of the goal is smaller or larger than its target $\overline{G}_g$. Since a goal cannot be underachieved and overachieved at the same time, then only one of the variables G_g^- and G_g^+ can be positive.

The objective function in the goal programming problem consists of a weighted sum of the deviations between the achievement of the goals and their targets. If the achievement of a goal should really be equal or greater than its target, then the relevant G_g^- variable is minimized. On the other hand, if the goal is such that the farmer wishes the achievement to be equal to or less than its target, the relevant G_g^+ variable is minimized. For goals whose achievement should be as close as possible to their target, then both G_g^- and G_g^+ are minimized. Let w_g denote the weight assigned to the gth goal, then the objective function can be written as

$$\min G = \sum_{g=1}^{r} w_g G_g^- + \sum_{g=r+1}^{s} w_g G_y^+ + \sum_{g=s+1}^{t} w_g \left(G_g^- + G_g^+ \right) \qquad (4.19)$$

The goals have been ordered in (4.19) so that the first r are lower bound goals, the $r + 1$ to s goals are upper bound goals, and the $s + 1$ to t goals are equality goals.

This formulation solves the problem of infeasibility. Targets may now be violated, but the model will seek to minimize the amount by which the achievement falls short of the target. A new problem arises though in the need to arrive at a set of weights for the goals. Rather than adhering to a single set of weights, a useful procedure is often to solve the model for different weights, and to present the farmer with information about the tradeoffs that exist between competing goals.

Goal programming assumes the existence of targets and attaches no value at all to the overachievement of a goal. Often a farmer may be more interested in achieving as large (or small) a value as possible for two or more goals. For example, he may wish to maximize cash income and leisure at the same time. There are computational procedures for solving models with more than one objective function, but these essentially reduce to procedures for exploring the optimal tradeoff frontier between competing goals.[6] A very simple approach is to take a weighted sum of the goals such as in

$$\max G = \sum_{g} w_g G_g \qquad (4.20)$$

where

$$G_g = \sum_{j} a_{gj} X_j$$

measures the achievement of the goal in the model. Again, by solving the model for different weights, useful information can be obtained about tradeoffs between competing goals.

4.7   APPROXIMATING SEPARABLE NONLINEAR FUNCTIONS IN LINEAR PROGRAMMING[7]

In this chapter (and in others that follow) we introduce nonlinear functions as the most complete way of specifying some economic relations in farm and sector models. However, if the resultant models are to be solved by linear programming, then linear approximating procedures are required. This section reviews ways of handling such nonlinear functions.

We confine our discussions to functions that are separable; that is, they can be written in the additive form $Y = \sum_j f_j(X_j)$. We further assume that nonlinear functions appearing in the objective function are concave (convex) if the problem is one of maximization (minimization), while those in the constraint set are of opposite curvature. These assumptions eliminate the possibility of local optimal solutions that cannot be handled with conventional linear programming computer codes. Finally, and without any loss in generality, we shall focus on approximating nonlinear concave functions which appear in the objective function of a maximizing problem.

The best-known procedure for linearizing a nonlinear function $Y = f(X)$ is illustrated in Figure 4.1. The function $f(X)$ is approximated by a series of linear segments (the dotted lines) which are defined over intervals $\overline{X}_i - \overline{X}_{i-1}$ on the X axis and corresponding intervals $\overline{Y}_i - \overline{Y}_{i-1}$ on the Y axis. Let s_i denote the slope of the linear segment in the ith interval, that is,

$$s_i = \frac{\overline{Y}_i - \overline{Y}_{i-1}}{\overline{X}_i - \overline{X}_{i-1}}$$

and define V_i as variables which measure the value of ΔX over the corresponding ith interval, such that $0 \le V_i \le \overline{X}_i - \overline{X}_{i-1}$. That is, V_i ranges from zero to the length of the ith interval. Now, since $Y = f(X)$ is to be maximized and the s_i are predetermined, then the following equation system:

$$\max Y^* = \sum_i V_i s_i \qquad (4.21)$$

subject to

$$X = \sum_i V_i \qquad (4.22)$$

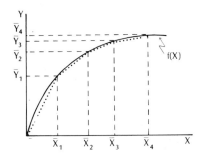

Figure 4.1 Linear segmentations of a nonlinear function.

and

$$0 \le V_i \le \overline{X}_i - \overline{X}_{i-1}, \text{ all } i, \qquad (4.23)$$

will provide a linear approximation to Y. Note that since the slope coefficients s_i decrease in value as X increases (because the function is concave), the V_i variables will always enter the solution in sequential order from left to right, and no modifications in the simplex method are required to ensure this.

Equations (4.21) through (4.23) can easily be incorporated into a linear programming model. Equation (4.22) is purely definitional and could be eliminated, if desired, by substituting $\Sigma_i V_i$ for X whenever this occurs in the programming problem. Clearly, the degree of accuracy of the approximation depends on the number of segments introduced, but the associated cost is an extra column (V_i) and upper bound row for each segment. While extra columns add little to computational costs with modern linear programming computer codes, extra rows are expensive. Consequently, the cost of introducing many nonlinear approximations would soon become prohibitive.

A more efficient method, from the computation point of view, is to work with $f(X)$ directly rather than with approximations to its slope. Define new variables W_i for each interval in Figure 4.1, such that $0 \le W_i \le 1$. These variables should be viewed as weights rather than as values of X. A linear approximation to $Y = f(X)$, under the maximization assumption, is then given by:

$$\max Y^* = \sum_i \overline{Y}_i W_i \qquad (4.24)$$

subject to

$$\sum_i W_i \le 1 \qquad (4.25)$$

and

$$X = \sum_i W_i \overline{X}_i \qquad (4.26)$$

$$W_i \ge 0 \qquad (4.27)$$

Apart from the definitional equation (4.26), only one constraint (4.25) is added, and this is not affected by the number of segments (hence, columns) introduced. This is why the method is superior to (4.21) to (4.23).

This formulation is identical to the first—that is, the values of Y^* obtained always lie on the segmented function in Figure 4.1. This is trivially true when one W_i is equal to 1 (say, W_3) and all the others are zero, since in this case $Y^* = W_3 \overline{Y}_3 = \overline{Y}_3$, which is a corner point on the segmented function, as seen in Figure 4.1. The equivalence is less obvious when the value of Y^* selected lies intermediate between two boundary points, and, in fact, Y^* will only lie on the segmented function if it is a linear combination of the two adjacent $\overline{Y}_i$ and $\overline{Y}_{i+1}$ boundary points (that is, when W_i and W_{i+1} are positive and all other Ws are zero). However, this will always be true given equation system (4.24) to (4.26), since any linear combination of nonadjacent W_is will lead to a value of Y^* which lies interior to the segmented function, and therefore requires more X to achieve the same value of Y^* (see Figure 3.6 and the associated discussion).

NOTES

1 Risk may also be an important consideration, but we defer this important topic until Chapter 5.
2 This section is of a more specialized and theoretical nature and might be omitted by readers whose interest is primarily in practical model building.
3 The term $\partial U/\partial Z$ is the marginal utility of income, λ, because the right hand side of (4.5) is income, and a unit increase in it changes the objective function U by the amount $\partial U/\partial Z$.
4 In this programming model the perfect labor market takes the form of having no constraints on the amount of labor that can be traded at fixed wage w.
5 See Romero and Rehman (1984) for a more detailed review.
6 Loucks (1975) provides a useful review.
7 This section draws heavily on Duloy and Hazell (1975), and the permission of Oxford University Press to use this material is gratefully acknowledged.

Chapter 5

Risk in the Farm Model

5.1 INTRODUCTION

Agricultural production is typically a risky business. Farmers face a variety of price, yield, and resource risks which make their incomes unstable from year to year. In many cases, farmers are also confronted by the risk of catastrophe. Crops and livestock may be destroyed by natural hazards such as hurricanes, floods, fire, or drought.

The types and severity of the risks confronting farmers vary with the farming system, and with the climatological, policy, and institutional setting. Nevertheless, agricultural risks seem to be prevalent throughout most of the world, and they are particularly burdensome to small-scale farmers in developing countries.

Numerous empirical studies have demonstrated that farmers typically behave in risk-averse ways (e.g., Binswanger 1980 and Dillon and Scandizzo 1978). As such, farmers often prefer farm plans that provide a satisfactory level of security even if this means sacrificing income on average. More secure plans may involve producing less of risky enterprises, diversifying into a greater number of enterprises to spread risks, using established technologies rather than venturing into new technologies and, in the case of small-scale farmers, growing larger shares of family food requirements.

Ignoring risk-averse behavior in farm planning models often leads to results that are unacceptable to the farmer, or that bear little relation to the decisions he actually makes. To resolve this problem, several techniques for incorporating risk-averse behavior in mathematical programming models have been developed in recent years. We shall review a number of these developments in this chapter, but will focus particularly on those methods that have proved useful at both the farm level and the aggregative sector model level.

5.2 PRINCIPLES OF DECISION MAKING UNDER RISK

In a risky world a farm plan no longer has a known income each year. Rather, there are many possible income outcomes and, in the mathematical programming context, the actual outcome each year depends on the realized values of all the c_j, a_{ij}, and b_i coefficients in the model.

Conceptually we can think of each farm plan (to be denoted by the vector X_v) as having a probability distribution of income $f(Y_v)$. If the number of possible outcomes of Y_v is finite then we can arrange the decision problem in the form of a payoff matrix as shown in Table 5.1.

A state of nature consists of a particular set of outcomes of all the c_j, a_{ij}, and b_i coefficients in the model, and these values determine a level of income for each alternative farm plan. In farm planning a state of nature typically corresponds to a particular type of year, e.g., a wet or dry year, or a high-price or low-price year.

Not all states of nature need be equally likely, and each may be assigned a probability p_t. Knight (1921) distinguished between risk and uncertainty on the basis of the state of knowledge about such probabilities. According to his definition if the probabilities are known, the decision problem is one of risk. In contrast, if the probabilities are unknown, the problem is one of uncertainty. This distinction is not particularly useful in farm planning since data for estimating income distributions are usually restricted to relatively small time-series samples, or to subjective anticipations held by the farmer. In either case one can only form estimates of the possible income outcomes and their associated probabilities. We use the word risk in this book to describe this more general state of ambiguity.

Table 5.1 An Illustrative Payoff Matrix

Alternative farm plans	State of nature			
	S_1	S_2	...	S_T
X_1	Y_{11}	Y_{12}	...	Y_{1T}
X_2	Y_{21}	Y_{22}	...	Y_{2T}
$\vdots$	$\vdots$	$\vdots$	...	$\vdots$
X_r	Y_{r1}	Y_{r2}	...	Y_{rT}

The decision problem for the farmer is to rank farm plans on the basis of their income distributions, and to select the one that best meets his goals. But given that an income distribution is a multivalued outcome, $(Y_{v1} \ldots Y_{vT})$, on what basis can they be ranked? Many alternative decision rules and theories have been developed in the literature to provide ways of ranking income distributions. These alternative methods typically use some measure of the variability, or spread, of the income distribution to provide a measure of risk, but some are more quantifiable than others. We shall restrict our coverage to the more quantifiable decision rules that have proved practical and useful in mathematical programming models.

The most established decision theory in economics is the expected utility theory (or the Bernoulli principle). Developed by von Neuman and Morgenstern (1944) this theory asserts a set of (reasonable) axioms about how an individual ought to order risky prospects, and then deduces the existence of an ordinal utility function $U(Y)$ which associates a single real number to any value of income Y. Furthermore, given any two farm plans X_1 and X_2, the theory predicts X_1 will be preferred to X_2 only if $E[U(Y_1)] > E[U(Y_2)]$, where E denotes the expected value. That is, X_1 is preferred to X_2 if the expected, or average, value of utility over all possible income outcomes is larger for X_1 than X_2.[1]

Compliance with the behavioral axioms of this theory does not restrict an individual's utility function $U(Y)$ to any particular functional form. Rather, a functional form can be chosen that best describes an individual's behavior. Because the theory predicts that risky prospects will be ranked by their expected utility, the choice of a functional form also determines the risk preferences of the individual. Suppose, for example, that a farmer's utility function is best described by the quadratic function

$$U(Y) = \alpha Y + \beta Y^2 \tag{5.1}$$

where α and β are constants. The relevant decision rule for ranking risky farm plans for the farmer is then

$$
\begin{aligned}
E[U(Y)] &= \alpha E[Y] + \beta E[Y^2] \\
&= \alpha E[Y] + \left(\beta E[Y^2] - \beta E[Y]^2 \right) + \beta E[Y]^2 \\
&= \alpha E[Y] + \beta V[Y] + \beta E[Y]^2
\end{aligned}
\tag{5.2}
$$

where $V[Y]$ denotes the variance of Y. By this rule the farmer should rank farm plans solely in terms of their expected (mean) income $E[Y]$ and their variance of income $V[Y]$. If $\alpha > 0$ and $\beta < 0$, then the farmer will prefer plans having higher expected income and lower variances of income. Or, put another way, for a given level of mean income, the farmer will prefer the farm plan that has the lowest variance of income.

Quadratic utility functions are one of many possible functional forms, each of which leads to its own decision rule for ranking risky farm plans. The problem facing the analyst is to choose the functional form that best describes a farmer's behavior. One of the exciting features of the expected utility theory is that methods of measuring an individual's utility function can be constructed from its axioms. Measurement requires playing a series of carefully designed gambling games with a farmer, the outcomes of which provide a series of observations along his utility function $U(Y)$. Regression analysis can then be used to provide the best fitting functional form as well as a set of estimates for its parameters. Several successful attempts to elicit individual utility functions have been reported in the literature (see Anderson, Dillon, and Hardaker, 1977, for a review). In many of these cases, quadratic utility functions appear to fit the data as well as most other functions (e.g., Officer and Halter, 1968).

Such elicitation of utility functions is not always practical, and many analysts simply assume a functional form that is computationally convenient. Then, in the absence of knowledge about the values of the function's parameters, a farm model may be solved for alternative parameter values, and the set of farm plans obtained offered to the farmer so that he can make the final choice. Another approach is to derive a set of plans corresponding to some past year and to select the parameter values that provide the closest match between the model's prediction and the farmer's actual farm plan.

Not all the decision rules proposed in the literature for risk analysis are consistent with the behavioral axioms of the expected utility theory. Some rules have been proposed because of their intuitive appeal, or because they have particularly attractive computational or data requirements that are valuable in applied modeling work. Such decision rules include the safety-first rules and game theory models.

Our discussion has focused on income risk. In principle, all risks involving c_j, a_{ij}, or b_i coefficients translate into income risk, and the use of a single utility function $U(Y)$ provides an integrated behavioral approach for selecting optimal farm plans. However, many modeling approaches treat risk in the objective function (the c_j coefficients) separately from risk in the constraint set (the a_{ij} and b_i coefficients). We shall largely follow this convention here, though where applicable we show how the two types of risk can be integrated into a single measure of income risk.

5.3 MEAN-VARIANCE (E, V) ANALYSIS

The expected income-variance criterion assumes that a farmer's preferences among alternative farm plans are based on expected income $E[Y]$ and associated income variance $V[Y]$. By convention, this is referred to as the E, V decision rule.

As we have seen, an E, V decision rule results from expected utility theory if a farmer has a quadratic utility function for income $U(Y)$. Unfortunately, a quadratic utility function is characterized by increasing absolute risk aversion, as well as having a maximum value beyond which the marginal utility of income actually declines. It has therefore been rejected as untenable by many theorists (e.g., Pratt, 1964). Despite this, the quadratic utility function can still provide an excellent second-order approximation to more desirable functions (Levy and Markowitz, 1979).

An alternative derivation of the E, V decision rule follows if the utility function is of the exponental form $U(Y) = 1 - e^{-\beta Y}$ and income Y is normally distributed (Freund 1956). In this case

$$E[U(Y)] = E[Y] - 1/2\beta V[Y] \qquad (5.3)$$

where β is a risk-aversion parameter. It might be expected that since farm income is often an aggregate of many independent sources of revenue and cost risks, then by the central limit theorem, it should be approximately normally distributed. And in many cases it is not possible to reject this hypothesis given the length of time series data available on farm incomes.

The computational advantages of the E, V model must be offset against its theoretical limitations. It can be solved by quadratic programming or by linear programming approximating techniques. Utility functions with preferred theoretical properties often have expected values that are difficult to evaluate numerically, and higher order polynomials that might be used to approximate more desirable functions can lead to nonconvex programming problems.

Given an E, V expected utility function, then for a risk averse farmer the iso-utility curves will be convex when plotted in E, V space (Figure 5.1). That is, along every iso-utility curve the farmer would prefer a plan with higher V only if E were also greater (i.e., $\partial E/\partial V > 0$), and this compensation must increase at an increasing rate with increases in V (i.e., $\partial E^2/\partial V^2 > 0$).

The farmer should then rationally restrict his choice to those farm plans for which the associated income variances are minimum for given expected income levels. The problem facing the farm analyst is to develop the set of feasible farm plans having the property that variance V is minimum for associated expected income level E. Such plans are called efficient E, V pairs

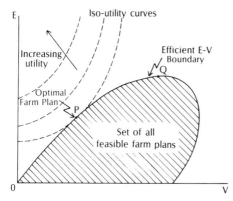

Figure 5.1 The optimal E, V farm plan

and they define an efficient boundary over the set of all feasible farm plans (segment OQ in Figure 5.1).

Given a set of efficient farm plans the acceptability of any particular plan to an individual farmer will depend on his preferences among various expected income and associated variance levels as described by his E, V utility function. When this function can be measured, a unique farm plan can be rigorously identified which offers the farmer highest utility. This is the efficient farm plan P in Figure 5.1.

When the parameters of the expected utility function are not known, then the best alternative seems to lie in obtaining the set of efficient farm plans and allowing the farmer to make the final choice. This approach is also more flexible in avoiding too rigid a specification of the utility function and perhaps compensates to some extent for situations where income variance is not the best measure of uncertainty. Further, if other socioeconomic factors enter the utility function in addition to E and V, the farmer is free to choose the plan he most prefers in relation to a multiplicity of goals.

5.4 QUADRATIC PROGRAMMING

The efficient E, V set of farm plans can be derived with the aid of quadratic programming. Consider a short-run planning problem in which only the c_j coefficients are stochastic. In this case farm overhead costs are constant and the income distribution of a farm plan is totally specified by the total gross margin distribution.

Let X_j denote the level of the jth farm activity, and let σ_{jk} denote the covariance of gross margins between the jth and kth activities (σ_{jk} will be the variance when $j = k$). Then the variance of total gross margin (and hence farm income) is[2]

$$V = \sum_j \sum_k X_j X_k \sigma_{jk} \qquad (5.4)$$

Equation (5.4) shows that the variance of total gross margin is an aggregate of the variability of individual enterprise returns, and of the covariance relationships between them. Covariances are fundamental for efficient diversification among farm enterprises as a means of hedging against risk (Markowitz 1959, Heady 1952). Combinations of activities that have negatively covariate gross margins will usually have a more stable aggregate return than the return from more specialized strategies. Also, a crop that is risky in terms of its own variance of returns may still prove attractive if its returns are negatively covariate with other enterprises in the farm plan.

To obtain the efficient E, V set it is required to minimize V for each possible level of expected income E, while retaining feasibility with respect to the available resource constraints. The relevant programming model to achieve this is as follows:

$$\min V = \sum_j \sum_k X_j X_k \sigma_{jk} \tag{5.5}$$

such that

$$\sum_j \bar{c}_j X_j = \lambda \tag{5.6}$$

$$\sum_j a_{ij} X_j \le b_i, \quad \text{all } i \tag{5.7}$$

and

$$X_j \ge 0, \quad \text{all } j \tag{5.8}$$

where $\bar{c}_j$ denotes the expected gross margin of the jth activity, and λ is a scalar. Since (5.5) is quadratic in the Xs, the model must be solved by a quadratic programming algorithm.

The sum $\sum \bar{c}_j X_j$ is expected total gross margin E, and which is set equal to a parameter λ. By varying λ over its feasible range through parametric procedures (see Sections 2.8 and 6.4), a sequence of solutions is obtained of increasing total gross margin and variance until the maximum possible total gross margin under the resource constraints has been attained. This maximum value corresponds to the standard linear programming problem of maximizing expected total gross margin subject to constraints (5.6) to (5.8). Solutions are obtained for critical turning points in the solution basis such that for the current total gross margin E, determined by λ, the variance V is minimum. These basic solutions are sufficient to define the entire efficient E, V boundary since efficient plans for intermediate levels of E can always be derived by linear interpolation on the adjacent turning point solutions.

To illustrate, consider the farm linear programming problem in Table 5.2. Expected total gross margin is to be maximized subject to land and labor constraints and to a rotation constraint which requires that the area planted to X_2 and X_4 cannot exceed the area planted to X_1 and X_3. The optimal solution

Table 5.2   An Illustrative Farm Model for Risk Programming

	Crop activities (ha)				
Row	X_1	X_2	X_3	X_4	RHS
Expected gross margin (pesos)	253	443	284	516	Maximize
Land (ha)	1	1	1	1	≤ 200
Labor (hours)	25	36	27	87	$\le 10,000$
Rotational requirement (ha)	-1	1	-1	1	≤ 0

Table 5.3 Activity Gross Margins and Their Variances and Covariances

	Crop activities			
	X_1	X_2	X_3	X_4
	Gross margins (pesos / ha)			
Year 1	292	-128	420	579
Year 2	179	560	187	639
Year 3	114	648	366	379
Year 4	247	544	249	924
Year 5	426	182	322	5
Year 6	259	850	159	569
Average	253	443	284	516
	Covariances (pesos)			
X_1	11,264	-20,548	1,424	-15,627
X_2	-20,548	125,145	-27,305	29,297
X_3	1,424	-27,305	10,585	-10,984
X_4	-15,627	29,297	-10,984	93,652

to this problem calls for 27.45 hectares of X_2, 100 hectares of X_3, 72.55 hectares of X_4, and provides an expected total gross margin of 77,996 pesos.

The farmer considers that this plan is too risky because X_2 and X_4, while very profitable on average, have highly variable gross margins. Gross margins for each crop are available for the past 6 years (Table 5.3), and these have been used to calculate the gross margin variances and covariances in the bottom part of the table. The variances for X_2 and X_4 are 125,145 pesos, and 93,652 pesos, respectively, and these are clearly much larger than the variances of X_1 and X_3 (11,264 pesos and 10,585 pesos, respectively).[3]

Using a quadratic programming algorithm, the set of efficient E, V farm plans was obtained (Table 5.4). There are four basic solutions in all, and the last one is the linear programming solution. Low levels of E correspond to lower levels of risk, and X_1 (a low-variance crop) figures prominently in Plan I.

Table 5.4 The Efficient E, V Farm Plans for the Example Problem

	Basic solution			
Farm plan	I	II	III	IV
E (pesos)	62,609	77,142	77,354	77,996
V (million pesos)	21.4	436.1	448.7	500.5
X_1 (ha)	68.67	4.32	—	—
X_2 (ha)	28.26	37.21	36.14	27.45
X_3 (ha)	88.23	95.68	100.00	100.00
X_4 (ha)	14.85	62.77	63.85	72.55

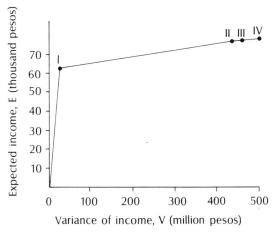

Figure 5.2 The efficient E, V frontier for the example problem.

In contrast, X_4 (a high-variance crop) is only present in Plan I at substantially reduced amounts. Interestingly, the areas of X_2 and X_3 do not change much in the solutions, even though these are the highest and the lowest variance crops, respectively. This result illustrates the important role that covariances play in determining efficient E, V solutions. The gross margins of X_2 and X_3 are negatively covariate (the covariance is $-27,305$ pesos), and when grown together their aggregate gross margin is considerably stabilized.

Figure 5.2 portrays the efficient E, V frontier for the farm problem. As is often the case in practice, the frontier is initially steep showing that E can be increased without much increase in V. But as reasonable levels of income are attained, the frontier quickly becomes flat. Additional E is then costly to obtain in terms of increased V, and only farmers who are less concerned about risk will choose points on the frontier near the linear programming solution.

5.5 LINEAR PROGRAMMING APPROXIMATIONS

The E, V model has proved popular in farm planning analysis, but the need to use a quadratic programming algorithm is often troublesome. Available computer codes with the necessary parametric option typically can only handle problems of limited dimensions, and some of these suffer severely from computer rounding errors if the number of basis changes is large.[4] To overcome this problem, several methods have been proposed for obtaining approximate solutions to the E, V problem through linear programming.

5.5.1 Separable Linear Programming

Thomas et al. (1972) proposed using separable linear programming. Equation (5.4) can be disaggregated into its variance and covariance terms as follows:

$$V = \sum_j X_j^2 \sigma_j^2 + \sum_{k \neq j} \sum_j X_j X_k \sigma_{jk}$$

where σ_j^2 denotes the variance of returns from the jth activity. Each of the X_j^2 terms can be linearized using the separable linear programming procedures described in Section 4.7.

A problem remains in linearizing the cross-products $X_j X_k$, and Thomas et al. seek to solve this through the following trick. Define new variables Z_{jk1} and Z_{jk2} such that $Z_{jk1} = 0.5\,(X_j + X_k)$ and $Z_{jk2} = 0.5\,(X_j - X_k)$. It follows that $X_j X_k = Z_{jk1}^2 - Z_{jk2}^2$, and hence

$$V = \sum_j X_j^2 \sigma_j^2 + \sum_{k \neq j} \sum_j \left(Z_{jk1}^2 - Z_{jk2}^2 \right) \sigma_{jk} \qquad (5.9)$$

Thomas et al. then suggest linearizing the Z^2 terms using the same separable linear programming procedures as used for the X^2 terms.

The approach suffers from the large number of linearizing activities that need to be added to the model. More importantly though, the objective function V (which is to be minimized) is no longer convex in all its variables. Since variances are always positive then the term $\sum_j X_j^2 \sigma_j^2$ is always convex. However, the remaining terms in (5.9) cannot all be convex because the Z_{jk1}^2 and Z_{jk2}^2 variables are of opposite signs. This means that the problem can only be solved by mixed integer linear programming algorithms.

5.5.2 The Marginal Risk Constrained Linear Programming Model

Chen and Baker (1974) developed Marginal Risk Constrained Linear Programming (MRCLP) as another computational alternative to quadratic programming. The motivation behind their method derives from the observation that an optimal solution to the quadratic programming problem (5.5) through (5.8) must satisfy the condition

$$\frac{\partial E[U(Y)]}{\partial X_j} \geq 0$$

for all $X_j > 0$. That is, no activity will be activated beyond the level at which its marginal expected utility has declined to zero.

Taking equation (5.3) as the relevant expected utility function, and substituting (5.5) for $V[Y]$ and (5.6) for $E[Y]$, then

$$\frac{\partial E[U(Y)]}{\partial X_j} = \bar{c}_j - \beta \sum_k X_k \sigma_{jk}$$

The MRCLP model is specified as:

$$\max Z = \sum_j \bar{c}_j X_j$$

such that

$$\bar{c}_j - \beta \sum_k X_k \sigma_{jk} \geq 0, \qquad \text{all } j \text{ for which } X_j \neq 0$$

and

$$\sum_j a_{ij} X_j \leq b_i, \qquad \text{all } i$$

$$X_j \geq 0, \qquad \text{all } j$$

The model is simply the standard linear programming problem (which maximizes expected income) to which has been added a set of marginal risk constraints. Unfortunately, the marginal risk constraints entail an "if" condition; they are only to be imposed for those activities that enter the basis. The problem cannot be solved as a single linear programming problem, and Chen and Baker developed a multistage approach that involves solving a sequence of linear programming problems. However, when completed, they claim the results are numerically very close to those obtained by quadratic programming.

5.5.3 The MOTAD Model

Another linear programming alternative for E, V analysis that has been widely used in practice was developed by Hazell (1971). This approach is most relevant when the variance of farm income is estimated using time series (or cross-sectional) sample data.[5] In this case the measure of income variance used in quadratic programming is only a statistical estimate of the true variance. As such, there is no reason why alternative estimates of the variance should not be used, and particularly those that can be calculated from linear estimators. Hazell proposed using variance estimates based on the sample Mean Absolute Deviation (MAD).

If sample data and classical procedures for estimating variances and covariances from samples are used, the estimated income variance in the quadratic programming model (equation 5.4) becomes[6]

$$\hat{V} = \sum_j \sum_k X_j X_k \left[(1/T - 1) \sum_{t=1}^{T} (c_{jt} - \bar{c}_j)(c_{kt} - \bar{c}_k) \right]. \qquad (5.10)$$

Here $t = 1$ to T denote T sample observations, and c_{jt} is the gross margin of the jth activity in the tth year with sample mean gross margin $\bar{c}_j$.

Taking the summation over t to the left and factoring, the estimated variance becomes

$$\hat{V} = (1/T - 1) \sum_t \left[\sum_j c_{jt} X_j - \sum_j \bar{c}_j X_j \right]^2$$

$$= (1/T - 1) \sum_t [Y_t - \bar{Y}]^2 \qquad (5.11)$$

That is, the variance of farm income for a given farm plan can be estimated as an aggregation of the sample variances and covariances of the individual activities (5.10), or it can more simply be obtained by calculating the farm income Y_t corresponding to each sample observation on the activity gross margins and estimating the variance of the single random variable Y (5.11).

This transformation allows the MAD estimator of the variance of Y to be used. The MAD estimator is

$$\tilde{V} = F\left\{(1/T)\sum_t \left|\sum_j c_{jt}X_j - \sum_j \bar{c}_j X_j\right|\right\}^2$$

$$= F\left\{(1/T)\sum_t |Y_t - \bar{Y}|\right\}^2 \tag{5.12}$$

where the expression in the curly brackets is the sample MAD, and F is a constant that relates the sample MAD to the population variance.[7] Specifically, $F = T\pi/2(T - 1)$, where π is the mathematical constant.

The attraction of the MAD estimator is that if we substitute (5.12) for (5.5) in the quadratic programming model, then a linear programming model can be derived. Let the deviation of farm income from its mean in year t be denoted by Z_t^+ if it is positive, and by Z_t^- if it is negative. Then

$$Z_t^+ - Z_t^- = \sum_j c_{jt}X_j - \sum_j \bar{c}_j X_j, \qquad \text{all } t \tag{5.13}$$

Note that Z_t^+ and Z_t^- are both nonnegative in this formulation, so they measure the absolute size of the deviation in income from its mean. Further, only one of them can be greater than zero each year; the deviation cannot be positive and negative at the same time.[8]

Now,

$$\sum_t (Z_t^+ + Z_t^-)$$

measures the sum of the absolute values of the income deviations for a farm plan, so the MAD estimator of the variance becomes

$$\tilde{V} = F\left\{(1/T)\sum_t (Z_t^+ + Z_t^-)\right\}^2.$$

Since F/T^2 is a constant for a given farm problem, we can divide $\tilde{V}$ through by F/T^2 to obtain

$$W = (T^2/F)\tilde{V} = \left\{\sum_t (Z_t^+ + Z_t^-)\right\}^2$$

It is also permissible to take the square root of W, since the ranking of farm plans by $W^{1/2}$ is the same as the ranking by W. We then have the following linear programming alternative to the quadratic problem (5.5) through (5.8).

$$\min W^{1/2} = \sum_t (Z_t^+ + Z_t^-) \tag{5.14}$$

such that

$$\sum_j (c_{jt} - \bar{c}_j) X_j - Z_t^+ + Z_t^- = 0, \qquad \text{all } t \tag{5.15}$$

and

$$\sum_j \bar{c}_j X_j = \lambda \tag{5.16}$$

$$\sum_j a_{ij} X_j \le b_i, \qquad \text{all } i \tag{5.17}$$

$$X_j, Z_t^+, Z_t^- \ge 0, \qquad \text{all } j, t \tag{5.18}$$

Since the objective function in the model is the Minimization Of the Total Absolute Deviations, Hazell called it the MOTAD model.

This model can be solved by parametric linear programming (see Section 6.4) to obtain the efficient E, V set of farm plans. Once these plans have been obtained the variance of their income can be calculated using the MAD estimator $\tilde{V} = (F/T^2)W$. Alternatively, if the variances and covariances of the activity gross margins are calculated, then the classical estimator in equation (5.10) can be applied to the known activity levels. The latter is to be preferred statistically since it has a smaller sampling variance (Hazell 1971, p. 58). It also avoids any errors that may arise from using Fisher's constant F when the income distributions are not normal.

A more compact version of the MOTAD model can be obtained. Note that the sum of the negative income deviations below the mean, $\sum_t Z_t^-$, must always be equal to the sum of the positive deviations above the mean $\sum_t Z_t^+$. It is therefore sufficient to minimize either of these two sums and to multiply the result by 2.0 to obtain $W^{1/2}$. This is easily done in the following MOTAD model (where we have chosen to minimize the sum of the negative deviations).

$$\min 0.5 W^{1/2} = \sum_t Z_t^- \tag{5.19}$$

such that

$$\sum_j (c_{jt} - \bar{c}_j) X_j + Z_t^- \ge 0, \qquad \text{all } t \tag{5.20}$$

and subject to (5.16) to (5.18).

Table 5.5   A MOTAD Model for the Example Problem

Rows	Crop activities (ha)				Negative deviation counters (pesos)						RHS
	X_1	X_2	X_3	X_4	Z_1^-	Z_2^-	Z_3^-	Z_4^-	Z_5^-	Z_6^-	
Objective function (pesos)					1	1	1	1	1	1	Minimize
Expected total gross margin (pesos)	253	443	284	516							$= \lambda$
Land (ha)	1	1	1	1							≤ 200
Labor (hours)	25	36	27	87							$\leq 10,000$
Rotational requirement (ha)	-1	1	-1	1							≤ 0
Risk rows (pesos)											
Year 1	39	-570	136	63	1						≥ 0
Year 2	-74	117	-97	123		1					≥ 0
Year 3	-138	205	82	-137			1				≥ 0
Year 4	-6	101	-35	408				1			≥ 0
Year 5	173	-261	38	-510					1		≥ 0
Year 6	6	408	-124	53						1	≥ 0

To illustrate, Table 5.5 shows the linear programming tableau for a MOTAD formulation of the farm problem in Table 5.2. Note that the entries for the crop activities in the risk rows—corresponding to equation (5.20)—are activity gross margin deviations from their sample means. These deviations must always sum to zero for each activity.

The results obtained by solving this problem through parametric linear programming are given in Table 5.6. There are five basic solutions in all, and the last one again corresponds to the standard linear programming problem of maximizing expected income. The income variances reported in the table were calculated using equation (5.10) after the optimal farm plans were obtained.

The MOTAD model typically provides an efficient set of farm plans that is very similar to the results obtained by quadratic programming. In Table 5.7 the quadratic programming and MOTAD model solutions for the example

Table 5.6   The MOTAD Model Results for the Example Problem

Farm plan	Basic Solution				
	I	II	III	IV	V
E (pesos)	62,769	73,574	77,329	77,529	77,996
V (million pesos)	22.1	267.6	459.8	474.9	500.5
X_1 (ha)	72.26	32.85	19.15	16.59	—
X_2 (ha)	26.80	28.03	28.46	26.80	27.45
X_3 (ha)	83.92	81.64	80.85	83.41	100.00
X_4 (ha)	17.02	57.48	71.54	73.20	72.55

Table 5.7   A Comparison of Results Obtained with the Quadratic Program and MOTAD Models for the Example Problem

Farm plan	Model[a]	I	II	III	IV
E (pesos)		62,609	77,142	77,354	77,996
V (million pesos)	Q	21.4	436.1	448.7	500.5
	M	22.0	448.9	461.6	500.5
X_1 (ha)	Q	68.67	4.32	—	—
	M	72.08	19.83	18.83	—
X_2 (ha)	Q	28.26	37.21	36.14	27.45
	M	26.73	28.44	28.25	27.45
X_3 (ha)	Q	88.23	95.68	100.00	100.00
	M	83.71	80.89	81.17	100.00
X_4 (ha)	Q	14.85	62.77	63.85	72.55
	M	16.97	70.84	71.75	72.55

[a]Q denotes the quadratic problem solutions which occurred at changes in basis, M denotes the corresponding MOTAD model solutions for the same levels of E.

problem are compared. The results are shown for the values of E corresponding to the basic solutions of the quadratic programming results reported in Table 5.4; the MOTAD farm plans were calculated by linear interpolation on adjacent basic solutions shown in Table 5.4. There are some discrepancies between the crop areas but these are not sufficient to have any marked effect on the corresponding variances. In fact, the E, V pairs are almost identical for the two models.

This similarity in results may seem surprising given that the sample MAD is a less efficient estimator of the population variance than the sample variance (Fisher 1920, Hazell 1971). However, the selection of efficient E, V farm plans only requires that the MAD be efficient at ranking alternative plans. Even if the estimate of V is incorrect for each farm plan, it is still possible to correctly rank them to identify the plan with the smallest value of V for each level of E. In a Monte Carlo simulation study of the MAD's ranking abilities, Thomson and Hazell (1972) found that the sample MAD is almost as good as the sample variance in ranking farm plans with normally distributed incomes, especially when the sample sizes are small. They also found that the MAD may sometimes outperform the sample variance when income distributions are skewed.

5.6   MEAN-STANDARD DEVIATION (E, σ) ANALYSIS

Closely related to the E, V model is the mean-standard deviation (or E, σ) model. Since σ is the square root of V, the efficient E, σ set of farm plans is identical to the efficient E, V set. It can therefore be obtained by quadratic

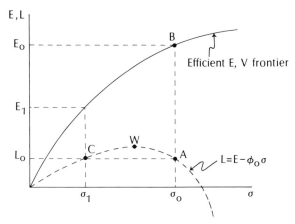

Figure 5.3 Relationship of efficient E, V and E, L Sets.

programming, or by linear programming alternatives such as MOTAD. One simply calculates the value of σ after the efficient farm plans have been obtained.

A useful decision rule rationalized by Baumol (1963) is the expected gain-confidence limit (E, L) criterion, where $L = E - \phi\sigma$ and ϕ (taken to be positive) is a risk-aversion parameter. Baumol argued that not all the plans in an efficient E, V set are reasonable for a prudent individual. In particular, plans with lower E and V are not always more secure than plans with higher E and V when the probability of a significant income shortfall is calculated.

If income is normally distributed, then for a specific value of ϕ, say ϕ_0, $L = E - \phi_0\sigma$ identifies a particular fractile of the income distribution for each farm plan. For example, if $\phi = 1.65$, then $L = E - 1.65\sigma$ identifies the 5% income fractile. A 5% income fractile is the value of income which, for a given income distribution $f(Y)$, will be exceeded 95% of the time. Baumol argues that a prudent individual (with risk parameter ϕ_0), should always select a farm plan that has the maximum value of E for a given value of $L = E - \phi_0\sigma$. The set of such farm plans comprises the efficient E, L set.

Figure 5.3 shows the relationship between the efficient E, V set and an efficient E, L set of plans. For any given ϕ, say ϕ_0, $L = E - \phi_0\sigma$ has a direct one-to-one correspondence with the efficient E, V frontier. Points on L and the efficient E, V frontier having the same value of σ also correspond to the same farm plan. Thus points A and B correspond to the efficient E, V farm plan having standard deviation σ_0 and mean income E_0.

Baumol's efficient E, L criterion requires that decision makers choose plans that have the largest value of E for given L. In Figure 5.3 this clearly restricts choice to those plans lying to the right of W. To see this consider plans C and A. Both have identical values of L, and hence are equally risky in terms of the probability of the same low income L_0. But plan A has a higher expected income E, (i.e., $E_0 > E_1$).

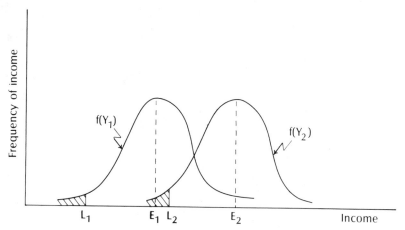

Figure 5.4 Income fractiles.

A popular adaptation of the E, L criterion is to assume that a farmer simply maximizes L given his risk aversion parameter ϕ. Thus in Figure 5.3, a farmer having $\phi = \phi_0$ will choose the plan associated with W. There are two rationalizations for this decision criterion.

If income is normally distributed, then for a specific value of ϕ, say ϕ_0, maximization of $L = E - \phi_0\sigma$ leads to selection of the farm plan having the largest value of the corresponding income fractile. Figure 5.4 shows two income distributions, $f(Y_1)$ and $f(Y_2)$, corresponding to two farm plans X_1 and X_2; both distributions are assumed to be normal. The fractiles corresponding to $\alpha = 0.05$ are shown as L_1 and L_2. In each case 5% of the area under the probability distribution lies to the left of the indicated fractile (the shaded areas).

If the two plans are ranked on the basis of the $L = E - 1.65\sigma$ criterion, then X_2 will be chosen because $L_2 > L_1$. This is equivalent to choosing the

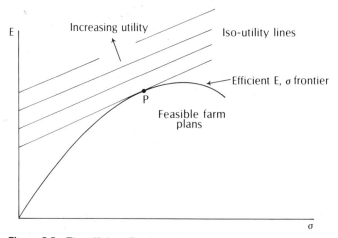

Figure 5.5 The efficient E, σ farm plan.

plan that has the largest income Y_0 such that $Pr\{Y_t \le Y_0\} = 0.05$. This formulation of the problem has been rationalized by Charnes and Cooper (1959), Kataoka (1963), and Sengupta and Portillo-Campbell (1970).

An alternative justification for maximizing $L = E - \phi\sigma$ arises when a farmer has an expected utility function $E[U] = E - \phi\sigma$. If the farmer is risk averse, then $\phi > 0$ and the iso-utility curves are linear and upward sloping in E, σ space (Figure 5.5). Once the efficient E, σ frontier is known, then knowledge of the risk aversion parameter ϕ leads to identification of the optimal farm plan P (Figure 5.5).

One attractive feature about the $L = E - \phi\sigma$ criterion is that ϕ is a number with an intuitive interpretation. For example, if income is normally distributed, then a ϕ value of 1.65 corresponds to the level of risk aversion tolerated by statisticians (or economists!) when performing one-tail, 5% confidence tests on selected hypotheses. If Sir Ronald Fisher had a ϕ parameter of 1.65, should we expect rational farmers to be much different?

The ϕ parameter can be estimated from direct elicitation of farmers' risk preferences. Using experimental methods, Dillon and Scandizzo (1978) obtained an average ϕ value of 0.9 for a sample of farmers in northeast Brazil. Moscardi and de Janvry (1977) imputed an average ϕ value of 1.12 for farmers in the Pueblo Project in Mexico. This value was derived from actual decision data and the first-order conditions for maximizing $E - \phi\sigma$ over an estimated production function.

Several researchers have also imputed values of ϕ by solving farm models for their efficient E, σ set of plans and selecting the value of ϕ that leads to the closest fit between the actual and predicted farm plans. Various ways of measuring the closeness of fit have been used, such as the mean absolute deviation of the differences in crop areas. This method of estimating ϕ has been more common with sector models than with individual farm models. Hazell et al. (1983), Simmons and Pomareda (1975), and Kutcher and Scandizzo (1981) have reported ϕ values ranging from 0.5 to 1.5 when derived in this way for aggregate models in Mexico and Brazil. Brink and McCarl (1978) reported ϕ values derived for individual farmers in the U.S. Corn Belt. They obtained values of less that 0.25 and concluded that risk preferences were not important.

There are two major problems with this approach to estimating ϕ. First, in using ϕ as a fine-tuning device to validate the model, there is a real possibility that ϕ may be biased by model misspecification and data errors. Second, if farmers have access to risk-sharing institutions such as crop insurance or futures markets, then their farm-planning decisions will not reflect their real risk preferences. Unless these risk-sharing possibilities are included in the model, ϕ is likely to be underestimated. This may explain the low ϕ values obtained by Brink and McCarl.

As a decision criterion, the E, σ model is subject to the same theoretical criticisms as the E, V approach. However, Tsiang (1972) has argued that the E, σ criterion is a good approximation to more desired decision criteria if the risk taken is "small" relative to the total wealth of the farmer. While this condition may easily be met for many commercial farms, it probably is not satisfied for small, subsistence farms in developing countries.

5.7 GAME THEORY MODELS

Following early studies by Swanson (1959), Walker, Heady, Tweeten, and Pesek (1960), and Dillon and Heady (1961), all the risks and uncertainty facing a farmer can be summarized as a composite "nature" component. Thus defined, nature can be considered an opponent in two-person zero sum games,[9] who, perhaps randomly rather than willfully, may financially undo a farmer in his selection of a farm plan. Many different decision criteria have been suggested to aid in selection of a farm plan, each superimposing its own utility assumptions on the model. The most commonly used decision criteria are the Wald maximin and the Savage regret.[10]

5.7.1 The Maximin Criterion

This criterion is based on the pessimistic view that whatever farm plan the farmer chooses, nature will do her worst and select the state of nature that minimizes the farmer's income from that plan. To illustrate, consider the following payoff matrix:

Farm plan	State of nature		
	S_1	S_2	S_3
X_1	100	40	80
X_2	50	60	30

The farmer may choose between farm plans X_1 or X_2, and for each plan there are three possible states of nature. The maximin criterion assumes that if the farmer selects plan X_1, then nature will select state S_2 and income will be 40. On the other hand, if the farmer selects X_2, nature will select S_3 and income will be 30. Under these circumstances, the appropriate strategy for the farmer is to select the plan that has the largest (maximum) outcome under the worst (minimum) state of nature; the maximin strategy. In our illustrative problem, the maximin strategy is to choose X_1 since its worst possible payoff is 40.

McInerney (1969) developed a linear programming model to derive the maximin solution for a constrained farm planning problem. Define M as the (unknown) worst possible outcome of farm income, then his model is

$$\max M \qquad (5.21)$$

such that

$$\sum_j c_{jt} X_j \geq M, \qquad \text{all } t \qquad (5.22)$$

and

$$\sum_i a_{ij} X_j \leq b_i, \qquad \text{all } i. \qquad (5.23)$$

$$X_j, M \geq 0, \qquad \text{all } j. \qquad (5.24)$$

Formulation of the model depends on identification of a finite number of states of nature. The model is therefore suitable when time series data are available on the activity gross margins, or when the gross margin outcomes for selected bad years can be elicited from farmers.

The maximin criterion is very conservative, and it often leads to farm plans with such low total gross margins on average in relation to overhead costs and family income needs that the criterion would not be acceptable. Nevertheless, the idea of minimizing the worst loss is appealing, and, unlike the E, V and E, σ models, higher incomes in favorable years are not penalized by this decision criterion.

To render the maximin criterion more useful, Hazell (1970) and Maruyama and Kawaguchi (1971) independently suggested adding the expected income equation

$$\sum_j \bar{c}_j X_j = \lambda \qquad (5.25)$$

to the model, and parameterizing λ to obtain an efficient E, M set of farm plans. The farmer could then choose the most favorable combination of E and M for his purposes, knowing that for any level of E, the plan offered has the minimum worst possible loss.

When plotted against the E, M axis, the efficient boundary is shaped as shown in Figure 5.6. The efficient E, M boundary is always concave, and the maximum attainable value of M is the value obtained from McInerney's

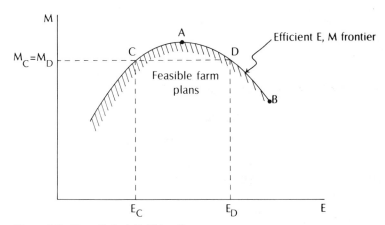

Figure 5.6 The efficient E, M frontier.

Table 5.8   A Maximin Tableau for the Example Problem

	Crop activities (ha)				Worst outcome	
	X_1	X_2	X_3	X_4	M	RHS
Objective function (pesos)					1	Maximize
Expected total gross margin (pesos)	253	443	284	516		$= \lambda$
Land (ha)	1	1	1	1		≤ 200
Labor (hours)	25	36	27	87		$\leq 10{,}000$
Rotational requirement (ha)	-1	1	-1	1		≤ 0
Risk rows (pesos)						
Year 1	292	-128	420	579	-1	≥ 0
Year 2	179	560	187	639	-1	≥ 0
Year 3	114	648	366	379	-1	≥ 0
Year 4	247	544	249	924	-1	≥ 0
Year 5	426	182	322	5	-1	≥ 0
Year 6	259	850	159	569	-1	≥ 0

model (plan A in Figure 5.6). The last solution (plan B) is always the standard linear programming solution in which E is maximized.

Only farm plans represented by segment AB in Figure 5.6 are rational for a farmer to consider. Any plan to the left of A (e.g., plan C) has the same value of M as a plan to the right of A (plan D), but its expected income E is smaller ($E_C < E_D$).

To illustrate, Table 5.8 is the tableau of the maximin model for the farm problem presented in Section 5.4. Solutions to the model for parametric increases in E are shown in Table 5.9. In this case the first nonzero solution has the largest value of M, and hence is the solution to McInerney's original model. This solution entails almost a 20% sacrifice in expected income compared to the maximum expected income attainable (solution V). On the other hand, income in the worst possible case is 60% larger.

Table 5.9   The Maximin Results for the Example Problem

Farm plan	Basic solution				
	I	II	III	IV	V
E (pesos)	65,316	70,364	73,267	75,182	77,996
M (pesos)	60,455	55,872	51,909	47,264	37,559
X_1 (ha)	86.32	114.19	100.00	100.00	—
X_2 (ha)	30.69	38.41	49.77	23.53	27.45
X_3 (ha)	55.77	—	—	—	100.00
X_4 (ha)	27.20	47.40	50.23	76.47	72.55

5.7.2 The Savage Regret (or Minimax) Criterion

This criterion is based on the assumption that a decision maker wishes to minimize the regret (or remorse) that he experiences when, after having made a decision, he is able to compare the outcome with what he could have achieved had he had perfect foresight.[11] For example, suppose that the tth state of nature will prevail. If the farmer could correctly anticipate all the activity gross margins corresponding to that state (c_{jt}, $j = 1$ to n), then he would adopt the farm plan that maximizes income

$$\sum_j c_{jt} X_j$$

Let this maximal value of income be denoted by Y_t^*. However, since the farmer rarely (if ever) has perfect foresight, he is likely to adopt an alternative farm plan that leads to a realized income Y_t. The difference $Y_t^* - Y_t$ measures the regret that the farmer might experience once the consequence of his decision is known.

Given this measure of regret, the Savage regret criterion focuses on the largest of these regrets over all states of nature, and calls for selection of the plan having the minimum value of the maximum regret (the minimax criterion).

Hazell (1970) proposed the following linear programming adaptation of the minimax criterion for farm planning:

$$\min R \tag{5.26}$$

subject to

$$Y_t^* - \sum_j c_{jt} X_j \leq R, \quad \text{all } t \tag{5.27}$$

and

$$\sum_j a_{ij} X_j \leq b_i, \quad \text{all } j \tag{5.28}$$

$$\sum_j \bar{c}_j X_j = \lambda \tag{5.29}$$

$$X_j, R \geq 0, \quad \text{all } j \tag{5.30}$$

Here R is the largest regret for a farm plan over all states of nature, and the farm plan to be chosen is that which has the minimum R. By including the expected income equation (5.29), λ can be parameterized to provide an efficient E, R set of plans. Each plan in the set has the property that, for its given level of E, it is the plan having the minimum largest possible regret the farmer could experience.

When plotted against the E, R axes, the efficient E, R boundary is always convex (Figure 5.7). Plan A has the minimum possible value of R, and plan B

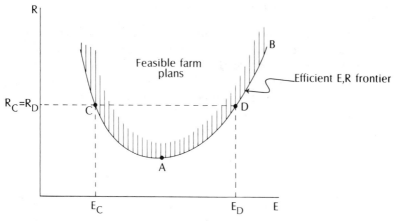

Figure 5.7   The efficient E, R frontier.

is again the linear program solution that maximizes E. Only efficient plans lying on segment AB are rational for a farmer to consider. Any efficient plan to the left of A is dominated by an efficient plan lying to the right of A. For example, D dominates C because it has a larger value of E for the same value of R.

To solve model (5.26) through (5.30) it is first necessary to calculate Y_t^* for each state of nature by solving a series of linear programming problems. An obvious limitation of the model is that the Y_t^* values must be recalculated for any experiment involving changes in the model c_j, a_{ij}, or b_i coefficients.

Table 5.10   A Minimax Regret Tableau for the Example Problem

| | Crop activities (ha) | | | | Largest regret | |
	X_1	X_2	X_3	X_4	R	RHS
Objective function (pesos)					1	Minimize
Expected total gross margin (pesos)	253	443	284	516		$= \lambda$
Land (ha)	1	1	1	1		≤ 200
Labor (hours)	25	36	27	87		$\leq 10{,}000$
Rotational requirement (ha)	-1	1	-1	1		≤ 0
Risk rows (pesos)						
Year 1	292	-128	420	579	1	$\geq 96{,}190$
Year 2	179	560	187	639	1	$\geq 80{,}431$
Year 3	114	648	366	379	1	$\geq 101{,}400$
Year 4	247	544	249	924	1	$\geq 108{,}159$
Year 5	426	182	322	5	1	$\geq 85{,}200$
Year 6	259	850	159	569	1	$\geq 110{,}900$

Table 5.11   The Minimax Regret Results for the Example Problem

Farm plan	I	II	III	Basic solution IV	V	VI	VII	VIII
E (pesos)	5,999	16,217	20,189	43,833	69,945	74,379	75,795	77,996
R (pesos)	101,341	87,730	83,373	58,909	32,459	36,484	40,050	47,641
X_1 (ha)	8.62	22.60	27.78	28.97	58.26	82.73	78.21	—
X_2 (ha)	8.62	15.87	16.10	24.14	35.10	41.87	24.38	27.45
X_3 (ha)	—	—	—	29.15	66.25	17.27	21.79	100.00
X_4 (ha)	—	6.72	11.68	33.97	40.39	58.12	75.62	72.55

Table 5.10 shows the tableau of the minimax regret model for our example problem. The parametric solutions for increases in E are given in Table 5.11. Plan V has the smallest possible value of regret R, hence only plans V through VIII are rational for a farmer to consider.

5.7.3   Features of Game Theory Models

Game theory decision criteria such as the maximin and minimax rules are attractive because they require less information about possible gross margin outcomes than the E, V or E, σ models. For example, they do not use information about the relative frequency (or probability) of occurrence of each state of nature. This means that large time series samples of activity gross margins are not important once the relevant states of nature are enumerated. Also, the maximin criterion only uses information about unfavorable gross margin outcomes, so there is no point in including states of nature in the model in which none of the activity gross margins are significantly smaller than their means.

One of the perceived advantages of the E, V and E, σ models is that they take explicit account of the covariance relations between activity gross margins. Game theory models can also incorporate these covariances, but only on an implicit basis. We have already seen in Section 5.5 that, when using sample data on activity gross margins, the variance of total farm income can be expressed either as an aggregation of the sample variances and covariances of the individual activities or as the variance of total farm income Y_t evaluated for each of the sample observations. The same information about the relationships among activity gross margins is contained in both approaches, but the latter depends on retaining the yearly observations as mutually exclusive sets of activity gross margin outcomes. In other words, it is not permissible to combine activity gross margins from different years in the same state of nature. This is an important consideration if the gross margin outcomes for any state of nature are to be elicited directly from the farmer. For example, construction of a worst possible state of nature using the lowest gross margin that the farmer can recall for each activity may be very misleading, because it is unlikely that the worst possible outcome for every activity would occur at the same time.

5.8 SAFETY-FIRST MODELS

The risk models we have considered so far are concerned with increasing a farmer's utility by minimizing an appropriate measure of the variability of farm income. Safety-first models have a different perspective. They are designed to help a farmer insure that he attains the minimum income necessary to meet his fixed costs (including credit repayment), and to meet his family's living costs each year. Safety-first models are most appropriate where the risk of catastrophe is large, either because of an inherently risky environment, or because the farmer is poor and has minimal reserves to fall back on in a bad year.

5.8.1 Roy's Safety-First Criterion

One of the earliest safety-first models was proposed by Roy (1952). Given that some minimal income Y_0 is required for the farm family to survive, Roy's criterion calls for selection of the farm plan that minimizes the probability that income Y_t could fall below Y_0. That is, choose the plan such that $Pr\{Y_t \leq Y_0\}$ is minimum.

Roy's criterion is not easily incorporated in a mathematical programming model. However, if farm income is normally distributed, then the optimal plan is identifiable as a member of the efficient E, V set. In fact, it is the plan corresponding to the point of tangency between Y_0 and the lower confidence limit $L = E - \phi\sigma$ that has its maximum at $E = Y_0$ (plan A in Figure 5.8). If the efficient E, V set of plans is first derived, the optimal plan for Roy's criterion can be identified by plotting lower confidence bands for different values of ϕ on graph paper until the required tangency with Y_0 is attained.

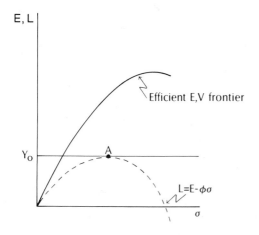

Figure 5.8 Roy's safety-first criterion.

5.8.2 Low's Safety-First Model

Low (1974) has proposed a modification of the maximin game model that selects the farm plan that has an income equal to or greater than Y_0 in every state of nature, and which maximizes expected income E. The model is defined as follows:

$$\max E = \sum_j \bar{c}_j X_j \tag{5.31}$$

subject to

$$\sum_j c_{jt} X_j \geq Y_0, \quad \text{all } t \tag{5.32}$$

and

$$\sum_j a_{ij} X_j \leq b_i, \quad \text{all } i \tag{5.33}$$

$$X_j \geq 0, \quad \text{all } j \tag{5.34}$$

The model has the same solution as the maximin model (5.21) through (5.24) if Y_0 happens to equal the maximum attainable value of M. It will also produce the standard linear programming solution for maximum E if Y_0 is sufficiently small that none of the constraints in (5.32) are binding.

A difficulty with Low's model is that there may not be a feasible solution if Y_0 is large relative to the maximum attainable E and/or if the farmer is operating in a high-risk environment. An alternative approach is to treat Y_0 as a target (as in goal programming) and to seek the farm plan that deviates the least from this target.

5.8.3 Target MOTAD

One model formulation that does this is Tauer's (1983) target MOTAD model.[12] This model is formulated as follows.

$$\max E = \sum_j \bar{c}_j X_j \tag{5.35}$$

subject to

$$Y_0 - \sum_j c_{jt} X_j - Z_t^- \leq 0, \quad \text{all } t \tag{5.36}$$

and

$$\sum_t p_t Z_t^- = \lambda \tag{5.37}$$

$$\sum_j a_{ij} X_j \leq b_i, \quad \text{all } i \tag{5.38}$$

$$X_j, Z_t^- \geq 0, \quad \text{all } j, t. \tag{5.39}$$

Table 5.12 A Target MOTAD Tableau for the Example Problem

Rows	Crop activities (ha)				Negative deviations from the target						RHS
	X_1	X_2	X_3	X_4	Z_1^-	Z_2^-	Z_3^-	Z_4^-	Z_5^-	Z_6^-	
Objective function											
(pesos)	253	443	284	516							Maximize
Land (ha)	1	1	1	1							≤ 200
Labor (hours)	25	36	27	87							≤ 10,000
Rotational requirement											
(ha)	−1	1	−1	1							≤ 0
Expected shortfall											
from target (pesos)					0.167	0.167	0.167	0.167	0.167	0.167	= λ
Risk rows (pesos)											
Year 1	292	−128	420	579	1						≥ 55,000
Year 2	179	560	187	639		1					≥ 55,000
Year 3	114	648	366	379			1				≥ 55,000
Year 4	247	544	249	924				1			≥ 55,000
Year 5	426	182	322	5					1		≥ 55,000
Year 6	259	850	159	569						1	≥ 55,000

The Z_t^- variables in (5.36) measure the value of any deviations in income below the target. These deviations are collected in (5.37) and multiplied by the probabilities of the states of nature in which they occur (the p_t) to give the expected sum of the deviations below the target income.

The model is set up to maximize E subject to achieving a satisfactory level (determined by λ) of compliance with the target income. By parameterizing λ, a set of efficient farm plans is obtained which, for any given level of compliance with the target income (as measured by $\Sigma_t p_t Z_t^-$), have the maximum possible value of E. A farmer who is most concerned about survival might well choose the plan having the smallest possible value of $\Sigma_t p_t Z_t^-$. But other farmers might prefer plans with higher levels of E providing $\Sigma_t p_t Z_t^-$ remains reasonably small.

A linear programming tableau for the target MOTAD model is shown in Table 5.12 using our example problem. In this case, we have stipulated a target

Table 5.13 The Target MOTAD Results for the Example Problem

Farm plan	Basic solution			
	I	II	III	IV
E (pesos)	71,003	73,585	75,182	77,996
λ (pesos)	0	644	1,289	2,907
X_1 (ha)	111.07	100.00	100.00	—
X_2 (ha)	40.91	45.40	23.53	27.45
X_3 (ha)	—	—	—	100.00
X_4 (ha)	48.02	54.60	76.47	72.55

income of 55,000 pesos. Also, in the absence of any additional information about gross margin outcomes other than the 6 years of sample data, the states of nature are treated as equally likely in the model. The results are shown in Table 5.13.

5.8.4 The Focus-Loss Model

A quite different approach to farm income security was developed by Boussard and Petit (1967). Rejecting probabilistic approaches to safety-first as impractical because of inadequate data and the need to assume normally distributed risks, they turned instead to a concept of focal loss developed by Shackle (1949, 1961). The focal loss of a risky activity is defined as the level of loss that a decision maker would be "very surprised" to realize. In practice, Boussard and Petit approximated focal loss values for different farm activities using "decennial catastrophies," i.e., the worst gross margin that might occur once in a decade. Given this "worst" gross margin (call it c_j^*) for each activity, and the expected gross margin, $\bar{c}_j$, the focal loss is defined as $f_j = \bar{c}_j - c_j^*$, all j.

For any farm plan, a maximum permitted loss (call it $LOSS$) is defined as the difference between expected total gross margin, $\sum_j \bar{c}_j X_j$, and the minimum income ($MINI$) required to cover farm fixed costs, essential family living costs, and debt repayment. That is,

$$LOSS = \sum_j \bar{c}_j X_j - MINI$$

Boussard and Petit then impose the requirement that no single activity may have a total focal loss $f_j X_j$ greater than $1/k$ of the maximum permitted loss for the farm plan. These constraints are $f_j X_j \leq 1/k \, (LOSS)$, all j. Table 5.14 shows a schematic tableau for the focus-loss model.

The focus-loss model can be solved by standard linear programming codes, and it requires relatively little information about possible gross margin outcomes. There are two major disadvantages to the approach. First, it ignores

Table 5.14 A Focus-Loss Model

	Crop activities				LOSS	RHS
	X_1	X_2	X_3	X_4		
Expected income	$\bar{c}_1$	$\bar{c}_2$	$\bar{c}_3$	$\bar{c}_4$		Maximize
Minimum income constraint	$\bar{c}_1$	$\bar{c}_2$	$\bar{c}_3$	$\bar{c}_4$	-1	$= MINI$
Activity constraints						
X_1	f_1				$-1/k$	≤ 0
X_2		f_2			$-1/k$	≤ 0
X_3			f_3		$-1/k$	≤ 0
X_4				f_4	$-1/k$	≤ 0

covariance relations between activity gross margins; the model assumes that the focal loss of each activity can occur in the same year. Second, the focal loss coefficients f_j and the value of k are inherently difficult to measure.

5.9   RISK IN THE CONSTRAINT SET

So far we have assumed that all the a_{ij} and b_i coefficients of a farm model are deterministic. This is not always a tenable assumption. Yield risks that affect gross margins are also likely to affect activity labor and machinery requirements. Fluctuations in input costs affect the capital requirements of the farm activities as well as gross margins. Independently of gross margin risks, a farmer may also face risks in resource supplies; for example, seasonal labor, water for irrigation, and forage supplies for livestock feed.

Risk in the constraint set can significantly affect the feasibility of a farm plan in any one year. Consequently, in seeking to find better farm plans in relation to a farmer's income objectives, the analyst must be sure that the plan will also be feasible at an acceptable risk level.

5.9.1   Discrete Stochastic Programming

Ideally, all the risks in the constraint set should be transferred into the objective function of a model and a single risk decision rule applied. If resources are freely tradable, then any stochastic discrepancies between the resource requirements of a farm plan and the resource supplies can be captured in the objective function through buying and selling activities.

Implementation of this concept requires explicit consideration of all the adjustments that should be made to a farm plan in each state of nature to overcome any infeasibilities. As a simple example, consider the Mayaland example in Table 5.15.

The farmer, who can grow corn or beans, faces three possible states of nature S_1, S_2, and S_3. Both the gross margins and the labor requirements of corn and beans vary with the state of nature. To make the problem more interesting, we also assume that the supply of labor depends on the state of nature.

The relevant risk decision rule is arbitrarily assumed to be the maximin criterion, hence the tableau is structured after Table 5.8. A new feature is the introduction of labor rows for each state of nature, and of labor hiring and selling activities in each of these states. These activities enable the model to hire or sell different amounts of labor in each state of nature. Each of the hiring and selling activities has an appropriate $+1$ or -1 entry in the relevant labor row, and a wage entry which adds or subtracts from total gross margin in the relevant state of nature. The variability in labor requirements and supplies is therefore transferred into the gross margin rows, and the maximin criterion is applied in the usual manner. Note that in calculating expected income E, the relevant wage entries under the labor activities are weighted by their probabilities of occurrence; in this case by equal weights of one third.

Table 5.15 A Discrete Stochastic Programming Problem

	Corn (ha)	Beans (ha)	Hire labor (months)			Sell labor (months)			Worst income outcome (pesos)	RHS
			S_1	S_2	S_3	S_1	S_2	S_3	M	
Objective function (pesos)									1	Maximize
Land (ha)	1	1								≤ 5.0
Labor (months)										
S_1	1.2	2.0	-1			1				≤ 15.0
S_2	1.6	1.9		-1			1			≤ 17.0
S_3	1.4	1.4			-1			1		≤ 17.5
Gross margins (pesos)										
S_1	1200	1400	$-w$			w			-1	≥ 0
S_2	1550	1207		$-w$			w		-1	≥ 0
S_3	1366	1050			$-w$			w	-1	≥ 0
Expected total gross margin (pesos)	1372	1219	$-1/3w$	$-1/3w$	$-1/3w$	$1/3w$	$1/3w$	$1/3w$		$= \lambda$

Models of this type are known as discrete stochastic programming (Cocks 1968) or stochastic programming with recourse. A key assumption is that some decisions (labor decisions in Table 5.15) are made after the state of nature is observed. This means that the farmer has scope for avoiding problems with infeasibilities or underutilized resources that might otherwise arise. This assumed sequencing of decisions is actually very descriptive of agriculture. A farmer does have to commit some resources for planting crops at the beginning of the growing season, but application of many inputs such as fertilizers, pesticides, or irrigation water typically occurs after the farmer has had time to gain new information about the season. As such, he can adjust the use of these inputs in an optimal way. Rae (1971a, 1971b) has shown how discrete stochastic programming can be used to model detailed sequences of decisions in farming.

The major difficulty of the approach is its hearty appetite for data, and the fact that models rapidly become very large because of the need to have separate rows and columns for many resources and activities in every state of nature.

When resources are not tradable, any risk in their use or supply cannot be transferred into income risk through buying and selling activities. Discrete stochastic programming models require the farm plans to be feasible for those resources in all states of nature. A similar result holds for more simplistic stochastic linear programming models in which the constraint set is duplicated for each state of nature.[13] That is, the constraint set becomes

$$\sum_j a_{ijt} X_j \le b_{it}, \qquad \text{all } i, t$$

Forcing feasibility under all circumstances is not to be generally recommended. It leads to conservative farm plans that may be incompatible with a farmer's risk-aversion behavior.[14] This is most likely to happen if the farmer has some recourse for resolving infeasibilities, but these options cannot be fully specified in the model.

5.9.2 Chance-Constrained Programming

Practical alternatives to discrete stochastic programming models include chance-constrained programming and goal programming (see Section 4.6). In both cases it is recognized that feasibility cannot always be assured, and that the best strategy is to try to minimize the risk of infeasibility while pursuing other income related objectives.

Chance-constrained programming, developed by Charnes and Cooper (1959), expresses the feasibility requirements in probabilistic terms. A chance constraint for the ith resource takes the form

$$Pr\left\{ \sum_j a_{ij} X_j \le b_i \right\} \ge 1 - \alpha_i \qquad (5.40)$$

where α_i is some prespecified probability (usually 10% or less). The constraint requires that the total requirements for the ith resource should not exceed its supply more than α percent of the time.

In order to incorporate (5.40) into a linear programming model, it is necessary to convert it into a legitimate linear inequality constraint. This is usually done by assuming that all the stochastic coefficients are normally distributed. To illustrate the method, suppose that the a_{ij} coefficients in (5.40) are stochastic with means $\bar{a}_{ij}$ and covariances $\text{cov}(a_{ij}, a_{ik})$, but that b_i is deterministic. The sum

$$\sum_j a_{ij} X_j$$

(which we shall denote by Z_i) is then a normally distributed random variable with mean

$$E[Z_i] = \sum_j \bar{a}_{ij} X_j$$

and standard deviation

$$\sigma_{zi} = \left[\sum_j \sum_k X_j X_k \text{cov}(a_{ij}, a_{ik}) \right]^{1/2}.$$

Equation (5.40) then becomes:

$$Pr\{ Z_i \le b_i \} \ge 1 - \alpha_i \qquad (5.41)$$

or equivalently

$$Pr\{ (Z_i - E[Z_i])/\sigma_{zi} \le (b_i - E[Z_i])/\sigma_{zi} \} \ge 1 - \alpha_i$$

Now $(Z_i - E[Z_i])/\sigma_{zi}$ is a standardized normal random variable with mean zero and standard deviation one, so tables for the cumulative normal distribution can be used to find, for any α_i, a constant K_α such that

$$Pr\{ (Z_i - E[Z_i])/\sigma_{zi} \le K_\alpha \} = 1 - \alpha_i \qquad (5.42)$$

Comparing (5.42) and (5.41), the chance constraint will be satisfied if

$$K_\alpha \le (b_i - E[Z_i])/\sigma_{zi}$$

or equivalently, if $E[Z_i] + K_\alpha \sigma_{zi} \leq b_i$. For example, if $\alpha_i = 0.05$, then $K_\alpha = 1.65$ and the constraint is $E[Z_i] + 1.65\sigma_{zi} \leq b_i$. Substituting in our full expressions for $E[Z_i]$ and σ_{zi}, the chance constraint (5.40) becomes

$$\sum_j \bar{a}_{ij} X_j + K_\alpha \left[\sum_j \sum_k X_j X_k \text{cov}(a_{ij}, a_{ik}) \right]^{1/2} \leq b_i \qquad (5.43)$$

Given sample data, all the covariances could be calculated and (5.43) added to a model. Unfortunately, the inequality is quadratic in the Xs, and so the problem can be solved only by quadratic programming.[15]

Following Wicks and Guise (1978), the problem can be linearized through the following MOTAD formulation.

$$\max E = \sum_j \bar{c}_j X_j \qquad (5.44)$$

such that

$$\hat{\sigma}_i = \left(2F^{1/2}/T \right) \sum_t Z_{it}^+, \qquad \text{all } i \qquad (5.45)$$

and

$$\sum_j \left(a_{ijt} - \bar{a}_{ij} \right) X_j - Z_{it}^+ \leq 0, \qquad \text{all } t \qquad (5.46)$$

$$\sum_j \bar{a}_{ij} X_j + K_\alpha \hat{\sigma}_i \leq b_i, \qquad \text{all } i \qquad (5.47)$$

$$X_j, Z_{it}^+, \hat{\sigma}_i \geq 0, \qquad \text{all } i, j, t \qquad (5.48)$$

Here $\bar{a}_{ij}$ denotes the sample mean value of the a_{ij}th coefficient and F is again Fisher's constant $\pi T/2(T - 1)$.

The Z_{it}^+ variables measure the amount by which the requirement of a farm plan for the ith resource in the tth year exceeds the average requirements for that resource, equation (5.46). In equation (5.45), these deviations provide a MAD estimator of the standard deviation of the plan's resource requirements. These estimates of σ_i are then entered in the chance constraint equations (5.46).

The MAD estimates of the standard deviations are included in the constraint set. Since these estimates will affect the choice of an optimal solution, they cannot be calculated after the solution has been obtained as we did with the MOTAD model in Section 5.5. The MAD is being used here to provide point estimates of the standard deviation as well as to rank farm plans, and it cannot be as reliable an alternative to quadratic programming as the parametric form of MOTAD presented in Section (5.5). Note also that the model will seek to minimize $\hat{\sigma}_i$ in those constraints in (5.47) that are binding.

Table 5.16 A MOTAD with RINOCO[a] Model

	Corn (ha)	Beans (ha)	Labor deviations (months)			$\hat{\sigma}$ (months)	RHS
			Z_1^+	Z_2^+	Z_3^+		
Expected total gross margin (pesos)	1372	1219					Maximize
Standard deviation of labor use (months)			1	1	1	−0.977	= 0
Labor (months)							
S_1	−0.2	0.23	−1				≤ 0
S_2	0.2	0.13		−1			≤ 0
S_3		−0.36			−1		≤ 0
Chance Constraint (months)	1.4	1.77				1.65	≤ 16.5

[a]Risky Input-Output Coefficients (after Wicks and Guise 1978).

This means that the corresponding Z^+ variables will be selected in a minimizing way, thereby fulfilling an essential requirement of the MOTAD approach.

Table 5.16 provides a simple illustration of the model using Mayaland data from Table 5.15. Only the labor portion of the tableau is shown, and an α value of 0.05 has been assumed. Since $T = 3$, then $F = 2.3571$ and $2F^{1/2}/T = 1.0235$. Equation (5.45) becomes

$$\hat{\sigma} = 1.0235 \sum_t Z_t^+$$

or

$$\sum_t Z_t^+ - 0.977\hat{\sigma} = 0$$

This explains the entry under $\hat{\sigma}$ in the second row of the table.

The model has been set up to maximize expected total gross margin, but other objective functions could be used, including an E, V or E, σ specification.

Despite the attractiveness of chance constraints, there are some major drawbacks to their use. First, if more than one chance constraint is to be incorporated in a model, then it is necessary to assume that the stochastic coefficients in each constraint are statistically independent of the stochastic coefficients in all the other constraints. Tractable methods for handling jointly dependent constraints have yet to be developed. Note that the coefficients within a constraint do not need to be statistically independent.

Second, even when two or more chance constraints are statistically independent, problems still arise in that the probability of all the constraints being feasible at the same time is the product of their individual probabilities. For example, if there are five chance constraints and each is to be satisfied with a probability of 0.95, then the probability that all five constraints will be satisfied at the same time is only $0.95^5 = 0.773$.

Third, a value of α has to be selected for each chance constraint. The chosen values may be inconsistent with the type and degree of risk averse behavior assumed in the objective function of the model. This problem can only be resolved through the kind of unified decision theory analysis offered by discrete stochastic programming.

Fourth, chance constrained programming provides no guidance as to what a farmer should do in the α percent of the years in which his plan will be infeasible. However, it is because the farmer does have recourse options, many of which are difficult to include in a model, that chance constraints are attractive.

NOTES

1 See Anderson, Dillon, Hardaker (1977, pp. 66–69) for an insightful review of the theory.

2 If X and Y are random variables then the variance of their sum is $V[X + Y] = V[X] + V[Y] + 2\,\mathrm{cov}[X, Y]$. Equation (5.4) is a generalization of this basic result.

3 The variances are always found along the diagonal of a variance-covariance matrix.

4 There have been some recent improvements, but improved algorithms are not widely available, particularly in developing countries.

5 The approach has been extended for use when subjective information can be elicited from farmers about possible income outcomes (Hardaker and Troncoso 1979).

6 We assume that the data are first adjusted for any trend or cyclical patterns.

7 The constant F was derived by Fisher (1920), and strictly speaking, it only holds for normally distributed random variables.

8 This assumes that Z_t^+ and Z_t^- will be selected in a minimizing way. This requirement is met when the estimated variance is minimized in a farm model. It is not met if the variance is maximized, hence a MOTAD approach is not applicable to a risk-loving farmer.

9 A zero sum game is one in which the sum of all winnings is equal to the sum of all losses among the players.

10 Kawaguchi and Maruyama (1972) developed farm planning models for additional decision criteria.

11 Readers who have ever invested in the stock market will appreciate the concept as the remorse felt at breakfast when reading the financial pages of the newspaper and realizing how much money they might have made (or saved) the previous day.

12 Tauer (1983) also shows that the target MOTAD model, unlike MOTAD, provides farm plans that are always second-degree stochastic dominant.

13 Low's safety-first model is a good example (see Section 5.8.2). In this case feasibility with respect to a minimum income constraint is imposed in all states of nature.

14 For a contrary view, see Hogan, Morris, and Thompson (1981).

15 If only b_i is stochastic, then the reader can easily verify that the chance constraint becomes

$$\sum_j a_{ij} X_j \leq E(b_i) - K_\alpha \sigma_{bi}$$

In this case the equation is linear in the Xs and can be included in a linear programming model.

Chapter 6

Solving the Model
on a Computer

The practical use of linear programming as a farm planning tool has been greatly advanced in recent years by the development of computer software packages based on the simplex method. These packages are widely available on modern computer systems and offer a cheap and efficient way to solve even large models. Most packages also provide the user with options for post-optimality analysis for exploring the stability of the solution to changes in the model's coefficients.

One of the most popular linear programming packages is IBM's MPSX (Mathematical Programming System Extended) package. A similar package in terms of the input/output formats is CDC's APEX package. In this chapter we describe how to set up a simple linear programming problem for MPSX and illustrate the procedures involved and the nature of the optimal solution with the simple Mayaland farm example. The discussion draws heavily on Stanton (1977), and is not intended to be an exhaustive treatment of the facilities of the MPSX package.[1]

6.1 PREPARATION OF A LINEAR PROGRAMMING PROBLEM FOR SOLUTION ON A COMPUTER

Submission of a linear programming problem for solution by MPSX requires the following sets of cards:

1 Job and Catalog cards
2 Program cards
3 Data input cards

6.1.1 The Job and Catalog Cards

These cards are unique for each computer system, hence they are not discussed here. They are required to indicate the job to be performed, space requirements, and the procedure to be followed.

6.1.2 The Program Cards

These cards tell the computer which options available in the MPSX package are to be used and specify the sequence that should be followed. Order is important in most cases if the linear programming problem is to be solved. A set of program cards that will solve a standard linear programming problem follows together with some comments on each card. All cards are punched starting in column 10.

Card	Comment
PROGRAM	Signifies the beginning of the program cards.
INITIALZ	Calls a basic set of instructions that are standard for handling all the program cards that follow.
TITLE('....')	This optional card allows a user to establish a title for the problem which will be listed at the top of each page of results in the computer output. The title may consist of up to 40 characters.
MOVE(XDATA, '....')	This card allows the user to designate the name of the data set that will be used and stored in the system. Up to 8 characters may be used.
MOVE(XPBNAME, '....')	This card allows the user to designate which problem is being run using a given data set. Up to 8 characters may be used in making up such names.
MOVE(XOBJ, '....')	This card allows the user to designate the name of the objective function row for the problem. It cannot have more than 8 char-

	acters and must be listed exactly the same way in the data input section.
MOVE(XRHS, '....')	This card designates the name of the right-hand side of the problem set. Again this name must be exactly the same as the one used in the data input section, and can consist of up to 8 characters.
CONVERT('SUMMARY')	Tells the computer to read the data input, convert it to a binary problem format and store the data in a problem file.
SETUP('MAX')	Indicates whether the linear programming problem is a maximization ('MAX') or minimization problem ('MIN'). Maximization is assumed if no statement is specified following SETUP.

At this point four optional cards may be included in the program deck to provide additional information to the user in the printout for the problem.

BCDOUT	Prints a listing of the data input that allows the user to review the data set analyzed by the computer.
PICTURE	Prints the basic matrix to be solved in diagrammatic form. All numbers other than ± 1 are converted to an alphabetic code according to their magnitude.
TRANCOL	Prints the basic matrix to be solved in numerical form. For most linear programming problems this is the most useful way to compare the data read into the computer with the original matrix constructed in setting up the problem.
CRASH	Provides a routine that establishes the most efficient starting point for solving the problem. For small problems it provides little assistance in reaching efficient solutions.

This is the end of this set of optional program cards for standard linear programming problems. The next two cards must be included for all programs.

PRIMAL	Invokes the optimizing procedure using the simplex method to search for the optimal solution.
SOLUTION	Directs that the optimal solution obtained be printed.

Another set of optional program cards may be introduced at this point to provide additional analytical material to interpret the original solution or to extend the analysis. These extensions include postoptimality procedures as discussed in Sections 6.3 and 6.4.

The remaining program cards that must be included are as follows:

EXIT	Provides directions to the computer that the problem set is completed.
PEND	Designates the end of the program card deck.

6.1.3 The Data Input Cards

These cards provide the computer with the necessary information about the problem to be solved. They are organized into three sections. A ROWS section defines the name of each of the constraints or rows in the problem, including the objective function. It also specifies the type of constraint. A COLUMNS section defines the activity names in the problem and indicates the data coefficients that are to be entered in each row. Up to two data entries are permitted per card. Finally, a RHS section provides information about the supplies of the fixed farm resources. Detailed instructions for the preparation of the data input cards now follow.

NAME	This card is always the first one in the data input deck. NAME is written starting in column 1. The name for the data deck, which must be the same as the name in the XDATA program card, is written starting in column 15.
ROWS	An initial card starting in column 1 designating that the cards that follow describe the rows of the problem. Each of the cards that follow have the following format:

Card Columns:	2 or 3	5–12
	Type of constraint	Row name

The type of constraint is coded as L = less than or equal to; G = greater than or equal to; E = equal to; or N = not constrained (such as the objective function). Row names can consist of up to 8 characters, and the name of the objective function row must correspond to the name in the XOBJ program card. The order of the rows does not effect the solution but does determine the order in which they appear in the results.

Table 6.1   Coded Program and Data Cards for the Mayaland Farm
MPSX Linear Programming Package

```
(JCL cards)
          PROGRAM
          INITIALZ
          TITLE('MAYALAND FARM')
          MOVE(XDATA,'MAYALAND')
          MOVE(XPBNAME,'PROB1')
          MOVE(XOBJ,'OBJ')
          MOVE(XRHS,'B1')
          CONVERT('SUMMARY')
          SETUP('MAX')
          BCDOUT
          PICTURE
          TRANCOL
          PRIMAL
          SOLUTION
          EXIT
          PEND
(JCL cards)
NAME              MAYALAND
ROWS
  N    OBJ
  L    LAND
  L    LABOR
  L    MULES
  L    MARKET

COLUMNS
          CORN      OBJ       1372.      LAND       1.
          CORN      LABOR        1.42    MULES      1.45
          BEANS     OBJ       1219.      LAND       1.
          BEANS     LABOR        1.87    MULES      1.27
          SORGHUM   OBJ       1523.      LAND       1.
          SORGHUM   LABOR        1.92    MULES      1.16
          PEANUTS   OBJ       4874.      LAND       1.
          PEANUTS   LABOR        2.64    MULES      1.45
          PEANUTS   MARKET       0.983

RHS
          B1        LAND         5.      LABOR     16.5
          B1        MULES       10.      MARKET      .5

ENDATA

(JCL cards)
```

COLUMNS   This card, which is punched beginning in column 1, designates the beginning of the data cards for the activities or columns of the linear programming problem. Each of the cards that follows has the following format:

Card Columns:	5–12	15–22	25–36	40–47	50–61
	Column name	Row name	Numerical data	Row name	Numerical data

Each column name can consist of up to 8 characters, and the row names must correspond to those in the ROWS section. Decimals must always be entered, and all the cards corresponding to one column should be grouped together.

RHS   The card RHS, punched beginning in column 1, designates that the cards that follow give the right-hand side values of the problem. The corresponding data cards are prepared as follows:

Card Columns:	5–12	15–22	25–36	40–47	50–61
	Right-hand side name	Row name	Numerical data	Row name	Numerical data

The right-hand side name must correspond to that in the XRHS program card. The row names must match those in the ROWS section, and decimals must always be included.

ENDATA   This card indicates that the data input has been completed.

To illustrate the preparation of a deck of cards for a linear programming problem, Table 6.1 shows the relevant cards for the Mayaland farm problem in Table 2.2.

6.2 INTERPRETATION OF THE SOLUTION OUTPUT

A problem submitted for solution using the MPSX Linear Programming Package yields a substantial number of pages of computer output if there are no errors and a solution is obtained. The amount of output is determined by the control cards and the size of the problem. In general, the relevant part of the printout consists of two parts.

    1 A listing and detailed description of the problem submitted, including a list of the job control cards, a check for major and minor errors in the data, and a printout of data if BCDOUT, PICTURE, or TRANCOL is requested.

2   The optimal solution.

The first page of the output of the optimal solution lists the number of iterations computed before an optimal solution was reached. In the case of the Mayaland farm example, only two iterations were required before the optimal solution was found. This is followed by a separate page reporting the final value of the objective function; 9319 pesos for the Mayaland farm.

The main printout of the solution consists of a ROWS and COLUMNS section. The ROWS section indicates the status of each of the constraint rows in the problem. It tells whether or not the limiting resources were fully used and lists the DUAL values, or shadow prices, for all the constraints that are used up to capacity.

For the Mayaland farm information is reported in five rows (Table 6.2). The first is the objective function, OBJ, and the other four are the farm constraints.

The columns headed ACTIVITY and SLACK ACTIVITY report the amounts of resources used in the solution, and the amounts of slack or unused resources, respectively. Thus in row 2 all the land was used, and in row 5 the market constraint has been used to the maximum permitted level. However, rows 3 and 4 show that 6.5338 months of labor and 4.0525 months of mules are left slack.

The columns headed LOWER and UPPER LIMIT simply restate the greater than (LOWER) or less than (UPPER) constraints of the problem. All the constraints in Table 6.2 were ≤ constraints.

The last column, DUAL ACTIVITY, reports the shadow prices (or dual values) for the fixed resources and constraints that are fully used. These shadow prices are calculated for each resource as the cost to the objective function value if one unit of the resource were withdrawn from use by increasing the corresponding slack activity by one unit. All the shadow prices are therefore negative. The shadow price for land in Table 6.2 is − 1523 pesos. This means that if the farmer were to lose 1 hectare of land then his maximum attainable total gross margin would decline by 1523 pesos. The negative of a shadow price indicates the maximum amount by which the model's objective function could be increased if an additional unit of the resource were to become available. Thus, in the case of land, 1523 pesos is the maximum rent that the farmer should be willing to pay for an extra hectare of land beyond his initial 5 hectares.

The shadow price on the market constraint is − 3409 pesos. The negative of this amount is the extra total gross margin that could be earned if the farmer could increase his peanut sales by 1 ton. This might be possible by investing in a truck, or by devoting more time to expanding the number of customers.

Table 6.2 MPSX / Computer Output — Status of Rows in Optimal Solution, Mayaland Farm Example

MPSX / 370   MAYALAND FARM

SECTION 1 – ROWS

NUMBER	ROW	AT	ACTIVITY	SLACK ACTIVITY	LOWER LIMIT	UPPER LIMIT	DUAL ACTIVITY
1	OBJ	BS	9319.47609	9319.47609 –	NONE	NONE	1.00000
2	LAND	UL	5.00000	.	NONE	5.00000	1523.00000 –
3	LABOR	BS	9.96623	6.53377	NONE	16.50000	.
4	MULES	BS	5.94751	4.05249	NONE	10.00000	.
5	MARKET	UL	0.50000	.	NONE	0.50000	3408.95219 –

Table 6.3 MPSX Computer Output — Status of Columns in Optimal Solution, Mayaland Farm Example

MPSX / 370   MAYALAND FARM

SECTION 2 – COLUMNS

NUMBER	COLUMNS	AT	ACTIVITY	INPUT COST	LOWER LIMIT	UPPER LIMIT	REDUCED COST
6	CORN	LL	.	1372.00000	.	NONE	151.00000 –
7	BEANS	LL	.	1219.00000	.	NONE	304.00000 –
8	SORGHUM	BS	4.49135	1523.00000	.	NONE	.
9	PEANUTS	BS	0.50865	4874.00000	.	NONE	.

119

The COLUMNS section of the computer output (Table 6.3) provides information about the optimal farm plan. Each of the farm activities is listed as a row in this output.

The column headed ACTIVITY reports the status of each activity in the final solution. Thus the optimal plan for the Mayaland farm consists of 4.491 hectares of sorghum, 0.509 hectares of peanuts, and zero hectares of corn and beans.

The entries in the column headed INPUT COST are simply the per hectare gross margins from the data input. The LOWER and UPPER LIMIT columns indicate any constraints that were imposed on the individual activity levels. The LOWER LIMIT values are all zero, implying that negative activity levels are not permitted. Positive LOWER LIMITS and finite UPPER LIMITS only become effective if the MPSX option BOUNDS is used. This option enables the user to specify upper or lower limits on any activity. It is a more efficient way of introducing such constraints than adding additional constraints in the ROWS and RHS sections. The last column headed REDUCED COST is similar to a shadow price for the resource constraints. It is the amount by which the objective function value would decline if a unit of the corresponding activity were forced into the solution. Equivalently, the negative of the REDUCED COST is the amount by which the activity per hectare gross margin would have to be increased before that activity is profitable enough to be included in the optimal farm plan. The gross margins would have to increase by 151 pesos and 304 pesos per hectare, respectively, for corn and beans before these activities could be included in an optimal solution. The reduced cost coefficients are of course zero for those activities already in the optimal plan.

6.3 POSTOPTIMALITY ANALYSIS USING THE MPSX OPTION RANGE

The MPSX option RANGE provides information about the stability of the optimal linear programming solution. Stability is tested under a *ceteris paribus* condition, whereby the effect of a change in a single coefficient is considered with all other coefficients held constant. The stability of the solution refers to the degree of variation in the coefficient that can be absorbed by the model before a change in basis occurs. A change in basis is said to occur when a new activity enters the solution, or one previously in solution drops out. The value of the coefficient at which the change in basis occurs is a critical turning point, and the change in a coefficient required to span two critical turning points is referred to as the range for that coefficient. Stability thus depends on the magnitude of the range for each coefficient under the *ceteris paribus* condition.

To obtain a RANGE printout along with the optimal solution, an additional card is inserted immediately after the SOLUTION card in the program cards section of the input deck (see Section 6.1). This card contains the word RANGE punched beginning in column 10.

Table 6.4 Computer Output — Rows at Limit Level; RANGE Analysis, Mayaland Farm Example

MPSX / 370   MAYALAND FARM
SECTION 1 – ROWS AT LIMIT LEVEL

NUMBER	ROW	AT	ACTIVITY	SLACK ACTIVITY	LOWER LIMIT / UPPER LIMIT	LOWER ACTIVITY / UPPER ACTIVITY	UNIT COST	LOWER COST / UPPER COST	LIMITING PROCESS	AT
2	LAND	UL	5.00000	.	NONE	0.50865	1523.00000 -		SORGHUM	LL
					5.00000	8.40301	1523.00000		LABOR	UL
5	MARKET	UL	0.50000	.	NONE	.	3408.952158 -		PEANUTS	LL
					0.50000	4.91500	3408.95215		SORGHUM	LL

Table 6.5 MPSX Computer Output — Columns at Limit Level; RANGE Analysis, Mayaland Farm Example

MPSX / 370   MAYALAND FARM
SECTION 2 – COLUMNS AT LIMIT LEVEL

NUMBER	COLUMN	AT	ACTIVITY	INPUT COST	LOWER LIMIT / UPPER LIMIT	LOWER ACTIVITY / UPPER ACTIVITY	UNIT COST	LOWER COST / UPPER COST	LIMITING PROCESS	AT
6	CORN	LL	.	1372.00000	.	13.06755 -	151.00000 -	INFINITY -	LABOR	UL
					NONE	4.49135	151.00000	1523.00000	SORGHUM	LL
7	BEANS	LL	.	1219.00000	.	130.67548 -	304.00000 -	INFINITY -	LABOR	UL
					NONE	4.49135	304.00000	1523.00000	SORGHUM	LL

Table 6.6 MPSX Computer Output — Rows at Intermediate Level; RANGE Analysis, Mayaland Farm Example

MPSX / 370 MAYALAND FARM
SECTION 3 - ROWS AT INTERMEDIATE LEVEL

NUMBER	ROW	AT	ACTIVITY	SLACK ACTIVITY	LOWER LIMIT	UPPER LIMIT	LOWER ACTIVITY	UPPER ACTIVITY	UNIT COST	LOWER COST	UPPER COST	LIMITING PROCESS	AT
3	LABOR	BS	9.96623	6.53377	NONE		7.72055		302.00000 -			CORN	LL
						16.50000		9.96623	INFINITY -			NONE	
4	MULES	BS	5.94751	4.05249	NONE		0.73754		1312.93115 -			LAND	UL
						10.00000		7.25000	520.68970 -			CORN	LL

Table 6.7 MPSX Computer Output — Columns at Intermediate Level; RANGE Analysis, Mayaland Farm Example

MPSX / 370 MAYALAND FARM
SECTION 4 - COLUMNS AT INTERMEDIATE LEVEL

NUMBER	COLUMN	AT	ACTIVITY	INPUT COST	LOWER LIMIT	UPPER LIMIT	LOWER ACTIVITY	UPPER ACTIVITY	UNIT COST	LOWER COST	UPPER COST	LIMITING PROCESS	AT
8	SORGHUM	BS	4.49135	1523.00000	.		9.48276 -		151.00000 -	1372.00000		CORN	LL
						NONE		5.00000	3351.00000 -		4874.00000	MARKET	UL
9	PEANUTS	BS	0.50864	4874.00000	.		INFINITY -		3351.00000 -	1523.00000		MARKET	UL
						NONE		0.50865	INFINITY -		INFINITY	NONE	UL

The additional printout generated by RANGE is organized in four sections. These are illustrated in Tables 6.4 to 6.7 using the Mayaland farm example.

6.3.1 Rows at Limit Level

This section (Table 6.4) reports on the stability of the constraints that are used up to their limit in the optimal solution. These are the resources or constraints that have nonzero shadow prices in the optimal solution. For the Mayaland farm these are the land and market constraints. Part of the table simply duplicates the information contained in the ROWS section of the optimal solution printout (Table 6.2). The new information of importance is reported in the column headed LOWER/UPPER ACTIVITY. This column shows the range in the b_i coefficient for each constraint over which the shadow price still holds—the two numbers reported for a row are the critical turning points for the solution basis. The activity levels will of course change as the supply of a limiting resource is changed, but the activities appearing in the solution basis will not change over this range.

In the case of the land, the shadow price of 1523 pesos per hectare would remain the same in the optimal solution if the land constraint were reduced from 5.0 to 0.508 hectares, or if it were increased to 8.403 hectares. This relatively wide range suggests that the optimal basis is robust with respect to land area. It also provides information of potential value to the farmer. For example, we could now advise our Mayaland farmer to pay up to 1523 pesos per hectare to rent an additional 3.403 hectares of land. However, if additional land renting were contemplated beyond 3.403 hectares, we could not advise on the rent to pay without solving a revised linear programming problem.

Similarly, the market constraint for peanuts has a shadow price of 3409 pesos per ton, and this shadow price holds over the range 0 to 4.915 tons. If the market constraint were increased to 4.915 tons the farmer could devote his entire 5 hectares to peanuts (see Table 2.2). This suggests that the farmer should attach high priority to ways of expanding his market for peanuts; each additional ton that he could sell would add 3409 pesos to his total gross margin.

The column headed LIMITING PROCESS provides information about the activity that would leave the solution basis at the critical turning point for each limiting resource. For example, if the available land were reduced to 0.508 hectares, then sorghum would be forced out of the optimal solution. On the other hand, if the available land were increased to 8.403 hectares, then labor would become a binding constraint and the slack labor activity would leave the basis.

If the market constraint for peanuts were reduced to zero, then peanuts would be forced out of the optimal basis. But if the market constraint were increased to 4.915 tons, sorghum would leave the optimal solution and the entire land area would be devoted to peanuts.

6.3.2 Columns at Limit Level

This section (Table 6.5) reports on the stability of those activities that appear at their limit levels in the optimal solution. The relevant activities are corn and beans which are at their lower limit level of zero.[2] We have already seen that these activities have nonzero REDUCED COSTS (Table 6.3), and these reduced costs are reported under the column headed UNIT COST in Table 6.5. They measure the amount by which an activity c_j coefficient would have to increase before the activity could enter the optimal solution. The new information reported in Table 6.5 pertains to the level at which an activity would enter the optimal solution if its c_j coefficient were increased by the required reduced cost. This information is to be found in the column headed UPPER ACTIVITY. For example, corn would enter the optimal solution if its gross margin were increased by 151 pesos to 1523 pesos per hectare (the UPPER COST), and it would enter the optimal solution at 4.491 hectares. Similarly beans would enter the optimal solution at 4.491 hectares if their gross margin were increased by 304 pesos to 1523 pesos per hectare.

The column headed LIMITING PROCESS shows that if corn or beans did enter the solution at 4.491 hectares then sorghum would be forced out of the solution to provide the necessary land. Since sorghum has a gross margin of 1523 pesos per hectare, this explains why the gross margin for corn or beans must increase to 1523 pesos per hectare if they are to enter the solution.

Table 6.5 also shows changes in activity levels corresponding to critical reductions in their gross margins. However, these are of little interest since the activity levels decline from zero to negative levels.

6.3.3 Rows at Intermediate Level

This section of the sensitivity analysis considers the constraints that were not used at capacity in the optimal solution (Table 6.6). These are the rows for labor and mules in the Mayaland farm example. In each case there is a slack capacity available so the shadow price is zero. The relevant information in Table 6.6 shows what happens if the b_i coefficients of these constraints are reduced below the level at which the resource is used in the optimal solution.

The optimal solution uses only 9.966 months of the available 16.5 months of labor. The LOWER ACTIVITY column in Table 6.6 shows that if the supply of labor were reduced to 7.72 months then a change in basis would result. With that amount of labor the LIMITING PROCESS column shows that corn, which requires least labor per hectare (Table 2.2), would enter the optimal basis. Corn would in fact exactly replace sorghum in the solution. Similarly the supply of mules could be reduced from 10.0 to 0.7375 months before a change in basis would occur. At 0.7375 months some land would become idle and hence the slack activity for land would enter the basis.

The UNIT COST entries in Table 6.6 indicate the amount of total gross margin foregone for each unit reduction in a resource below the level at which it is employed in the optimal solution. Each month reduction in labor below

9.966 months would cost 302 pesos, and the value holds for each month until labor has been reduced to 7.72 months. Similarly with mules, each month reduction below 5.948 months would cost 1312.93 pesos, and this value holds for each month reduction until there are only 0.7375 months of mules left.

6.3.4 Columns at Intermediate Level

This section (Table 6.7) reports on the stability of those activities included in the optimal solution at nonzero levels. The column headed LOWER/UPPER COST shows the range in activity gross margins for which the current basis remains optimal.

Sorghum has a gross margin of 1523 pesos per hectare and at that level 4.491 hectares enter the optimal solution. However, sorghum would remain in the basis even if its gross margin were reduced by 151 pesos (the entry in the UNIT COST column) to 1372 pesos (the LOWER COST entry). If the gross margin for sorghum fell below 1372 pesos per hectare then corn would become sufficiently attractive relative to sorghum to enter the basis (see the LIMITING PROCESS column). On the upside, the gross margin for sorghum could increase to 4874 pesos per hectare before a change in basis would occur. At that level of profitability, sorghum would displace peanuts in the optimal solution and the slack activity for the market constraint would enter the basis.

Table 6.7 also shows that peanuts are a stable crop. Their gross margin would have to fall from 4874 to 1523 pesos per hectare before they would leave the optimal basis (they would be replaced in the basis by the slack activity for the market constraint). On the other hand, the optimal basis remains unchanged for any sized increase in their gross margin as shown by the infinity entry in the UPPER COST column. This is because of the market constraint on peanuts.

Note that in all these results it is always assumed that only one coefficient is changed at a time from its initial value. RANGE cannot be used to analyze the stability of the solution with respect to simultaneous changes in more than one coefficient.

6.4 POSTOPTIMALITY ANALYSIS USING PARAMETRIC PROGRAMMING

Parametric programming is one of the most important methods of further analysis after an initial optimum solution is obtained. This option allows one to consider the impact of a sequence of incremental changes in any of the model coefficients. Any a_{ij}, b_i, or c_j can be varied systematically and changes in the optimal solution studied. The technique is useful for additional sensitivity analysis of an optimal solution where it is desired to explore the stability of the solution for values of coefficients lying beyond critical values identified in the MPSX RANGE analysis. Also, by varying c_j or b_i coefficients, it is a powerful way to derive product supply or resource demand functions from a farm or sector model. It is also a useful tool in risk analysis as we saw in Chapter 5.

There are five basic options available in the MPSX package:

PARAOBJ   Considers changes in one or more coefficients in the objective function, others held constant

PARARHS   Considers changes in one or more RHS value, all other coefficients held constant

PARARIM   Considers simultaneously changes for coefficients in both the objective function and the RHS

PARACOL   Considers changes in one or more a_{ij} coefficients for a specific activity

PARAROW   Considers changes in one or more a_{ij} coefficients for a specific constraint

The first two of these options are the ones most commonly used in applied economic analysis, and they form the subject of our present discussion.

6.4.1 Basis Changes or Fixed Intervals

There are two ways to approach problems using the parametric options. One is to establish a fixed interval of change for the coefficient parameterized and then determine the optimal solution for successive values of that coefficient. This is the fixed interval option. For example, the amount of land available to the Mayaland farmer is 5.0 hectares. One could look at the optimal solutions obtained as the available land increases by intervals of 0.1 hectares. In this case the computer would solve and print for the initial supply of 5.0 hectares, and then successively provide solutions for 5.1 hectares, 5.2 hectares, and so on to an upper limit of say 10.0 hectares, all other coefficients held constant at their original values.

The second option is to instruct the computer to print solutions only at basis changes when a coefficient is parameterized. Using the example just considered, the available land is initially set at 5.0 hectares. After printing the initial optimal solution, the program prints a solution only when a change in basis occurs. That is, when the increase in the available land induces a new activity to enter the basis. A range of land areas is specified initially and the procedure stops when the maximum land area has been reached.

It is this second alternative which is of greatest value in economic analysis using linear programming. A particularly useful property of such parametrically derived solutions is that the solution corresponding to any noncritical value of the parameterized coefficient can always be derived by linear interpolation between adjacent basic solutions. Thus the set of basic solutions provides complete information about the optimal solution corresponding to any value of the coefficient within the prescribed range. With the fixed interval approach however, solutions corresponding to basis changes are only captured by chance, and linear interpolations between adjacent solutions may prove misleading. In the examples that follow the suggested program calls for printing solutions at basis changes only.

6.4.2 An Example Using PARAOBJ

Suppose that in the Mayaland farm example it is desired to know the supply function of sorghum for the farm over a range of possible price changes. To obtain this supply function we must systematically vary the price of sorghum over the relevant range of prices.

The initial gross margin for sorghum (Table 2.2) is 1523 pesos per hectare. Suppose this gross margin is derived as follows:

> Yield of sorghum = 1.00 ton/hectare
> Price of sorghum = 1760 pesos/ton
> Revenue = (1.0)(1760) = 1760 pesos/hectare
> Direct production costs = 237 pesos/hectare
> Gross margin = 1760 − 237 = 1523 pesos/hectare

Suppose also that the range of prices of interest is 1000 to 5000 pesos per ton. If we substitute this latter price into the gross margin calculation, then the range of gross margins we need to consider is 763 to 4763 pesos per hectare.

To obtain the required solutions for the Mayaland farm using the basis change approach, the program and data cards are set up as shown in Table 6.8. If one compares this set of cards with those in Table 6.1 for the standard linear programming problem, many of them are the same. The new program and data cards and their function are described below.

Card	Comment
MOVE(XCHROW,'CHSOR')	This card identifies the name of a change row; in this case CHSOR. The name is optional and may consist of up to 8 characters. The chosen name must also be used on cards now added to, or changed, in the DATA deck. For this example a total of three changes are introduced into the data deck. In the ROWS section following the objective function OBJ, a new card is introduced: N CHSOR. In the columns section, the coefficient for sorghum in the OBJ row is changed to 763.0. This is the new initial gross margin. In addition, a unit coefficient is entered for sorghum in the CHSOR

row. The positive sign on this coefficient indicates that the gross margin for sorghum is to be parameterized over increasing values. A -1.0 coefficient would lead to the gross margin being successively reduced.

XPARDELT=0.0

This card fixes the interval at which solutions are to be printed. It is always set equal to 0.0 when solutions are required at basis changes only.

XPARMAX=4000.0

This card defines the maximum increase to be considered for the coefficient being parameterized. In our example we wish the gross margin for sorghum to be increased from 763 pesos to 4763 pesos, or a total increment of 4000 pesos.

XPARAM=0.0

This card indicates that parameterization should start at the initial value for the coefficient.

XFREQ1=1

This card alerts the computer to carry out the command that follows at intervals of one (for each change in basis).

MVADR(XDOFREQ1,PRINTSOL)

This is the key program card for printing solutions at basis changes.

PARAOBJ

This is the program card calling for the set of parametric options to be performed using all the previous commands.

PRINTSOL SOLUTION

This calls for printing each solution following the PARAOBJ option.

6.4.3   Interpreting the Computer Output for PARAOBJ

The output for parametric programming has the same format as discussed for the standard linear programming run in Section 6.2. The first solution printed is the optimal one for the initial set of coefficients in the objective function. Note though that in the example we have reduced the initial gross margin for sorghum to 763 pesos per hectare. A sequence of optimal solutions are then printed, each corresponding to a basis change as the gross margin for sorghum is increased to the next critical value. The value of the gross margin for sorghum at which the basis change occurs is also indicated. The last solution printed is always the solution for the final value established (PARMAX) for the parameterized coefficient.

Table 6.8   Mayaland Example of Use of PARAOBJ Program and Data Cards for MPSX

```
(JCL cards)
          PROGRAM
          INITIALZ
          TITLE('MAYALAND CHANGING SORGHUM PRICE')
          MOVE(XDATA,'MAYALAND')
          MOVE(XPBNAME,'PROB2')
          MOVE(XOBJ,'OBJ')
          MOVE(XRHS,'B1')
          MOVE(XCHROW,'CHSOR')
          XPARDELT = 0.0
          XPARMAX = 4000.0
          XPARAM = 0.0
          CONVERT('SUMMARY')
          SETUP('MAX')
          PRIMAL
          SOLUTION
          FREQ1 = 1
          MVADR(XDOFREQ1,PRINTSOL)
          PARAOBJ
PRINTSOL  SOLUTION
          EXIT
          PEND

(JCL cards)
NAME            MAYALAND
ROWS
 N    OBJ
 N    CHSOR
 L    LAND
 L    LABOR
 L    MULES
 L    MARKET

COLUMNS
      CORN      OBJ        1372.      LAND      1.
      CORN      LABOR         1.42    MULES     1.45
      BEANS     OBJ        1219.      LAND      1.
      BEANS     LABOR         1.87    MULES     1.27
      SORGHUM   OBJ         763.      CHSOR     1.
      SORCHUM   LAND          1.      LABOR     1.92
      SORGHUM   MULES         1.16
      PEANUTS   OBJ        4874.      LAND      1.
      PEANUTS   LABOR         2.64    MULES     1.45
      PEANUTS   MARKET        0.983

RHS
      B1        LAND          5.      LABOR    16.5
      B1        MULES        10.      MARKET     .5

ENDATA

(JCL cards)
```

**Table 6.9   Basic Solutions for Changes in the Price of Sorghum,
Mayaland Farm Example**

	Initial solution	First basis change	Final solution
Price of sorghum (pesos / ton)	1000	1609	5000
Gross margin for sorghum (pesos / ha)	763	1372	4763
Total gross margin (pesos)	8641.28	8641.28	23871.46
Crop areas (ha)			
Corn	4.491	—	—
Beans	—	—	—
Sorghum	—	4.491	4.491
Peanuts	0.509	0.509	0.509
Slack activities			
Land (ha)	—	—	—
Labor (months)	8.779	6.534	6.534
Mules (months)	2.750	4.052	4.052
Market (tons)	—	—	—

Table 6.9 shows the sequence of solutions obtained for the Mayaland example in Table 6.8. In this case there is only one basis change as the sorghum price is parameterized from 1000 to 5000 pesos per ton. This change in basis occurs when the gross margin of sorghum is 1372 pesos per hectare; equivalent to a sorghum price of 1609 pesos per ton. At that price sorghum displaces corn from the solution. Since there are no further basis changes, the last solution printed is the same as the previous one.

6.4.4   An Example Using PARARHS

Instead of parameterizing one or more coefficients in the objective function, it is sometimes useful to study the impact of changing the availability of one or two key resources or restrictions listed among the RHS. For example, in the Mayaland example, it may be desired to study the impact on the optimal farm plan of changes in the amount of land available.

The procedure to institute parametric programming on a key RHS coefficient is analogous to that for PARAOBJ, but now a change column is introduced instead of a change row. A new card for the change column is added in the RHS section of the input deck. The name of the change column may be described using up to eight characters, but it must conform exactly with the name used in the program deck.

The new data card to change the available land in the Mayaland example might read as:

CHLAND   LAND   1.0

where CHLAND is the name of the change column and is punched starting in

Table 6.10 Mayaland Example of Use of PARARHS Program Cards for MPSX

```
         PROGRAM
         INITIALZ
         TITLE('MAYALAND CHANGING LAND RHS')
         MOVE(XDATA,'MAYALAND')
         MOVE(XPNAME,'PROB3')
         MOVE(XOBJ,'OBJ')
         MOVE(XRHS,'B1')
         MOVE(XCHCOL,'CHLAND')
         XPARDELT = 0.0
         XPARMAX = 5.0
         XPARAM = 0.0
         CONVERT('SUMMARY')
         SETUP('MAX')
         PRIMAL
         SOLUTION
         XFREQ1 = 1
         MVADR(XDOFREQ1,PRINTSOL)
         PARARHS
PRINTSOL SOLUTION
         EXIT
         PEND
```

column 5. This new card is inserted in the RHS section of the deck immediately after all the B1 cards.

The program cards for the Mayaland example are given in Table 6.10. This program parameterizes the available land from its initial value of 5.0 hectares to a maximum of 10.0 hectares. The program also calls for solutions to be printed at each change in basis.

NOTES

1 IBM publishes its own manuals describing how to use the MPSX package.
2 Activities may enter at nonzero limit levels when the MPSX option BOUNDS is used.

Part Two

The Sector Model

Chapter 7

The Economic Structure of the Sector Model

7.1 THE SECTOR AS AN ECONOMIC UNIT

In Part I of this book, the microeconomic foundations were established for the product supply side of agricultural models. In this chapter and the next the analysis is carried from the farm level to the sector level. Spatial distinctions on the supply side and consumer demand functions are introduced. Factor supply functions also are introduced, and product and factor prices now are determined by supply and demand considerations rather than being fixed.

In moving to the sector level of analysis, it becomes necessary to define market forms in the models: competitive, monopolistic, oligopolistic, monopsonistic, etc. While the study of market forms traditionally falls in the domain of microeconomics, the sector is a separate level of analysis that is distinct from both the micro level and the economy-wide level. One of the main characteristics of a sector model is that it includes all sources of supply and demand for the products of the sector. The supply and demand sources may be considerably aggregated, for example, into a few producing regions and into national consumer demand functions, but nevertheless a sector model is comprehensive in this regard. It includes international trade possibilities as well when they are relevant.

On the other hand, sector models are not equally comprehensive for all factors of production. Only economy-wide models are complete in their descriptions of domestic factor markets. A sector model typically will include one or more factors that are sector-specific in the short or medium run (such as land and irrigation water in agricultural models), but it also will include factors that are mobile across sectors (capital, hired labor).

Implicitly or explicitly, every sector model's structure contains the following five elements:

1   A description of producers' economic behavior, that is, their decision rules on output composition and scale. In agriculture, the motives of profit maximization and risk aversion usually figure importantly in the decision rules, but other considerations may be important as well (such as production for home retentions in subsistence agriculture).

2   A description of the production functions, or technology sets, available to producers in each region. These functions relate yields to inputs, and they need to be differentiated by farming regime (irrigated vs. nonirrigated, livestock vs. annual crops vs. perennial crops, etc.). In dualistic agricultural sectors, different groups of producers may have very different options in technology and even in the crops they may grow. A subsistence farmer in rainfed areas may not be able to grow all the crops that a farmer with irrigation can, and he may not have access to the same degree of mechanization. Thus, appropriate differentiation of the technology sets can be important for making the model as realistic as possible. Also, depending on the agroclimatic conditions and farming customs, in some cases multiproduct production functions need to be specified.

3   A definition of the resource endowments held by each group of producers. These endowments refer chiefly to land, irrigation supplies, and family labor, although for some models it also is important to include initial stocks of tree crops, livestock, and farm machinery. Even with the same technology sets, variations in resource endowments will lead to differences in farmer response, in terms of their output levels and mixes.

4   A specification of the market environment in which the producer operates. As noted, this specification will include market forms plus associated consumer demand functions, and it will include statements about which inputs are effectively available in perfectly elastic or inelastic supply. It can include simple stepped supply functions where they are appropriate, such as a two-part market for short-term credit, with a limited amount of institutional credit available at a subsidized rate and an unlimited amount available on the informal credit market at a higher rate. Another element of the market environment is the cost of marketing and processing agricultural products. Often the marketing costs will vary spatially, and such variations should be included in the model. Finally, the market environment also includes possibilities for international trade and the corresponding import supply functions, export demand functions, export quotas, etc. In

most cases, the import supply functions are simple, that is, perfectly elastic at a given c.i.f. price, but it is important to make an explicit decision about each component of the market environment.

5   A specification of the policy environment of the sector. In this case, for example, values are needed for rates of input subsidy (and for amounts of inputs available at the subsidized rates) and a specification is needed for output subsidies when they are relevant. Frequently the latter take the form of a guaranteed minimum price, which means a horizontal demand function at the guaranteed price. This kind of demand function can be entered into the model alongside the usual downward-sloping market demand function, and the guaranteed price will become effective only if the market price would otherwise fall below it. To construct the model, it is not necessary to know the rates of input subsidy, only the subsidized prices, but to be able to make policy experiments involving possible variations in subsidy rates it is necessary to know the initial rates. Import quotas and tariffs also fall in the category of policy instruments, but export quotas are included in the description of the market environment, for they are beyond the reach of purely domestic policy.

These five specifications define a sector model, and they also define the sector as an economic unit. The sector has economy-wide characteristics, such as prices that are not fixed and completeness as regards sources of supply and demand. It also contains elements of micro theory, such as production functions and producers' decision rules. And it has a policy dimension that is relevant both for understanding the functioning of the sector and for conducting policy experiments. From a policy viewpoint, the sector has a fairly clearcut identity, especially in the case of agriculture, for many policy instruments are sector-specific. From a product viewpoint, the sector is well defined also, for it is complete in the treatment of the specified products. The boundaries are less clear-cut for factors, but installed productive capacity always is sector-specific in the short and medium run.

The sector's boundaries can be ambiguous as regards households. Frequently a given household will have members working in more than one sector, and they may receive nonwage income (remittances, rents) from other sectors. A complete sector model may need variables or parameters defining the opportunity costs of factors in other sectors to permit correct determination of factor prices. However, it does not need a complete specification of incomes of the households in the sector. The consumer demand portion of a sector model refers to all demands for the products of the sector, and not to all the consumer demands of the households that are primarily engaged in the sector. In other words, the model includes all demands for agricultural products, but not all demands by farming households. This distinction becomes especially relevant for regional submodels in a sector, where it is necessary to derive, by indirect means, the demand curves facing the producers of that region, as opposed to the demand curves of the families living in that region.

Thus, the sector as defined here has a clear economic identity, and its behavior can be defined by well-known tools of analysis such as production and consumption theory, trade analysis, the theory of risk-averse behavior, and analysis of fiscal choices. A sector analysis can be carried out without a model,[1] but the sector is a highly interdependent and multivariate entity, so often it is helpful to use a model to study the sector's interlinked reactions to policy change or to other external changes.

Agriculture is a sector in which the main variables are unusually interdependent. On the supply side, the products within a producing region often compete for the same local resources of soils, water, labor, and capital.[2] The farm or district can be viewed as a multiproduct firm, and in many cases the product mix of that firm is sensitive to prices and other variables. In addition, different districts and regions compete with each other for access to the same national and international markets. For these reasons, there usually is marked interdependence among products on the supply side of the sector. To put it in other terms, there often are many cross-elasticities of supply that are significantly different from zero, and they may differ by region for the same pairs of products. As remarked in Chapter 1, the available data series, at least for developing countries, usually are not sufficient to permit statistical estimation of the complete set of supply elasticities; hence the popularity of the process analysis approach which is the topic of this book.

Other significant sources of economic interdependence in the sector are found on the demand side, where product substitution is common (especially among oilseeds and also among forage crops), and where there may be multiple markets for a single good. And of course there is interdependence among supply and demand in the determination of prices.

An illustrative example of these linkages is found in the case of cotton. The cultivation of cotton yields two joint products: cotton fiber and cottonseed oil. The oil competes with other edible oils, such as safflower, corn, sesame, soybean, and linseed oils, and hence the market price of cottonseed oil is very much influenced by the production costs and cultivation conditions for these other crops. It also depends on the demand growth for oils for both human and livestock uses. The cotton fiber faces its own domestic markets (with competing fibers), and both oils and cotton fiber enter into international trade as well. Hence, a medium-term projection regarding the profitability of cotton production depends on rather complex factors on the demand side, not to mention cotton's competition with other crops for resources on the supply side.

In this brief sketch of the basic elements of sector analysis, and therefore of a sector model, attention has been confined to static elements. The investment decision is ignored for the time being, as a matter of convenience in exposition. Investment analysis was introduced in Chapter 4 and it is discussed again in Chapter 12. The exposition in this chapter and in Chapters 8 and 9 deals with the static structure of the model (based on a complete cropping year), which in any case is a part of most investment models. The principles of policy analysis with sector models are introduced in Chapter 12.

7.2   TWO LEVELS OF DECISION PROBLEMS

Frequently the policy problem is visualized in terms of alternative allocations of public resources, toward specified ends of policy. Sometimes it is cast in terms of finding the production patterns that will contribute most to the creation of employment or to foreign exchange earnings or to the promotion of other goals. Conceiving of the policy problem in either of these ways is incomplete and is not likely to lead to realistic prescriptions for policy, for there is an important omission: the analysis of the degree to which the sector will respond to policy changes.

Achieving the ends of policy via reallocations of public resources requires the cooperation of farmers. Even in highly centralized economies there are limits to the extent that governments can dictate cropping patterns and other production decisions, much less in market-oriented economies. Therefore, finding the "optimal" cropping patterns from a viewpoint of policy may not be very useful unless ways are also found to induce farmers to adopt those cropping patterns.

To state it another way, agricultural decision problems involve choices on at least two levels. At one level (the macro level) a policy maker is trying to decide how best to allocate funds in the face of more than one objective, and also in the face of uncertainty about what all the allocational consequences will be. This uncertainty really is uncertainty about how farmers, ranchers, and others will respond to the contemplated policy change. At the other level, the micro level, farmers have their own decision problem: how best to respond to the new policy environment, given their own objectives and limitations of action.

In order to solve the macro (or policy) problem, the uncertainty about micro responses has to be reduced. In other words, some means of simulating the probable response of farmers is required before the policy decision is taken. This statement may seem to be a truism, but it is common practice in project appraisal to assume that producers will adopt the "improved technology" or the "higher-value crops" without inquiring into producer decision rules and constraints which might affect the adoption decision. The usual way to simulate producer decisions is to build a model that reflects their constraints, opportunities, and objectives, and then to solve it under varying assumptions about the policy environment affecting producers. Agricultural producers differ widely in their resources, wealth endowments, and economic opportunities, so an adequate investigation of producer response to policy changes requires models of several representative farms.

To evaluate policy options, a key analytic question concerns the modeling of producers' responses to new technologies, greater resource endowments, and altered relative prices. Understanding consumers' responses can be an important part of the problem as well, depending on the circumstance, but the producers' behavior question always is present. This question is so basic (and still not well enough answered!) that it has been the principal focus of applied agricultural modeling work.

It could be argued that effort should be devoted to formal modeling of the policy problem: to maximize a weighted set of policy objectives, subject to specification of policy options and their consequences, and subject to constraints that limit the degrees of freedom for policy action. Sometimes that is in fact a fruitful approach (Chapter 12), but usually it is more productive to orient the analytic effort toward providing a better understanding of the potential responses of producers. The reason is simple: until producers' responses are better understood, the consequences of policy actions cannot be specified for the policy decision model.

Thus in analytic terms, the policy problem can be decomposed into the following two problems: (1) the problem of allocation of public resources under goals and constraints, given predictions of how farmers will react to each possible allocation, and (2) the problem of predicting farmers' reactions. The second problem almost always is the more difficult for the analyst, and accordingly is the focus of attention in this book. As noted in Chapter 1, the first problem may be called normative and the second positive, or the first prescriptive and the second descriptive.

7.2.1 A Mathematical Formulation

Both problems may be expressed as optimization problems. To gain some insight into the ways in which they are linked, it may be useful to write the problems formally in mathematical notation. A formal description of the problem contains four basic components: the policy goals and objective function, the available policy instruments, the constraints on the policy instruments, and the sector's reactions to policy changes. If the set of policy instruments were to include, for example, input and output subsidies, then the principal constraint on these instruments would be the budgetary funds available to finance the subsidies. For sake of illustration, let us assume that the principal objectives of policy are generating more agricultural employment and earning more foreign exchange via agricultural exports. They can be denoted X_0^e and X_0^h, respectively, and are the elements of X_0, the vector of policy objectives. Let the instruments be a corn (maize) subsidy X_2^m, a wheat subsidy X_2^w, and a cotton subsidy X_2^c, where X_2 is the vector of instrument variables. The corresponding cropping activity levels (in acres or hectares) can be denoted X_1^m, X_1^w, and X_1^c, respectively, where X_1 is the vector of activity levels.

If only those three crops are considered, the policy optimization problem then has the following shape:

$$\max_{X_2} Z = f\left(X_0^e, X_0^h \right) = w_e X_0^e + w_h X_0^h \tag{7.1}$$

subject to:

definitions of values of the policy objectives

$$X_0^e = e_m X_1^m + e_w X_1^w + e_c X_1^c \qquad (7.2\text{a})$$

$$X_0^h = h_m X_1^m + h_w X_1^w + h_c X_1^c \qquad (7.2\text{b})$$

reaction functions for producers

$$X_1^m = f_m(X_2^m, X_2^w, X_2^c) \qquad (7.3\text{a})$$

$$X_1^w = f_w(X_2^m, X_2^w, X_2^c) \qquad (7.3\text{b})$$

$$X_1^c = f_c(X_2^m, X_2^w, X_2^c) \qquad (7.3\text{c})$$

constraint on government budgetary resources

$$k_m X_2^m + k_w X_2^w + k_c X_2^c \le g \qquad (7.4)$$

Equation (7.1) is the policy makers' objective function, where w_e and w_h are the policy "preference weights" as regards the two goals of employment creation and foreign exchange earned.[3] Equations (7.2a) and (7.2b) provide the links between the policy goals and the farmers' decisions on cropping levels. The coefficients e_m, e_w, and e_c express the amount of employment required per hectare for each of the three crops. Likewise, the h_j ($j = m, w, c$) denote the foreign exchange earned (through exports) or saved (through import substitution) per hectare cultivated in each crop. Some of the h_j may be zero but all of the e_j must be positive.

Equations (7.3a) through (7.3c) are the "reaction functions," showing how farmers' planting decisions are influenced by the subsidy instruments.[4] In general, the decisions on any one crop are influenced by the amount of subsidy in all crops, because it is the relative profitability of crops that influences cropping patterns. Finally, equation (7.4) is the government's budget constraint for outlays on subsidies. The coefficients k_j are the costs per hectare of the subsidy instrument, and the limit g is the available subsidy budget in monetary terms.

For this illustrative policy problem, equations (7.1) through (7.4) provide a complete analytic description, but equations (7.3a) through (7.3c) are "black boxes." Most of the effort in sector modeling is devoted to illuminating the contents of these black boxes. Of course, usually the policy problem is more complex than this example suggests, and so before broaching the sector model per se it may be useful to essay a more complete treatment of the policy problem. In essence, it is a two-level optimization problem, and the reaction functions can be decomposed into their constituent components, which are farmers' objective functions and the constraints faced by farmers. Letting the subscript 1 represent the producers' level of decisions and the subscript 2 represent the policy level, the problems may be expressed as follows:[5]

$$\max_{X_2} Z_2 = f_2(c_2' X_0) \qquad (7.5)$$

subject to

$$kX_2 \le g \tag{7.6}$$

$$\underset{X_1 | X_2}{\text{maximize}}\, Z_1 = f_1(c_1' X_1) \tag{7.7}$$

$$A_{11} X_1 + A_{12} X_2 \le b \tag{7.8}$$

$$-I X_0 + A_{21} X_1 + A_{22} X_2 = 0 \tag{7.9}$$

$$-a_1' I X_2 + c_1 = 0 \tag{7.10}$$

$$X_0,\, X_1,\, X_2 \ge 0 \tag{7.11}$$

where X_0 is a vector of target variables (policy objectives, such as income growth, income redistribution, foreign exchange earnings, etc.)

X_1 is a vector of farmers' decision variables (production levels and mixes, input allocations, etc.)

X_2 is a vector of policy instrument variables

f_2 is a policy objective function

f_1 is a descriptive (farmers') objective function

k is a vector of costs of public programs (including staff time requirements)

g is a vector of policy resources, i.e., tax revenues and government staff resources

b is a vector of resource endowments and other constraint values for the descriptive problem

a_1 is a vector of subsidies or other instruments which directly affect the farmers' objective function weights

c_1 is the set of coefficients in the descriptive objective function for farmers

c_2 is the set of policy weights, previously denoted by w.

In this reasonably typical case, the model is structured so that

1 Only the target variables X_0 are of interest in the policy makers' objective function f_2

2 Only the descriptive choice variables X_1 affect the descriptive objective function f_1

3 A_{11} is a technological matrix of unit resource requirements for the farmers' decisions

4 The matrix A_{12} expresses the effect of the policy instrument variables X_2 on resource availability (a policy that increases resource availability, such as investment in new irrigation supplies, is represented by a negative element of A_{12})

5 The matrix A_{21} represents the effects of descriptive variables X_1 on target variables X_0 (e.g., if greater employment is a policy target, then A_{21} may contain coefficients showing the labor input requirements per unit of production of each crop)

6 A_{22} is a matrix of the direct effects of the policy variables X_2 on the target variables X_0 (in many cases, this matrix would be zero and so policies would have to achieve their impacts indirectly, that is, through the matrices A_{12} and A_{21})

The variables the policy maker controls are different than the variables the farmer controls, i.e., the domains of maximization of f_2 and f_1 differ. If this were not the case—if policy makers could control directly the production variables X_1—then the problem collapses to the case of pure centralized planning, and only the objective function f_2 is relevant. As the centralized planning formulation is not very useful in reality, the overall policy problem is better described as the two-level problem given by equations (7.5) through (7.11).

Unfortunately for purposes of analysis, the problem (7.5) through (7.11) is not generally solvable directly, because it rarely has a convex feasible set, although local optima can be found.[6] Indirect methods can be used to solve the two-level problem approximately (see Chapter 12) but first it is necessary to develop the structure of the descriptive problem given in equations (7.7), (7.8), and (7.11). One of the primary theses of this book is that the descriptive problem can be set up and analyzed in the form of an optimization model, while remaining fully consistent with the institutional framework of decentralized decision making. As will be seen, the nature of the model's objective function (f_1 in equation 7.7) is crucial to the decentralized framework. Before getting to the objective function, the next three sections discuss other issues involved in moving from farm-level models to sector-level models.

7.3 SELECTION OF REPRESENTATIVE FARMS AND REGIONS

7.3.1 The Aggregation Issue

In the transition from farm-level to sector-level analysis aggregation bias arises because all farms are not alike. Ideally, a model should be constructed for every individual farm, and all the individual models linked together to form the sector model. Let the vector X_i^* denote the optimal solution to ith farm model, then the optimal solution to the sector model would be

$$X_1^* = \sum_i X_i^*$$

In this case the aggregation is exact.

In practice it is not feasible to model each individual farm, and the sector model must be based on representative farms, or on aggregate regional or farm type models. The representative farm approach involves classifying the universe of farms into a smaller number of homogeneous groups, and constructing a model for a "representative" farm from each group. These farm models are then aggregated in the sector model using the number of farms in each group as weights. Let X_h^* denote the optimal solution to the hth representative farm model and let n_h denote the number of farms in the group. Then the sector model solution will be[7]

$$X_2^* = \sum_h n_h X_h^*$$

If we compare this with the solution obtained by the ideal method (X_1^*), then aggregation bias is said to exist if $X_2^* \neq X_1^*$ or, equivalently, if

$$\sum_i X_i^* \neq \sum_h n_h X_h^*$$

Using the number of farms in each group as weights is the correct aggregation procedure if the representative farms are defined as the arithmetic mean farms for their groups. If other types of representative farms are chosen, such as median or modal farms, then the weighting procedure may have to be rather more complex.

The aggregate regional approach involves aggregating the resources of a homogeneous region or area (not necessarily involving contiguous land) and modeling these aggregated variables as a single large farm. This approach is identical to the representative farm approach if representative farms are defined as arithmetic mean farms for the same regions or areas.

As an example of the nature of aggregation bias, consider the following two farm problems, each with two cropping activities X_1 and X_2:

Farm A	X_1	X_2	RHS
Profit	60	90	Maximize
Resource 1	1	2	≤ 5
Resource 2	1	1	≤ 5

Farm B	X_1	X_2	RHS
Profit	100	90	Maximize
Resource 1	1	2	≤ 10
Resource 2	2	1	≤ 5

The optimal strategy for farm A is to grow 5 units of X_1, while farm B should grow 5 units of X_2. For farm A the profit is 300 while for farm B the profit is 450.

Suppose now we were to take the aggregate farm to represent farms A and B in a sector model. The aggregate farm problem would be as follows, with relabeling of the cropping activities:

Aggregate Farm	X_1	X_2	X_3	RHS
Profit	60	90	100	Maximize
Resource 1	1	2	1	≤ 15
Resource 2	1	1	2	≤ 15

The optimal solution to this problem is 15 units of X_1 for a total profit of 900; an amount which exceeds the sum of the profits obtained from the individual farm models. This outcome illustrates the fact that aggregation bias is always in an upward direction: it overstates resource mobility by enabling farms to combine resources in proportions not available to them individually, and it carries the implicit assumption that all the aggregated farms have equal access to the same technologies of production. (This point is taken up again in Chapter 11.)

7.3.2 Criteria for Farm Classification

Aggregation bias can only be avoided (or minimized) if farms are classified into groups or regions which are defined according to rigid theoretical requirements of homogeneity. The most comprehensive set of conditions have been established by Day (1963a).

Let the linear programming model of the ith farm be written in matrix notation as:

$$\max c_i' X_i$$

subject to

$$A_i X_i \leq b_i$$
$$X_i \leq 0$$

Further let the aggregate or representative farm model be denoted in the same way but without i subscripts. Then Day has shown that only farms satisfying the following three conditions should be grouped together if aggregation bias is to be avoided:

1 $A_i = A$
2 $c_i = \mu_i c$
3 $b_i = \lambda_i b, \lambda_i \geq 0$

Day termed the first requirement "technological homogeneity," and it requires that each farm have the same production possibilities, the same type of resources and constraints, the same levels of technology, and the same level of managerial ability.

The second requirement demands that individual farmers in a group hold expectations about unit activity returns that are proportional to average expectations. Day termed this requirement "pecunious" proportionality.

The third requirement is that the constraint vector of the programming model for each individual farm should be proportional to the constraint vector of the average or aggregate farm. Day termed this requirement "institutional" proportionality. This requirement is strictly necessary only for those constraints that will be binding in the model solution, but since these can rarely be identified beforehand, it is usually necessary to demand institutional proportionality in all constraints.

Day's conditions are usually sufficient to guarantee unbiasedness because they ensure that $X_i^* = \lambda_i X^*$ for all farms. Strict sufficiency requires two additional things. First that the representative farm, if used, be defined as the arithmetic mean farm, so that

$$\sum_i \lambda_i = 1$$

Second, that none of the individual farm models be degenerate, since then the choice of X_i^* is unknown and arbitrary. This problem was pointed out by Spreen and Takayama (1980).

Day's requirements are very demanding, and several authors have tried to derive less stringent conditions. Theoretical approaches, such as those developed by Sheehy and McAlexander (1965), Miller (1966), and Lee (1966), are based on the underlying reasoning that an optimal solution to a linear programming model can be stable even when many of the coefficients are perturbed. We explored this concept in Chapter 6 under post-optimality analysis and noted that there is usually a range for each coefficient over which it can be varied without inducing a change in the optimal basis. Clearly, as long as the farms included in a group all have coefficients lying within tolerated ranges of the solution basis of the average farm model, then their optimal solution vectors may still all be proportional.

The problem with this approach is that the tolerable ranges for the coefficients are unique for a single optimal solution. Hence, farms that can be grouped together for one experiment with a representative farm model may have to be regrouped for any other experiment. Since one cannot possibly know in which group to classify individual farms for each experiment without knowledge equivalent to knowing the optimal solution vector for each farm, aggregation criteria based on this approach have not proved useful.

It is also possible for an aggregate farm model to give an unbiased solution even when the individual farm solutions are not proportional (Paris and Rausser, 1973). However, the conditions under which this can happen change from one solution to another and so it is again difficult to provide *ex ante* guidelines for classifying farms in sector models that are intended for numerous policy experiments.

In another approach methods have been sought to provide for grouping farms so as to minimize rather than eliminate aggregation bias. Buckwell and Hazell (1972), for example, suggest grouping farms in agroclimatically similar areas and by the type of products produced to ensure a reasonable degree of conformity to Day's requirements of technological and pecunious homogeneity. They then suggest the use of statistical clustering techniques to assign farms to a limited number of groups on the basis of their resource endowment ratios. The method ensures that the institutional homogeneity requirement is met as closely as possible for a prespecified number of farm groups.

Another approach proposed by Kennedy (1975) has applicability when farms initially can be classified in groups that meet the first two of Day's requirements and when the ratios of farm resources available within groups vary on account of farm size. Kennedy proposes that linear regressions be estimated for each group relating farm RHS vectors to a single resource measuring farm size. These estimated equations are then included in the aggregate model, and the farm size variable is parameterized to identify the series of optimal solutions corresponding to critical farm sizes. Estimates of aggregate supply are then obtained using this series of solutions and the number of farms falling within each of the critical farm size intervals. The main difficulty with this approach is that aggregate commodity supplies cannot be made endogenous in the model to permit joint determination of outputs and prices. It also is necessary to parameterize the sector model for each policy experiment and to recalculate the number of farms in each critical size group.

7.3.3 Other Considerations

In practice, the aggregation criteria usually are reduced to grouping farms according to a few simple rules. Chief among those rules are (1) similar proportions in resource endowments, (2) similar yields, and (3) similar technologies. The first rule most often means similar land-to-labor ratios, that is, grouping farms by size class. Among other things, grouping farms in this way will help the model more accurately to show which farms engage in labor-saving techniques, such as mechanization of plowing and other operations.

The second rule means at minimum putting irrigated and nonirrigated farms into separate classes, and it also means looking out for differences in climate, soils, and elevation which alone (apart from the technology employed) cause significant yield differences. Usually, but not always, on a sector-wide basis climate (rainfall), slope of the land, and elevation are more important criteria than soil types per se.

The third rule means separating farms according to predominant crops. For example, farms with yam-based cropping patterns in the south of Nigeria clearly belong in a different category than sorghum-millet-groundnut farms in northern Nigeria. Also, some of the technologically more backward areas of a sector simply may not have the household wealth or know-how to grow more sophisticated crops or to use more demanding technologies. Farms in such areas should be placed in a separate category and the production vectors specified should reflect a narrower range of options. This is a form of technological dualism and to the extent that it is a part of reality, it should be incorporated in the model structure. (Clearly, one of the experiments that can be conducted with such a model is to explore the consequences for production, prices, farm income, the rural income distribution, etc. of better access to improved technologies on the part of poorer farmers.)

Several other criteria can be important for defining producer classes, depending upon the issues to be studied. For irrigation studies, the plot's position along the canal (relative distance from the canal head) can be important. Variations in land tenure can influence producers' incentives and also their access to resources (such as institutional short-term credit). The soil type is in principle an important criterion, but, with some exceptions, introduction of that criterion in addition to the others leads to too many farm categories to be manageable from a computational viewpoint. Predominant soil types can, however, be used to differentiate subregions within each agroclimatic region, and the prevailing soil types allowed to influence the corresponding average yield coefficients. Another characteristic that can be important is proximity to major market centers, which determines the producer's marketing costs and hence his net farm gate price. Usually, however, spatial variations in farm gate prices are already included in the model's regions that are established by other criteria, so that price variations alone are not needed to determine regional boundaries.

Survey techniques and subsequent clustering can improve the selection of categories of producers, but no matter how well designed, surveys will never provide the complete answer to this selection question. Surveys must be designed according to static criteria—on the characteristics of the sampled population that are of interest. But ultimately, for the model, the most interesting characteristic is a less static one—namely, how producers respond to policy change—and that characteristic cannot be measured until the model is built and available for use.

7.4   THE STRUCTURE OF A BASIC SECTOR MODEL

Sector models display enormous diversity, as they should, given the world-wide diversity of agriculture and the variations over time in policy concerns. This diversity makes it difficult to set out a completely general statement concerning the proper structure of sector models, and so the exposition will start with typical elements of basic sector models. The following two chapters introduce more detail regarding demand and marketing parameters, and Chapter 10 deals with the treatment of risk.

The main operational implication of the previous section is that one of the first steps in the construction of an agricultural model is the designation of regions and representative farms. This designation is always strongly circumscribed by the availability of data. Also, it should be borne in mind that decision makers usually have their own "mental models" of a small set of representative producers. Since one aim of the modeling exercise is to improve their implicit analyses, in practice the selection of representative producers should be based on a variety of criteria.

As the representative units are defined, their resource endowments need to be tabulated as well. For agriculture, the pertinent resource endowments include land, irrigation supplies, family labor, livestock herds, existing perennial plants, agricultural machinery, and the intangible resource of degree of access to outside resources.

The next step is to define the production technologies available to each representative producing unit. Some interesting issues arise in this regard. First, as previously noted, technological dualism is an important feature of the agricultural sector in almost all countries. Thus it cannot be assumed that all producers have access to the same production function in the short run or medium run. Production techniques available to poorer farmers are likely to have smaller input coefficients for farm machinery and agrochemicals, and the yields may be lower as well. Usually, subsistence farmers have fewer cultivation choices than commercial farmers. That is, subsistence farmers have less choice as regards alternative crops and the range of production techniques. Subsistence farmers typically grow only staple foods, in large part for home consumption, whereas the more commercial farmers, who can finance the purchase of modern inputs, can choose between staple foods and a range of industrial and export crops.

Second, in the short or medium run, a continuous production function (Cobb-Douglas, CES, or otherwise) may not be a very accurate representation of reality at the micro level. Discrete choices represented by alternative crop budgets of input/output vectors (or linear combinations thereof) usually are more realistic. For example, when a farmer moves from animal traction power to the hire of tractor services, initially he often will use the hired machinery only for land preparation, or possibly, depending on the crop, for both land preparation and harvesting. These are discrete choices, and intermediate choices usually are not meaningful. In this case the continuous production function is an approximation to the reality of discrete functions, and not vice-versa.[8] Modeling production functions in discrete form is called process analysis or activity analysis.[9] In the event that the information on production comes in the form of continuous production functions, Chapter 11 shows how to translate that information into process analysis vectors.

The activities of a sector model include producing, marketing, purchasing for consumption or other domestic final use, supplying inputs, importing, and exporting. Following the notation of previous chapters, production activities are denoted by the symbol X. It is necessary to add subscripts denoting the product (j), the technology (t), the farm type (h), and the location or region (r). Marketing activities are denoted by T, for transportation and transformation (processing), domestic purchases by D (for demand), imports by M, and exports by E. The input supplying activities vary in notation according to the particular input.

Corresponding to these variables, the basic equations of a sector model may be grouped into four types: supply-demand balances, resource restrictions and other restrictions, miscellaneous equations, and the objective function. Supply-demand balances always will hold as equalities in the solution, even if they are written as inequalities.[10] Restrictions always are written as inequalities and they may have slack in them in the solution.

Supply-demand balances are needed at both regional and national levels and are specified for both inputs and outputs. The manageability of sector models is enhanced considerably if pricing and costing activities are kept separate from the production activities, even though this requires use of additional supply-demand balances. Early sector models frequently contained coefficients representing the net economic or financial return to each production activity. This procedure is incompatible with endogenous output prices, and makes it awkward to perform experiments by varying input prices; changing a single price of fertilizer, for example, could require changing hundreds of net-return coefficients. For these reasons, the exposition in this book makes frequent use of supply-demand balances, even if the supply is characterized by a trivial one-step, fixed-price supply function.

The simplest sector model can be sketched by positing more than one producing region, product demand functions, and resource restrictions as follows:

Model 7.1
commodity balances

$$-\sum_t \sum_r y_{jtr} X_{jtr} + D_j \le 0, \quad \text{all } j \qquad (7.12)$$

resource restrictions

$$\sum_j \sum_t a_{kjtr} X_{jtr} \le b_{kr}, \quad \text{all } k, r \qquad (7.13)$$

objective function

$$\max Z = \sum_j f(D_j) \qquad (7.14)$$

Model 7.1 is shown in schematic tableau format in Table 7.1 for the case of two regions. As in Chapter 2, each variable in the model is represented by a column in the tableau, and the columns are in turn presented in three groups: production in regions 1 and 2 and demand. In mathematical programming, the words "activity," "column," "variable," and "column variable" are interchangeable. In the tableau, each rectangle containing a symbol represents a set of nonzero coefficients, that is, cases in which the given column variable enters

Table 7.1   Presentation of a Simple, Two-Region Sector Model

Constraints	Activities			
	Production region 1 X_{jt1}	Production, region 2 X_{jt2}	National demand D_j	
Commodity balances	$-y_{jt1}$	$-y_{jt2}$	1	≤ 0
Resource restrictions, region 1	a_{kjt1}			$\leq b_{k1}$
Resource restrictions, region 2		a_{kjt2}		$\leq b_{k2}$
Objective function			$f(D_j)$	Maximize

the given equation. The production columns have yield entries $[y_{jtr}]$ in the commodity balance rows and resource requirements $[a_{kjtr}]$ in the resource constraint rows, where k denotes the type of resource. The intersections of the demand activities and the commodity balances are the quantities demanded for the national market. In this initial sector model, the nature of the objective function is left undefined except to specify that it is a function of the quantities sold of all products. A more explicit form of the objective function is developed later in the chapter.

This introductory model serves to introduce two concepts which are basic to a sector model but do not appear in the farm-level model: supply-demand equilibrium conditions (commodity balances) and differentiation of supply sources. Here the supply sources are called regions, but they could as well be farm size classes, irrigated vs. nonirrigated farms, or other categorizations. Now suppose large and small farms (indexes 1 and 2, respectively) are distinguished within region 1. As noted previously, even if the available technologies of production were the same for the two size classes, a representative small farm could be expected to produce a different output mix than a representative large farm, owing to the fact that the relative resource endowments (ratios of land to family labor) differ between the two farms. Therefore, it often is useful to introduce farm size distinctions to enhance the realism (predictive ability) of the model.

With a farm size distinction, region 1's production column would look as in Table 7.2. Notice that adding the farm size dimension increases the number of resource restrictions but usually not the number of commodity balances. Also, as noted, even if the two sets of columns for large and small farms are identical in terms of the coefficient values, the two sets of output mixes in the solution may differ. But owing to the technological dualism mentioned previously, the two sets of columns are not likely to be identical; in fact, among other things, the large farm (or commercial farm) section of the matrix may have more column vectors than the small farm (or subsistence farm) section does.

Table 7.2   Mini-Tableau Concerning Farm Size Classes

	Region 1 Activities		
	Production, large farms (Size 1)	Production, small farms (Size 2)	
Commodity balances	$- y_{jt11}$	$- y_{jt12}$	
Resource restrictions, large farms	a_{kjt11}		$\leq b_{k11}$
Resource restrictions, small farms		a_{kjt12}	$\leq b_{k12}$

7.5   A MORE COMPLETE MODEL

7.5.1   Enriching the Market Specification

The next step in making the model more interesting and realistic is to introduce purchased current inputs, and therefore input balances, together with marketing costs and international trade activities. By introducing these components, we actually are arriving at a reasonably complete skeleton of a sector model, although some important items, such as risk and risk aversion, still are omitted. At this level of generality, marketing is construed to include transportation and processing as well as marketing per se.

Since marketing costs differ spatially, marketing activities must be added for each region (although not necessarily for each farm size class within a region). In consequence, the supply-demand balances for agricultural commodities need to be specified at both regional and national levels. At the regional level those balances refer to the movement of raw farm products from the farm gate to the marketing and processing centers. At the national level, those balances equate the supply of processed products to retail demand. Foreign trade activities enter the national balances but not the regional balances. Similarly, input balances now need to be introduced for each region, to ensure that the derived demands for inputs in the production processes are consistent with the conditions of input supply and cost.

With these considerations in mind, the revised sector model looks as follows in algebraic form, with the purchased inputs denoted by subscript f:

Model 7.2

national commodity balances (j)

$$-\sum_{r} y_{jr}^{*}T_{jr} - M_{j} + D_{j} + E_{j} \leq 0, \qquad \text{all } j \qquad (7.15)$$

regional commodity balances ($j \times r$)

$$-\sum_t \sum_h y_{jtrh} X_{jtrh} + T_{jr} \leq 0, \qquad \text{all } j, r \tag{7.16}$$

input balances ($f \times r$)

$$\sum_j \sum_t \sum_h a_{fjtrh} X_{jtrh} - J_{fr} \leq 0, \qquad \text{all } f, r \tag{7.17}$$

resource restrictions ($k \times r \times h$)

$$\sum_j \sum_t a_{kjtrh} X_{jtrh} \leq b_{krh}, \qquad \text{all } k, r, h \tag{7.18}$$

export limits (j, for those j that are exportable)

$$E_j \leq \bar{e}_j, \text{ all } j \text{ which are exportable} \tag{7.19}$$

objective function (1)

$$\max Z = -\sum_j \sum_r \Delta_{jr} T_{jr} - \sum_f \sum_r P_{fr} J_{fr}$$
$$+ \sum_j f(D_j) + P_j^e E_j - P_j^m M_j \tag{7.20}$$

Some additional notation has been required. The asterisk denotes the yield coefficients for the marketing and processing activities; y_{jr}^* is the output (in tons, say) of the joint marketing-processing activity, per ton of raw material input from the farm, for region r. The variable T_{jr} is the corresponding activity level, i.e., how many tons of raw farm product were marketed and processed. The marketing and processing activities play the role of transferring commodities from the regional level (areas of production) to the national level.

For Model 7.2, the maximum number of equations in each category is indicated in parentheses after the equation's label. For example, there are at most $j \times r$ regional commodity balances, where in this case j indicates the number of crops (as well as serving as a crop subscript) and r indicates the number of regions. The actual number of equations in this category will be less, because not all crops are grown in all regions.

The model now contains input supply variables J_{fr} by input and region, where the subscript f indicates the type of input. The marketing (and processing) costs are denoted by Δ_{jr} and the input costs are denoted by P_{fr}. Similarly, export and import prices are P_j^e and P_j^m, respectively. The commodity balance equations, the resource restrictions, and the export limits always are stated in physical units. Most of the input balances are as well, but some may be stated in monetary terms so that the input coefficients reflect input

Table 7.3 Tableau for a Less Simple Sector Model

	Region 1 production		Marketing, region 1	Input supply, region 1	Region 2 production	Marketing, region 2	Input supply, region 2	Domestic demand	Exports	Imports	RHS
	large farms	small farms									
	X_{jf11}	X_{jf12}	T_{j1}	J_{j1}	X_{jf2}	T_{j2}	J_{j2}	D_j	E_j	M_j	
National commodity balances			$-y_{j1}^*$			$-y_{j2}^*$		-1	1	-1	≤ 0
Region 1 commodity balances	$-y_{jf11}$	$-y_{jf12}$	1								≤ 0
Region 2 commodity balances					$-y_{jf2}$	1					≤ 0
Region 1 input balances	a_{fjf11}	a_{fjf12}		-1							≤ 0
Region 2 input balances					a_{fjf2}		-1				≤ 0
Region 1 resource restrictions, small farms		a_{kjf12}									$\leq b_{k11}$
Region 1 resource restrictions, large farms	a_{kjf11}										$\leq b_{k12}$
Region 2 resource restrictions					a_{kjf2}						$\leq b_{k2}$
Export limits									1		$\leq \bar{e}$
Objective function			$-\Delta_{j1}$	$-P_{j1}$		$-\Delta_{j2}$	$-P_{j2}$	$f(D_j)$	P_j^e	$-P_j^m$	Maximize

costs per hectare. In this last case, the corresponding input prices become unity.

Table 7.3 shows an illustrative model corresponding to equations (7.15) through (7.20). In this two-region example, the farm size distinction has been maintained in region 1, but it is assumed that farms are homogeneous in region 2. Marketing costs are assumed to vary by region but not by farm size —this assumption could be altered readily. Notice the identity matrices (I or − I); as a model becomes larger these matrices tend to become more frequent. As the discussion of the components of sector models becomes more specific, it will seldom prove convenient to use complete tableaus, but portions of tableaus ("mini-tableaus") will be used extensively hereafter.

7.5.2 Enriching the Supply Specification

The brevity of both the equations and the tableau conceals much of the richness of detail that is found in many sector models, particularly on the supply side. While the matrices of a_{fj} coefficients for purchased inputs are not likely to have many rows, the matrices of a_{kj} resource input coefficients often have many more rows, because it can be important to distinguish resource availability by season or for even shorter intervals. As discussed in Chapter 3, the timing of agricultural activities is crucial. If a model is specified with only annual labor availability, it may appear that there is substantial surplus labor when in fact seasonal shortages of labor may make derived production levels infeasible. Similarly, the possibilities of cultivating two or more crops per year cannot be accommodated with a model containing only annual land constraints. Seasonal land constraints may not be sufficient either, for in order to evaluate which crop combinations are possible it is necessary to know in which month each first-season crop is harvested and in which month each second-season crop is planted. Some annual food crops occupy the land as little as 3 or 4 months, others as much as 9 months.

For these reasons, it is a common practice to specify the land and labor constraints on a monthly basis. Irrigation water, when available, also is usually included in monthly form, although for irrigation-specific models, biweekly or even weekly irrigation rows have sometimes been used.[11] Time thus enters the model as a characteristic of resource inputs, in addition to any inter-annual specifications. By using dated inputs, it is possible to distinguish options with alternative planting dates for the same crop. Such options might appear as column vectors with identical coefficients except that some of the coefficients appear in different rows, for different months. In the notation used here, these options constitute different technologies and hence are distinguished by different values of the subscript t. With time-dated inputs, matrices of a_{kj} coefficients are large—in fact they account for most of the coefficients on the supply side of a model.

Model 7.2 does not allow for intercropping, sometimes called crop consortiums. To allow for this phenomenon, the indexes for production activities have to be differentiated from the indexes for crops. If the subscript j is now used to denote production activities and the index i, crops, then the regional commodity balances (7.16) can be rewritten as follows:

$$- \sum_j \sum_t \sum_h y_{ijtrh} X_{jtrh} + T_{ir} \leq 0, \quad \text{all } i, r \qquad (7.16a)$$

Notice that the yield coefficients and the marketing-processing activities now are indexed by crop, but the production activities continue to be identified as activities—in some cases multicrop activities. Likewise equations (7.15), (7.19), and (7.20) have to be rewritten so that all subscripts j change to i. Equations (7.17) and (7.18) do not change with the introduction of intercropping. In some cases, intercropping can be an important characteristic of the sector. It is the dominant form of cropping in Nigeria and other countries of West Africa. A recent survey of some 300 farmers in northern Nigeria (Bauchi State) encountered over 100 different intercrop combinations!

From the viewpoint of economic theory, the three basic points to recognize about model 7.2 are that (1) it contains implicit domestic supply functions, (2) it contains implicit functions for the derived demands for inputs, and (3) with an appropriate definition of the objective function this model can simulate a market equilibrium outcome under endogenous prices. We now take up these points below.

7.5.3 The Nature of Supply Response in a Sector Model

Given that the model contains (possibly very many) alternative techniques of production, it must also contain a range of costs of production. Those costs may be divided into two components: cash outlays for purchased inputs, including hired labor, and the opportunity costs of fixed resources.[12] If the alternative production activities for a given crop are arrayed in increasing order with respect to cost of purchased inputs, then they can be viewed as forming a sequence of steps on a stepped supply function. However, there is yet another characteristic to the implicit supply function. As the activity level of one production vector increases—that is, as supply expands while remaining at the same level of unit costs for purchased inputs—other crops are being displaced, and this displacement affects the opportunity cost of fixed resources. As the given crop expands in output in the short run, it uses land and other resources that previously went to other crops. Initially, the least profitable of the other crops will be displaced, and gradually crops that are increasingly profitable will be displaced. This means that the opportunity cost of fixed resources is rising, even over portions of the supply function where the unit costs of purchased inputs are constant.

The true implicit supply function in an agricultural programming model looks like the upper solid line in Figure 7.1. The lower solid line represents the changing marginal cash costs as technologies are changed and the upper line

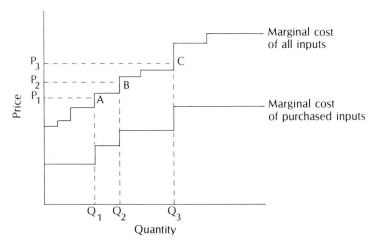

Figure 7.1   A mathematical programming supply function.

includes the opportunity cost of fixed resources. There are more steps on the upper line. The dotted vertical lines are drawn at quantities where the unit cost of purchased inputs changes. Technology changes in the aggregate may be forced by limits on the availability of irrigation water, by limited land endowments in the regions with more productive soils, by limited numbers of farmers with superior management techniques, and so forth. The first, least-cost segments on the supply function could refer to production under irrigation in a highly fertile region, the second group of segments, to irrigated production in a slightly less fertile region, etc., until the last segments represent rainfed production on poor soils. The number of different production vectors included in the model for a given crop places a lower bound on the number of steps in the supply function.

The domestic supply function in Figure 7.1 is implicit in the model, but it can be traced out—made explicit—by simple parametric solutions of the model. Imagine a series of solutions in which the downward-sloping demand function for one product is replaced by a horizontal demand function—a fixed price. Let that price be varied over levels P_1, P_2, and P_3 in successive solutions. As illustrated in Figure 7.1, the corresponding quantities in the solutions would be Q_1, Q_2, and Q_3, and the solutions would have revealed points A, B, and C on the supply function. By exploring enough such solutions, the supply function can be traced out with any desired degree of precision.

The arc elasticity of supply normally will vary along different segments of such a function, and that behavior is more realistic than the assumption of a constant elasticity which frequently is imposed in econometric estimation. Other aspects of the model which bear on the realism of the implicit supply functions are discussed in chapter 11. Strictly speaking, the function shown in Figure 7.1 is a supply response function, not a supply function. A supply function is defined under the condition that prices of inputs and other outputs are held constant. However, as the function of Figure 7.1 is traced out, the output and therefore prices of competing and complementary crops will change as well.

A usual condition for the supply response function to be upward sloping within a region and farm class is that there be more column vectors for production than there are crops. In other words, there must be multiple technologies per crop, and each of the yield matrices must be rectangular. If there is only one technology per crop the yield matrices in the model will be square, and within each farm class the supply side of the model would behave like an input/output model; that is, factor substitution could occur only via changes in the output mix. At the extreme, with one representative farm for the entire sector and a square yield matrix, the programming model reduces to an input/output model of agriculture with a single production column per crop. With multiple farm types but square yield matrices for all the farm types, then factor substitution is possible by changing the composition of output over farm types, as well as within farm types, but factor substitution via on-farm technology or technique change is not captured.

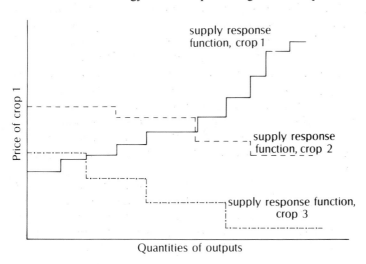

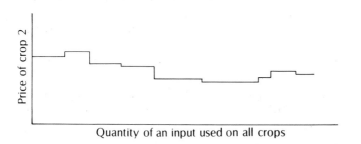

Figure 7.2 Supply response functions implicit in a sector model.

To be able to capture true technology-driven factor substitution at the farm level, rectangular yield matrices are required. A good sector model must be based on farm-level information, yet it is used primarily to address sector-wide issues and to derive more aggregate relationships, such as supply functions. In this respect, a sector model may be seen as a device for translating micro-level information into more aggregate economic statements.

By virtue of including input/output coefficients and alternative cropping possibilities for the representative farm, the sector model is able to provide other kinds of information about the supply function in Figure 7.1. It can be used to trace out cross-supply functions, even though cross-elasticity terms are not part of the model's data input. It is also possible to quantify the additional requirements for purchased inputs associated with a given increase in supply. In this respect, the model is perhaps more useful for analyzing the structure of supply response than it is for computing supply elasticities.

For example, if the policy planners desire to induce greater production of maize, it can be helpful to provide them with the consequences in terms of decreased production of wheat, sorghum, soybeans, and other competing crops. Owing to the presence of crop rotation practices and multiple cropping, the production of some crops actually may increase as maize production increases. Also, it may be important to know how the total demand for labor, fertilizer, short-term credit, or other inputs changes as the output of maize increases. The sector's supply function is really a vector which shows how several outputs and inputs will change as the price of one output is altered. Figure 7.2 illustrates components of such a supply response vector.

7.5.4   The Nature of Input Demand in a Sector Model

In analogous fashion to the tracing out of a supply response function, a sector model may be used to trace out numerically the input demand functions. Imagine an experiment in which the sector model is solved several times under successively lower prices of irrigation water. In each new solution, the model would tend to use more irrigation-intensive technologies for at least some of the crops, and it also would tend to shift the cropping pattern toward more water-intensive crops. The net effect would be a greater demand for water for the given amounts of land and labor resources. The same solutions of the model would provide information on the regional cropping patterns at each level of overall water use. Figure 7.3 shows a hypothetical function for the derived demand for an input which could be constructed via successive solutions of Model 7.2. Notice that whereas the output price is placed on the vertical axis of Figure 7.2, it is the input price that is on the vertical axis of Figure 7.3.

With movements along the horizontal axis of Figure 7.3, the output levels and prices of many products will be changing. Since output prices in general react to every change in an input price, and output levels respond to these price changes, the input demand function is likely to have more steps than a single product supply function, for comparable ranges of input use. The input

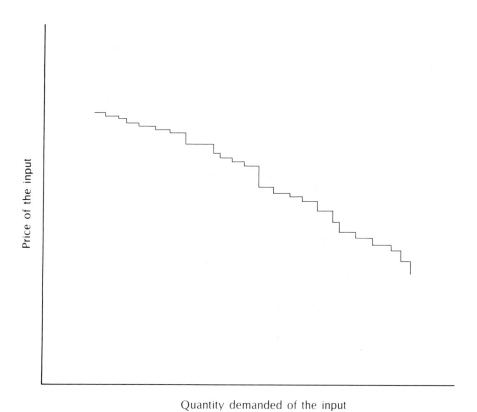

Figure 7.3   A sector model's implicit function for the derived demand for an input.

demand function is drawn so that it does not touch the vertical axis, to illustrate the fact that in most cases the model's solution space will not include zero values of input use.

All the implicit functions illustrated above may be constructed (via model solutions) not only for the sector as a whole but also for any particular region, farm size class, or other grouping within the sector. The tracing out of implicit functions is one of the uses to which a sector model may be put. These and other uses are discussed in Chapter 12; the relevant point for the present discussion is that the functions shown in Figures 7.1 to 7.3 are part of a sector model's structure, even though they are not known when the model is being constructed.

7.6   DEMAND FUNCTIONS AND MARKET EQUILIBRIUM

Thus far the nature of the models' demand functions has been left unexplored. In this section, the basic concepts are introduced; Chapter 8 shows how to define and compute the parameters in the columns in the demand section of the tableau. The early generations of agricultural models had either fixed prices (infinitely elastic demand curves) or fixed demand quantities (infinitely inelastic demand curves). Often the sector planning problem was posed in the form of seeking the least-cost way—least-cost spatial cropping patterns—for meeting "required" deliveries to final consumption. This kind of paradigm is appropriate to centrally planned economies, but it clearly is of limited use in market economies. When prices are free to vary, the quantities demanded are not fixed but change in response to price, and therefore in response to variations in the cost of production.

Introducing demand functions into the model forces a reconsideration of the model's objective function. When demand functions are present, it is necessary to define the market forms; a simple cost-minimizing objective function will not suffice to drive the model to, say, a competitive equilibrium outcome. Export-maximizing, employment-maximizing, and other policy-oriented objective functions will not do the job either. They may lead to solutions that give the export-maximizing and employment-maximizing cropping patterns, but they will not give clues as to how to induce farmers to adopt those patterns. It is necessary to give specific content to the function f_1 in equation (7.7), and thereby make the model a descriptive tool of analysis.

The most basic market form is the competitive one. As used here, a competitive market means only one thing: that no producer has a sufficiently large scale of operations to be able to influence the market price. It is sometimes called the atomistic market in which each producer is a price-taker, even though at the aggregate level prices are influenced by the volume of production. When used in this sense, the competitive market does not mean that there are no market imperfections. Prices may vary substantially over different locations, owing to imperfect market channels—poor transportation facilities in some areas, lack of market information, local monopoly of marketing, inadequate storage facilities, etc. Nor does competition mean that producers are necessarily only profit maximizers. They may be risk averse, they may produce primarily for home consumption, and they may have other objectives in place of, or in addition to, profit maximization.

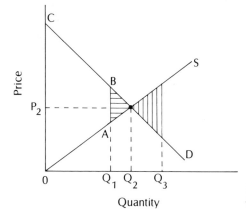

Figure 7.4 Maximizing the area between the demand and supply function.

For the case of a competitive market in this sense, Samuelson (1952) was the first to show that there exists a maximization model that will simulate the market outcome under downward-sloping demand functions. His concern was with spatial equilibrium, but his basic insight applies equally well to markets at a point in space. The essence of his demonstration was that the model's objective function needs to correspond to the sum of producer and consumer surplus, i.e., the area between the demand and supply functions. As Figure 7.4 shows, maximizing that area will drive the model to the competitive outcome in price and quantity (P_2, Q_2). If the solution were to be at quantity Q_1, the objective function's value would be $OABC$, and the objective function could have been increased by the horizontally hatched area by moving to quantity Q_2. Similarly, if the model goes to Q_3, the objective function is diminished from its maximum value by the vertically hatched area. Thus, if it is desired that the model's solution replicate a competitive market outcome, then only one objective function is known to be admissible: the area between the supply and demand functions.

In retrospect, this discovery may seem rather obvious, but making it operational in a model involves some less obvious steps. One hurdle to be overcome is how to measure that area when the supply function is implicit—when it is unknown beforehand. Another hurdle concerns the mathematical form of the expression for the area. Since it involves triangles, it must include terms in price times quantity. But both price and quantity should be endogenous, and in linear programming two endogenous variables cannot be multiplied together.

One solution to the second problem is to use a quadratic programming algorithm. Another solution is to use techniques that are called grid linearizations. Both approaches are reviewed in Chapter 8, with more emphasis placed on the linear version since linear programming still is the most widely available optimization algorithm on a world-wide basis. Also, the linearized version has some useful features not found in the quadratic version, such as dual variables that correspond to the value of consumer surplus and convertibility into a general equilibrium model. These issues are discussed in Chapters 8 and 9.

The equilibrium point at which the model arrives via this maximization procedure represents a partial equilibrium rather than a general equilibrium. It is partial because, although prices are endogenous, incomes are not. Were incomes also endogenous, the position of the model's demand functions (in price-quantity space) would shift as incomes changed, but in sector models the demand functions are fixed. Extensions of the sector model to the general equilibrium case have been developed by Norton and Scandizzo (1981) and they are reviewed in Chapter 9.

NOTES

1 See, for example, Fletcher et al. (1970).
2 In the Mexican agricultural model CHAC (see Chapter 12), there are about 30 products, and in some regions 15–20 products are produced.

3   As discussed in Chapter 12, a surprising amount of useful policy analysis can be conducted without necessarily knowing the values of the preference weights.

4   In the literature on bilateral monopoly and oligopoly, there is considerable discussion of reaction functions in the context of bargaining.

5   This brief exposition is adapted from Candler and Norton (1977) and Norton and Schiefer (1980).

6   See Candler and Norton (1977) and Candler, Fortuny-Amat, and McCarl (1981). Pursuing iterative solution procedures for the two levels of decision making leads into the realm of multilevel planning; see for example, Heal (1973).

7   Here the subscripts 1 and 2 no longer refer to the descriptive and policy problems.

8   N. Georgescu-Roegen has written extensively on the conceptual foundations of discrete production functions. See his 1969 and 1972 articles.

9   The pioneering essays in process analysis are contained in T. Koopmans's 1951 volume.

10 There are two reasons for writing supply-demand balances as inequalities rather than equalities. One is that economic theory allows for surplus production (and costless disposal) at the equilibrium price. Another reason is that existing algorithms tend to converge to a solution on the computer faster when the balance equations are written as inequalities, even though they hold as equalities *ex post* in the solution.

11 Purchased inputs (with the exception of hired labor in some cases) are not usually given a monthly or seasonal dimension, because their physical availability usually is not limited.

12 This distinction is very useful in sector programming models, but notice that it does not correspond to the input/output distinction between intermediate inputs and primary factors. Hired labor is a primary factor in input/output terminology, but in sector models it belongs in the category of purchased inputs rather than fixed resources.

Chapter 8

Modeling Market Equilibrium

8.1 THE MODEL'S OBJECTIVE FUNCTION

In the previous chapter, the general structure of a sector model was developed but the exposition stopped short of an explicit algebraic statement of the objective function. This chapter focuses on the model's objective function and the specification of consumer demand functions. Its principal aims are to develop the theory relating to the objective function and to show how to implement it numerically.

Formally, there are two ways of deriving the objective function that will push the model to an equilibrium solution: via the geometry of producer and consumer surplus and via algebraic proof. The geometric approach is used first. It is helpful to think of the Samuelsonian objective function as comprising two components: the total area under the demand function and the area under the supply function. The first component enters the objective function with a positive sign and the second with a negative sign, so that their algebraic sum is the sum of producer and consumer surplus. The total area under the demand function in turn may be decomposed into consumer surplus and the gross margin of producers. Thus, there are three areas in all. They are illustrated in Figure 8.1, where they are the triangle A (consumer surplus), the

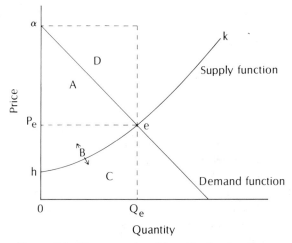

Figure 8.1 The geometry of the objective function.

rectangle B (gross margins), and the irregularly shaped area C (area under the supply function). This last area of course represents the total costs of production. The area B is the rectangle OP_eeQ_e; C is defined as $OheQ_e$; and A is the triangle $\alpha P_e e$. Area B includes area C but, as noted, the two enter the objective function with opposite signs. Their difference $B - C$ is producer surplus, so that the Samuelsonian objective function is $A + B - C$.

To facilitate the analysis, the demand function in Figure 8.1 is drawn as a straight line. In this case, at the equilibrium solution (P_e, Q_e), the value of the objective function Z can be expressed as follows:

$$Z = A + B - C$$
$$= \tfrac{1}{2}(\alpha - P_e)Q_e + P_eQ_e - C \qquad (8.1)$$

The same basic expression holds for any price-quantity pair that lies on the demand function, so the subscript e may be dropped. In its place, the product subscript j may be introduced. Also, the area C may be represented by a supply function, or total cost function, $C(Q_j)$, with $C'(Q_j) > 0$ and $C''(Q_j) > 0$. The curve hk in Figure 8.1 is the marginal cost function $C'(Q_j)$. Following the usual definition of the producer surplus, the cost function refers only to purchased inputs, i.e., cash outlays on the part of producers.[1] Therefore, the objective function becomes, for a single good,

$$Z_j = \tfrac{1}{2}(\alpha_j - P_j)Q_j + P_jQ_j - C(Q_j) \qquad (8.2)$$

Utilizing the working assumption of linearity of demand, the inverse demand function can be written

$$P_j = \alpha_j - \beta_jQ_j \qquad (8.3)$$

where β_j is a positive constant equal to the absolute value of the slope of the demand function.

Combining (8.2) and (8.3) yields the following expression:

$$Z_j = \tfrac{1}{2}(\beta_j Q_j)Q_j + (\alpha_j - \beta_j Q_j)Q_j - C(Q_j)$$
$$= (\alpha_j - \tfrac{1}{2}\beta_j Q_j)Q_j - C(Q_j) \qquad (8.4)$$

Notice that Z_j now is a quadratic expression in Q_j, even with linear demands. Effectively, the objective function has been defined along the horizontal axis of Figure 8.1. It equally could have been defined along the vertical axis, that is, only in prices instead of quantities.[2]

For the special case of linear demand functions, equation (8.4) is the proper objective function for a market-simulating linear programming model. A simple proof will show that this assertion is correct. To set up the model for the proof, let us distinguish between production S_j and sales Q_j. Referring to the notation of Chapter 7, but assuming for the moment that there is only one production technology, then production of good j is

$$S_j = y_j X_j$$

As before, the unit requirements of fixed resources in production can be denoted by a_{kj}, and resource availability by b_k, for k types of resources.

With these notational conventions, the simple sector model corresponding to Model 7.1, with multiple goods, can be rewritten with an explicit objective function:

Model 8.1

$$\max Z = \sum_j \left(\alpha_j - \tfrac{1}{2}\beta_j Q_j\right)Q_j - \sum_j C(S_j) \qquad (8.5)$$

such that

$$Q_j - S_j \le 0, \qquad \text{all } j \qquad [\pi_j] \qquad (8.6)$$

$$\sum_j a_{kj} X_j = \sum_j (a_{kj}/y_j)S_j \le b_k, \qquad \text{all } k \qquad [\lambda_k] \qquad (8.7)$$

$$Q_j, S_j \ge 0, \qquad \text{all } j. \qquad (8.8)$$

The terms in brackets at the right are the dual variables (shadow prices) corresponding to each primal equation. The last equation is the set of nonnegativity constraints. Equation (8.6) is the set of commodity balances, and (8.7) is the set of resource restrictions. Model 8.1 can be solved with quadratic programming algorithms.

To show that this little model's solution corresponds to the competitive equilibrium outcome under demand functions characterized by (8.3), we examine the first-order conditions for an optimal solution. The Lagrangean function is

$$\mathcal{L} = \sum_j \left(\alpha_j - \tfrac{1}{2}\beta_j Q_j \right) Q_j - \sum_j C(S_j)$$

$$- \sum_j \pi_j [Q_j - S_j] - \sum_k \lambda_k \left[\sum_j (a_{kj}/y_j) S_j - b_k \right] \qquad (8.9)$$

Apart from the feasibility requirements, the necessary Kuhn-Tucker conditions are:

$$\frac{\partial \mathcal{L}}{\partial Q_j} = \alpha_j - \beta_j Q_j - \pi_j \le 0, \qquad \text{all } j, \qquad (8.10)$$

$$\frac{\partial \mathcal{L}}{\partial S_j} = -C'(S_j) + \pi_j - \sum_k (a_{kj}/y_j)\lambda_k \le 0, \qquad \text{all } j. \qquad (8.11)$$

For the cases in which demand and supply are nonzero, these equations imply that

$$\pi_j = \alpha_j - \beta_j Q_j = P_j \qquad (8.12)$$

and

$$P_j = \pi_j = C'(S_j) + \sum_k (a_{kj}/y_j)\lambda_k \qquad (8.13)$$

Equation (8.12) says that, at the optimal solution, the model's shadow prices on the commodity balances are equal to the corresponding commodity prices. Equation (8.13) says that, also at the optimum, each commodity price is equal to the corresponding marginal cost of production. The marginal costs are defined as including both the explicit costs of purchased inputs at the margin $(C'(S_j))$ and the opportunity costs of fixed resources at the margin. The dual variable λ_k measures the marginal opportunity cost of resource k: by definition, it is the increment in consumer and producer surplus that would arise from the availability of an additional unit of resource k. In a competitive market this is the valuation of resource k.[3] The ratio a_{kj}/y_j is the amount of resource k required per unit of product j. Hence the second term on the right-hand side of (8.13) is the resource opportunity cost of an additional unit of product j.

Price equaling marginal cost of production is of course the fundamental characteristic of a competitive market. This demonstration has shown that the optimal solution to the programming model 8.1 corresponds to the equilibrium outcomes of a set of competitive markets. Furthermore, the supply functions in these competitive markets are defined so that the costs of production include both cash costs and opportunity costs. Recall that it was noted in

Chapter 7 that the supply functions in these models are implicit. Nevertheless, through numerical experiments with the model the supply functions can be made explicit.

The area under the demand function can of course be expressed as an integral. For multiple products, the objective function in its most general form is as follows:

$$Z = \sum_{j=1}^{n} \int_0^{Q_j} \phi_j \left(Q_j | Q_{j+i} = 0, \text{ all } i = 1 \text{ to } n - j \right) dQ_j - C(Q) \quad (8.14)$$

where $\phi_j(Q)$ is the inverse demand function for the quantity consumed of commodity j, Q_j. If the commodity demands are independent, then (8.14) simplifies to

$$Z = \sum_j \int_0^{Q_j} \phi_j(Q_j) \, dQ_j - C(Q). \quad (8.14a)$$

Further, if each $\phi_j(Q_j)$ is linear, that is, $P_j = \alpha_j - \beta_j Q_j$, all j, then integration of (8.14a) leads to the expression in (8.5). It is readily seen in (8.14a) that the first term on the right is simply the sum of areas under the single commodity demand functions.

The existence of interdependences in demand, or cross-price effects, accounts for the more complicated integral expression in (8.14). The integrals still measure the areas under the commodity demands, but to avoid double counting of areas across markets due to the cross-price terms, the integrals must be defined in a special way. The integrations are performed in sequence, and the integral for the jth market is evaluated while setting the quantities of all remaining commodities in the sequence to zero, i.e., with $Q_{j+1}, Q_{j+2}, \ldots, Q_n = 0$. Aspects of (8.14) are discussed in Courant (1936, p. 353), Willig (1979), and Yaron, Plessner, and Heady (1965).

In order to be sure that (8.14) is well-defined, the original demand functions have to be of such a form that the inverse demand functions exist, and at the same time the original functions have to be meaningful from a viewpoint of utility theory. The former requirement is known as the integrability condition, that is, being able to integrate the demand functions back to a utility function (Chapter 9 discusses this requirement in more detail). In general, this pair of requirements cannot be met satisfactorily. Zusman (1969) has shown that a resolution is possible only if symmetry of the demand functions is assumed, that is, only if the matrix of cross-price terms is symmetric. He points out that this is a strong requirement, and with empirical demand systems it will be met only if the goods are closely related in demand, have low income elasticities, and constitute a minor share of the consumer's expenditures."

As this book aims to present models that can be readily implemented numerically, the general expression (8.14) is not used, and instead the objective function (8.5) and extensions thereof are employed. In addition, for the purposes of the exposition in this chapter, the cross-price terms are assumed to be not only symmetric, but zero in value, so that demand functions of the form (8.3) may be used. Methods of handling nonzero cross-price terms are taken up in Chapter 9.

The next section shows how to linearize efficiently the quadratic objective function (8.5) so that model 8.1 can be solved as a linear programming problem. Linear programming algorithms are more widely available than nonlinear algorithms, and in some cases the sheer size of a model makes a linear formulation essential. In addition to these computational considerations, the linear model has some other advantages for model specification. Among its dual variables are variables which directly measure consumer surplus. Also the linear version leads conveniently into extensions for handling nonzero cross-price effects and nonzero income effects. Finally, the linear version can also be used to approximate nonlinear demand functions.

8.2   A LINEAR PROGRAMMING FORMULATION

Before entering into the details of the linear model's structure, and its properties, it is worth mentioning that, if no cross-price terms are contemplated, the demand side of the model can be built up from three pieces of data per demand function: the own price elasticity, the initial (base-year) price and the initial quantity. One additional data entry is required per cross-price term. In section 8.3 below, some suggestions are made regarding ways to use these initial data in calculating the models' coefficients.

8.2.1   A Linear Approximation to the Objective Function

The principal distinguishing feature of the linear programming formulation is that choices along the demand function are specified *a priori* in numerical form. For a given product, the model's solution involves a decision like whether to sell (to consumers) 100 tons, 120 tons, 140 tons, etc., or some interpolated amount between two of those values. With each quantity sold, the total area under the demand function (to be denoted by W) also is specified *a priori*, so that the model is selecting from among pairs (W_s, Q_s) that are explicitly linked.[4]

To illustrate this approach to building the model, suppose the demand function (8.3) is, in numbers,

$$P = 50 - 0.10Q \tag{8.15}$$

And suppose also that in the short run Q is almost certain to lie in the range

100 to 200. In that case, for $Q_1 = 100$

$$W_1 = \alpha Q_1 - \tfrac{1}{2}\beta Q_1^2$$
$$= (50)(100) - \tfrac{1}{2}(0.10)(100)^2 = 4500 \qquad (8.16)$$

Similarly, for $Q_2 = 110$, $W_2 = 4895$, and for $Q_3 = 120$, $W_3 = 5280$. Thus, the model will be asked to choose among the following options, each of which represents a point on the demand function:

	1	2	3	
W:	4500	4895	5280	...
Q:	100	110	120	...

and it may also choose a linear combination of any two of those values. Recall that the model's solution will be such that price = marginal cost of production, so implicitly the price at points 1, 2, 3, etc., will be compared with costs of production, which are recorded elsewhere in the model, before the final choice is made among points on the demand curve.

Since the points 1, 2, 3 represent alternative choices, they become activities in the model. Customarily, they are given the symbol D, for demand. Thus, in the illustration above, the model would include activities D_1, D_2, D_3, etc., associated with quantities sold of 100, 110, 120, etc., respectively.

These quantities are total quantities sold, not incremental quantities. Therefore the model cannot be permitted to choose, say, both points 2 and 3, but rather one of them or some linear combination thereof. To enforce this requirement the additional constraint is needed that the sum of the D activities does not exceed unity. It might appropriately be called the linear combination constraint, but by usage it has become known as the convex combination constraint.

By adding this constraint and the symbols for the variable names, the example above may be converted into a small tableau for the demand side of the model as follows:

	D_1	D_2	D_3	...	RHS
Objective function Z	4500	4895	5280	...	Maximize
Supply-demand balance[5]	100	110	120	...	≤ 0
Convex combination constraint	1	1	1	...	≤ 1

The model's solution may contain $D_1 = 1$ and $D_2 = D_3 = 0$; or $D_1 = D_3 = 0$ and $D_2 = 1$; or $D_1 = 0.4$, $D_2 = 0.6$, $D_3 = 0$; or any other combination consistent with the convex combination constraint. If the model were to choose $D_2 = 1$, the solution would be selecting the second point in the relevant range of the demand function. The associated quantity of sales is 110 tons, but the variable D_2 itself does not represent the quantity. Thus, although the model contains demand functions, neither price nor quantity is an explicit

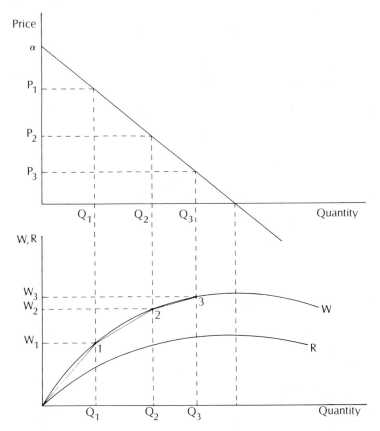

Figure 8.2 The demand function and the objective function.

variable in the model—unless it is desired to add equations for purely accounting purposes which measure those concepts.

Figure 8.2 shows the area under the demand curve (W) in relation to the demand function in the linearized case. The model's choices are among variables that represent points like 1, 2, and 3 on the W function. The associated quantities are found on the horizontal axes of both diagrams in the figure, and the corresponding prices and values of W are found on the vertical axes. The model is not operating along the envelope W but rather along the piecewise linear frontier connecting the origin with points 1, 2, and 3. Clearly, by increasing the number of points specified in a given interval, the piecewise linear approximation to W can be made closer. The model's solution may include more than one point (more than one variable D_s), but it will not include more than two, and those two will be adjacent points. By utilizing two nonadjacent points, or a linear combination of three or more points, the solution would be located on a piecewise linear frontier below the one shown in Figure 8.2. That would be an inefficient solution, as a greater value of W and hence Z could be obtained from the same value of Q by utilizing only one point or two adjacent points.

In most applications, it is convenient to add to the tableau another row which serves as an accounting equation for gross income (revenue of producers). To do that, values are taken from the function R in Figure 8.2 for each designated point on the demand function. In algebra, for the jth product,

$$R_j = (\alpha_j - \beta_j Q_j)Q_j = P_j Q_j \qquad (8.17)$$

Note that the expression for revenue differs from the expression for area only in the absence of factor $1/2$ before the β_j. In our one-product example, for $Q = 100$, 110, and 120, the corresponding values of R are 4000, 4290, and 4560. Hence the complete tableau would read as follows:

	D_1	D_2	D_3	Y	RHS
Objective function	4500	4895	5280 $\cdots$		Maximize
Producer incomes row	4000	4290	4560 $\cdots$	-1	$= 0$
Supply-demand balance	100	110	120 $\cdots$		≤ 0
Convex combination constraint	1	1	1 $\cdots$		≤ 1

The new variable Y is the accounting variable for producer gross incomes. If total costs of production are subtracted, it may be converted into a variable representing producer net incomes.

8.2.2 Interpretation of the Shadow Prices

In these tableaus, as demonstrated earlier, the shadow price on the supply-demand balance equals the product price. The shadow price on the convex combination constraint also has a convenient interpretation; it turns out to be a measure of the total consumer surplus. To show this, model 8.1 is transformed to include a linearized objective function both in terms of W and $C(Q)$, and, for each product, a convex combination constraint. As in Chapter 7, alternative production technologies are reinstated with t subscripts. At this simplified level of treatment, the complete linear model now looks as follows:

Model 8.2

$$\max Z = \sum_j \sum_s \omega_{js} D_{js} - \sum_j \sum_t c_{jt} X_{jt} \qquad (8.18)$$

such that

$$-\sum_t y_{jt} X_{jt} + \sum_s \theta_{js} D_{js} \leq 0, \quad \text{all } j \quad [\pi_j] \qquad (8.19)$$

$$\sum_j \sum_t a_{kjt} X_{jt} \leq b_k, \quad \text{all } k \quad [\lambda_k] \qquad (8.20)$$

$$\sum_s D_{js} \leq 1, \quad \text{all } j \quad [\mu_j] \qquad (8.21)$$

$$X_{jt}, D_{js} \geq 0, \quad \text{all } j, t, s \qquad (8.22)$$

In model 8.2, the symbol ω_{js} denotes the value of the area under the demand curve at point s on the demand curve for product j. It corresponds to the figures 4500, 4895, and 5280 in the immediately foregoing illustration. The symbol θ_{js} denotes the associated quantities; they are 100, 110, and 120 in the example. The variables D_{js} may not exceed unity in value. They are the choice variables regarding position on the demand function. The convex combination constraint forces the model's solution to be located on or below the demand function. But it is inefficient to lie below the demand function, for with the same quantity sold a greater value of Z can be attained by being on the demand function. Hence constraint (8.21) effectively dictates that the model's optimal solution will lie on the demand function, provided, of course, that it is feasible to do so.

Apart from the feasibility requirements, the necessary first-order conditions for an optimal solution to model 8.2 are as follows:

$$\frac{\partial \mathcal{L}}{\partial D_{js}} = \omega_{js} - \theta_{js}\pi_j - \mu_j \leq 0, \qquad \text{all } j, s \qquad (8.23)$$

and

$$\frac{\partial \mathcal{L}}{\partial X_{jt}} = -c_{jt} + y_{jt}\pi_j - \sum_k a_{kjt}\lambda_k \leq 0, \qquad \text{all } j, t. \qquad (8.24)$$

Multiplying (8.23) by D_{js} and summing it over s,

$$\sum_s \omega_{js}D_{js} - \left(\sum_s \theta_{js}D_{js}\right)\pi_j - \left(\sum_s D_{js}\right)\mu_j \leq 0, \qquad \text{all } j. \qquad (8.25)$$

By (8.21), and the fact that it is inefficient to be at a point below the demand function,

$$\sum_s D_{js} = 1 \qquad (8.26)$$

Also, by definition

$$\sum_s \theta_{js}D_{js} = Q_j \qquad (8.27)$$

and

$$\sum_s \omega_{js}D_{js} = W_j \qquad (8.28)$$

Substituting (8.26), (8.27), and (8.28) into (8.25), then for each commodity for which there is some positive amount of production and sales, it follows that

$$W_j - Q_j\pi_j = \mu_j \qquad (8.29)$$

For these same nonzero activities, equation (8.24) can also be arranged as

$$\pi_j = \frac{\sum\limits_{k} a_{kjt}\lambda_k + c_{jt}}{y_{jt}} \qquad (8.30)$$

Equation (8.30) says that π_j is equal to the marginal (unit) cost of production for each technology t used. The first term in the right-hand side numerator is the marginal opportunity cost of the fixed resources employed in the production of good j. The second term is the marginal cost of purchased inputs (which are fixed in price but perfectly elastic in supply). Both terms are expressed per acre, hectare, or some other unit of area, so when they are divided by the unit yield y_{jt} the result is marginal cost per ton (or per other unit of output measurement).

Since the model's solution must lie on the demand function, and since the maximand is consumer plus producer surplus, then, as in model 8.1, marginal cost will be equal to price in the solution. Hence π_j is the product price.

Returning to (8.29), the term W_j is the total area under the demand function (area A and B in Figure 8.1) and $Q_j\pi_j = R_j$ is producer revenue (area B in that figure). Therefore μ_j must equal area A, or consumer surplus.

The convex combination constraint plays a controlling role in defining the demand function. Increasing the right-hand side value of the convex combination constraint for product j by an amount ε^* would enable the sum of the D_{js} in the optimal basis to attain a value of $1 + \varepsilon^*$. This would effectively multiply the Q, W, and R values by $1 + \varepsilon^*$, for the same price level. In other words, the demand function is rotated rightward by the percentage ε^*, as shown in Figure 8.3, where $\varepsilon^* = (d_1 - d_0)/d_0$.

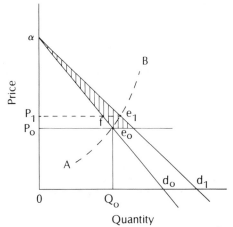

Figure 8.3 Rotating the demand function.

This rotation procedure is taken up in Chapter 9 in the context of income and cross-price effects. For the present, the rotation concept may be used to show geometrically that μ_j must be equal to consumer surplus. If the supply function were horizontal at P_0, then the rotation of the demand function would increase the objective function's value by the amount of the cross-hatched area in Figure 8.3. This area can be identified readily as additional consumer surplus, and therefore the increment in Z per unit increment in the right-hand side of equation (8.21) is consumer surplus. This ratio of increments also defines the dual variable associated with (8.21), or μ_j.

Of course, in most cases the supply function will be upward sloping, as shown by the dashed line AB in Figure 8.3, and rotation of the demand function would cause the price to rise from P_0. There would be a reallocation of area $P_0 e_0 f P_1$ from consumer to producer surplus, but since the two surpluses are summed in the objective function, its value is not affected by the reallocation. The net addition to the objective function is the area $\alpha e_0 e_1$, which is almost entirely consumer surplus. In the limit, as the rotation becomes small, it can be seen from the diagram that the share of the net addition corresponding to consumer surplus approaches 100%. A dual variable is a limit concept, defined for infinitesimally small changes in the right-hand side value of an equation. Therefore, in the limit μ_j, which measures the net addition to the objective function, is pure consumer surplus.[6]

While linear demand functions have been used throughout this exposition, nonlinear functions pose no additional problems. The only requirement is that the W-function in Figure 8.2 be convex from above throughout the relevant range of quantities. The area under the curve at each preselected point can be calculated either directly or via triangles and rectangles for a piecewise linear approximation to the curve, as shown in Figure 8.4. In that figure, the superscripts u and l represent upper and lower limit values, respectively, for the relevant range of the demand function.

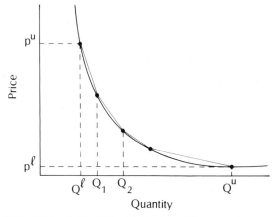

Figure 8.4 A nonlinear demand function.

8.3 CALCULATING THE COEFFICIENTS IN THE TABLEAU

In the case of the linearized demand function, the steps required for calculating the coefficients in the tableau can be described briefly. As mentioned above, without taking into account cross-price effects the starting parameter values needed for each demand function are three: the own-price elasticity of demand (η_j), the initial price (P_{j0}) and the initial quantity (Q_{j0}).

The first step is to calculate the parameters α_j and β_j of the linearized inverse demand function.

$$\beta_j = -\frac{dP_j}{dQ_j} = -\frac{P_{j0}}{\eta_j Q_{j0}} > 0 \tag{8.31}$$

and

$$\alpha_j = P_{j0} + \beta_j Q_{j0} > 0 \tag{8.32}$$

Next, the relevant range of the demand function is measured. For most applications, it has been found that a range of $(P_j^l, P_j^u) = (.5P_{j0}, 2P_{j0})$ is adequate, but depending on the circumstances the model builder may wish to alter that range. The range is then translated to the quantity axis:

$$Q_j^l = \frac{\alpha_j - P_j^u}{\beta_j} \tag{8.33}$$

$$Q_j^u = \frac{\alpha_j - P_j^l}{\beta_j} \tag{8.34}$$

and a check is needed to be sure that Q_j^l is nonnegative. If it is not, the price range needs to be revised. (Of course, the range may be established on the quantity axis from the outset, but in practice it usually proves easier to make appropriate judgments on the range via the price axis.)

The next step is to establish the length of segments between points on the demand function; that length depends on Q_j^u, Q_j^l, and the number of segments. Most recent applications have utilized eleven segments although more are utilized in some cases. The segment length is then

$$k_j = \frac{Q_j^u - Q_j^l}{n-1} \tag{8.35}$$

where n is the number of segments. The quantities at each point on the function are

$$\theta_{j0} = Q_j^l$$
$$\theta_{j1} = Q_j^l + k_j$$
$$\theta_{j2} = Q_j^l + 2k_j$$
$$\vdots$$
$$\theta_{j10} = Q_j^l + 10k_j = Q_j^u \tag{8.36}$$

Finally, the values of W and R for each point are calculated on the basis of the foregoing information:

$$W_{js} = \omega_{js} = \alpha_j \theta_{js} - \tfrac{1}{2}\beta_j \theta_{js}^2 \tag{8.37a}$$

$$R_{js} = \rho_{js} = \alpha_j \theta_{js} - \beta_j \theta_{js}^2. \tag{8.37b}$$

A small example of these calculations is reproduced from the first version of the CHAC model (see Chapter 11), for the case of tomatoes:

$$\eta_j = -0.4, \ P_{j0} = 0.1150 \ \text{(in ten thousand pesos/ton)}$$
$$Q_{j0} = 436.818 \ \text{(in thousand tons)}$$

Step 1

$$\beta_j = -\frac{P_{j0}}{\eta_j Q_{j0}} = 0.000658$$

$$\alpha_j = P_{j0} + \beta_j Q_{j0} = 0.402426$$

Step 2

$$P_j^u = 0.2300$$

$$P_j^l = 0.0575$$

$$Q_j^u = \frac{\alpha_j - P_j^l}{\beta_j} = 524.2037$$

$$Q_j^l = \frac{\alpha_j - P_j^u}{\beta_j} = 262.0456$$

Step 3

The segment length is

$$k_j = \frac{Q_j^u - Q_j^l}{10} = 26.2158$$

and therefore the quantities at each point are

$$\theta_{j0} = 262.0456$$
$$\theta_{j1} = 288.2614$$
$$\theta_{j2} = 314.4772$$
$$\vdots$$
$$\theta_{j10} = 524.2037$$

Step 4

Samples of the objective function entries and revenue values are:

	Point 0	Point 1
ω_{js}	82.8622	88.6657
ρ_{js}	60.2705	61.3276

Two remarks on numerical procedures emerge from this example. One is that the units of measure should be scaled so that unduly large or small coefficients in the matrix are avoided. The other is that, even though the original parameter estimates (the η_j, P_{j0} and Q_{j0}) may not be known with much accuracy, it is important to carry the computations of the model's coefficients to a few decimal places to avoid spurious nonconvexities and other numerical problems.

8.4 MARKETING AND MARKET IMPERFECTIONS

The basic apparatus is now complete for building models that determine prices endogenously on the basis of consumer behavior (demand functions), producer behavior (production technologies and resource endowments), and competitive market-clearing processes. As discussed earlier, competition here means that no single producer can influence the market price by varying his output. Competition can still determine prices even in the presence of some types of market imperfections, such as transportation inadequacies and imperfect flows of market information. In this section, the incorporation of such market imperfections in a model of competitive markets is reviewed.

8.4.1 Differences in Regional Transport Costs

A typical kind of market imperfection is exaggerated farm-to-market transportation costs for a remote producing region. This circumstance results in permanently lower farm-gate prices for producers in the more remote region, and hence in lower farm incomes there. Such a phenomenon may be incorporated in the model via marketing and transportation activities. Following the notation of Chapter 7, let these activities be denoted by the symbol T. Then model 8.2 can be modified by the addition of regional commodity balances, with the marketing-transportation activities playing the role of transferring products from the regional balances to the national balances.

Model 8.3[7]

$$\max Z = \sum_j \sum_s \omega_{js} D_{js} - \sum_j \sum_r \sum_t c^1_{jrt} X_{jrt} - \sum_j \sum_r c^2_{jr} T_{jr} \qquad (8.38)$$

such that

$$-\sum_t y_{jrt} X_{jrt} + T_{jr} \leq 0, \quad \text{all } j, r \qquad [\pi_{jr}] \qquad (8.39)$$

$$-\sum_r T_{jr} + \sum_s \theta_{js} D_{js} \leq 0, \quad \text{all } j \qquad [\pi_j] \qquad (8.40)$$

$$\sum_j \sum_t a_{kjrt} X_{jrt} \leq b_{kr}, \quad \text{all } k, r \qquad [\lambda_{kr}] \qquad (8.41)$$

$$\sum_s D_{js} \leq 1, \quad \text{all } j \qquad [\mu_j] \qquad (8.42)$$

$$D_{js}, X_{jrt}, T_{jr} \geq 0, \quad \text{all } j, s, r, t \qquad (8.43)$$

The cash-outlay costs are now broken into two categories: production costs per hectare (c^1) and marketing costs per ton of product marketed (c^2). Notice that model 8.3 includes regional prices (π_{jr}) and national prices (π_j) for the same commodity j. A priori, it is expected that the marketing costs will enter into the determination of the interregional price differentials. The relevant first-order conditions for an optimal solution are as follows:

$$\frac{\partial \mathcal{L}}{\partial D_{js}} = \omega_{js} - \theta_{js}\pi_j - \mu_j \leq 0 \tag{8.44}$$

$$\frac{\partial \mathcal{L}}{\partial X_{jrt}} = -c^1_{jrt} + y_{jrt}\pi_{jr} - \sum_k a_{kjrt}\lambda_{kr} \leq 0 \tag{8.45}$$

$$\frac{\partial \mathcal{L}}{\partial T_{jr}} = -c^2_{jr} - \pi_{jr} + \pi_j \leq 0 \tag{8.46}$$

Equation (8.44) is identical to equation (8.23), which was derived from model 8.2. Equation (8.45) differs from (8.24) only in the superscript on the cost term and in the use of regional subscripts. Equation (8.46) is new.

From equation (8.46) it follows immediately that if marketing and transportation take place from region r, then the dual variables display the following relationship:

$$\pi_{jr} = \pi_j - c^2_{jr} \tag{8.47}$$

That is, the regional price is lower than the national price by the amount of marketing and transportation costs c^2_{jr}. The greater the latter costs, the greater the interregional price differentials.[8] Interestingly, interregional differences in production costs do not figure in the determination of the price differentials. This implies that regions with higher production costs or lower yields will receive lower levels of income per unit of product harvested and marketed.

Model 8.3 can be used to analyze two sources of economic dualism (or interregional differences in income levels): market imperfections and productivity differentials. Or, in the event of no true market imperfections, geography's contribution to transportation and marketing costs can have the same kind of influence. Again, instead of, or in addition to, regions, the model may have farm size classes, and the same procedures and conclusions would be applicable.

8.4.2 Distinguishing Between Retail and Wholesale Prices

So far the concept of product price has been used extensively without discussing its nature, except to say that it is a farm-gate price. Once marketing activities are introduced it is preferable to distinguish farm-gate prices from retail (or urban wholesale) prices. In that regard, the π_{jr} are better interpreted as farm-gate prices and the π_j as retail (or urban wholesale) prices. When this distinction is made, the demand functions are defined for the prices π_j and not the farm-gate prices. At this stage, care must be exercised to define net farm income on the basis of the appropriate set of prices. It is most conveniently defined by starting with the retail prices, but then subtracting both marketing and production costs, so that effectively the income calculation is based on farm-gate prices. If a farm-income accounting row were added to model 8.3, it would read as follows:

$$\sum_j \sum_s \rho_{js} D_{js} - \sum_j \sum_r \sum_t c^1_{jrt} X_{jrt} - \sum_j \sum_r c^2_{jr} T_{jr} - Y = 0 \qquad (8.48)$$

where Y denotes aggregate net producer income and ρ_{js} is the parameter corresponding to the R-function in Figure 8.2 for product j and point s on the demand function. Notice that no dual variable is posited for equation (8.48). The model's solution would be identical were that equation dropped, and so its shadow price is always zero.

8.4.3 Introducing Regional Demand Curves

Thus far the demand functions have been assumed to be national in character, but it is more realistic to specify market-clearing behavior by region, along with opportunities for interregional arbitrage in commodities. This step is usually not taken because of the implications for model size. However, it is increasingly recognized as a useful step in the direction of improving model realism. It also permits net farm incomes to be defined by region within the model.[9] In terms of model structure, specifying the model with regional demand functions requires regional convex combination constraints and also marketing-transportation activities for pairs of regions r and r'. The modified model is as follows:

Model 8.4

$$\max Z = \sum_j \sum_r \sum_s \omega_{jrs} D_{jrs} - \sum_j \sum_r \sum_t c^1_{jrt} X_{jrt} - \sum_j \sum_r \sum_{r' \neq r} c^2_{jrr'} T_{jrr'} \qquad (8.49)$$

such that

$$- \sum_t y_{jrt} X_{jrt} - \sum_{r'} T_{jr'r} + \sum_{r'} T_{jrr'}$$
$$+ \sum_s \theta_{jrs} D_{jrs} \leq 0, \qquad \text{all } j, r \qquad [\pi_{jr}] \qquad (8.50)$$

$$\sum_j \sum_t a_{kjrt} X_{jrt} \leq b_{kr}, \qquad \text{all } k, r \qquad [\lambda_{kr}] \qquad (8.51)$$

$$\sum_s D_{jrs} \leq 1, \qquad \text{all } j, r \qquad [\mu_{jr}] \qquad (8.52)$$

$$\sum_j \sum_s \rho_{jrs} D_{jrs} - \sum_j \sum_t c^1_{jrt} X_{jrt}$$
$$- \sum_j \sum_{r'} c^2_{jr'r} T_{jr'r} - Y^r = 0, \qquad \text{all } r \qquad (8.53)$$

$$D_{jrs}, X_{jrt}, T_{jrr'} \geq 0, \qquad \text{all } j, r, s, t, r' \qquad (8.54)$$

In model 8.4, the national commodity balances have disappeared in favor of regional balances only. Likewise, there is no "national" price but only a set of regional prices. As in model 8.3, resource endowments are regional. The variable $T_{jrr'}$ denotes shipment of product j from region r to region r'. In defining the regional net farm income variable Y^r (via equation 8.53), the costs of interregional shipments had to be assigned either to the shipping region or to the receiving region. In this case, the convention was adopted that these costs are assigned to the receiving region.[10]

A set of regional income variables has been gained in model 8.4, but the distinction between farm gate and retail prices has been lost. To recover that distinction, two levels of commodity balances need to be introduced for each region: producer-level balances (production balances) and consumer-level balances (consumption balances). To accomplish this change, the principal modification needed is to replace equation (8.50) with the following pair of equations:[11]

$$- \sum_t y_{jrt} X_{jrt} + T_{jr} \le 0, \quad \text{all } j, r \quad \left[\pi^1_{jr} \right] \qquad (8.50a)$$

$$- T_{jr} - \sum_{r'} T_{jr'r} + \sum_{r'} T_{jrr'}$$
$$+ \sum_s \theta_{jrs} D_{jrs} \le 0, \quad \text{all } j, r \quad \left[\pi^2_{jr} \right] \qquad (8.50b)$$

Also, the objective function must be augmented with the term $- \sum_j \sum_r c^2_{jr} T_{jr}$. Now the model contains a distinction between intraregional marketing and shipping (T_{jr}) and its interregional counterpart $(T_{jrr'})$. Also, a distinction has been made between regional farm-gate prices (π^1_{jr}) and regional retail prices (π^2_{jr}).

A slightly more realistic treatment of the marketing activities would allow for the physical wastage that occurs for most products, especially fresh fruits and vegetables, in the course of marketing and transportation. If the waste percentages are known, then this factor may be taken into account by a further modification of (8.50b) as follows:

$$- u_{jr} T_{jr} - \sum_{r'} u_{jr'r} T_{jr'r} + \sum_{r'} u_{jrr'} T_{jrr'}$$
$$+ \sum_s \theta_{jrs} D_{jrs} \le 0, \quad \text{all } j, r. \quad \left[\pi^2_{jr} \right] \qquad (8.50c)$$

The wastage percentage for local marketing is $(1 - u_{jr})$ and for interregional marketing it is $(1 - u_{jr'r})$. In the latter case, the shipping region r' ships out one unit and the receiving region r gets $u_{jr'r}$ units.

8.4.4 Processing Activities

In terms of formal structure, processing activities look very much like the marketing-transportation activities that have been presented above. In fact, in some cases it is useful to combine marketing, transportation, and processing in one activity. These activities are best compared in tableau format. The following tableau shows a marketing-transportation activity as it appears in model 8.3 or model 8.4:

Equation	T_{jr}	Equation number in model (8.3)
Objective function	$-c_{jr}^2$	(8.38)
Production balance	$+1$	(8.39)
Consumption balance	$-u_{jr}$	(8.40)

(In model 8.3, the parameter $u_{jr} = 1.0$.) The tableau for a processing activity would look exactly the same, in terms of both row names and coefficients. If T_{jr} is read as a processing activity, then the raw material input is one unit (from the production balance) and the corresponding physical output is u_{jr} units. For example, in milling wheat, a ton of grain may yield 800 kilograms of processed flour, ignoring the bran by-product. The total cost per ton processed is c_{jr}^2.

Given this identity of structure, it is possible to form a single activity which represents processing, marketing, and transportation. The main motivation for doing so lies in simplification of the data requirements for the model. If data are available on farm-gate prices of the raw products and retail prices of the processed products, plus information on the conversion/wastage factors u_{jr}, then the unit cost of all stages of marketing, transportation, and processing is calculated simply, as follows:

$$c_{jr}^2 = u_{jr} P_{jr}^s - P_{jr}^f \qquad (8.55)$$

where P_{jr}^s is the retail sales price and P_{jr}^f is the farm-gate price. If national, rather than regional, demand functions are used, then the retail price symbol does not have a regional subscript.

When the processing activity yields joint products, then (8.55) has to be modified:

$$c_{jr}^2 = \sum_i \left(u_{jr}^i P_{jr}^{s,i} \right) - P_{jr}^f \qquad (8.56)$$

where i is the index of the joint products that result from the processing activity. In this case, the above tableau for T_{jr} has to be altered to allow for entries in as many consumption balances as there are joint products i.

By incorporating these representations of marketing, processing, and transportation activities into the model, the model becomes much more useful. It now can be used to help evaluate the effects of programs aimed at improving the economic efficiency of those activities. The model's solution will show the effects of such improvements in terms of changes in farm-gate and consumer prices, changes in production levels, cropping patterns, and rates of input use, changes in farm income and employment, and, in some cases, changes in the agricultural foreign trade balance.

8.4.5 On-Farm Consumption of Foods

A "market imperfection" that is commonly encountered in developing countries is the practice of retaining substantial quantities of harvested food for home consumption, even though relative farm-gate prices would appear to suggest that it is more profitable to cultivate commercial crops. To some extent this behavior is a manifestation of risk aversion where basic nutrition is concerned, but it is also a function of the cost of marketing crops. By not consuming the farm's own harvest of staple foods, the farm family may pay 30% to 50% more than the farm-gate price when replacement food is purchased over the year in local markets. Thus the true opportunity cost of substituting commercial crops for staple foods is not the farm-gate price of staples, but rather their local retail price.

These considerations, which reinforce the tendency toward production for home retentions, can be incorporated in farm-level and sector models.[12] For those regions and farm size groups in which home retentions are significant, the following equation can be added to the model, for subsistence crop j:

$$\sum_{t} y_{jrt} X_{jrt} + V_{jr} \geq H_{jr} \qquad [\gamma_{jr}] \qquad (8.57)$$

where V_{jr} signifies the farm family's purchases of the subsistence good. The right-hand side constant H_{jr} is the annual requirement of the good that is needed for home consumption purposes.[13]

Correspondingly, the objective function and the farm income accounting equation both need to be modified with the addition of the term $-\Delta_{jr} V_{jr}$, where Δ_{jr} is the difference between the price farm families pay for purchases of the subsistence good and the price they receive for its sale at harvest. The shadow price γ_{jr} is then equal to $-\Delta_{jr}$.

The developments presented in this section have illustrated ways in which market imperfections can be introduced into a model whose prices are determined by competitive market-clearing processes. Model builders should be able to extend these approaches as required to deal with particular cases of market imperfections they encounter.

8.5 HISTORICAL ANTECEDENTS IN THE LITERATURE[14]

The story behind the material in this chapter began when Enke (1951) posed the problem of finding the competitive equilibrium levels of interregional product flows and prices. He ingeniously proposed solution by using an electrical analog, a system of interconnected batteries. Since the typical economist is not a competent electrician, the profession's interest was stirred more by Samuelson's mathematical formulation a year later, in which he pointed out the possibility of formulating the problem as a maximization problem.

Samuelson (1952) viewed his maximand, the "net social payoff," as an artifice whose usefulness lay simply in driving a programming model solution to the equilibrium quantity marketed at each location. He explicitly rejected any welfare interpretation of the maximand. Although Samuelson gave the first mathematical formulation, his suggestions on procedures for solution did not go beyond trial-and-error iterations. A decade later Smith (1963) showed that the same problem could be cast as the minimization of rents to fixed resources, which he felt was a more natural way of looking at the workings of a competitive market. Smith, too, dealt with the market for a single product, so questions of interdependence in demand were not considered.

Meanwhile, attempts at developing manageable, numerical procedures for solution were being made outside the optimization framework. Fox (1953) appears to have been the first to carry out a computational procedure for competitive equilibrium (for the case of a multiregion, feedgrain economy). Given estimated parameters of regional demand functions, Fox followed an iterative method to arrive at market-clearing prices and shipments. A few years later, Judge and Wallace (1958) and Tramel and Seale (1959) similarly proposed iterative, nonoptimizing tatonnement procedures for finding the equilibrium solutions for the interregional shipments problem. Ho and King (1972) developed a modified computer program for the Tramel and Seale spatial equilibrium algorithm which accommodates a variety of independent functional forms.

Also in the numerical context, Heady and others had been concurrently developing spatial linear programming models in which interregional demands were fixed nationally or regionally (see, for example, Heady and Egbert 1959). In these studies the dual solution was sometimes used to discuss supply prices, but market equilibrium prices were not obtained. A later example of this approach is Piñeiro and McCalla's study of Argentine agriculture (1971).

The first attempts to explicitly introduce price-responsive demand functions into a linear programming model also led to iterative solution methods. In these cases a linear programming solution was calculated at each iteration. For example, Schrader and King (1962) maximized producers' revenue at each iteration and successively revised prices to eventually attain the market-clearing solution. This procedure can be workable for some simple models, but, when the model becomes large or when many products are included, the iteration procedure becomes excessively time consuming.

Of course, iterations were adopted because the objective function is inherently nonlinear in this kind of problem: it is some function of price $\times$ quantity, where both factors are endogenous. Takayama and Judge (1964a, 1964b) were the first to solve the spatial equilibrium problem directly with quadratic programming under linear, interdependent demand functions.[15] However, their procedures required the supply functions to be explicit. In the

Takayama-Judge formulation, the objective function is clearly identified as the sum of the consumer and producer surpluses. For computational methods, Takayama and Judge showed that a modified simplex algorithm of Wolfe can be applied through reformulation of the problem as a primal-dual linear program. In practice, however, this algorithm is not nearly as powerful as the simplex algorithm itself.

Yaron, Plessner, and Heady (1965) distinguished between the following multiproduct cases: (1) independent demand, (2) interdependent demands with fulfillment of the integrability conditions, and (3) interdependent demands without fulfillment of the integrability conditions. For case 1, they showed how linear programming solution techniques could be applicable via stepwise approximation of the demand curves, and they provided welfare interpretations of the objective function. For case 2, they established a quadratic programming formulation along the lines of Takayama and Judge and again stressed the welfare interpretation. For case 3, they used a primal-dual formulation and pointed out that the welfare interpretation breaks down, a point that lends force to satisfying integrability conditions. No computations were presented. Takayama and Judge (1971, Chapter 12) also addressed the integrability problem.

Hall, Heady, and Plessner (1968) applied a multiregional quadratic programming model to U.S. agriculture and obtained estimated prices that were lower than actual prices.[16] Shortly thereafter, Guise and Flinn (1970) used the quadratic formulation in an application to derive competitive allocations and prices of irrigation water for an agricultural district.

The work up to this point may be summarized as follows: the single-period (static) market demand structures had been fully worked out conceptually, in general optimizing models, for solutions treating prices and quantities as endogenous. On the computational side, however, although linear programming had been used for single-product models, little progress had been made on efficient, single-solution procedures. Also, the procedures required that the supply functions be known beforehand, that is, activity analysis technology sets could not be used for the supply side of the model. Hence, for multiproduct and activity analysis models it was not yet practical to use linear programming, which, by virtue of the computational advantages of the simplex algorithm, would permit complex and detailed formulations on both the supply and demand sides.[17] And, for multiproduct models with interdependence in demand, no simplex formulation had been established.

Without taking into account interdependence in demand, Martin (1972) spelled out in detail the piecewise linear specification of product demand and factor supply functions in a linear programming model of competitive markets. Although Martin gave a systematic presentation of the procedure, national and regional multiproduct models that included stepped demand functions and the surplus-maximizing objective had already been developed in Europe. A national model was developed for France, as discussed by Farhi and Vercueil (1969) and Tirel (1971). About the same time, a regional model designed to yield the competitive market solution in prices and quantities was formulated for the Moldavian region of the USSR and was reported by Mash and Kiselev (1971). These apparently were the first sectoral linear programming models to give the competitive equilibrium solution without iterations. Neither, however, considered interdependence in demand, and their stepped approximation technique led to models that are much larger in row dimension than models developed using the procedure followed in this chapter.

In their work on the CHAC model of Mexican agriculture, Duloy and Norton (1973a, 1975) developed an efficient linearization procedure that utilizes the grid linearization techniques of Miller (1963). An advantage of their approach is that the linear approximation may be made arbitrarily close without increasing the number of rows in the model. They also presented a procedure for dealing with interdependence in demand that is based on specification of alternative commodity bundles in consumption. (That procedure is reviewed and extended in Chapter 9.) Finally, they integrated the demand functions with activity analysis supply sets. For the most part, the representations of this chapter constitute a review and extension of their work. Hazell (1979) developed the corresponding procedures which are discussed in Chapter 9 for replicating equilibria in factor markets.

The general equilibrium model presented in Chapter 9 was developed by Norton and Scandizzo (1981). During its development stage it was applied to an economy-wide analysis of Korea by Hong (1980). A subsequent application was made by Willett (1982) for the United States.

Detailed literature surveys that cover some of the topics in this book are found in Norton and Schiefer (1980), McCarl and Spreen (1980), and Kutcher and Norton (1982). The first two articles are more technical in content, and the last one provides more of an overview of the nature and uses of these models, with brief summaries of three case studies. The article by Norton and Schiefer contains some 150 references to works in this field.

NOTES

1 The producer surplus is the return (or rent) to fixed factors.
2 Takayama and Judge (1964a, 1964b, 1971) work along the price axis rather than along the quantity axis.
3 We prefer not to ascribe welfare connotations to the objective function Z, but for the interested reader Willig (1976) showed that under many plausible circumstances the sum of surpluses is a very close approximation to the true welfare measure, which is either the compensating variation (CV) or the equivalent variation (EV).
4 The objective function Z is then $W - C(Q)$.
5 Recall from Chapter 7 that outputs enter the supply-demand (commodity) balances with negative signs.
6 The magnitude of μ_j in the limit is $\Delta Z/\varepsilon^* d_0$, for very small ε^*. In linear programming algorithms, the dual variable's magnitude is scaled so that the denominator of the above expression is one unit of the corresponding RHS. But

for equation (2.1), the RHS is 1.0, so one unit is the entire RHS, and therefore μ_j is total, not incremental, consumer surplus.

7 Model 8.3 corresponds to Table 7.3, without the foreign trade activities.

8 The cost term c_{jr}^2 also can reflect the lack of timely marketing information and/or the lack of adequate storage facilities in the producing location.

9 They can also be calculated *ex post*, on the basis of the information in the solution.

10 In a model with large numbers of regions and/or products, it may be desirable to rule out many interregional shipment possibilities on *a priori* grounds, to prevent the model from becoming too large.

11 Regional demand functions and regional production and consumption balances are included in the recent agricultural model for Turkey of Norton and Gencaga (1985).

12 More complete approaches to modeling farm food consumption are developed in Chapter 4.

13 This formulation of the problem assumes that farm family food retentions are included in the estimated market demand parameters. That is, Q_{js} in Section 8.3 includes the quantity of the jth product consumed by farm households as well as total sales. Locating the demand curves in this way allows farm family consumption to respond to market prices.

14 This section is adapted, with permission of the Johns Hopkins University Press from Norton and Solís (1983).

15 With nonlinear demand functions, the problem is of a higher order than quadratic.

16 They attribute the discrepancies to omission of fixed costs in the model and to the fact that supply-control and price support programs in the real world distort prices away from the competitive equilibrium levels. They appear to overlook the fact that both aggregation and specification biases could distort prices in a downward direction by overstating productive efficiency and, hence, placing the supply curve to the right of its proper location. Given the generally inelastic demands for agricultural products, this bias would show up more significantly in prices than in quantities, which is what their results display.

17 The relative ease of handling large-scale models by means of linear programming is especially relevant to the construction of sector-wide planning models, in which incorporation of considerable detail by location and product is almost unavoidable if useful results are to be obtained.

Chapter 9

Modeling Market Equilibrium: Extensions

9.1 INTRODUCTION

This chapter provides a number of extensions to the equilibrium theory for programing models that was developed in the preceding chapter. The topics covered are noncompetitive market forms, demand functions in a regional model, the incorporation of cross-price effects, endogenous input prices, and extensions to general equilibrium. The modeling of land markets is discussed in the subsection on endogenous input prices.

The material in this chapter and the following one completes the technical foundations of the sector model. The reader more interested in applications may wish to skip ahead to Chapters 11 to 13; Chapters 9 and 10 can be used as needed for references regarding technical issues that arise in the course of building a model.

9.2 NONCOMPETITIVE MARKET FORMS

As discussed earlier in the book, one of the major features of sector models with explicit demand structures is that they contain well-defined market forms. Normally, agricultural markets are competitive in the sense that no single producer can influence the market price by varying his output level; however, cases do exist of monopolistic behavior. Such cases can be reflected in the model's structure by appropriate modification of the objective function.

Monopolistic behavior can be simulated by replacing the demand area component (W) of the objective function with the expression for producer revenue. Recall that gross revenue is given by the function R in Figure 8.2 and by equation (8.17). For the programming model, it is given by the numerical value of the expression

$$\sum_j \sum_s \rho_{js} D_{js} = \sum_j \left(\alpha_j Q_j - \beta_j Q_j^2 \right) \tag{9.1}$$

which appears as part of equation (8.48). Use of this objective function leads to a solution with a higher price and a lower quantity sold than in the competitive case. A model may be constructed with a competitive market specification for some products and a monopolistic specification for others.

In a recent article, Nelson and McCarl (1984) have shown that various forms of oligopoly may be modeled by further changes in the objective function. Let the first term in the objective function be rewritten (for product j) as:

$$W_j' = \alpha_j Q_j - \nu_j \beta_j Q_j^2 \tag{9.2}$$

If $\nu_j = 1$, the model simulates the monopolistic equilibrium with its optimal solution; if $\nu_j = \frac{1}{2}$, the competitive equilibrium is being simulated. For the case of Cournot oligopoly, extended to n firms, Nelson and McCarl (1984) have demonstrated that

$$\nu_j = \frac{n + 1}{2n} \tag{9.3}$$

Clearly, as $n \to \infty$, $\nu_j \to \frac{1}{2}$, which means that perfect competition is reached in the limit. When $n = 1$, $\nu_j = 1$, which is the monopoly case.

9.3 DEMAND FUNCTIONS IN A REGIONAL MODEL

Model (8.4) in the preceding chapter is national in scope and contains regional demand functions which refer to the consumption behavior of the residents of each region. If added horizontally they sum to the national demand functions. A very different type of demand function is appropriate for a model that focuses on supply behavior in only one region. The demand functions faced by producers in the region rarely correspond to the demand functions of the residents of the region, for local consumption needs may also be met by purchasing products from other regions. And conversely, some of the demands for local production may arise in other regions.

As Kutcher (1972, 1983) has shown, demand functions facing producers in a region depend not only on local demand but also on the supply functions of producers in other regions. Composite demand functions are needed for a regional model, and they cannot be estimated directly from market data. In this section, the appropriate composite demand functions are derived under alternative assumptions. (The derivation is a simplification of Kutcher, 1983.)

National production can be decomposed into its regional components

$$Q = Q_1 + Q_2 \tag{9.4}$$

where subscript 1 represents the region in the model and subscript 2 represents the aggregate of all other regions not included in the model.

The problem is to derive the demand function facing the region's producers, $P = f(Q_1)$, using information about a supply shift in region 1, the accompanying supply response in region 2, and the national demand function. In Figure 9.1, the problem is to find the slope of the demand function connecting points E and E' before and after the region 1 supply curve has shifted from S_1 to S_1', where D represents the national demand function, and D^1 the demand function facing the region.

Let ΔP denote the absolute value of the change in price, then the elasticity of the demand function facing the producers of region 1 can be expressed as

$$\eta_1 = \frac{Q_{10} - Q_{11}}{\Delta P} \cdot \frac{P_0}{Q_{10}} \tag{9.5}$$

Since by definition $Q_{11} = Q_1 - Q_{21}$, and $Q_{10} = Q_0 - Q_{20}$, (9.5) can be

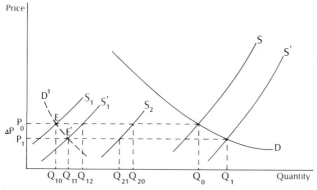

Figure 9.1 Shifts in regional supply functions.

expanded as

$$
\eta_1 = \frac{Q_0 - Q_1}{\Delta P} \cdot \frac{P_0}{Q_{10}} - \frac{Q_{20} - Q_{21}}{\Delta P} \cdot \frac{P_0}{Q_{10}}
$$

$$
= \eta_N \frac{Q_0}{Q_{10}} - \sigma_2 \frac{Q_{20}}{Q_{10}} \tag{9.6}
$$

where η_N denotes the national demand elasticity, and σ_2 is the supply elasticity of region 2.

Now $Q_0/Q_{10} = 1/K$ where K is the ratio of region 1 output to national output. Further, $Q_{20}/Q_{10} = (Q_{20}/Q_0)(Q_0/Q_{10}) = (1 - K)(1/K)$. Substituting into (9.6), this becomes

$$
\eta_1 = \eta_N \cdot \frac{1}{K} - \sigma_2 \cdot \frac{1 - K}{K} \tag{9.7}
$$

Three principal points emerge from the foregoing. First, the demand function facing a region's producers can be calculated, and it depends on the national demand parameters and also on parameters of the supply functions in the rest of the sector. Second, in the limit, as the supply elasticity in the rest of the sector approaches perfect elasticity ($\sigma_2 \to \infty$) and the region's share in output becomes small, the elasticity of demand facing the sector approaches infinity ($\eta_1 \to -\infty$). This would correspond, for example, to the case of a traded good in a small country situation. Third, in the other limit, if supply is not responsive in the rest of the sector ($\sigma_2 = 0$), then the elasticity of the demand function facing the region is equal to a simple transform of the national elasticity:

$$
\eta_1 = \eta_N \frac{1}{K} \tag{9.8}
$$

9.4   CROSS-PRICE EFFECTS

9.4.1   Demand Mixtures

Thus far the demand side of the programming models has been based on a simple kind of demand function in which quantities depend only on own prices. Income effects and cross-price effects have been ignored. This formulation is incomplete and hence unrealistic, but before rushing into more complex formulations it should be pointed out that there are many circumstances in which the simpler approach is a reasonable one for applied purposes.

Specifically, if the agricultural sector is a small part of the economy, in terms of shares of GNP or GDP, then the income effects would be very much second-order effects. In other words, the *change* in agricultural income indicated by the model's solution would be a sufficiently small part of income in the entire economy that the position of the demand curves would not be materially affected by taking that change into account. Similarly, cross elasticities of demand for specific products often are sufficiently small that they can be safely ignored (e.g., the corn-pineapple cross elasticity).

However, there are circumstances in which it is desirable to include these effects in the model's structure. Making the income effects endogenous leads to a general equilibrium model, and that topic is treated in a later section of this chapter. The cross-price effects are discussed here.

In developing model formulations to handle cross-price effects it is important to be aware of the empirical context. In some cases (rather few), cross elasticities are known from previous studies. More frequently, the relevant cross elasticities are not known, but it is known that substitution occurs readily among particular sets of goods. Oilseeds and forage crops are two examples.

In this last case, it sometimes is useful to handle the substitution possibilities via prior specification of alternative commodity bundles, or demand mixes. The demand can be specified in terms of the aggregate commodity, such as oilseeds in general, and that demand can be satisfied with varying combinations of safflower, sesame, cottonseed, etc.

Following Duloy and Norton (1973b), Table 9.1 illustrates such substitution possibilities. In the commodity balances, the coefficients $\theta_{im}Q_s$ denote the amount of commodity i consumed in mixture m, on segment s of the demand curve. The θ coefficients are shares that sum to unity, and Q_s is the total quantity consumed of all goods in the mixture at demand segment s. The θ are invariant over segments. For example, for $Q_s = 1.0$, the quantities consumed of safflower, sesame, and cottonseed oil on a given segment of the oilseeds demand curve might be as follows:

	Mixture 1	Mixture 2	Mixture 3
Safflower	.2	.1	.3
Sesame	.1	.1	.3
Cottonseed	.7	.8	.4

In drawing up this little example, two assumptions implicitly have been made: (1) that there are limiting values on the proportions of each crop in the mixture, e.g., safflower and sesame each will constitute no less than 10% of the mixture, and cottonseed no less than 40%; and (2) that the three goods are perfect substitutes for each other in the physical sense that one kilogram of any of them can substitute for one kilo of another.

The indifference curves that characterize such a specification are downward sloping straight lines, truncated at the limiting values. In this example the marginal rates of substitution (slopes) along the indifference curves are

Table 9.1 Substitution Effects in Demand

	Production	Demand segment 1			Demand segment 2			RHS
		Safflower ω_{11}	Sesame ω_{21}	Cotton ω_{31}	Safflower ω_{12}	Sesame ω_{22}	Cotton ω_{32}	
Objective function								Maximize
Commodity balance:								
Safflower	$-y_1$	$\theta_{11}Q_1$	$\theta_{12}Q_1$	$\theta_{13}Q_1$	$\theta_{11}Q_2$	$\theta_{12}Q_2$	$\theta_{13}Q_2$	≤ 0
Sesame	$-y_2$	$\theta_{21}Q_1$	$\theta_{22}Q_1$	$\theta_{23}Q_1$	$\theta_{21}Q_2$	$\theta_{22}Q_2$	$\theta_{23}Q_2$	≤ 0
Cotton seed	$-y_3$	$\theta_{31}Q_1$	$\theta_{32}Q_1$	$\theta_{33}Q_1$	$\theta_{31}Q_2$	$\theta_{32}Q_2$	$\theta_{33}Q_2$	≤ 0
Convexity		1	1	1	1	1	1	≤ 1

− 1.0. The linear indifference curve is not likely to be acceptable over a wide range of values, but sometimes it can be useful for small changes around the observed values.

The marginal rate of substitution (MRS) of − 1.0 is less likely to be acceptable than the linearity of the indifference curve. A more reasonable value of the MRS can be found by introducing additional information in the form of prices. Recall that in equilibrium, the price line must be tangent to the indifference curve. In the case of a linear indifference curve, this condition implies that the price line is identical to a line whose slope is the MRS. Hence the desired MRS is given by the negative of the ratio of prices (in the base year).

Suppose that the price ratio were 1 : 1.2 for safflower and sesame, respectively, and 1 : 1.4 for safflower and cottonseed, respectively. Then, if mixture 1 in the above example represents the observed proportions, mixtures 2 and 3 could be derived as follows:

	Mixture 1	Mixture 2	Mixture 3
Safflower	.2	[.129 / 1.03 = .125]	[.171 / .842 = .203]
Sesame	.1	[.100 / 1.03 = .097]	[.271 / .842 = .322]
Cottonseed	.7	[.800 / 1.03 = .777]	[.4 / .842 = .475]

The new proportions in mixture 2 are derived via the following sequence of steps: (1) cottonseed's share is raised from 0.7 to 0.8, to represent the possibility of greater concentration in that product; (2) for this mixture, the increase in cottonseed is taken out of safflower consumption, at the stated MRS of 1 : 1.4, which implies a decrease in safflower's share of 0.071 for the cottonseed increase of 0.100; (3) the new row shares are normalized so that they sum to unity. Similar steps were carried out to find the new shares in mixture 3, except that the change in cottonseed's share is distributed over both safflower and sesame.

To span the relevant mathematical space of possibilities as efficiently as possible, each mixture should contain at least one extreme share, i.e., a crop at its maximal or minimal share. For three goods x, y, and z, no more than six mixtures will suffice to span the space:

For x at its maximum:
y at max *or* z at min
z at max *or* y at min
For y at its maximum
z at max *or* x at min

And similarly for x, y at their minimum values. The "or" statement is necessary because setting two shares at their maximum values may drive the third one to a negative value.

9.4.2 Price-Weighted Aggregation

The foregoing procedures are applicable when physical aggregation rather than economic aggregation is used. If a kilogram of vegetable oil has the same usefulness, or gives the same satisfaction in consumption regardless of which plant it came from, then physical aggregation is appropriate. However, if the substitutable goods are not perfectly homogeneous in this sense, then the aggregate should be established by economic criteria, that is, by using price weights. The aggregation problem arises because the demand function is defined over the aggregate good, with a corresponding aggregate price. The demand mixtures show alternative ways of disaggregating the aggregate demand in terms of specific commodities, but the demand functions are not defined for those commodities.

Under physical aggregation, for any mixture m the aggregate good is

$$Q_{ms} = \sum_i Q_{ims} = \sum_i \theta_{im} Q_s \qquad (9.9)$$

and since
$$\sum_i \theta_{im} = 1.0 \text{ for all } m$$

$$Q_{ms} = Q_s \text{ all } m \qquad (9.10)$$

Under economic aggregation,

$$Q_{ms} = \frac{\sum_i \overline{P}_i Q_{ims}}{\sum_i \overline{P}_i} \qquad (9.11)$$

where the $\overline{P}_i$ are observed prices. In this case, the shares in Table 9.1 have to be redefined as

$$\theta_{im}^* = \frac{\theta_{im} \sum_i \overline{P}_i}{\sum_i \theta_{im} \overline{P}_i} \qquad (9.12)$$

where the θ_{im} are the physical shares, as before. Only in this way can we derive the required condition that the price-weighted quantity of the aggregate commodity is independent of the commodity mix. Since $Q_{ims}^* = \theta_{im} Q_s$,

$$Q_{ms} = \frac{\sum_i \overline{P}_i Q_{ims}}{\sum_i \overline{P}_i} = \frac{\left(\sum_i \overline{P}_i \theta_{im}^*\right) Q_s}{\sum_i \overline{P}_i}$$

$$= \frac{\left[\sum_i \overline{P}_i \left[\dfrac{\theta_{im} \sum_i \overline{P}_i}{\sum_i \theta_{im} \overline{P}_i}\right]\right] Q_s}{\sum_i \overline{P}_i} = Q_s \qquad (9.13)$$

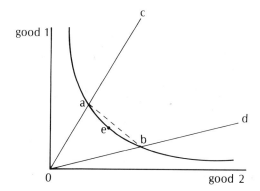

Figure 9.2 A linear indifference curve for a limited range of substitution.

which is the desired result. (See Duloy and Norton, 1973b.) In this case, the construction of the model proceeds as before, except that the θ_{im} in Table 9.1 are replaced by the θ_{im}^*. Forage crops, fruits, vegetables, and food grains are common examples of crop groups that would require an economic aggregation approach.

The demand mixtures represent a fairly workable approach to incorporating demand substitution possibilities, but they do have the drawback of distorting the commodity prices in the dual solution. Figure 9.2 gives a geometric representation of substitution possibilities inherent in Table 9.1. The substitution surface is the line segment ab, which is a linearized portion of the indifference curve between the rays Oc and Od. The solution almost certainly will lie at one of the extreme points a or b. If it is at a, for example, then more of good 1 can be produced and sold only by moving outward along the ray Oc. In other words, selling more of good 1 implies, at the margin, also selling more of good 2. A Leontief consumption technology (fixed proportions) characterizes the marginal behavior. This result implies that the marginal cost of producing good 1 will be equal to the price of good 1 plus the marginal profit (or loss) involved in producing good 2 in the required proportion. This "price + cross profit" term will be the shadow price on the commodity balance, and it will be the determinant of producer decisions.

A way to reduce this distortion is to expand the number of demand mixtures to include points like e in Figure 9.2. If point e is included, then there would be two linear segments along the indifference curve: a straight line connecting a and e, and a straight line connecting e and b. Such a procedure could be carried further, and points outside the rays Oc and Od could be included as well. The distortion is reduced because if the solution is at point e, more of good 1 can be sold by selling less of good 2. In other words, the goods still are substitutes, rather than complements, as they were at the margin in the previous case. With more points along the indifference curve, the solution still may lie in a corner, so that the previous objection still holds, but the frequency of that behavior should be reduced.

Will the model choose point e in preference to a linear combination of points a and b? Yes, for the reason that at point e it can satisfy the demand at a given segment on the demand function by selling less of both goods, and hence by producing less of both. The quantity and price of the aggregate of goods 1 and 2 would remain the same, but costs of production would be lower.

This practical implication of this expanded procedure is that more alternative demand mixtures should be included in the model, and not just those that represent upper and lower bounds on the shares of individual products. But here an empirical difficulty arises: how are we to know the marginal rates of substitution between a and e and between e and b? In the initial procedure of positing only a single, linear indifference curve segment, it was assumed that base year relative prices provided the necessary information on the (single) MRS.

In the absence of knowledge about the complete demand system, the indifference curve itself cannot be known, but there is a possible way of constructing the curve empirically. *If* there is sufficient historical variation in relative prices, and *if* historically the relative quantities varied in a regular way with relative prices (that is, more consumption of good 1, vis-à-vis good 2, was associated with a lower relative price of good 1), then possibly the indifference curve may be constructed by using those relative prices and relative quantities. We leave this as a topic for further exploration by others.

9.4.3 Cross Elasticities

In some cases, a matrix of cross elasticities may be known, or they may be known only for a subset of the goods in the model. In the quadratic model, the cross elasticities are incorporated simply by changing the first term in the objective function to read

$$W = Q'A - \tfrac{1}{2}Q'BQ \qquad (9.14)$$

where now Q is a vector of quantities consumed, A is a vector of demand intercepts, and B is a matrix of cross-price slopes. The slopes can be defined from the elasticities readily:

$$B_{ij} = \frac{-1}{\eta_{ij}} \frac{\bar{P}_j}{\bar{Q}_i} \qquad (9.15)$$

where η_{ij} is the cross elasticity and the bars represent observed values. Note that the elasticity refers to the percentage change in Q_i with respect to a change in P_j, but that the slope is defined from the inverse demand function, so it is $\Delta P_j / \Delta Q_i$.

As noted in Chapter 8, use of the quadratic model is restricted to the case in which the cross-price slopes are symmetric. The maximand (9.14) will represent the sum of the areas under the demand functions only if symmetry holds. Recalling equation (8.14), the area is given by the expression

$$W = \sum_{i=1}^{n} \int_0^{Q_i} \left(P_i | Q_{i+j} = 0, \text{ all } j = 1 \text{ to } n - i \right) dQ_i \qquad (9.16)$$

where, in the case of linear demand functions,

$$P_i = a_i - \sum_j b_{ij} Q_j$$

A two-good example will illustrate why symmetry is necessary. The result of the integration in (9.16) is indeed expression (9.14); see Yaron, Plessner, and Heady (1965). Let us work back, however, from (9.14) to P_i for the two-good case.

$$\frac{\partial}{\partial Q_1} \left[Q'(A - \tfrac{1}{2} BQ) \right] = \frac{\partial}{\partial Q_1} \left[A_1 Q_1 + A_2 Q_2 - \tfrac{1}{2} B_{11} Q_1^2 - \tfrac{1}{2} B_{12} Q_1 Q_2 \right.$$
$$\left. - \tfrac{1}{2} B_{21} Q_1 Q_2 - \tfrac{1}{2} B_{22} Q_2^2 \right]$$
$$= A_1 - B_{11} Q_1 - \tfrac{1}{2} B_{12} Q_2 - \tfrac{1}{2} B_{21} Q_2 \qquad (9.17)$$

If $B_{12} = B_{21}$, then (9.17) becomes

$$\frac{\partial}{\partial Q_1} Q'(A - \tfrac{1}{2} BQ) = A_1 - B_{11} Q_1 - B_{12} Q_2 = P_1 \qquad (9.18)$$

and hence maximization of (9.14) is the same as maximization of (9.16). However, if $B_{12} \neq B_{21}$, then that is not the case. Zusman (1969) discusses these issues further.

9.4.4 Cross-Price Effects in Linear Programming

One way of avoiding the symmetry requirement in specifying the linear cross-price model is to introduce endogenous shifts in the position of each demand curve, according to the cross effects.[1] If the price of good 2 increases by 20% and the cross-price elasticity with respect to good 1 is -0.10, then the demand curve for good 1 should rotate leftward by 2%. That is, at any initial price, the quantity demanded of good 1 would be 2% less.

The rotation of the demand curve is accomplished by altering the convex combination constraint (as discussed below for income effects in the context of the general equilibrium model). In the original version of the model, the right-hand side value of the convex combination constraint is 1.0. If it is 1.2, the demand curve is rotated rightward by 20%; if it is 0.8, the curve is rotated leftward by 20%. To make the rotation endogenous, the incremental term appears on the left-hand side:

$$\sum_s D_{is} - \sum_{j \neq i} \eta_{ij} \dot{P}_j \leq 1 \qquad (9.19)$$

where $\dot{P}_j$ represents the percentage change in the price of good j.

To make this equation usable in the linear programming model, the percentage change variable has to be expressed in another form:

$$\dot{P}_j = \left(\frac{1}{P_{j0}}\right)P_j - 1 \qquad (9.20)$$

where P_{j0} is the observed base-year value of the price and hence can be regarded as a predetermined parameter. Also, in order to introduce the price variable into the primal solution, the demand functions have to be written explicitly in the primal.

With these introductory comments, the linear model with cross-price effects may be written as follows:

$$\max Z = \sum_i \sum_s \omega_{is} D_{is} - \sum_i \sum_t c_{it} X_{it} \qquad (9.21)$$

subject to
resource constraints

$$\sum_i \sum_t a_{kit} X_{it} \le b_k \qquad [\lambda_k] \qquad (9.22)$$

commodity balances

$$-\sum_t y_{it} X_{it} + \sum_s \theta_{is} D_{is} \le 0 \qquad [\pi_i] \qquad (9.23)$$

convex combination constraints

$$\sum_s D_{is} - \sum_{j \ne i}\left(\frac{\eta_{ij}}{P_{j0}}\right)P_j \le 1 - \sum_{j \ne i}\eta_{ij} \qquad [\mu_i] \qquad (9.24)$$

demand functions

$$\frac{1}{Q_{i0}}\sum_s \theta_{is} D_{is} - \sum_j\left(\frac{\eta_{ij}}{P_{j0}}\right)P_j = 1 - \sum_j \eta_{ij} \qquad [\gamma_i] \qquad (9.25)$$

The terms in brackets at the right are again the dual variables corresponding to each primal equation. Equation (9.24) follows from substituting (9.20) into (9.19). The demand functions are written in percentage change form, also utilizing (9.20). The first term on the left in (9.25) is equal to one plus the percentage change in the quantity demanded.

The first-order conditions for the model (9.21) through (9.25) are as follows:

$$\frac{\partial \mathscr{L}}{\partial D_{is}} = \omega_{is} - \theta_{is}\pi_i - \mu_i - \left(\frac{\theta_{is}}{Q_{i0}}\right)\gamma_i \leq 0 \qquad (9.26)$$

$$\frac{\partial \mathscr{L}}{\partial X_{it}} = -c_{it} - \sum_k a_{kit}\lambda_k + \pi_i \leq 0 \qquad (9.27)$$

$$\frac{\partial \mathscr{L}}{\partial P_j} = \sum_{i \neq j} \eta_{ij}\mu_i + \sum_i \left(\frac{\eta_{ij}}{P_{j0}}\right)\gamma_i = 0 \qquad (9.28)$$

Without loss of generality, all the initial prices P_{j0} may be set equal to unity. With this condition, when the system is evaluated at the solution that reproduces the base year (so that $\theta_{is} = Q_{i0}$ for the optimal segments), (9.26) becomes

$$\omega_{is} - \theta_{is}\pi_i - \mu_i - \gamma_i = 0 \qquad (9.29)$$

The exact equality is used to signify that the dual system is being evaluated for the basic primal variables.

From (9.27), again π_i = marginal cost. To derive sufficient conditions, it is assumed that price = marginal cost = π_i. Therefore, from (9.29), $\mu_i + \gamma_i$ = consumer surplus associated with good i.

If the solution does reproduce the base year, then each demand equation collapses to the trivial identity $1 = 1$, which is a redundant expression, and so $\gamma_i = 0$. Therefore, under this condition, μ_i = consumer surplus, as in the case of the model with no cross-price terms. That is, when the demand equations are not rotated endogenously, the new system reverts to the simpler specification in dual as well as primal.

These properties suggest that a sufficient condition characterizing the solution to (9.21) through (9.25) is that the term $(\theta_{is}/Q_{i0})\gamma_i$ in (9.26) represent the incremental consumer surplus associated with the endogenous rotation of the demand curve. This interpretation is shown in Figure 9.3, where $\alpha D'$ is the rotated demand function. In that figure, the initial value of consumer surplus μ is shown as the crosshatched area. The incremental value $(\theta_s/Q_0)\gamma$ is given by the area $(\alpha f e_1) - (P_1 P_0 e_0 f)$.

In closing this section, it should be remarked that this linearized cross-price specification has not yet been fully tested in a comprehensive sector model. It would appear to be most useful in circumstances in which a few important cross elasticities are known (but not necessarily symmetric) and the others are assumed to be approximately equal to zero.

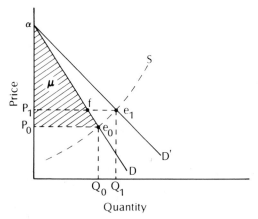

Figure 9.3 Consumer surplus under a rotated demand curve.

9.5 ENDOGENOUS INPUT PRICES

So far we have focused on methods of endogenizing product prices in the sector model, but the same principles apply to factor markets as well. In the case of product markets, the demand functions were given *ex ante* and the supply functions were implicit in the model's structure. For factor markets, the reverse holds: the factor supply functions are specified beforehand, and the corresponding demand functions are implicit in the production activities of the model.

The supply functions for many factors are simple, being either perfectly inelastic or perfectly elastic. For the sector as a whole, or for regions within the sector, land is a factor that typically is perfectly inelastic in the short run. Irrigation water fits in the same category. Fertilizers and other agrochemicals are examples of inputs that usually are perfectly elastic in supply at the given price. However, there are cases of factor supply functions that fall between these two extremes. Labor supply often is elastic but not perfectly elastic. In developing countries, short-term credit is another example, for often institutional credit is subsidized and nonbank credit is not, and there may be several kinds of the latter, each with its own price. Effectively, credit is characterized by an upward-sloping stepped supply function.

For inputs in perfectly elastic supply, their cost is subtracted from the objective function in the model and there is no restriction on their availability. For inputs in inelastic supply, the cost is not explicit in the primal formulation but their availability is limited; consequently the dual solution will include variables that measure their opportunity cost. The following illustrative model shows both cases, with product demands set as perfectly elastic for simplicity:

$$\max Z = \sum_j P_j Q_j - \sum_i c_i J_i \tag{9.30}$$

such that

$$- \sum_t y_{jt} X_{jt} + Q_j \leq 0, \quad \text{all } j \quad [\pi_j] \quad (9.31)$$

$$- J_i + \sum_j \sum_t a_{ijt} X_{jt} \leq 0, \quad \text{all } i \quad [\delta_i] \quad (9.32)$$

$$\sum_j \sum_t a_{kjt} X_{jt} \leq b_k, \quad \text{all } k \quad [\lambda_j] \quad (9.33)$$

In this model, the inputs in perfectly elastic supply are denoted by the variable J_i and their unit costs are c_i. Otherwise the notation is as above.

In the solution, the shadow price of product j, π_j, will be equal to the fixed price P_j, and the shadow price of input i, δ_i, will be equal to the fixed unit cost c_i. As before, λ_j will measure the opportunity cost of the resources that are available in perfectly inelastic supply.

To analyze the case of factors whose supply functions are upward sloping, one such factor, N (for labor), will be distinguished from the other inputs.[2] Define labor's unit cost w and its supply function as

$$w = \alpha^* + \beta^* N \quad (9.34)$$

Then the total wage bill is

$$wN = \alpha^* N + \beta^* N^2 \quad (9.35)$$

One approach is to include the total wage bill (with a negative sign) in the objective function, as is done for the terms $-c_i J_i$. However, this formulation leads to a solution in which the last laborer hired is paid more than earlier laborers, that is, a discriminating monopsonist solution. It will be argued later that there are circumstances in which this formulation is in fact the appropriate one, but of course there are circumstances for which it would be inappropriate. To see that the discriminating monopsonist solution results, the objective function (9.30) can be revised:

$$\max Z = \sum_j P_j Q_j - \sum_i c_i J_i - \alpha^* N - \beta^* N^2 \quad (9.36)$$

and an additional constraint can be added:

$$\sum_j \sum_t n_{jt} X_{jt} - N \leq 0 \quad [\lambda_n] \quad (9.37)$$

Now the relevant first-order necessary conditions are, for the model (9.31) through (9.33) and (9.36) through (9.37):

$$\frac{\partial \mathscr{L}}{\partial X_{jt}} = y_{jt}\pi_j - \sum_i a_{ijt}\delta_i - \sum_k a_{kjt}\lambda_k - n_{jt}\lambda_n \leq 0 \tag{9.38}$$

$$\frac{\partial \mathscr{L}}{\partial N} = -\alpha^* - 2\beta^* N + \lambda_n \leq 0 \tag{9.39}$$

$$\frac{\partial \mathscr{L}}{\partial Q_j} = P_j - \pi_j \leq 0 \tag{9.40}$$

$$\frac{\partial \mathscr{L}}{\partial J_i} = -c_i + \delta_i \leq 0 \tag{9.41}$$

From (9.38), (9.40), and (9.41) the relation between price and cost of any nonzero activity may be derived as

$$P_j = \frac{\sum_i a_{ijt} c_i + \sum_k a_{kjt}\lambda_k + n_{jt}\lambda_n}{y_{jt}} \tag{9.42}$$

where the equality follows from the assumption that (9.38) through (9.41) are defined for basic primal variables. This relation holds for technologies t that appear in the optimal basis. The numerator is the sum of marginal costs of production per unit activity level of X_{jt} (e.g., per hectare). Dividing by the yield y_{jt} converts this cost into an expression for cost per ton. The question concerns the last term in the numerator: what is the nature of the labor cost? From (9.39) it follows that, if labor inputs are used,

$$\lambda_n = \alpha^* + 2\beta^* N = \frac{\partial(wN)}{\partial N} \tag{9.43}$$

Thus λ_n is the marginal cost of labor, not the average cost, which is

$$AC_N = \frac{\alpha^* N + \beta^* N^2}{N} = \alpha^* + \beta^* N = w \tag{9.44}$$

It follows that products are being priced in the model on the basis of labor's marginal cost, not its average cost, hence the optimal solution's supply of labor will correspond to the intersection of the (implicit) demand function and the marginal cost function, as illustrated in Figure 9.4. In that figure the crosshatched area corresponds to the monopsonistic profits. The subscript m on w and N denotes the monopsonistic solution, and c, the competitive solution.

In order to model the competitive solution, the objective function (9.36) must be modified to include the area under the factor supply function,

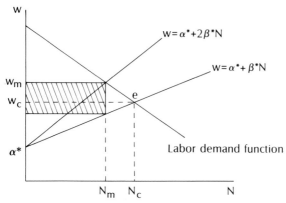

Figure 9.4 Labor market equilibrium situations.

analogous to the inclusion of the area under the product demand function in Sections 8.1 and 8.2. The area under the labor supply function is

$$\int_0^N (\alpha^* + \beta^*N)\, dN = \alpha^*N + \tfrac{1}{2}\beta^*N^2 \qquad (9.45)$$

Therefore the revised objective function is

$$\max Z = \sum_j P_j Q_j - \sum_i c_i J_i - \alpha^*N - \tfrac{1}{2}\beta^*N^2 \qquad (9.46)$$

To see that this formulation gives rise to the competitive outcome for the labor market, it is necessary only to look at the revised version of the first-order condition (9.39):

$$\frac{\partial \mathscr{L}}{\partial N} = -\alpha^* - \beta^*N + \lambda_n \le 0 \qquad (9.47)$$

When labor is employed in nonzero amounts, then

$$\lambda_n = \alpha^* + \beta^*N = w \qquad (9.48)$$

and in the model labor now is costed at the market wage (labor's average cost) rather than at a higher level.

This specification of factor markets involves a quadratic term, but it may be linearized for use in linear programming models by the introduction of segmentation variables. In this case, they are denoted N_s, with $\sum_s N_s \le 1$. Let γ_s^n denote the amount of labor supplied at point N_s on the supply function, and ω_s^n the corresponding value of $\tfrac{1}{2}\beta^*N^2 = \tfrac{1}{2}\beta^*(\gamma_s^n)^2$. Then the objective function of the model can be rewritten as

$$\max Z = \sum_j P_j Q_j - \sum_i c_i J_i - \alpha^*N - \sum_s \omega_s^n N_s \qquad (9.49)$$

and the following additional equations are needed:

$$\sum_s \gamma_s^n N_s - N = 0 \qquad (9.50)$$

$$\sum_s N_s \leq 1 \qquad (9.51)$$

The shadow price on equation (9.51) now is equal to the surplus accruing to labor, (area $\alpha^* w_c ew$ in Figure 9.4), calculated up to the quantity of labor supplied in the solution.[3]

The monopsonist solution may be appropriate for the case of farm family labor vs. hired labor. In the short run, farm family labor may have restricted mobility in the job market, for once the crop is planted the family is unlikely to migrate permanently to an urban area until the crop is harvested. And in rural areas few part-time jobs may be available. Therefore, it often is observed (especially in developing countries) that in the short run family labor will work on their own farms at tasks that have a marginal productivity below the market wage (although well above zero!). The corresponding specification of the model is a two-step labor supply function in which family labor occupies the first step, and hired labor occupies the second step. In that case, the implicit wage paid to family labor during the growing season actually is less than the market wage, so the family unit is behaving as a discriminating monopsonist with respect to its own labor, although it reaps the monopsonistic profits as well.

In the foregoing treatment of factor markets, the factor supplies are taken as exogenous to the model. By implication the factor supply functions refer to factors not productively employed elsewhere in the sector. The model specification is different when labor is hired away from one farm to work on another farm, or when land is rented out from one farm to be used as part of the operation on another farm. In that situation, both the factor supply function and the factor demand function are endogenous, so the previous method of formulating the model is not applicable.

An appropriate method for this last case involves specification of a transfer activity representing the exchange of a factor, along with the associated transaction cost. An illustration is developed in the context of renting land, denoted L_r, between two farm groups labeled 1 and 2. To allow the possibility of land transfers via rental, land constraints for the two classes of farms are written as follows:

$$\sum_j \sum_t l_{jt1} X_{jt1} + L_r \leq L_1 \qquad [\lambda_1] \qquad (9.52)$$

$$\sum_j \sum_t l_{jt2} X_{jt2} - L_r \leq L_2 \qquad [\lambda_2] \qquad (9.53)$$

Since the payment of rent is a pure income transfer between the two classes of

Table 9.2 Mini-Tableau for Land Rental

	L_{12}	L_{21}
Group 1 land constraint	1.0	− 1.0
Group 2 land constraint	− 1.0	1.0
Objective function	$-c^r$	$-c^r$

farms, it is not necessary to enter the rental value of the land in the model's objective function. However, the rental payment and receipt should be entered in the income rows if these are specified separately for the two classes of farms.

The relevant first-order necessary condition with respect to the rental variable is

$$\frac{\partial \mathscr{L}}{\partial L_r} = -\lambda_1 + \lambda_2 \leq 0 \tag{9.54}$$

If $L_r > 0$, then, in the absence of restrictions on the rental market, rental will take place until $\lambda_2 = \lambda_1$, that is, until the productivity of land in the two farm classes is equated.

It may not be known beforehand in which direction the rental transaction will take place, so it may be necessary to posit variables for both directions, for rental from group 1 to group 2 (L_{12}) and for rental from group 2 to group 1 (L_{21}). The mini-tableau for this pair of rental variables is shown in Table 9.2.

9.6 EXTENSIONS TO GENERAL EQUILIBRIUM

9.6.1 Preliminary Considerations

Rotations of the demand function were discussed in Chapter 8, in the context of interpreting the dual variable associated with the convex combination constraint, and again earlier in this chapter, for the inclusion of cross-price effects. Later, in Chapter 12, exogenous rotations are made in order to represent the increases in demand that are associated with growth of incomes over time. If the rotations can be made endogenous, as functions of income levels, then the model becomes general equilibrium rather than partial equilibrium in nature. In a partial equilibrium model, the solution determines a point *on* a fixed demand function. In a general equilibrium model, the solution determines both the position *on* the demand curve and the position *of* the demand curve.

However, before this step can be taken, a number of problems need to be resolved. First, the demand for agricultural products depends on nonagricultural incomes as well as agricultural incomes, so some representation of other sectors in the economy is required. Second, factor productivities, as described by the shadow prices on the resource constraints, need to be related to factor incomes. Third, the factor prices need to be related to output prices in a systematic way. Fourth, factor incomes need to be translated into household incomes. And fifth, the relation between household incomes and consumer expenditures needs to be governed by a budget constraint.

The resolution of these problems leads to considerable modification of the models presented thus far, but the general and partial equilibrium models can be considered members of the same family of models, even if distant cousins. They share the following structural features: (1) both models include commodity balances and resource constraints, and in equilibrium the corresponding shadow prices indicate product prices and factor prices; (2) both models are based on activity analysis production functions; and (3) the implementation of both models proceeds by stating the product demand functions in explicit numerical form and by including as variables the choices of alternative points on the demand functions.

In the following exposition, the goods index i represents both agricultural and nonagricultural goods, but for applications that emphasize agriculture, the crops and livestock products could be represented with considerably more disaggregation. At the extreme, the nonagricultural economy could be represented by a single aggregate good and a corresponding input/output production vector. The model presented here is taken from Norton and Scandizzo (1981).

Any general equilibrium model includes the following four elements: (1) a specification of technology and producer behavior, including resource limitations; (2) commodity balances to provide for market clearing; (3) a description of how income is formed and distributed; and (4) specifications of consumer demand behavior. In this model, the specification of producer behavior includes equations that set price equal to (or less than) marginal costs, reflecting the hypothesis of profit maximization. Other hypotheses could be substituted for this one, for example mark-up pricing, via modifications of the price–marginal cost equation.

If the demand functions are not homogeneous of degree zero, then household budget constraints will not be satisfied automatically, and so those constraints need to be added to the model explicitly. Incomes are assumed to be formed on the basis of factor endowments and factor prices. The endowments are exogenous and the prices are endogenous. Thus the incomes of different population groups or social groups depend in part on their endowments of labor and capital; some groups effectively hold only labor endowments, some only capital, and some hold both. The model's specification can be enriched and made more realistic by differentiating labor by skill. (See Hong, 1980, for such an application of this kind of model.)

When these new elements are added to the specification of the model, the previous objective function no longer is valid. It is replaced by another kind of market-simulating function, a function that consists of the difference between the aggregate value of final sales and the aggregate value of factor endowments (with the latter valued at their marginal products). In competitive equilibrium, abstracting from the role of the government, this function has a zero value. In the general equilibrium programming model, its feasible values are either zero or negative. Hence in the model it is maximized, so that the optimal solution gives it a zero value.

9.6.2 A Simple General Equilibrium Model

To develop the algebraic statement of the general equilibrium model, the required sets and subscripts are as follows:

$$i, j = 1, \cdots, n \qquad \text{goods}$$
$$h = 1, \cdots, v \qquad \text{income groups}$$
$$k = 1, \cdots, m \qquad \text{resources}$$
$$t = 1, \cdots, z \qquad \text{production technologies}$$

(Note that the income groups are not necessarily income strata; they can be functional groups.)

The variables are:

P_i price
Q_{ih} quantity consumed
R_k marginal value product of a resource
X_{it} quantity produced (measured in units of product)
Y_h income.

and the parameters are

B_k, B_{hk} resource endowments
d_{ikt} resource input/output requirement in production
s_{ijh} cross-price demand parameter (slope)
c_{ih} demand parameter (slope) with respect to income
a_{ih} demand intercept

Note that

$$\sum_h B_{hk} = B_k$$

For the sake of clarity, the general equilibrium model discussed here is quite simple in economic structure. There is no foreign trade, no government, and no savings or investment. More detailed and realistic versions are found in Hong (1980) and Norton, Scandizzo and Zimmerman (1986).

The model is first presented in nonlinear form and then in linearized form. The first equation of the model is the supply-demand balance, or commodity balance:

$$-\sum_t X_{it} + \sum_h Q_{ih} \leq 0 \qquad (9.55)$$

This equation is the same as the corresponding equation in the partial equilibrium models, except that the demand variable now is indexed for income (household) groups.

The resource constraint is identical to that used in the partial models:

$$\sum_i \sum_t d_{ikt} X_{it} \leq B_k \tag{9.56}$$

and incomes are defined on the basis of the shadow prices on those constraints:

$$Y_h - \sum_k B_{hk} R_k \leq 0 \tag{9.57}$$

This last equation is conceptually an equality and will hold as such in the optimal solution. It is written here as an inequality simply for computational convenience.

An important feature of the general equilibrium model is that it contains an explicit price variable in the primal. The presence of this variable is necessary in order to be able to write the condition that price equals marginal cost for each good produced at a positive level in the solution. The price variable may be captured for use in the primal by writing out the demand function in explicit form. Here that function is written in its linear version:

$$Q_{ih} - \sum_j s_{ijh} P_j - c_{ih} Y_h = a_{ih} \tag{9.58}$$

Given the price variables P_j, the household budget constraint may now be written:

$$\sum_i Q_{ih} P_i - Y_h \leq 0 \tag{9.59}$$

This equation is the model's first nonlinear relation; it is the kind of nonlinearity known as a bilinear form.

The last constraint in the model is the marginal cost-pricing condition:

$$P_i - \sum_k d_{ikt} R_k \leq 0 \tag{9.60}$$

This equation says that economic profits will be zero for technologies of production used in the optimal basis, and they will be negative for technologies not used. For the technologies used, it is equivalent to Euler's condition. Jones (1965) also requires an explicit statement of the marginal cost pricing condition in his "simple general equilibrium models." Provided that the number of goods equals or exceeds the number of resources, equation (9.60) effectively establishes the values of the factor prices R_k, which then are used in determining incomes via (9.57). Thus a condition on the structure of the model is that there be at least as many goods as resources ($n \geq m$).

As stated thus far, the model normally would contain more variables than equations (depending on the dimensionality of the various sets). Specifically, there are $nv + nz + n + v + m$ variables and $nv + nz + n + 2v + m$ constraints. However, it is likely that only n of the nz constraints (9.60) will hold as equalities. If that is true, then for the model to have more than one feasible solution, we need $nz > n + v$. In most applications, this requirement will be satisfied with room to spare.

To select the optimal solution out of the many feasible solutions, the objective function is required:

$$Z = \sum_i \sum_h Q_{ih} P_i - \sum_k B_k R_k \qquad (9.61)$$

The same nonlinearity that appeared in (9.59) is found in the objective function.

In models like this, it turns out that the primal and dual solutions are equal up to a factor of proportionality. Let π_i be the shadow price on the commodity balances and λ_k the shadow price on the resource constraints. Then in the optimal solution

$$\frac{\pi_i}{P_i} \cong \frac{\pi_j}{P_j} \qquad (9.62)$$

and

$$\frac{\pi_i}{P_i} \cong \frac{\lambda_k}{R_k} \qquad (9.63)$$

This property, along with the degree of approximation, is discussed in Norton and Scandizzo (1981).

Some related models are those of Shubik (1977), Yaron (1967), and Plessner (1957). Shubik pointed out that an appropriate model with the maximand (9.61) guarantees the efficient outcome in prices and quantities, but his paper did not discuss computational issues. In Yaron's case, income was predetermined, so his model was a partial equilibrium model in the static sense, although he updated its demand parameters for lagged changes in income. His model did not include equations (9.57), (9.58), or (9.59). Plessner's model is similar to Yaron's, but it omits income from the demand functions and does not include equations (9.57) or (9.59). In a real sense, however, the general equilibrium model presented above is a generalization of the partial equilibrium optimization models of Samuelson (1952), Takayama and Judge (1964a), and Duloy and Norton (1973a).

9.6.3 A Linear Version

It would appear straightforward to linearize the expressions (9.59) and (9.61) by means of first-order approximations. However, such approximations have the property that the approximation error increases the further the solution departs from the initial equilibrium conditions. Experiments have shown that the optimization procedure exploits this property, and consequently in the solution equation (9.59) does not hold even approximately.

A better linearization may be derived by techniques of grid linearization, which have the property that the approximation error is independent of the numerical solution values. Grid linearization requires prior specification of the relevant range of values along, say, the demand and revenue functions. It also requires use of variables that represent interpolation weights among the predetermined grid points. Such a linearization has in fact been used already in Chapter 8 in regard to the demand variables and the corresponding values of farm income and the objective function, and also earlier in this chapter for the cross-elasticity problem.

The main features of the linearization below are (1) this use of grid linearization, and (2) the use of the convex combination constraints to rotate the demand functions. As before, an $x\%$ rightward rotation of the demand function is represented by an increase of the right-hand side to $1.0 + x\%$. And in the general equilibrium model the $x\%$ term is shifted to the left-hand side of the equation, so that the rotation may be endogenous.

This procedure is developed with an example related to income growth. Suppose that the income growth (in %) is denoted by the variable $\dot{Y}$, and that the income elasticity of demand for good i is denoted by ε_i. Then the percentage rotation of the demand curve is $\varepsilon_i \dot{Y}$, and in the partial equilibrium model the convex combination constraint would become

$$\sum_s D_{is} \le 1 + \varepsilon_i \dot{Y} \qquad (9.64a)$$

or

$$\sum_s D_{is} - \varepsilon_i \dot{Y} \le 1 \qquad (9.64b)$$

where, as before, the subscript s indicates the point on the demand curve.

Very similar procedures apply to the convex combination constraint in the general equilibrium model. To make them operational, the percentage change variables need to be defined. Suppose the base-year value of income were Y_0. Then

$$\dot{Y} = \left(\frac{1}{Y_0} \right) Y - 1 \qquad (9.65)$$

where the factor in parentheses is a known parameter.

Combining (9.64b) and (9.65), the convex combination constraint becomes

$$\sum_s D_{is} - \varepsilon_i\left(\frac{1}{Y_0}\right)Y \leq 1 + \varepsilon_i \qquad (9.66a)$$

or

$$\sum_s D_{is} - \varepsilon_i^* Y \leq 1 + \varepsilon_i \qquad (9.66b)$$

where $\varepsilon_i^* = \varepsilon_i/Y_0$. The demand interpolation variable D_{is} now may have a value greater than one.

This version of the constraint is the same as that given in (9.72) below, except that a similar procedure has been followed to incorporate the demand-shifting effects of cross-price behavior, and also subscripts have been added to indicate income groups.

With these introductory comments, the full linearized general equilibrium model may be written out, as follows:

commodity balances

$$\sum_h \sum_s \theta_{ihs} D_{ihs} - \sum_t X_{it} \leq 0 \qquad (9.67)$$

Note that $Q_{ih} = \sum_s \theta_{ihs} D_{ihs}$

resource constraints

$$\sum_i \sum_t d_{ikt} X_{it} \leq B_k \qquad (9.68)$$

No change has been made here; this equation is identical to (9.56).

income distribution equations

$$Y_h - \sum_k B_{hk} R_k \leq 0 \qquad (9.69)$$

Again, there is no change from the nonlinear version.

demand functions

$$-\left(\frac{1}{Q_{ih0}}\right)\sum_s \theta_{ihs} D_{ihs} + \sum_j \eta_{ijh}\left(\frac{1}{P_{j0}}\right)P_j + \varepsilon_{ih}\left(\frac{1}{Y_{h0}}\right)Y_h = -1 \qquad (9.70)$$

The coefficients η_{ijh} represent the own-price and cross-price elasticities of demand. This equation is derived from the expression of a demand function in terms of percentage-change variables and elasticities:

$$\dot{Q}_{ih} = \sum_j \eta_{ijh}\dot{P}_j + \varepsilon_{ih}\dot{Y}_h \qquad (9.71)$$

convex combination constraints

$$\sum_s D_{ihs} - \varepsilon_{ih}\left(\frac{1}{Y_{h0}}\right)Y_h - \sum_{j \neq i} \eta_{ijh}\left(\frac{1}{P_{j0}}\right)P_j = 1 + \eta_{iih} \qquad (9.72)$$

As in the partial model, this equation forces the solution to lie on the demand curve; however, in this case it may rotate endogenously. In the third term on the left-hand side the summation is taken over $j \neq i$ because only cross-price effects, and not own-price effects, are included in the rotation. The right-hand term η_{iih} results from the difference

$$\varepsilon_{ih} - \sum_{j \neq i} \eta_{ijh}$$

(See the comment below on the homogeneity condition for the demand parameters.) It also results from use of expressions like (9.65) above to incorporate percentage changes in the price and income variables.

household budget constraints

$$\sum_i \sum_s \rho_{ihs}D_{ihs} - Y_h \leq 0 \qquad (9.73)$$

The coefficient ρ_{ihs} represents the area under the marginal revenue function down to point s on the demand curve; that is, it is producer income for sales at point s. It is the same ρ that was used in Chapter 8. Now the bilinear form has been linearized via grid techniques. Whatever approximation error that is present can be reduced simply by increasing the number of points s in a given interval.

marginal cost pricing conditions

$$P_i - \sum_k d_{ikt}R_k \leq 0. \qquad (9.74)$$

This equation also is identical to its counterpart in the nonlinear model.

objective function

$$Z = \sum_i \sum_h \sum_s \rho_{ihs}D_{ihs} - \sum_k B_k R_k \qquad (9.75)$$

Note the use of ρ (area under the marginal revenue function) instead of ω (area under the demand function). In the partial equilibrium model, use of ρ generates a solution that replicates the monopolistic outcome. It doesn't do so here because of the presence of the marginal cost pricing conditions, which are characteristic of the competitive market. (Monopolistic producers set their prices above marginal costs.)

This completes the algebraic description of the linearized general equilibrium model. An advantage of this model is that it simulates the general equilibrium outcome with a single linear programming solution, unlike the methods of Manne, Chao, and Wilson (1978) and Ginsburgh and Waelbroeck (1975), which require iterative solution procedures.

Clearly, this model needs a set of initial conditions in order to be applied. The commodity balances and the other constraints do not have to be satisfied in the initial conditions, but it is necessary that the demand parameters be estimated or computed in such a way that in the initial conditions the restrictions of Engel aggregation, homogeneity, and Cournot aggregation are satisfied:

$$\sum_i \varepsilon_i \alpha_{ih} = 1, \; \alpha_{ih} = \frac{P_{i0} Q_{ih0}}{Y_{h0}} \tag{9.76}$$

$$\sum_j \eta_{ijh} = -\varepsilon_{ih} \tag{9.77}$$

$$\sum_i \alpha_{ih} \eta_{ijh} = -\alpha_{jh} \tag{9.78}$$

Note that if the solution deviates from the initial conditions in the budget shares, then these conditions are not necessarily satisfied with the solution values of prices, quantities, and incomes. Another advantage of this model is that the demand functions are not required to be symmetric in the cross-price effects.

To introduce intermediate goods into the model, the commodity balances and the marginal cost pricing conditions have to be modified. Let $\hat{a}_{ijt}$ be an input/output coefficient from a rectangular (I-A) Leontief matrix. Then the commodity balances become

$$\sum_h \sum_s \theta_{ihs} D_{ihs} - \sum_j \sum_t \hat{a}_{ijt} X_{jt} \leq 0 \tag{9.79}$$

and the marginal cost pricing conditions become

$$\hat{a}_{iit} P_i - \sum_j \hat{a}_{jit} P_j - \sum_k d_{ikt} R_k \leq 0 \tag{9.80}$$

This brief discussion suffices to present the general equilibrium variant of the models discussed in this book. Space limitations prevent pursuing this topic further. A sample application, proofs, and other comments are found in Norton and Scandizzo (1981).

NOTES

1 An alternative approach to dealing with asymmetric problems is discussed by Takayama and Judge (1971).
2 Most of the exposition in the remainder of this section follows Hazell (1979).
3 The proof of this assertion is straightforward. First, substitute equation (9.50) into (9.49) and (9.37), so that everywhere the variable N is replaced by

$$\sum_s \gamma_s^n N_s$$

Let the dual variable for equation (9.51) be denoted σ_n. Then the relevant first-order condition is

$$\frac{\partial \mathscr{L}}{\partial N_s} = -\alpha^* \gamma_s^n - \omega_s^n + \gamma_s^n \lambda_n - \sigma_n \leq 0$$

If labor is used, it follows that $\sigma_n = \gamma_s^n(\lambda_n - \alpha^*) - \omega_s^n$. Further, since $\lambda_n = w$, and by definition, $\gamma_s^n = N$ and $\omega_s^n = \frac{1}{2}\beta^* N^2$, then $\sigma_n = (w - \alpha^*)N - \frac{1}{2}\beta^* N^2$. In Figure 9.4, $(w - \alpha^*)N$ is equal to area $(w_c - \alpha^*)N_c$, and $\frac{1}{2}\beta^* N^2$ is the area under the supply function $w = \alpha^* + \beta^* N$ but above α^*. The difference between these areas is equal to the area $\alpha^* w_c e$.

Chapter 10

Risk in the Sector Model

10.1 INTRODUCTION

Agricultural production, particularly in developing countries, is generally a risky process, and considerable evidence exists to suggest that farmers behave in risk-averse ways. Yet until quite recently, considerations of risk were rarely incorporated into regional or sectoral planning models. Rather, farmers were assumed to behave in a risk-neutral, profit maximizing way.

Explicit representations of risky outcomes and farmer's attitudes toward them are straightforward when commodity prices are specified exogenously to the model. In this case the regional or sectoral model can be treated as a large farm (or a number of large farms), and any of the methods discussed in Chapter 5 are relevant. However, if prices are to be endogenously determined in the model, then assumptions of risk and risk-averse behavior at the farm level can lead to considerable complexity in the choice and interpretation of the aggregate model objective function.

On theoretical grounds, neglect of risk-averse behavior in agricultural sector models can be expected to lead to important overstatements of the output levels of risky enterprises (often reflected in overly specialized cropping patterns), hence also to overestimates of the value of important resources (for example, land and irrigation water). These biases may be particularly large in models of low-income agriculture in which risk aversion is likely to be greatest.

A crucial issue in the development of methods for incorporating risk and risk averse behavior into price endogenous sector models lies in appropriate specification of the market to be simulated. The nature of market equilibrium under risk is a complex subject that has only recently received much attention in the literature.[1] Furthermore, the results depend very much on the assumptions made about the way in which farmers form their price and yield forecasts each year, and on the nature of the stochastic components involved.

At present, the only practical method that has been developed for including price and yield risks in the objective function of agricultural sector models with endogenous prices was devised by Hazell and Scandizzo (1974, 1977). Their model, which provides the necessary modification of the market simulation procedures described in Chapters 8 and 9, requires three key assumptions. First, the initial source of risk lies in yields, and it is the resultant fluctuations in output that cause variability in prices. Second, farmers operate in a competitive environment and they maximize E, V or E, σ utility. Third, production is lagged, that is, farmers have to commit their resources each year before prices and yields are known. Before considering the Hazell-Scandizzo method we first review some key characteristics of risky markets and show how the way in which farmers form their price forecasts affects the market equilibrium.

10.2 MARKET EQUILIBRIUM UNDER RISK

10.2.1 Specification of the Market

Consider the following simple, linear model of the market for a risky commodity:

demand function

$$D_t = \alpha - \beta P_t \tag{10.1}$$

supply function

$$S_t = \lambda y_t P_t^* \tag{10.2}$$

market clearing condition[2]

$$D_t = S_t \tag{10.3}$$

and $E[y_t] = \bar{y}$, $V(y_t) = \sigma^2$, and $\text{Cov}(y_t, P_t^*) = 0$ for all t. Here y_t is stochastic yield, P_t^* is the price anticipated by farmers at the time of making production decisions, and α, β, and λ are positive constants.

This model has two key features. First, the anticipated price P_t^* is the relevant forecast of price P_t made by farmers at the time of committing their

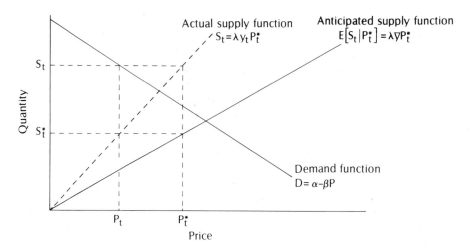

Figure 10.1 A market with multiplicative risk.

inputs for period t. Typically, in agricultural production, there will be a lag between such decisions and the realization of production. As such, P_t^* incorporates anticipations about both actual yield y_t and the total quantity supplied to the market. The assumption that $\text{Cov}(y_t, P_t^*) = 0$ rules out the possibility of perfect forecasts (in which case the model would collapse to a simultaneous specification) and implies that only the mean and variance of yield is known at the time of making decisions.

Second, the stochastic yield term is specified in a multiplicative way in the supply function. This specification is preferred to an additive risk model because it is the input decisions, and particularly the choice of land area, that are responsive to price, while actual output is the product of the resources allocated and their productivity. For example, in the linear programming context, the anticipated quantity supplied of a commodity is $S_t^* = \bar{y}X$ where X is the activity level (which is a function of P_t^*) and actual quantity supplied is $S_t = y_t X$. Another realistic feature of a multiplicative yield term is that it leads to an increasing variance of output with increasing input use. That is, $V(S_t) = \lambda^2 \sigma^2 P_t^{*2}$, and this increases with anticipated price. However, the coefficient of variation is constant and equal to $\sigma/\bar{y}$.

The structure of the market is portrayed geometrically in Figure 10.1. Each year producers form anticipations (or forecasts) about price and yield that lead, in the aggregate, to the anticipated output $E[S_t|P_t^*] = \lambda \bar{y} P_t^*$. The anticipated supply function in Figure 10.1 shows the level of anticipated output corresponding to any anticipated price P^*. Note that unlike previous figures in this book, quantity now appears on the vertical axis, and price appears on the horizontal axis.

Actual quantity supplied in year t is $S_t = \lambda y_t P_t^*$. The multiplicative random yield rotates the supply function in a random fashion. At time t producers are assumed in Figure 10.1 to have anticipated the price P_t^*, and to plan so that in aggregate they produce an anticipated output S_t^*. However, actual yield is y_t and so realized output and price are S_t and P_t, respectively.

Since the market clears each year, actual price is

$$P_t = \frac{1}{\beta}(\alpha - \lambda y_t P_t^*) \qquad (10.4)$$

Further, since yield is stochastic, then P_t is also stochastic. This presents a difficulty in defining a market equilibrium since, unlike the deterministic case, it can no longer be characterized by a single price-quantity pair. Rather, the market clearing price has a probability distribution, and this distribution depends on the distribution of both yield and anticipated price. A market equilibrium must now be defined in terms of some convergent property of the probability distribution of price. There are a number of possible concepts to chose from (Turnovsky 1968), but we need only consider convergence in mean price here. This price is defined as

$$\lim_{t \to \infty} E[P_t] = \frac{1}{\beta}\left(\alpha - \lambda \bar{y} \lim_{t \to \infty} E[P_t^*]\right) \qquad (10.5)$$

and it exists only if, with the passage of enough time, the mean price settles down to a fixed value.[3]

10.2.2 Farmers' Price Forecasts

The difficulty we now face is that the expected market clearing price in equilibrium is not unique, but depends on the kinds of price anticipations held by farmers. This can easily be seen in equation (10.5) since $\lim E[P_t^*]$ may take on different values depending on how P_t^* is formed.

Two types of price expectations behavior are of special interest. The first type are unbiased forecasts of the expected market clearing price $E[P_t]$. Such forecasts, which we shall call expected price forecasts, include weighted averages of past prices, i.e.,

$$P_t^* = \sum_i \omega_i P_{t-i}$$

where ω_i are weights satisfying $\sum_i \omega_i = 1$. Forecasts of this type are widely used in applied economics; they include the Nerlovian adaptive expectation models and the naive cobweb model in which producers are assumed to project the previous period's price. Hazell and Scandizzo (1975) have shown that, in the context of a market model with multiplicative yield risks, unbiased forecasts of $E[P]$ are not socially efficient. Further, if farmers really forecast in this way then important welfare gains may sometimes be obtained through policies aimed at optimally distorting the market price from its equilibrium value.

The reason expected price forecasts are inefficient is that they ignore covariance relations between price and yield.[4] Actual per hectare revenue in year t is $R_t = P_t y_t$. Taking the expected value, then,

$$E[R] = E[Py]$$
$$= E[P]\bar{y} + \text{Cov}(P, y) \qquad (10.6)$$

Now if farmers make independent estimates of $E[P]$ and $\bar{y}$, their anticipated per hectare revenue is $E[P]\bar{y}$, and this is clearly a biased forecast of the expected revenue if $\text{Cov}(P, y)$ is not zero. In a closed market, such as drawn in Figure 10.1, $\text{Cov}(P, y)$ is necessarily negative. Consequently, if farmers anticipate $E[P]\bar{y}$ they will overestimate the returns, and will produce too much of the risky commodity on average.

In a competitive market in which the individual farmer has no measurable impact on the aggregate supply, his best forecast of returns is the revenue forecast in (10.6). If we divide this per hectare return by the average yield $\bar{y}$, the resultant measure of anticipated return per unit of output is comparable to a price forecast; it is defined in similar units, e.g., pesos per ton. This price forecast,

$$P^* = E[Py]/\bar{y} \qquad (10.7)$$

which we shall call the unit revenue forecast, embodies full information about the mean price, the mean yield, and the price-yield covariance. It is a rational forecast for the farmer, and as Hazell and Scandizzo (1977) have shown, it is also the price forecast that maximizes social welfare.

10.2.3 Expected Market Equilibrium Price

We consider now the expected market equilibrium prices corresponding to the two types of price forecasts.

Suppose that as a forecast of expected price, farmers simply project the previous year's price, that is, $P_t^* = P_{t-1}$. Then, using equation (10.5),

$$\lim E[P_t] = (1/\beta)(\alpha - \lambda \bar{y} \lim E[P_{t-1}])$$

Assuming the market converges so that $\lim E[P_t] = \lim E[P_{t-1}]$, then

$$\lim E[P_t] = \frac{\alpha}{\beta + \lambda \bar{y}} \qquad (10.8)$$

This same price arises if farmers anticipate any other unbiased forecast of $E[P_t]$.

The equilibrium price in (10.8) happens to be the intersection price between demand and anticipated supply ($\bar{P}$ in Figure 10.2). To see this, equate $D = \alpha - \beta P$ and $E[S] = \lambda \bar{y} P$ and solve for P. The result is $P = \alpha/(\beta + \lambda \bar{y})$.

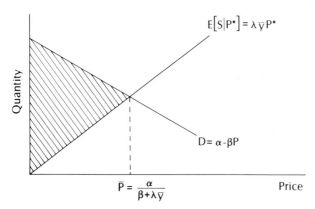

Figure 10.2 The market equilibrium.

To simulate this price in a mathematical programming model, then following the procedures developed in Chapter 8, the appropriate model maximand should be the area under the demand curve minus the area under the anticipated supply (the shaded area in Figure 10.2). In the notation of our market model, this area is

$$W_1 = \int_0^{\bar P}(\alpha - \beta P)\, dP - \int_0^{\bar P} \lambda \bar y P\, dP$$
$$= \alpha \bar P - 1/2(\beta + \lambda \bar y)\bar P^2 \qquad (10.9)$$

Maximizing (10.9) with respect to $\bar P$ leads to

$$\frac{\partial W_1}{\partial \bar P} = \alpha - (\beta + \lambda \bar y)\bar P = 0$$

or

$$\bar P = \alpha/(\beta + \lambda \bar y)$$

which is indeed the intersection price in equation (10.8).

An interesting point about area W_1 in (10.9) is that it is an *ex ante* measure of the sum of the producer and consumer surplus. It is the aggregate surplus that would arise if actual yield y_t happened to equal the mean yield $\bar y$.

Turning now to the expected market equilibrium price corresponding to the unit revenue forecast, we again suppose that farmers are naive and project the previous year's unit revenue $P_t^* = P_{t-1}y_{t-1}/\bar y$. The market clearing price in year t is then

$$P_t = (1/\beta)(\alpha - \lambda y_t(P_{t-1}y_{t-1})/\bar y) \qquad (10.10)$$

Multiplying through by y_t and taking the expected value leads to

$$E[P_t y_t] = \alpha \bar y/\beta - \lambda E[y_t^2]E[P_{t-1}y_{t-1}]/\beta \bar y$$

If the market converges so $\lim E[P_t y_t] = \lim E[P_{t-1} y_{t-1}]$, then

$$\lim E[P_{t-1} y_{t-1}] = \alpha \bar{y}^2 / (\beta \bar{y} + \lambda E[y^2]) \qquad (10.11)$$

Using equation (10.11) and taking the limit of the expected value of $E[P_t]$ in equation (10.10), one obtains

$$\lim E[P_t] = \frac{\alpha(\beta \bar{y} + \lambda \sigma^2)}{\beta(\beta \bar{y} + \lambda E[y^2])} \qquad (10.12)$$

This same price results for any other unbiased forecast of $E[P_t y_t]/\bar{y}$, including weighted averages of past unit revenues.

The equilibrium price in (10.12) is different from the limiting value of $E[P_t^*]$. Using (10.11) this latter price is

$$\lim E[P_t^*] = \lim E[P_{t-1} y_{t-1}]/\bar{y} = \alpha \bar{y}/(\beta \bar{y} + \lambda E[y^2])$$

and which is smaller than (10.12) because

$$\frac{\lim E[P_t]}{\lim E[P_t^*]} = (\beta \bar{y} + \lambda \sigma^2)/\beta \bar{y} = 1 + \frac{\lambda \sigma^2}{\beta \bar{y}} > 1$$

The unit revenue forecast is not therefore an unbiased forecast of the expected market clearing price; it underestimates the expected market clearing price.

Hazell and Scandizzo (1977) have shown that to simulate the market equilibrium price corresponding to unit revenue forecasts with a mathematical programming model, then the appropriate model maximand is the expected value of the realized, or *ex post*, sum of the producers' and consumers' surplus. Specifically, the relevant maximand is

$$W_2 = E\left[\int_0^{P_t}(\alpha - \beta P)\, dP\right] + E\left[P_t S_t - \int_0^{P^*} \lambda \bar{y} P\, dP\right] \qquad (10.13)$$

The first term in (10.13) is the average value of the realized, or *ex post*, consumer surplus. The second term is the average profit, or surplus, accruing to farmers. Each year this profit is actual revenue $P_t S_t$, less the cost of inputs as measured by the area under the anticipated supply function between zero and the anticipated price P^*.

Evaluating (10.13), then

$$W_2 = \alpha E[P_t] - 0.5\beta E[P_t^2] + \lambda E[P_t y_t]P^* - 0.5\lambda \bar{y} P^{*2} \qquad (10.14)$$

Maximizing (10.14) with respect to the optimal anticipated price P^* gives

$$\frac{\partial W_2}{\partial P^*} = \lambda E[P_t y_t] - \lambda \bar{y} P^* = 0$$

or

$$P* = \frac{E[P_t y_t]}{\bar{y}} \tag{10.15}$$

As required, this is the unit revenue expectation of equation (10.7).

Hazell and Scandizzo (1975) argue that W_2 is the relevant measure of social welfare in the kind of risk market modeled here. Consequently, the unit revenue forecast is the socially optimal price forecast since it is the anticipated price that maximizes W_2.

10.3 FARM LEVEL ASSUMPTIONS FOR AGGREGATE RISK MODELING

The sector model formulation developed in Chapter 8 assumes that farmers maximize profits in a competitive but riskless environment. In order to introduce risk in the sector model it is first necessary to make some alternative assumptions about decision making behavior at the farm level.

To simplify matters we initially confine the basic source of risk to yields. The $n \times 1$ vector of products for the hth individual farm is then

$$Q_h = N_h X_h$$

where N_h is an $n \times n$ diagonal matrix of stochastic yields with jth diagonal element y_{hj}, and X_h is an $n \times 1$ vector of activity levels.

Stochastic yields imply stochastic supply functions, and hence lead to stochastic market prices at the sectoral level. It is assumed, however, that input costs and the market demand structure remain nonstochastic, and that the farm linear programming constraints are not affected. Risk in the constraint set could be introduced using any of the techniques discussed in Chapter 5, and special problems arise at the sectoral level only if any of the stochastic constraints include prices that are endogenously determined in the model.

It is further assumed that individual farmers are averse to risk and that their behavior conforms to maximization of a single period E, σ utility function. Consequently, the objective function for the hth individual farm model is

$$\max u_h = E[P'Q_h] - c'_h X_h - \phi_h V[P'Q_h]^{1/2} \tag{10.16}$$

where X_h, P, and c_h are $n \times 1$ vectors of activity levels, product prices, and unit costs respectively, $E[P'Q_h]$ and $V[P'Q_h]^{1/2}$ are the mean and standard deviation of farm revenue, and ϕ_h is a risk aversion parameter.

To enumerate (10.16) more fully it is necessary to introduce some assumptions about the nature of farmers' perceptions of the parameters of the joint price and yield distribution, that is, of $E[P'Q_h]$ and $V[P'Q_h]$. In Section 10.2 we considered two particular ways of formulating expectations about

$E[P'Q_h]$. These were independent price and yield forecasts, so that $E[P_j^*Q_{hj}]$ $= P_j^* \bar{y}_{hj} X_{hj}$ for the jth activity, and unit revenue expectations with $E[P_j^*Q_{hj}]$ $= E[P_j y_{hj}] X_{hj} = r_{hj}^* X_{hj}$, where r_{hj}^* denotes the anticipated revenue for the jth activity. We also showed that these two types of expectations lead to different equilibria in terms of the asymptotic values of expected market clearing prices and outputs. Consequently, different model specifications are required to simulate the market equilibria corresponding to these two behavioral modes. It is also evident that there are doubtless alternative ways of subjectively formulating $V[P'Q_h]$ and that these may lead to convergence to different equilibrium values. However, to simplify the analysis, we assume that these expectations are always formed in a rational way and that they converge to statistically observable relationships at market equilibrium. Specifically, we assume that $V[P'Q_h] = X_h' V[P'N_h] X_h = X_h' \Omega_h X_h$ where Ω_h is a covariance matrix of unit revenues for the activities. That is, the i, jth element of Ω_h is $\omega_{hij} = \text{Cov}[P_i y_{hi}, P_j y_{hj}]$

10.3.1 The Optimal Farm Level Decisions

Given these assumptions, then the hth farm problem is

$$\max u_{h1} = P^{*'} E[N_h] X_h - c_h' X_h - \phi_h (X_h' \Omega_h X_h)^{1/2} \qquad (10.17)$$

subject to

$$A_h X_h \leq b_h \qquad (10.18)$$

if farmers anticipate prices and yields independently. However the problem is

$$\max u_{h2} = r_h^{*'} X_h - c_h' X_h - \phi_h (X_h' \Omega_h X_h)^{1/2} \qquad (10.19)$$

subject to (10.18) if farmers anticipate unit revenue forecasts.

Forming the relevant Lagrangean functions, these are

$$\mathcal{L}_1 = P^{*'} E[N_h] X_h - c_h' X_h - \phi_h (X_h' \Omega_h X_h)^{1/2} + v_h' (b_h - A_h X_h) \quad (10.20)$$

and

$$\mathcal{L}_2 = r_h^{*'} X_h - c_h' X_h - \phi_h (X_h' \Omega_h X_h)^{1/2} + v_h' (b_h - A_h X_h) \qquad (10.21)$$

for the price and revenue models, respectively. Then, from the necessary Kuhn-Tucker conditions for an optimal solution, it follows that for any $X_{hj} > 0$,

$$\frac{\partial \mathcal{L}_1}{\partial X_{hj}} = P_j^* \bar{y}_{hj} - c_{hj} - \phi_h (X_h' \Omega_h X_h)^{-1/2} \sum_i \omega_{hji} X_{hi} - \sum_k v_{hk} a_{hkj} = 0$$

for the price model, and

$$\frac{\partial \mathcal{L}_2}{\partial X_{hj}} = r_{hj}^* - c_{hj} - \phi_h (X_h' \Omega_h X_h)^{-1/2} \sum_i \omega_{hji} X_{hi} - \sum_k v_{hk} a_{hkj} = 0$$

for the revenue model. Rearranging terms, X_{hj} will be produced until

$$P_j^* \bar{y}_{hj} = c_{hj} + \sum_k v_{hk} a_{hkj} + \phi_h (X_h' \Omega_h X_h)^{-1/2} \sum_i \omega_{hji} X_{hi} \qquad (10.22)$$

if farmers anticipate prices and yields independently, but

$$r_{hj}^* = c_{hj} + \sum_k v_{hk} a_{hkj} + \phi_h (X_h' \Omega_h X_h)^{-1/2} \sum_i \omega_{hji} X_{hi} \qquad (10.23)$$

if farmers anticipate unit revenues.

The right-hand sides of equations (10.22) and (10.23) are identical and are risk counterparts to the classical marginality rules for output determination in a deterministic firm. For each product produced, anticipated marginal revenue per hectare is equated to expected marginal cost. The expected marginal cost comprises direct costs c_{hj}, plus expected opportunity costs as reflected in the dual values of the fixed resources used by that activity, plus a marginal risk term $\phi_h (X_h' \Omega_h X_h)^{-1/2} \sum_i \omega_{hji} X_{hi}$. This risk term is another cost, namely, the additional expected return demanded by farmers as compensation for taking risk. If farmers could participate in an insurance program that removed all revenue risk, then the marginal risk term in equations (10.22) and (10.23) is the marginal premium the farmer should be willing to pay to participate in that program.

10.3.2 The Effect of Risk

If we assumed risk neutrality ($\phi_h = 0$), the marginal risk term in equations (10.22) and (10.23) would disappear. Positive values of ϕ_h, which correspond to risk-averse behavior, lead to different output levels in the model solution, and, since $X_h' \Omega_h X_h$ is necessarily positive, the direction of change from risk neutrality depends critically upon the sign of

$$\sum_i \omega_{hji} X_{hi}$$

Crops that have large revenue variances or revenues that are positively correlated with the revenues for most other crops, or both, will tend to have a positive marginal risk term, and this will lead to a lower output under risk-averse behavior. In contrast, crops that have small revenue variances and negatively correlated revenues with most other crops will tend to have a negative marginal risk term, and hence their output will be increased under risk-averse behavior.

To show the effect of risk-averse behavior on the valuation of the sth scarce resource, we can arrange equations (10.22) and (10.23) as

$$v_{hs} = \left[P_j^* \bar{y}_{hj} - c_{hj} - \phi_h (X_h' \Omega_h X_h)^{-1/2} \sum_i \omega_{hji} X_{hi} - \sum_{k \neq s} v_{hk} a_{hkj} \right] / a_{hsj}$$
$$(10.24)$$

and

$$v_{hs} = \left[r_{hj}^* - c_{hj} - \phi_h (X_h' \Omega_h X_h)^{-1/2} \sum_i \omega_{hji} X_{hi} - \sum_{k \neq s} v_{hk} a_{hkj} \right] / a_{hsj} \quad (10.25)$$

respectively. Clearly, the imputed value of the sth resource for the jth nonzero activity will be greater or smaller than its value under risk neutrality depending again on the sign of $\sum_i \omega_{hji} X_{hi}$.

It is apparent from the similarity of equations (10.22) and (10.23) that differences in supply response between price and revenue expectations behavior arise from differences between $P_j^* \bar{y}_{hj}$ and r_{hj}^*. As we have seen in equation (10.6), these two terms differ by the covariance between price and yield, $\text{Cov}[P_j, y_{hj}]$. If this covariance is negative (positive), then revenue expectations will lead to lower (higher) output than when price expectations are held.

We turn now to the problem of formulating price-endogenous models that can simulate the market equilibria corresponding to price and revenue expectations behavior.

10.4 INTRODUCTION OF RISK IN THE SECTOR MODEL

Let X, Q, N, c, A, b, and Ω be defined as suitable aggregates of farm level X_h, Q_h, N_h, c_h, A_h, b_h, and Ω_h matrices. Also, let Φ be a suitable aggregate of the farm level risk parameters ϕ_h. Guidelines for forming many of these aggregates are discussed in Chapter 7, and typically aggregates are formed for a number of regions or representative farms when constructing a sector model. To simplify notation here, we assume a single group of farm level aggregates.

In addition to the aggregation requirements discussed in Chapter 7, special requirements must also be met in constructing Ω and Φ. These aggregates must be chosen so that

$$\Phi (X' \Omega X)^{1/2} = \sum_h \phi_h (X_h' \Omega_h X_h)^{1/2} \qquad (10.26)$$

that is, so that the aggregate level of risk adjustment calculated in the sector model is equal to the sum of individual risk adjustments over all farmers. Without this condition, covariance relationships between farms could be exploited in the sector model in seeking efficient crop diversification, and this would be inconsistent with the competitive behavior assumed. At present, practical aggregation procedures to satisfy (10.26) have yet to be worked out, and it is usually simply assumed that all farms in a group have identical Ω_h and ϕ_h.[5]

As in previous chapters, we assume the linear demand system

$$P = \alpha - BQ \qquad (10.27)$$

where α is an $n \times 1$ vector of intercepts, and B is a symmetric $n \times n$ matrix of own-price and cross-price terms. Since Q is now stochastic, the vector of expected prices is $E[P] = \alpha - BE[Q]$.

10.4.1 The Price Expectations Model

Consider now the following objective function for the sector model:

$$\max Z_1 = X'E[N](\alpha - 0.5BE[N]X) - c'X - \Phi(X'\Omega X)^{1/2} \quad (10.28)$$

The term $X'E[N](\alpha - 0.5BE[N]X)$ is the sum of areas under the demand curves given an expected supply of $E[Q] = E[N]X$, that is,

$$\int_0^{E[Q]} (\alpha - BQ) \, dQ.$$

Further, the term $c'X + \Phi(X'\Omega X)^{1/2}$ is total costs, which should equal the sum of areas under the (implicit) anticipated supply functions. Equation (10.28) therefore measures the *ex ante* sum of the producer and consumer surplus. Given the discussion in Section 10.2, the maximum value of Z_1 should provide the point where the demand and anticipated supply schedules intersect. That is, maximization of (10.28) provides the equilibrium values of expected prices and quantities corresponding to expected price forecasting behavior.

To verify this, specify the aggregate constraint set $AX \leq b$, and form the Lagrangean function

$$\mathcal{L}_1 = X'E[N](\alpha - 0.5BE[N]X) - c'X - \Phi(X'\Omega X)^{1/2} + v'(b - AX)$$

where v is a vector of dual values. From the necessary Kuhn-Tucker conditions,

$$\frac{\partial \mathcal{L}_1}{\partial X} = E[N]\alpha - E[N]BE[N]X - c - \Phi\Omega X(X'\Omega X)^{-1/2} - A'X \leq 0. \qquad (10.29)$$

Using $E[P] = \alpha - BE[N]X$ and rearranging,

$$E[N]E[P] \leq c + \Phi\Omega X(X'\Omega X)^{-1/2} + A'v \qquad (10.30)$$

the jth component of which is

$$\bar{y}_j E[P_j] \leq c_j + \Phi(X'\Omega X)^{-1/2} \sum_i \omega_{ji} X_i + \sum_k v_k a_{kj} \qquad (10.31)$$

The left-hand side of (10.30) is the vector of expected per hectare revenues assuming that farmers make independent forecasts about prices and yields, and that their anticipated prices are unbiased forecasts of the expected market clearing prices in equilibrium. The right-hand side of (10.30) is the sum of expected marginal cost curves over all farmers [the jth component in (10.31) is the sum of the right-hand sides of equations like (10.22)]. That is, it is the vector of aggregate anticipated supply functions. The inequality in (10.30) states that in aggregate, farmers should operate on average around points on the anticipated supply functions which lie at or above the intersections with demand. Clearly, by the complementary slackness conditions, optimality occurs at the intersection point for all nonzero activities in the solution, and then $E[P]$ is the intersection price vector.

10.4.2 The Revenue Expectations Model

We turn now to the formulation of the counterpart model which provides the competitive market equilibrium for revenue expectations.

Recall that in Section 10.2 it was shown that maximization of an *ex post* measure of the sum of producers' and consumers' surplus leads to revenue expectations. Not surprisingly, this *ex post* measure of welfare is also the relevant maximand for obtaining the expected prices and quantities corresponding to market equilibrium when farmers act on the basis of revenue expectations.

The relevant maximand is

$$\max Z_2 = E[X'N(\alpha - 0.5BNX)] - c'X - \Phi(X'\Omega X)^{1/2} \quad (10.32)$$

This maximand differs from (10.28) in that the term $E[X'N(\alpha - 0.5BNX)]$ is the expected sum of the areas under the demand curves given actual supplies $Q = NX$. That is,

$$E\left[\int_0^Q (\alpha - BQ)\right] dQ$$

compared to

$$\int_0^{E[Q]} (\alpha - BQ) \, dQ$$

in (10.28).

The difference between the two objective functions can be made more explicit by expanding the relevant term in (10.32) as follows:

$$
\begin{aligned}
E[X'N(\alpha - 0.5BNX)] &= X'E[N]\alpha - 0.5X'E[NBN]X \\
&= X'E[N]\alpha - 0.5X'(E[N]BE[N] + V[NBN])X \\
&= X'E[N](\alpha - 0.5BE[N]X) - 0.5X'V[NBN]X
\end{aligned}
$$

where $V[NBN] = E[NBN] - E[N]BE[N]$ is a covariance matrix of weighted yields with ijth element $\sigma_{ij}\beta_{ij}$, and σ_{ij} denotes the covariance of yields between crops i and j, and β_{ij} denotes the cross-price demand coefficient. Thus, the two objective functions differ only by the term

$$0.5X'V[NBN]X = 0.5\sum_i \sum_j X_i X_j \sigma_{ij}\beta_{ij} \tag{10.33}$$

Since this term will always be nonnegative, for a given model the maximum value of (10.32) must be equal to or less than the maximum value of (10.28).

To show that (10.32) provides the equilibrium solution for revenue expectations behavior, form the Lagrangean function

$$\mathcal{L}_2 = X'E[N]\alpha - 0.5X'E[NBN]X - c'X - \Phi(X'\Omega X)^{1/2} + v'(b - AX) \tag{10.34}$$

where v is again a vector of dual values. Apart from the feasibility conditions $AX \leq b$, the necessary Kuhn-Tucker conditions imply that

$$E[N]\alpha - E[NBN]X \leq c + \Phi\Omega X(X'\Omega X)^{-1/2} + A'v \tag{10.35}$$

From the assumed demand structure, the vector of market clearing prices in any one year is $P = \alpha - BNX$. Premultiplying by the diagonal matrix of yields N, the vector of unit revenues r is then $r = NP = N\alpha - NBNX$. Now, providing that farmers form their anticipations about r^* in such a way that, in equilibrium $r^* = E[r] = E[N]\alpha - E[NBN]X$ (as would happen if they took a weighted average of past revenues), then the left-hand side of (10.35) can be written as $E[r]$, and thus at optimality, expected unit revenue must be equal to or less than marginal cost for each activity. Complementary slackness conditions require that equation (10.35) hold as a strict equality for all nonzero X_j, in which case expected marginal revenue equals marginal cost at optimality. Assuming aggregation in the model is exact, then this condition is identical to that derived for the farm problem in (10.23).

10.5 LINEAR PROGRAMMING APPROXIMATIONS

The aggregate models with the objective functions defined in (10.28) and (10.32) are quadratic programming problems. Because of the large dimensions of any realistic sector model and the difficulties that still exist with quadratic programming computer codes in solving large problems, it is desirable to linearize these models.

10.5.1 Linearizing the Risk Term

Both objective functions contain the risk term $\Phi(X'\Omega X)^{1/2}$. Since this term is to be minimized, it can be linearized using a MOTAD approach as discussed in Chapter 5.

Let $r_{jt} = P_{jt} y_{jt}$ denote the tth year's observation on the revenue of the jth activity X_j, $t = 1, 2, \ldots, T$, and let $\bar{r}_j$ denote the sample mean revenue for the activity over the T years. Then the MAD estimator of the standard deviation of income is

$$\sum_t \left| \sum_j (r_{jt} - \bar{r}_j) X_j \right| s/T \qquad (10.36)$$

where $s = (T\pi/2(T-1))^{1/2}$ is the square root of Fisher's constant (see Chapter 5).

To obtain a linear programming formulation, define variables $Z_t^- \geq 0$ for all t such that

$$\sum_j (r_{jt} - \bar{r}_j) X_j + Z_t^- \geq 0,$$

where $\sum_j (r_{jt} - \bar{r}_j) X_j$ measures the deviation in total revenue from the mean, $\sum_j \bar{r}_j X_j$, for the tth set of revenue outcomes. If the Z_t^- variables are selected in a minimizing way for each t, either $Z_t^- = 0$ when $\sum_j (r_{jt} - \bar{r}_j) X_j$ is positive, or Z_t^- measures the absolute value of the negative deviation in total revenue when $\sum_j (r_{jt} - \bar{r}_j) X_j$ is negative. Consequently, $\sum_t Z_t^-$ measures the sum of the absolute values of the negative deviations. Since the sum of the negative deviations around the mean is always equal to the sum of the positive deviations for any random variable, it follows that $2\sum_t Z_t^-$ is the sum of absolute deviations in total revenue and hence the MAD estimate of $(X'\Omega X)^{1/2}$ is $(2s/T)\sum_t Z_t^-$.

In summary, the appropriate linear programming subproblem to minimize $\Phi(X\Omega X)^{1/2}$ is

$$\min \Phi(2s/T) \sum_t Z_t^-$$

such that

$$Z_t^- + \sum_j (r_{jt} - \bar{r}_j) X_j \geq 0, \qquad \text{all } t$$

Since it is useful to have a direct measure of the estimated value of σ in the model solution, it is generally worthwhile to add an identity row and column to calculate $\hat{\sigma}$. This variant of the problem is:

$$\min \Phi\hat{\sigma} \qquad (10.37)$$

such that

$$Z_t^- + \sum_j (r_{jt} - \bar{r}_j) X_j \geq 0, \qquad \text{all } t \qquad (10.38)$$

and

$$\hat{\sigma} = K\sum_t Z_t^- \qquad (10.39)$$

where $K = 2s/T$ is a constant.

The reliability of this method compared to using quadratic programming directly on $\Phi(X'\Omega X)^{1/2}$ has already been discussed in Chapter 5. The problem is similar to the Wicks-Guise MOTAD formulation of chance constraints in that the MAD estimator is being used as a point estimator of the standard deviation as well to rank plans on the basis of their estimated standard deviation for given E. The reliability of the approach therefore depends on the efficiency of the MAD as a point estimator of the standard deviation.

10.5.2 Linearizing the Expected Price Form

The objective function for the expected price forecasting model contains the quadratic term $X'E[N](\alpha - 0.5BE[N]X)$. This can be written as $\overline{Q}'(\alpha - 0.5B\overline{Q})$ where $\overline{Q} = E[Q] = E[N]X$ is the vector of mean quantities. This term can be linearized using the Duloy and Norton techniques described in Chapter 8.

To incorporate the approach here, consider the simplest case in which B is diagonal, implying that the product demands are independent. Then, letting V_j denote the area under the demand curve from zero to $\overline{Q}_j$ for the jth product,

$$\overline{Q}'(\alpha - 0.5B\overline{Q}) = \sum_j \left(\alpha_j \overline{Q}_j - \beta_j \overline{Q}_j^2\right)$$

$$= \sum_j V_j.$$

Now V_j is a quadratic, concave function in $\overline{Q}_j$ and, since the objective function is to be maximized, V_j can be approximated by a series of linear segments as described in Section 4.7.

Define a discrete number of intervals on the $\overline{Q}_j$ axis and assign specific values of $\overline{Q}_j$, say $\overline{Q}_{ij}$, as the boundary points for the intervals. To each of these interval boundary points is then assigned a value of $V_j = \alpha_j \overline{Q}_{ij} - \beta_j \overline{Q}_{ij}^2$, which will be designated by v_{ij}. Then, by defining weighting activities V_{ij} such that $0 \le V_{ij} \le 1$, the term $\overline{Q}'(\alpha - 0.5B\overline{Q})$ can be replaced by the linear programming subproblem.

$$\max \sum_j \sum_i v_{ij} V_{ij} \qquad (10.40)$$

such that

$$X_j \bar{y}_j - \sum_i \bar{Q}_{ij} V_{ij} \geq 0, \qquad \text{all } j \tag{10.41}$$

and

$$\sum_i V_{ij} \leq 1, \qquad \text{all } j \tag{10.42}$$

10.5.3 Linearizing the Expected Unit Revenue Form

The objective function for the revenue expectations model contains the quadratic term $E[Q'(\alpha - 0.5BQ)]$ where $Q = NX$ is the vector of realized quantities. It has already been seen that this objective function differs from the corresponding objective function for price expectations only by the quadratic term $0.5X'V[NBN]X$. One approach to linearizing $E[Q'(\alpha - 0.5BQ)]$ is therefore to use separable linear programming techniques to linearize $0.5X'V[NBN]X$ and to subtract this term from the linearized formulation of (10.28). However, when B is diagonal, Hazell and Pomareda (1981) have shown that a simpler approach can be taken.

Since $Q_j = X_j y_j$, then $E[Q_j] = \bar{Q}_j = X_j E[y_j]$ and $X_j^2 = \bar{Q}_j^2 / E[y_j]^2$. Further, since $Q_j^2 = X_j^2 y_j^2$, then $E[Q_j^2] = X_j^2 E[y_j^2] = \bar{Q}_j^2 (E[y_j^2]/E[y_j]^2) = \bar{Q}_j^2 (1 + C[y_j]^2)$, where $C[y_j]$ is the coefficient of variation of yield. That is, $C[y_j]^2 = V[y_j]/E[y_j]^2 = (E[y_j^2] - E[y_j]^2)/E[y_j]^2$. Now if B is diagonal,

$$\begin{aligned} E[Q'(\alpha - 0.5BQ)] &= \bar{Q}'\alpha - 0.5E[Q'BQ] \\ &= \bar{Q}'\alpha - 0.5\sum_j \beta_j E[Q_j^2] \\ &= \bar{Q}'\alpha - 0.5\sum_j \beta_j \bar{Q}_j^2 \big(C[y_j]^2 + 1 \big) \\ &= \bar{Q}'(\alpha - 0.5BD\bar{Q}) \end{aligned}$$

where D is a diagonal matrix with jth diagonal element $C[y_j]^2 + 1$. Since D is a matrix of constants then $G = BD$ can be calculated as part of the input to the model. The G matrix remains diagonal and the term $\bar{Q}'(\alpha - 0.5G\bar{Q})$ can be linearized using the Duloy-Norton method.

To summarize, if B is diagonal, the linearized sector models corresponding to expected price and unit revenue forecasting behavior are:

$$\text{max} = \sum_j \sum_i v_{ij} V_{ij} - \sum_j c_j X_j - \Phi \hat{\sigma} \tag{10.43}$$

such that

$$X_j \bar{y}_j - \sum_i \bar{Q}_{ij} V_{ij} \geq 0, \qquad \text{all } j \tag{10.44}$$

Table 10.1   A Linearized Sector Model with E, σ Behavior

Constraint and text equation numbers	Production activities $X_1 \cdots X_n$	Activities to linearize areas under demand $V_{11} \cdots V_{1k} \cdots V_{n1} \cdots V_{nk}$	Negative deviation counters for revenue $Z_1^- \cdots Z_T^-$	$\hat{\sigma}$	RHS
Objective function (10.43)	$-c_1 \cdots -c_n$			$-\Phi$	Maximize
Commodity balance constraints (10.44)					
Crop $j = 1$	$\bar{y}_1$	$-\bar{Q}_{11} \cdots -\bar{Q}_{1k}$			≥ 0
$j = n$	$\bar{y}_n$	$-\bar{Q}_{n1} \cdots -\bar{Q}_{nk}$			≥ 0
Convex combination constraints (10.45)					
Crop $j = 1$		$1 \cdots 1$			≤ 1
$j = n$		$1 \cdots 1$			≤ 1
Revenue deviation constraints (10.46)					
Year $t = 1$	$r_{11} - \bar{r}_1 \cdots r_{n1} - \bar{r}_n$		1		≥ 0
$t = T$	$r_{1T} - \bar{r}_1 \cdots r_{nT} - \bar{r}_n$		1		≥ 0
$\hat{\sigma}$ identity (10.47)			$K \cdots K$	-1	$= 0$
Resource constraints (10.48)	(A matrix)				$\leq b$

and

$$\sum_i V_{ij} \leq 1, \qquad \text{all } j \tag{10.45}$$

$$Z_t^- + \sum_j (r_{jt} - \bar{r}_j) X_j \geq 0, \qquad \text{all } t \tag{10.46}$$

$$\hat{\sigma} = K \sum_t Z_t^- \tag{10.47}$$

$$AX \leq b \tag{10.48}$$

where V_{ij}, X_j and Z_t^- are the unknown activity levels, and $K = 2s/T$ is a constant.

The difference between the two models is that $v_{ij} = \alpha_j \overline{Q}_{ij} - \beta_j \overline{Q}_{ij}^2$ when expected price forecasts are specified, but $v_{ij} = \alpha_j \overline{Q}_{ij} - \beta_j (C[y_j]^2 + 1)\overline{Q}_{ij}^2$ when unit revenue forecasts are specified.

Table 10.1 shows the layout of the linear programming tableau corresponding to equations (10.43) to (10.48).

10.6 AN *E, V* FORMULATION

So far we have assumed that producers maximize E, σ utility. However, the model can be adapted to simulate the expected market clearing prices and quantities corresponding to the market equilibrium in which producers maximize E, V utility instead (Hazell and Scandizzo, 1974).

If producers maximize the utility function $E[u] = E - \Theta V$ (see Chapter 5), then the relevant sector model objective functions for expected price and unit revenue forecasting behavior are, respectively,

$$\max Z_1 = X'E[N](\alpha - 0.5BE[N]X) - c'X - \Theta X'\Omega X \tag{10.49}$$

and

$$\max Z_2 = E[X'N(\alpha - 0.5BNX)] - c'X - \Theta X'\Omega X \tag{10.50}$$

where Θ is an appropriate aggregate of the individual farm risk parameters.

To linearize these problems, it is merely necessary to modify Table 10.1 to approximate the square of $\hat{\sigma}$ using the Duloy and Norton method. Define variables W_i, $i = 1$ to k, corresponding to k intervals over the possible range of values of $\hat{\sigma}$. For each interval end point, assign values $\hat{\sigma}_i$ and $w_i = \hat{\sigma}_i^2$. The subproblem minimize $\Theta X'\Omega X$ is then replaced by the linear programming subproblem.

$$\min \Theta \sum_i w_i W_i \tag{10.51}$$

such that

$$\sum_i W_i \leq 1 \tag{10.52}$$

**Table 10.2 Relevant Part of the
Tableau for the Linearized Sector Model with E, V Behavior**

Constraint and text equation number	Negative deviation counters for revenue Z_1^-	...	Z_T^-	$\hat{\sigma}$	Activities to linearize $\hat{\sigma}^2$ W_1	...	W_k	RHS
Objective function (10.43 modified with 10.51)					$-\Theta w_1$	...	$-\Theta w_k$	Maximize
Revenue deviation constraints (10.46)								
Year $t = 1$	1							≥ 0
$\vdots$		$\ddots$						$\vdots$
$t = T$			1					≥ 0
$\hat{\sigma}$ identity (10.47)	K	...	K	-1				$= 0$
$\hat{\sigma}$ balance (10.53)				1	$-\hat{\sigma}_1$	...	$-\hat{\sigma}_k$	≤ 0
Convex combination (10.52)					1	...	1	≤ 1

and

$$\hat{\sigma} = \sum_i \hat{\sigma}_i W_i \qquad (10.53)$$

Table 10.2 shows the relevant part of the modified tableau for the sector model. Since the production set $(X_1 \cdots X_n)$ and the activities to linearize the areas under the demand curves are not changed, this part of the tableau is not repeated from Table 10.1. Note that the entry in the objective function under $\hat{\sigma}$ has been deleted in Table 10.2. The disutility cost of risk now enters the objective function under the activities that linearize $\hat{\sigma}^2$.

10.7 EMPIRICAL ESTIMATION OF RISK PARAMETERS

The Hazell-Scandizzo models require estimation of a revenue covariance matrix Ω, and of the aggregate risk-aversion parameters Φ or Θ for each region or representative farm in the model. Both present difficult challenges.

10.7.1 Estimation of an Ω Matrix

Typically, the only available data on revenue variability are time-series data on prices and yields, by crop, for such aggregates as counties, irrigation districts, crop reporting districts, or states. In using such data it is first necessary to remove any trend or other systematic movement in prices or yields so that variations in the data reflect true stochastic variations. Use of ordinary least squares regression on the price and yield series separately is usually best, and detrended revenue is then calculated as the product of detrended yield and price. Note though that MOTAD approximations require that the deviations of the detrended revenues from their mean sum to zero for each activity. If prices and yields are detrended separately it is usually necessary to adjust the resultant revenue series to ensure that the revenue deviations do sum to zero. This is easily done by subtracting any nonzero mean from each detrended revenue observation.

There are two problems in using aggregate time-series data to estimate an Ω matrix. First, the Ω matrix should be an appropriate aggregate of the covariance matrices subjectively perceived by farmers at market equilibrium, and this may well differ from observed statistical relations. If we reasonably assume that farmers' anticipations about Ω are unbiased, and that the relevant markets converge in the variance and mean of price, then the expected value of Ω should, with the passage of enough time, converge to a unique matrix Ω^*. The problem is that available samples of time-series data may not provide an accurate estimate of Ω^*, and hence model solutions will not reflect the true equilibrium situation.

If the time-series data are obtained from a relatively stable period (i.e., there is little trend in relative prices or cropped areas), then the error may be relatively small. However, the problem can be quite serious when Ω is estimated with data from less stable periods. A related problem is that the estimated Ω matrix is not appropriate where policy interventions simulated by the model lead to different expected prices. These problems arise because the elements of Ω are not invariant with respect to changes in the mean prices.[6]

If the expected prices in the equilibrium solution are different from the sample mean prices used in calculating Ω, then Ω should be revised. This can be done through an iterative procedure proposed by Hazell and Pomareda (1981). If, at the k th iteration, the i, j th element of Ω has mean prices $\bar{P}_{ik}$ and $\bar{P}_{jk}$, and these differ from the equilibrium prices $E[P_{ik}]$ and $E[P_{jk}]$ obtained in the corresponding k th model solution, then $E[P_{ik}] - \bar{P}_{ik}$ and $E[P_{jk}] - \bar{P}_{jk}$ are added to the sample price observations for the i th and j th crops, the relevant i, j th element of Ω is recalculated (or the relevant deviations in the MOTAD formulation are recalculated), and a new solution is obtained. This procedure is repeated until $E[P_{ik}] - \bar{P}_{ik}$ and $E[P_{jk}] - \bar{P}_{jk}$ converge to approximately zero for all the elements of Ω. In practice, Ω typically converges in three or four iterations.

The second problem in using aggregate time-series data is that the estimated Ω invariably underestimates the degree of risk confronting individual farmers. As such, the aggregation condition $\Phi(X'\Omega X)^{1/2} = \Sigma_h \phi_h (X_h'\Omega_h X_h)^{1/2}$ is unlikely to be met (see Section 10.4).

Consider two random variables X and Y having identical variances, σ^2, and correlation coefficient, ρ. Let Z denote a weighted sum of X and Y, that is, $Z = \alpha X + (1 - \alpha)Y$ where $0 \leq \alpha \leq 1$. Then the variance of Z is $V[Z] = \alpha^2\sigma^2 + (1 - \alpha)^2\sigma^2 + 2\alpha(1 - \alpha)\text{Cov}(X, Y)$. Noting that $\text{Cov}(X, Y) = \rho\sigma^2$ and collecting terms,

$$V[Z] = [1 + 2\alpha(\alpha - 1)(1 - \rho)]\sigma^2$$

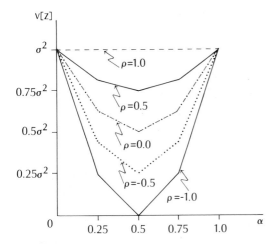

Figure 10.3 The bias inherent in aggregate measures of risk.

Figure 10.3 shows the relationship between $V[Z]$ and α for different values of ρ. If X and Y are perfectly and positively correlated (i.e., $\rho = 1.0$), then $V[Z] = \sigma^2$ for all values of α. However, for any other value of ρ, $V[Z]$ will be smaller than σ^2 whenever $0 < \alpha < 1$.

The relevance of this finding is immediate. If X and Y are taken to be the revenue of a crop grown on two different farms, then any aggregate measure of this revenue, Z, will underestimate the true variance of the crop's revenue unless the revenues for the two farms are perfectly and positively correlated. For modeling purposes, the solution to this problem is to group farms together that have highly correlated revenues for each crop.

10.7.2 Estimation of Φ or Θ

Ideally, the risk-aversion parameters should be formed as suitable aggregates of measured farm level risk parameters. The aggregation of individual utility functions is a troublesome business, especially for expected utility theory where preferences are ranked using ordinal indexes that are only defined up to a linear transformation. Many utility functions cannot be aggregated. Quadratic utility functions, for example, cannot be added, so there is little point in eliciting parameters from individual farmers for these functions if the overall purpose is to estimate an aggregate risk aversion parameter.

One of the attractions of the $E - \phi\sigma$ and $E - \theta V$ decision criteria is that their parameters (ϕ and θ) are invariant to linear transformations in the underlying utility functions. This is because these parameters are the slopes of the relevant indifference curves between E and σ or V. Consequently, a viable approach to estimating the aggregate parameters Φ or Θ is to elicit values of these parameters for a sample of individual farmers, and then to simply average them (e.g., Dillon and Scandizzo 1978).

A more common approach is to parameterize a sector model for different values of Φ or Θ and then to choose the value of the parameter that gives the best fit between the model's predicted cropping pattern or prices and the actual values observed in some base period. For example, see Hazell et al. (1983), Simmons and Pomareda (1975), and Kutcher and Scandizzo (1981).

Some of the problems of this approach to estimating Φ or Θ have already been discussed in Chapter 5, but when prices are endogenous to the model additional complications arise. First, the base year selected may not correspond to an equilibrium situation, in which case the chosen value of the parameter may be biased.

Second, we have already seen that the market equilibrium corresponding to expected price forecasting behavior is different from the equilibrium corresponding to unit revenue forecasts. Hazell and Scandizzo (1977) found (see also Chapter 13) that the market equilibrium solutions corresponding to unit revenue forecasts are more risk efficient for given levels of Φ or Θ. Selection of a best-fitting value of Φ or Θ could therefore lead to quite different results depending on the kind of price forecasting behavior assumed in the model. Without knowledge of how farmers actually form their expectations, then Φ or Θ remain largely indeterminate.

NOTES

1 See for example, Newbery and Stiglitz (1981), and Scandizzo, Hazell and Anderson (1984).
2 For simplicity, we ignore storage.
3 We shall ignore the required conditions for convergence. These are discussed in Bergendorff, Hazell, and Scandizzo (1974).
4 See Scandizzo, Hazell and Anderson (1984) for a full treatment of this issue.
5 It is also necessary to assume that the revenues of each activity are perfectly and positively correlated across all farms in a group (see Section 10.7).
6 Let $\tilde{P}_j = P_j + k$ with k constant, then $\text{Cov}[\tilde{P}_j y_j, P_i y_i] = \text{Cov}[P_j y_j, P_i y_i] + k \, \text{Cov}[y_j, P_i y_i]$, and since the last term is not zero the covariance is affected by changes in k.

Chapter 11

Construction and Validation of Sector Models

11.1 STARTING POINTS IN BUILDING THE MODEL

Chapters 3 through 5 have provided the basic analytics of the farm-level model, and Chapters 7 through 10 have done the same for the sector-level model. Following on the exposition in those chapters, this chapter presents a number of practical aspects of building a sector model. The topics include the structure and nomenclature of the overall model, developing the product supply side of the model, the input supplying activities, data for both the supply and demand sides, specifications for the livestock subsector, data reconciliation, model validation, and model management.

The topics in this chapter, and the discussion of them, have arisen out of experience with model-building exercises in a number of countries. Any attempt to develop an applied model inevitably leads to questions regarding many of these issues. This chapter is designed to assist the practitioner by presenting selected procedures and suggestions that have been found useful in quadratic and linear models, for they differ only in the objective function and in the treatment of the demand activities.

Where does one begin in working on a model? The starting point is a review of the concerns of an interested party in a policy-making position. This person is a client, or a sponsor, or a correspondent in the more traditional sense of that word, and his or her participation from the outset is vital. Without a sponsor who represents continuity of interest, and an institutional home for the model, there is little point in building an applied model.

The concerns of the sponsor help guide decisions on the model's structure. If, for example, the allocation of investment funds for irrigation is an important issue, then the model ought to have regional and subregional distinctions for irrigated (and potentially irrigable) areas, and it would need irrigation water balance equations at monthly or even finer intervals. If livestock development is a major concern, then the model ought to have considerable detail not only on livestock options but also on feed grains and forage crops. A sector programming model typically is not focused on a single issue but rather on a set of related issues, so the specification has to be as general as possible for those issues.

In almost all cases, regional distinctions of some kind are important to include in the model because yields, production technologies, and even cultivable crops usually vary significantly over regions.[1] In addition, in some cases the regional incidence of policy measures is in itself of interest to policy makers. Farm size categories may be required if any of the following statements are true: (1) there is significant variation in farm sizes in the sector, (2) cropping patterns and rates of input use vary significantly by farm size class, and (3) policy makers are concerned about the incidence of policy by farm size class. All these statements are of course tempered by the availability of data.

Again in almost all cases, a fairly large number of crops will be required in the model. The CHAC model for Mexico contains 29 products, TASM II for Turkey about 65 products, the Egyptian agroeconomic model 23 products, and the model of northeast Brazil 22 products (including three types of livestock feed). The reason for the multiplicity of products is that the supply functions in the sector usually cannot be represented properly without taking account of all the important sources of competition among crops for the use of resources. It is highly unlikely that fewer than 8 or 10 crops will suffice for a sector model.[2]

For the model's structure, then, the starting point is the designation of the regions and products, and possibly the farm size groups or other farm stratifications. On this basis, the structure of the matrix can be sketched out in preliminary form. The model's column vectors, or variables, probably will include at a minimum the following sets: production activities for crops and possibly livestock; activities for regional accounting of production and/or marketing and processing; input supplying activities (including risk accounting activities); domestic demand activities; foreign trade activities; and miscellaneous accounting activities for items such as farm income. (See Table 7.3.) Activities in addition to this minimum set may include interregional labor migration activities and activities to define alternative livestock feed rations. The production variables of course will be differentiated by product, technology, farm stratum, and region. Note that, as pointed out in Chapter 3, technological variations can have many dimensions, including ones as simple as variations in the planting and harvesting dates, and variations in proximity to the water source in gravity-fed irrigation systems.

Immediately after the products and technologies and farm groupings are defined, the next step is to define the inputs to production and their corresponding balances and constraints, including seasonality where relevant. Applied models have included inputs on weekly, biweekly, monthly, quarterly, and annual bases. Monthly specifications appear to be the most common, followed by quarterly. The disaggregation of input types again depends on the issues to be analyzed. For example, some models contain specific types of inorganic fertilizers (products or nutrients), and others contain just total fertilizer.

Except for the objective function, all the model's equations (rows) can be classified according to the dichotomy of balances and constraints. Balances are required in order to equate supply and demand, where the quantities of both are endogenous to the system, or to perform summations and other accounting roles. Balances always hold as equalities in the solution, even though they may be written as inequalities in some cases. Constraints (or restraints, restrictions, limits, or bounds, in other terminologies) are inequalities that represent limitations on the availability of resources and institutional and behavioral bounds. They do not necessarily hold as equalities in the solution.

Another useful distinction regarding the equations is whether they apply at the national, regional, or subregional ("local") level. The columns of the model may be grouped in the same three-way classification. Figure 11.1 illustrates the structure of the matrix according to that three-way classification. (It may be a four-way or five-way classification or more, depending on how many subregion distinctions are made, such as districts, canal commands, farm sizes, etc.). In that figure, the blocks $X1$ to $X4$ represent the production input/output coefficients in each of four subregions. Subregions (or districts) 1 and 2 constitute region 1, and subregions 3 and 4 constitute region 2. Resource constraints and input balances cut through the unlined part of blocks $X1$ to $X4$. Additional local (subregional) equations are indicated by the lines below each block and they are labeled $LE1$ to $LE4$. Examples include the risk accounting equations. The corresponding local columns are labeled $LC1$ to $LC4$. Examples of the local column variables would be the risk variables but they would also include variables for local input supplies, such as agricultural machinery and irrigation water.

The regional equations and column variables are indicated as $RE1$, $RE2$, and $RC1$, $RC2$. The national equations and columns are NE and NC, respectively. Examples of regional equations would be accounting balances for regional inputs (short-term credit in some cases) and regional supply-demand balances for products. The latter would cover the disposition of farm-level outputs as far as regional marketing and processing activities. Accordingly, the corresponding regional columns typically would include processing and marketing columns[3] and also supplying activities for those inputs which are

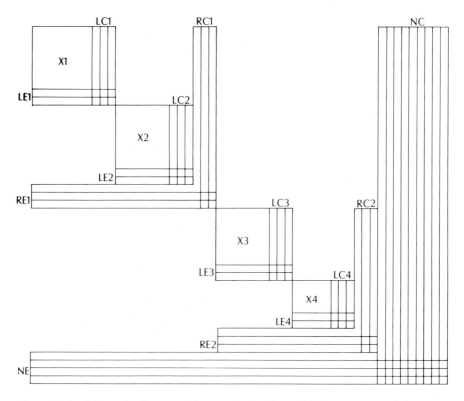

Figure 11.1 Schematic diagram of the structure of the matrix in a sector model.

available by region, or which exhibit interregional differences in prices. The national equations (*NE*) govern the use of inputs supplied on a national basis, if any, and the supply-demand equilibrium for products at the consumer level. The national columns include domestic demands for products, foreign trade activities, and supplies of the national inputs.

In establishing the list of equations, it should be noted that the conventions on seasonality do not need to be uniform. For example, depending on the climate, it is possible that irrigated lands are used 12 months a year and nonirrigated only 8 months. Therefore, off-season land availability may be irrelevant for the latter. Similarly, there may be periods of the year, such as the periods of land preparation and planting, when tasks need to be accomplished quickly and labor will be hired for that purpose, even though labor is in surplus supply most of the rest of the year. In order to be able to simulate the labor-hiring behavior during such periods, the labor constraints may need to be biweekly or even weekly, whereas monthly or bimonthly constraints may suffice for the rest of the year. (Chapter 3 discusses this point in more detail). If the model had ten regions, two farm size classes, and weekly constraints on family labor, the family labor component of the model alone would comprise at least $20 \times 52 = 1040$ equations. In contrast, judicious variation of the seasonality of the constraints, with weekly constraints for only one or two periods in the year, probably could reduce the number of those equations to $20 \times 12 = 240$.

In practice, the seasonality of constraints on land, labor, and water depends in large part on the nature of the available data. Cost-of-production data ("farm budgets") are available for at least the principal crops in virtually every country in the world. However, frequently they lack detail on the timing of inputs, so the model team has to look elsewhere for complementary information on timing. Data issues are discussed at greater length subsequently.

In specific terms, the model's equations are likely to include at least the following minimal set:

A Local equations[4]
  1 Seasonal constraints on land and, for irrigated localities, water.
  2 Seasonal balances for labor, to equate supply with demand, where supply normally includes at least two kinds of labor: family and hired.
  3 Seasonal constraints on the availability of family labor.
  4 Seasonal balances for draft animal and machinery services.
  5 Risk accounting balances (optional).
  6 Short-run constraints on endowments of machines, livestock and tree crops (optional). If livestock are in the model, then livestock feed balances need to be included.
B Regional equations
  7 Supply-demand balances at the producer level (governing the disposition of output from the farm gate to the first stage of marketing and processing).
  8 Balances for the supplies of regional inputs (perhaps credit, hired labor, contract agricultural machinery services).
  9 Constraints on the regional supplies of those inputs (optional). For labor, constraints on regional supplies may be accompanied by inter-regional migration activities.
C National equations
  10 Balances for nationally supplied inputs, that is, inputs with a uniform national price and uniform availability: perhaps fertilizer, agrochemicals, and credit. Also the accounting balance for other unspecified costs.
  11 Where appropriate, national constraints on the availability of inputs. Care must be taken with this class of constraints. It is not always the physical availability of, say, fertilizers and tractors that is the limiting factor, but rather the economics of using them and the farmer's ability to finance their costs.
  12 National supply-demand balances for products at the consumer level.
  13 If the model is linear, convex combination constraints for the demand variables (see Chapter 8).

14 Export quotas and other bounds on international trade activities.
15 The objective function.

As may be seen from Figure 11.1, the act of defining the equations also implies definition of many of the column variables. For example, if short-term credit is a regional input, then variables for the supply of credit are needed at the regional level. If it is a national input, then those variables are needed at the national level.

Thus, the first stages in building the model per se are: (1) listing the products and inputs and deciding on the spatial categories (farm groups), and (2) developing in preliminary form the list of equations and variables. These lists will typically be revised in the course of building the model, but it is important to get them down in preliminary form at the outset.

11.2 NOMENCLATURE AND UNITS

The other matters that require early decisions are model nomenclature and the units of the variables and equations. Nomenclature is especially important, not only for making the model readily interpretable, but also because in defining the nomenclature one is going a long way toward defining the structure of the model. Defining the nomenclature begins with defining the sets of the model. Three of the sets already have been mentioned; they are as follows, with the more usual conventions on their indexes:

1 products, j
2 regions, r
3 subregional or local units (including farm size categories), f or h

Following the discussions in earlier chapters, at least four more sets are relevant to the supply side of the model:

4 purchased inputs, i
5 fixed resources, k
6 technologies, t
7 seasons, m

On the demand side of the model, the products sold constitute a different subset of the product set $\{j\}$, because the processing activities change the form of the product and yield by-products. For example, processing wheat yields flour and bran; the unprocessed wheat also may be used in small amounts for livestock feed, so the single product on the supply side becomes three products on the demand side. In the linear model, the points (segments) on the demand curves constitute yet another set:

8 demand function points, s

With these conventions, in the computer version of the model, a variable representing sales on a point on the demand function often is written D_{jrs}, where r takes on a default value (such as 0 or 9) in the case of national demand functions. Alternatively, if all demand functions are specified at the national level, the demand variables are D_{js}. In some cases the demand variables have been written DEM_{js}. The model builder may prefer to use a different set of symbols; these are examples of frequently used ones. Other commonly used symbols are X for production, P or T for processing (transformation) activities, E for exports, M for imports, and J for input supplies. Inputs are few enough that often they are given their own primary symbol instead of being prefixed by J and differentiated by values of the subscript i. Examples are FER (or $FERT$) for fertilizer, $MACH$ for agricultural machinery, LAB for labor, IRR (or WAT) for irrigation, CRD (or $CRED$) for short-term credit, $DRAF$ for draft animal services, and $OTHR$ for other costs. Generally, mnemonic naming conventions should be used, because there will be many occasions in which the model's matrix will be studied, for purposes of checking and making revisions, even if a matrix generator is used. One of the authors once had the experience of reviewing a model whose variables were named $P1$ through $P300$! The process of review took several times longer than it would have if mnemonic abbreviations had been used.

Abbreviations are required because the formats for data inputs into linear programming packages allow only eight characters to represent names of variables and equations (Chapter 6). Further, other special symbols inevitably creep into the nomenclature. An illustration is provided by the symbol for supplies of irrigation water in the Mexican model CHAC. In some of the irrigation districts, water is supplied by both gravity (G) and pump (P) irrigation, so, for example, irrigation supplied by gravity flows in District A (Río Colorado) in the month of May is denoted AWAT5G.[5] Whatever the symbolic conventions, they should be established early, even though they almost certainly will undergo revision before the model is completed.

Units of measure also merit some thought, because the data inputs to the computer should be neither very small numbers nor very large numbers. Solution algorithms work more efficiently if the numbers in the model are of similar magnitudes, and also the model's inputs and outputs are more readable if that is the case. For readability, it is most convenient to formulate the vectors for technologies of production in units that agronomists and agricultural economists are most accustomed to. This facilitates considerably the process of review of the model's inputs by other specialists. The basic unit is land as input to production. In most countries, each production vector is defined per hectare, although other units that are similar in magnitude to hectares are used as well (acres in the United States and Great Britain, chongbo in Korea, carreaux in Haiti, relongs in Malaysia, etc.). A typical production vector, then, will report output in tons, labor inputs in man-days, tractor inputs in machine-hours or machine-days, fertilizer in kilograms or tons, irrigation inputs in 10,000 cubic meters (one hectare covered to a depth of one meter), or similar units, in all cases all on a per hectare basis.

Given that production vectors are defined in these more or less natural units, scaling the model's outputs is accomplished in other areas of the model. If production activities represent hectares, then usually the right-hand sides (endowments) of land are entered in the model in thousand hectares. To avoid inconsistencies, it usually is preferable to express all right-hand side values in thousands, so that the entire model is scaled by a factor of one thousand. This means, among other things, that if a production activity appears in the solution with, say, a value of 7.3, it corresponds to 7300 hectares in that crop and technology. Mathematically, if the programming constraints are written

$$AX \leq b \qquad (11.1)$$

then the right-hand side scaling consists of dividing b by one thousand (in this case). Thus, if the problem is to be the same, it must be the case that the units of b are raised by a factor of one thousand. Since the elements of A are unchanged, X must be divided by one thousand, and therefore its units are increased by the same factor.

Another place in the model where scaling frequently occurs is in the input-supplying activities, usually for fertilizer and credit but often for other inputs as well. If fertilizer inputs are in kilograms, and the country's total use of inorganic fertilizers is in the range of one million to fifty million tons, which is likely, then without scaling the fertilizer supplying activities could be in the billions of kilograms in magnitude. To avoid that outcome, each fertilizer supply activity is defined as providing one thousand or one million kilograms. An alternative solution is to state fertilizer inputs in tons—so that a typical farm may apply, say, 0.250 units of fertilizer per hectare—and to state fertilizer supplies in thousands of tons.

Table 11.1 presents a stylized model which illustrates some of these conventions regarding units. That model is simplified to two regions and two crops, wheat and beans. Region 1 produces both crops and region 2 produces only beans. Two alternative technologies are available for producing wheat in region 1, based on variations in fertilization levels; the labor input varies slightly also, mainly because of the higher harvest associated with the higher rate of fertilization. Region 2's bean yields are higher than those of region 1.

The nomenclature convention for the production activities has the regional index immediately after the "X" and the technology index after the crop code. The regional fertilizer supply activities are denoted $FERr$, $r = 1, 2$; and the regional marketing-processing activities are denoted $TrWHE$ and $TrBEA$. Wheat becomes flour in the course of processing, so the wheat demand activities are $DFLOs$, for three points ($s = 1, 2, 3$) on the demand function. Usually, in an actual model, more points on each demand function are preferred. It is common to use eleven points—one midpoint and five on each side. To save space, the demand for beans is not shown in the diagram.

Table 11.1 Tableau of a Simplified Model to Illustrate Units of Measurement

Rows	X1WHE1	X1WHE2	X1BEA1	FER1	T1WHE	T1BEA	X2BEA1	FER2	T2BEA	DFLO1	DFLO2	DFLO3	RHS
LAND11	1.0	1.0											≤ 4000.0
LAND12	1.0	1.0	1.0										≤ 4000.0
LAND13	1.0		1.0										≤ 4000.0
LAND14	1.0		1.0										≤ 4000.0
LAB11	8.0	8.0											≤ 105,600.0
LAB12	15.0	18.0	17.0										≤ 105,600.0
LAB13	15.0	16.0	12.0										≤ 105,600.0
LAB14			18.0										≤ 105,600.0
BFER1	0.100	0.200	0.100	−1000									≤ 0
BP1WHE	−1.4	−1.6			1.0								≤ 0
BP1BEA			−0.7			1.0							≤ 0
LAND21													≤ 3000.0
LAND22							1.0						≤ 3000.0
LAND23							1.0						≤ 3000.0
LAND24							1.0						≤ 3000.0
LAB21													≤ 39,600.0
LAB22							19.0						≤ 39,600.0
LAB23							13.0						≤ 39,600.0
LAB24							20.0						≤ 39,600.0
BFER2							0.120	−1000					≤ 0
BP2WHE													≤ 0
BP2BEA							−0.9		1.0				≤ 0
CBFLO					−0.8					6037.5	5250.0	4462.5	≤ 0
CBBEA						−0.99			−0.99				≤ 0
CCFLO										1.0	1.0	1.0	≤ 1.0
OBJ	−0.175				−.055	−.08	−0.175		−0.08	6414.9	5355.0	4362.1	Maximize

On the resource side, the model is simplified to only land and family labor, and quarterly constraints are imposed on each resource. The constraint names are of the form *LANDrm* and *LABrm*, where *r* is the region and *m* the quarter. The balance row for fertilizer is *BFERr*, and the producer-level balance rows for the products are *BPrWHE* and *BPrBEA*. At the national level, there are commodity balances for flour and beans, the convex combination constraint for wheat, and the objective function.

In the production activities, the units are as mentioned: hectares of land, man-days of labor, and tons of fertilizer and product. The right-hand side values of land and labor have been scaled by dividing them by a factor of one thousand, so that the regional land endowments are 4000 and 3000 instead of four million and three million hectares. The labor endowments were calculated by procedures similar to those used in practice: it is assumed that surveys reveal the average labor force in a farm family to be 2.0 adult-equivalent laborers, and each laborer can supply 22 days per month, or 66 days per quarter. Thus, if the average farm size is 5 hectares, the (scaled) labor endowment in region 1 is $4000 \div 5 \times 2.0 \times 66 = 105,600$, in thousand man-days available per quarter. Similarly, if the average farm size in region 2 is 10 hectares, the quarterly labor endowments in that region are 39,600, in thousand man-days.

The marketing-processing activities also are expressed in tons of product and their costs are in monetary units. Notice that the wheat-to-flour conversion ratio is assumed to be 80% and also that a 1% loss ratio is assumed in the course of transporting and marketing beans. Scaling again is performed on the fertilizer column, so that tons are converted to thousands of tons in the fertilizer coefficients of the left-hand side of the tableau.

Given the scaling of units of the right-hand side, the solution is read in units which are one thousand times larger than the units of the tableau. Production activities are read in thousands of hectares, e.g., an *X* value of 2000 means 2 million hectares. Similarly, in the solution the activities for marketing and processing are read in thousands of tons, and the activity for supply of fertilizers is read in millions of tons.

The demand activities have no units; their values are pure numbers which cannot exceed unity in the static solution. (A value of 1.0 for a demand activity means the solution is located exactly at that point on the demand function.) Therefore, it is convenient to exempt the right-hand sides of the convexity constraints from the scaling procedure. Even though the demand activities themselves do not have units, the coefficients in the intersection of the demand columns and the commodity balance rows do have units, and those units must be consistent with the unit conventions on the supply side of the model. In the case of Table 11.1, if the activity T1WHE were to appear in the optimal solution with a value of 1.0, that would signify the marketing and processing of one thousand tons of wheat. In that case, the coefficient -0.8 would be interpreted as 800 tons of flour. In this example, it happens that the demand coefficients also are in thousands of tons, for the base year consumption of flour in our hypothetical economy was 5.25 million tons, and the demand variables were designed so that the midpoint variable corresponds to the base year situation.[6]

A column has clear-cut units, but the units may vary along a row. For the rows, arithmetic consistency is required among the units of the variables and the values of the coefficients. For example, a simple production-level commodity balance may be written

$$-y_1 X_1 - y_2 X_2 + 1.0T + wH \leq 0 \qquad (11.2)$$

where the ys are yields, the Xs are production activities, T is the processing and marketing activity, w is a livestock feed coefficient, and H is the size of the local livestock herd. The agricultural product may be sold for processing and marketing elsewhere, or it may be used in raw form for livestock feed. The unit conventions among both the variables and the coefficients need to be consistent, and one way to ensure consistency is to check that (11.2) can be satisfied (as a strict equality) with the observed values for the base year. For this example, suppose the base year production was 340,000 tons, derived from the following values:

$$y_1 = 1.2 \text{ tons/ha}$$
$$y_2 = 1.1 \text{ tons/ha}$$
$$X_1 = 100,000 \text{ ha}$$
$$X_2 = 200,000 \text{ ha}$$

Correspondingly, let the uses be 200,000 tons for processing and 140,000 tons for livestock feed, with a herd of 100,000 head.

One possible rendering of (11.2) in numbers is then:

$$-1.2 \times 100,000 - 1.1 \times 200,000 + 200,000 + 1.4 \times 100,000 = 0 \quad (11.3)$$

The coefficients now have units of tons/ha in the two left-hand terms, and tons/head on the right. The units of the variables are hectares (Xs), tons (T) and head (H). Suppose, on the other hand, that the whole model's right-hand side had been scaled uniformly by 1000. Then the equation would read

$$-1.2 \times 100 - 1.1 \times 200 + 200 + 1.4 \times 100 = 0 \qquad (11.4)$$

and all the units of the variables would be in thousands of the previous units.

A more complicated case arises if, as a result of specifications elsewhere in the model, it already is established that the Xs are in hectares and T is tons but H is in thousand head. Then the coefficient w will have to be adjusted to maintain consistency. The equation must be changed to read

$$-1.2 \times 100,000 - 1.1 \times 200,000 + 200,000 + 1,400 \times 100 = 0 \quad (11.5)$$

because the herd variable cannot be other than 100 (in thousand head). The units of w now are tons per thousand head, or kilograms per head.

Another way to check the consistency of units is to write out a units equation for both the coefficient units and the variable units. In the case of (11.5), the units equation is

$$-\left(\frac{\text{tons}}{\text{ha}} \times \text{ha}\right) - \left(\frac{\text{tons}}{\text{ha}} \times \text{ha}\right) + \text{tons}$$
$$+ \left(\frac{\text{tons}}{\text{thousand head}} \times \text{thousand head}\right) = 0$$

With cancellations, all terms are in tons, which is the indication of consistency.

The objective function's units may be established independently of the other units in the model. In this case, to keep the magnitudes of the coefficients in reasonable ranges, the units of the objective function have been set at millions of dollars. Hence, in Table 11.1 if demand activity DFLO2 were equal to 1.0 in the optimal solution, then 5.25 million tons would be sold and the associated area under the demand function would be $5.355 billion. (As a check, the value of that amount of flour sales, at the base year price of $170/ton, would be $892.5 million, and we know beforehand that the demand area should be greater than the value of sales, but not several orders of magnitude greater.) To be consistent, the cost entries in the objective function must have the same units. Thus the fertilizer coefficients in the tableau imply that 1000 tons of fertilizer cost $0.175 million, or, in more familiar terms, fertilizer costs $175 per ton. Had the fertilizer supplying activity not been scaled, but instead left in units of tons, the objective function coefficient would have been -0.000175, which is a smaller number than is desirable. Similarly, wheat costs (according to the tableau) $55/ton to process into flour and to market, and beans cost $80/ton to market.

While this example is hypothetical, the unit conventions it illustrates are typical of sector models. It is worthwhile to give some consideration to units at the beginning of a modeling exercise. Otherwise, confusion over units is likely to arise, and part-way through the modeling exercise a halt will have to be called to sort out units and revise coefficients accordingly!

11.3 THE SUPPLY SIDE OF THE MODEL

The development of vectors for the supply side of the model has been reviewed in some detail in Chapter 3. Here attention is confined to a few additional issues which arise at the sector level. After they are presented and discussed, some observations are made regarding the data requirements for the supply side of the model.

To pick up a theme from Chapter 7, it is important that the supply side contain sufficient detail with regard to production alternatives. It probably is a useful rule of thumb that the number of production vectors should be at least six or eight times, and preferably at least ten times, the number of products in the model. While the majority of the production vectors will not enter the optimal basis in any one solution, the model's ability to respond to changes in resource endowments and relative prices is determined in large part by the range of alternative production vectors that it contains. In the terminology of production economics, moving from one technology vector per product to several is equivalent to moving from the L-shaped Leontief isoquant to several points along an isoquant which has some curvature.

Usually the specification of alternative technologies is based on field-level observations of farming practices. For example, in the course of economic development in rural areas, mechanization will be introduced in the cultivation of grains and oilseeds before in vegetables, fruits, fibers, and root crops. Thus, for a developing country, the mechanization options should be spelled out more fully for grains and oilseeds. Similarly, a farmer's first step in mechanization usually is the renting of tractor services for land preparation, and the second step is using machinery for harvesting (depending on the crop). It is usually only after these steps are taken that mechanized techniques are contemplated for seeding and other operations (Bassoco and Rendón 1973), although in East Asia use of a mechanical sprayer for herbicides and pesticides may predate the use of mechanical traction power.

If a country's agriculture exhibits a range of techniques of production, from traditional, nonmechanized techniques onward, the foregoing observations provide some useful tips about constructing the production vectors. The first alternative to the totally mechanized technique would be a vector that is identical in all respects to the original one except that the inputs of labor and draft animals for land preparation are replaced with inputs of (less) labor and machinery. Unless there is clear evidence that mechanical plowing affects yields, say by deeper furrows, the usual procedure is to maintain identical yields in the two vectors. In this way, two points are specified on a three-dimensional isoquant surface, whose axes are labor, machinery use, and draft animal services. By continuing these steps, alternative technology vectors of increasing sophistication can be constructed.

In specifying a sufficient range of optional technologies, it may be necessary to go beyond those actually observed for a given class of farmers. Suppose that, in a developing country, small rainfed farms in remote areas use only animal traction power. However, the modeler wants to allow for the possibility that a sufficient rise in income could lead the farmer to rent tractor services for land preparation, perhaps to economize on his time so that he can spend more time in off-farm occupations. In that case, the modeler need know only (1) the coefficients of the original, nonmechanized vector, and (2) the coefficients for plowing in the alternative ways (in hours per hectare of machinery, animals, and labor). The latter usually are known fairly well by field experts. The original vector can then be modified by substituting the plowing coefficients from the partially mechanized technology for the corresponding original coefficients. These illustrations are applicable only to certain cases, but the same principles of developing the technology vectors can be applied more generally.

The model's structure is amenable to incorporation of data from a variety of sources, including, whenever possible, econometric estimates of parameter values. Usually there are not sufficient degrees of freedom in the data set to estimate all the parameters in the supply side of a programming model, which tend to number in the hundreds or thousands. However, that does not mean the available estimates cannot be used in combination with other kinds of data. To illustrate this possibility, suppose that a Cobb-Douglas function had been estimated for machinery and labor inputs per hectare, for, say, the grains subsector. The Cobb-Douglas exponents can be used to define the possibilities for machinery-labor substitution, with other inputs and outputs held constant.

Let the estimated function be, for a given crop,

$$y = al^{\alpha}m^{\beta} \qquad (11.6)$$

and let an observed technology have values y_0, l_0, and m_0 for the output per hectare and inputs of labor and machinery, respectively. To find points along the Cobb-Douglas isoquant, a simple procedure is to select a series of values of l, *ex ante*, and then to use (11.6) to compute the corresponding values of m while holding y constant. For example, let l vary in increments of 10% so that the following seven values are available to the model:

$$l_0, \quad l_1 = 1.10l_0, \quad l_2 = 1.20l_0, \quad l_3 = 1.30l_0$$
$$l_4 = 0.90l_0, \quad l_5 = 0.80l_0, \quad l_6 = 0.70l_0$$

For each l_t, the corresponding value of m is

$$m_t = \left(\frac{y_0}{al_t^{\alpha}} \right)^{1/\beta} \qquad (11.7)$$

These seven pairs of numbers (l_t, m_t) define the isoquant shown in Figure 11.2.

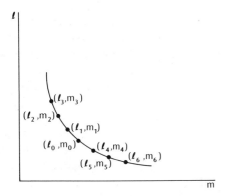

Figure 11.2 Points on an isoquant for labor and machinery inputs.

Table 11.2 Mini-Tableau for Input Substitution

	X	X_0	X_1	X_2	X_3	X_4	X_5	X_6	RHS
Isoquant definition row	1	$-y_0$	$-y_0$	$-y_0$	$-y_0$	$-y_0$	$-y_0$	$-y_0$	≤ 0
Labor input balance		l_0	l_1	l_2	l_3	l_4	l_5	l_6	≤ 0
Machinery input balance		m_0	m_1	m_2	m_3	m_4	m_5	m_6	≤ 0
		g_{10}	g_{10}	g_{10}	g_{10}	g_{10}	g_{10}	g_{10}	
Other input balances		$\vdots$	$\vdots$	$\vdots$	$\vdots$	$\vdots$	$\vdots$	$\vdots$	≤ 0
		g_{n0}	g_{n0}	g_{n0}	g_{n0}	g_{n0}	g_{n0}	g_{n0}	
Land constraints		1	1	1	1	1	1	1	$\leq L$
Production-sales balance	-1								≤ 0

The seven pairs of factor input combinations are entered into a programming table in Table 11.2. The table is a partial one, so only the first row is shown in its entirety, but the column vectors are complete. Recall that y_0 is the base-year yield. The total production of the crop in question is given in the solution by the value of the variable X. Its units are output units (tons, bushels, thousands of tons, etc.). Each of the variables X_t represents the amount of land farmed under technology t (point t on the isoquant). The isoquant definition row sums the total production (in tons: hectares multiplied by the yield y_0), and the variable X transfers that production to the production-sales balance—the supply-demand balance at the level of primary production. The coefficients for other inputs are constant across the technological variations, as are land inputs. There can be multiple land constraints, for months or seasons.[7]

In the optimal solution, either a single technology vector will have a nonzero value, or two adjacent technology vectors will have nonzero values. If the optimal basis contained more than two technology vectors, or two nonadjacent ones, that would be equivalent to locating on a point above the isoquant in Figure 11.2, such as a point on a straight line connecting (l_3, m_3) and (l_6, m_6). Such a point would represent the same output per hectare (y_0) as points along the isoquant, but it requires more inputs per hectare than the points below it and to the left of it that are located on the isoquant. In other words, such a point is inefficient, and hence it will not be selected in the optimal solution.

In Chapter 3 there are other examples illustrating the use of information which may be obtained by econometric means, such as input response functions.

These approaches to specifying production vectors reflect economists' tendency to think in terms of smooth, continuous functions for factor substitution, albeit translated into discrete form for the programming model. However, smooth, independent variations of inputs may not characterize the relevant choices in the real world. It may be, for example, that variations in machinery use and fertilizer use do not occur independently. In some circumstances, all farmers who mechanize already will be applying more than the minimal amounts of fertilizer, so that the option of substituting machinery for draft animals while still applying minimal (or zero) fertilizer does not make sense. Yet if all the technological variants are constructed systematically as illustrated above, such an option would be included in the model.

If these concerns are important, an alternative procedure is to build up the supply side of the model on the basis of observations of representative farms. Continuing the same example, among the representative farms presumably there would be some that used nonmechanized traction and little fertilizer, and others that used machinery plus substantial amounts of fertilizer, but presumably none that used machinery plus little fertilizer.

The representative-farm approach may be more realistic as regards input combinations, but it has two drawbacks. First, it will not allow for technologies (in a given region or farm class) beyond those that are observed, and for experiments with hypothetical future policies it may be important to allow for farm responses that include intensifying technologies beyond the observed levels. Second, using vectors representing actual farms undoubtedly will lead to a situation in which many of the vectors are inefficient, that is, dominated by at least one other vector. In this situation, a smaller model (with fewer column vectors) could generate the same solutions, but with many production vectors it is a laborious task to attempt to detect *a priori* the inefficient ones, and hence it usually is not worth the effort.

In the end, whether to use constructed vectors or observed vectors, or some combination of the two, is a matter of judgment for the model-building team. Economists probably overstate the continuity of input substitution possibilities, but field experts probably overstate the discreteness of choices in the real world.

It often is assumed that economic growth and development leads to continuously higher rates of application of modern inputs in agriculture, and so the specification of models tends to be weighted toward the more input-intensive variants of observed practices. However, there are cases in which development causes declining input use and declining yields. An obvious case is declining terms of trade for agriculture, that is, reductions in the ratio of output prices to input prices. A specific example of that syndrome is the not-infrequent circumstance in which the farmer finds off-farm work which is more profitable than his farming activities. He may then find it worthwhile to spend less time weeding and performing other crop tending activities. If this behavior is significant on a regional or sector basis, average yields can decrease, for some crops. This illustration is a reminder to be aware of the circumstances for which the model is being built when developing its coefficients.

When the model includes different farm size classes or other kinds of farm groupings, care should be taken in differentiating the production technologies over those classes. The observation that smaller farms tend to use less mechanized techniques is not necessarily explained by lesser access to mechanization but rather by relative factor endowments and factor prices. A smaller farm has more family labor per hectare than a larger farm, and family labor often is cheaper (calculating implicit wages) than hired labor. Thus it is rational for the family farm to utilize more labor-intensive techniques of production. For modeling, the implication is that the specification of available techniques should not differ much among farm size classes, but normally the expectation is that the optimal choice of techniques should differ. The more mechanized techniques should be specified for smaller farms as well, even though they probably would not be used in the base-year solution. To put it another way, a model that allowed only the less mechanized techniques on smaller farms would tend to reflect accurately the base-year choice of technique, but it could not represent responses to significant changes in relative factor prices, such as those caused by greater opportunities for off-farm earnings.

As a final practical note on the product supply side of the model, it is perhaps worth mentioning that one of the more common sources of inaccuracy in the coefficients is underestimating the "miscellaneous" costs of production. These costs are diverse and hence difficult to capture in standard questionnaires, but they often can add up to 10% or more of total production costs. Some items in this category are the cost of replacing and repairing implements, the time spent maintaining on-farm irrigation channels, the time in applying organic fertilizers (and sometimes their purchase cost), farm association fees, time and costs of postharvest on-farm transportation, time and costs of repairing on-farm storage facilities, machinery repair costs, the cost of crop insurance (if not specified separately), and the unanticipated extra labor occasioned by the effects of bad weather. Many regular reports on crop budgets tend to underestimate the aggregate of these costs, so the model builder may wish to make special inquiries in this area.

11.4 INPUT SUPPLIES AND INPUT PRICES

As discussed in Chapter 7, it is useful to separate input supplying activities, and their costs, from the production activities, so that the production columns in the sector model have no cost entries in the objective function. In the model as it has been developed thus far, each input has its balance row and its supplying column(s). The advantages of this specification are that: (1) input supplies can be both costed and bounded if appropriate, (2) multistep, upward sloping input supply functions can be introduced,[8] and (3) changes in input prices or supply conditions can be introduced simply, often by changing one parameter in the model instead of changing hundreds or thousands of aggregate cost coefficients for all the production vectors. There is another advantage of this specification, and that is clarity of structure in the tableau. Even when the model is built with matrix generators, time must be spent in examining a listing of the tableau itself to check that all coefficients are as they should be and in the right places. (See Section 11.9 below on model management.) When the tableau is examined, the checking process is aided by having each

Table 11.3   Mini-Tableau for Current and Capital Charges on Machinery Use

	MACH	KMACH	CAP	RHS
Machinery input balance	− 1			≤ 0
Machinery capitalization row	1	− 23.0		≤ 0
Capital accounting row		23.0	− 1	≤ 0
Objective function	− c		− r	Maximize

coefficient represent a single, clear concept. If several changes in price assumptions have been made since the model first was built, it is not a simple matter to check the revised aggregate cost coefficients.

Input supplying activities can take many forms, depending on the economics of the situation, and four of them are illustrated in the following paragraphs. In Table 11.3, the mini-tableau takes account of the fact that the cost of using machinery can be decomposed into current operating costs and capital costs. Such a decomposition can facilitate experiments with the interest rate in the model, so that changes in the interest rate affect only one component of the cost of tractor services. The activity $MACH$ supplies machinery services (in units of hours) at an operating cost of c dollars per hour; demands for machinery services are not shown in the tableau but they appear in the machinery input balance, under the cropping activities, with a positive sign. The activity $KMACH$ represents the use of capital which is implicit in the use of the machine. The capitalization row converts hours of use into dollars of capital value, on the basis of the machine's purchased price and its expected economic working lifetime in hours of use. The capital value then is entered into a capital accounting row that will include capital used elsewhere in the sector. The total value of capital used is represented by the value of the variable CAP. The interest charges in the objective function (r) are registered via CAP.

To derive the illustrative coefficient of 23, the following assumptions were used: the machine costs \$46,000 and it gives 2000 hours of use in a normal economic lifetime. Thus each hour of service implies the use of $46,000/2000 =$ \$23 worth of capital. Accordingly, the capital charge in the objective function for an hour of service effectively is $23r$. The units of the activity $KMACH$ are units of capital use, expressed in units of service, which are hours. In other words, $KMACH$ represents capital use after it has been converted by a stock-flow factor. The units of CAP are monetary units.

Another treatment of the stock-flow problem is given in Table 11.4. There the demands for machinery services are seasonal (quarterly), and therefore the supplies of services are also. But the ability to supply the services is limited by the initial capital stock plus the purchases ($PMACH$) of machinery. The coefficient m is a different expression of the stock-flow relationship; it is the maximum number of hours of expected use per quarter associated with a physical unit of machinery.[9] A unit costs P_m to purchase, and hence its capital

Table 11.4   Mini-Tableau for Machinery Use and Purchase

	MACH1	MACH2	MACH3	MACH4	PMACH	RHS
Quarterly machinery input balances	-1					≤ 0
	-1					≤ 0
			-1			≤ 0
				-1		≤ 0
Quarterly machinery stock-flow constraints	1				$-m$	$\leq mS$
		1			$-m$	$\leq mS$
			1		$-m$	$\leq mS$
				1	$-m$	$\leq mS$
Objective Function	$-c$	$-c$	$-c$	$-c$	$-rP_m$	Maximize

charge is rP_m. The initial stock of machines is S. As in Table 11.3, the operating costs per hour of service are summarized in the coefficient c.

With the formulation of Table 11.4, depending on the seasonal pattern of demand, there is likely to be excess machinery capacity in some seasons. Excess capacity is manifested in the solution by one or more of the stock-flow constraints being nonbinding. With sufficiently high returns to machinery use in peak periods, purchases of machinery could occur even in the presence of excess capacity in one or more seasons. In this event, there are possible economies to exploit if additional off-seasonal uses for the machinery could be found.

Irrigation provides the next example of input supply activities, as shown in Table 11.5. That table illustrates a situation in which irrigation is provided from storage in a reservoir. The gross inflows to the reservoir each season are denoted F_i, and the plus signs under the production activities represent

Table 11.5   Mini-Tableau for Irrigation Supplies with Water Storage Options

	Production activities	Irrigation by season		Storage: Interseasonal water transfer		RHS
Supply-demand balances for water	$+ + + \ldots$	-1		1		≤ 0
	$+ + + \ldots$		-1	$-.99$	1	≤ 0
	$+ + + \ldots$			-1	$-.99$	≤ 0
Constraints on water availability		1		1		$\leq F_1$
			1		1	$\leq F_2$
				1		$\leq F_3$
Objective function		$-c$	$-c$ $-c$			Maximize

coefficients of demand for water. The current inflows can be used either for current irrigating, or they can be stored one month. Multimonth storage takes the form of a sequence of one-month storage activities. Since current irrigating and storage represent the two alternative uses of current inflows, they both enter the monthly constraints on water availability. Irrigation has a cost to the user, which may be a levy to cover the system's operating and maintenance costs. That cost (per unit) is shown as $-c$ in the objective function. There also is a current cost associated with storage, in the form of evaporation of the water behind the dam. In this illustrative tableau, evaporation is assumed to be 1.0% per month, hence the storage of one unit of water yields an availability of 0.99 units the next month.

In cases of resource inputs whose availability is fixed in the short run, such as land and family labor, a question arises as to whether the input should be priced explicitly in the primal version of the model. The discussion in Section 1 of Chapter 8 shows that the model's cropping pattern is based on an implicit rent which reflects the opportunity cost of the fixed inputs. In the case of land, the implicit opportunity cost is its productivity in the highest-valued agricultural use. Is it not double counting also to include a land rent in the specification of the primal tableau? The answer is no, because in the presence of an explicit land rent the shadow price of land will represent the difference between the marginal value product of land and its explicit rental charge. The true economic rent would then be the shadow price plus the rental charge.

The presence of a rental charge will place a constraint on the uses to which the land may be put. The land will not be cultivated with technologies that generate a marginal value product of land that is lower than the rental charge. If the land is rented in actuality, that constraint is reasonable and is likely to be followed, at least approximately, in the real world. If the land is owned, will a farmer cultivate it under practices that will drive its marginal product to zero, or at least below prevailing rental charges? The answer will vary with the circumstances, but in most cases it will also be no. The reason is

Table 11.6   Mini-Tableau for Inclusion of Land Rental Charges

	Production activities			Land use activities			RHS
Supply-demand	+ + + ...		−1				≤ 0
balances	+ + + ...			−1			≤ 0
for land	+ + + ...					−1	≤ 0
Constraints			1				≤ L
on land				1			≤ L
availability						1	≤ L
Objective function			$-r_l$	$-r_l$		$-r_l$	Maximize

that the farmer almost always has the option of renting out the land, and that option establishes the opportunity cost of his land. Hence he is unlikely to drive its marginal product below that level. These considerations suggest that whether or not an explicit rental charge should be included depends on the circumstances being modeled, but very often it would be appropriate to do so.

When the rental charge is included, it may be useful to change the land constraints in the previous tableaus to land balances, and to add separate constraints. Table 11.6 shows the revised configuration. The explicit rental is r_l and the land availability is L, which is the same every season. Alternatively, the modeler may prefer to attach the rental charges directly to the cropping activities, but in that case there could be a large number of rental coefficients, and in experiments the modeler may wish to change them or to vary them over size classes.

For inputs of family labor, which usually is not paid an explicit wage, inclusion of a factor price in the primal model is equivalent to specifying a positive vertical intercept on the labor supply function. It says that at a zero wage—or for activities with a zero marginal value product—the supply of labor will be zero. In parallel with the case of land, to determine this intercept price, the relevant question is: what is the minimum return for which family labor will work? That return, or implicit wage, is almost certainly greater than zero, but it also is likely to be less than the market wage. During the cropping season, family labor is a semifixed factor of production, since the family stands to lose a lot by abandoning the crop after it has been planted. Some members of the family may work at temporary nonagricultural jobs, but in most cases some will stay on the farm until the harvest is collected. The question about the minimum return for which they will work is not easy to answer; it is an area where estimation would be helpful—estimation of production functions which include, separately, family and hired labor. Some simulations with the CHAC model suggested that, for Mexico, the implicit wage (or reservation wage) for family labor was 30–70% of the market wage, and lower in rainfed areas than in irrigated areas. This last conclusion presumably reflects the fact that irrigated areas are generally more prosperous, and hence through multiplier effects they have generated more local off-farm work opportunities.

In some contexts in developing countries, it is important to differentiate family labor by the categories of adult males, adult females, and children. Some field tasks are traditionally performed by children (in Egypt, for example) and some are traditionally performed by women (in Nigeria, for example). In specifying the labor component of the model, there is a corresponding choice between differentiating the demand for labor and differentiating it on the supply side. Under the first alternative, the model has separate coefficients in the production activities denoting demand for male labor, female labor, and/or child labor (see Section 3.5). Under the second alternative, the demand is simply for labor (by task or season), but on the supply side there are different classes of family labor, each with its own endowment and its own opportunity cost (reservation wage). In this second case, if the tasks or seasons are disaggregated finely enough, the model solution should match up the lower-cost labor with the lower productivity tasks.

The choice between the two specifications depends on whether (1) certain tasks will be performed only by certain types of labor, perhaps for cultural reasons, regardless of relative productivities and opportunity costs, or (2) the assignment of labor to tasks is indeed a function of productivities and costs. Situation 1 would indicate choosing the first alternative, and situation 2 the second one.

In the second specification, with labor differentiated only on the supply side, the description of technologies has to be complete enough to show the productivity of each task. For example, it may be necessary to have alternative production vectors which are more and less intensive in manual weeding operations, and which differ accordingly in their yields per hectare. Such a specification allows the model implicitly to evaluate the marginal productivity of weeding labor, and therefore to assign the appropriate types of labor to that task. In the absence of this kind of information on technological options, it may be preferable to use the first labor specification, which assigns types of labor to tasks *a priori*, even though the second one may be preferable from a viewpoint of economics.

Table 11.7 shows a mini-tableau with different types of labor on the supply side, and with technological options on the demand side. The two production vectors $X1$ and $X2$ refer to the same product, and family labor (LF) "hiring" activities are shown for men (M) and women (W), by month. The reservation wages are c_m and c_w, respectively. In most (but not all!) societies, $c_m > c_w$. The second production vector, $X2$, utilizes less weeding labor (in June) and therefore has a lower yield. Harvest labor is lower also (in September), as it is assumed to be proportional to the size of the harvest. Depending on the price of the product and the relative share of labor costs in

Table 11.7 Mini-Tableau with Male and Female Labor

	$X1$	$X2$	$LFM4$	$LFM6$	$LFM9$	$LFW4$	$LFW6$	$LFW9$	RHS
Labor balance, April	15	15	-1			-1			≤ 0
Labor balance, June	8	4		-1			-1		≤ 0
Labor balance, Sept.	20	17			-1			-1	≤ 0
Production balance	-2.0	-1.7							≤ 0
Objective function			$-c_m$	$-c_m$	$-c_m$	$-c_w$	$-c_w$	$-c_w$	Maximize

Notes: LFM_t denotes male family labor by month; LFW_t denotes family labor of women by month. Their corresponding daily reservation wages are c_m and c_w. In the crop production activities $X1$ and $X2$, labor requirements are in person-days, and the monthly field tasks are as follows: April, plowing and planting; June, weeding; September, harvesting. The yields in the production balance are in tons per hectare. In this table, the labor hire activities are not complete because their entries in the labor constraints are not shown.

total costs, if c_w were sufficiently lower than c_m, it would be optimal to produce via $X2$ rather than $X1$, and in any case it might be optimal to assign female labor to the weeding tasks in June, so that $LFW6 > 0$ and $LFM6 = 0$ in the solution.

This brief discussion of input supplying activities shows that the model structures are flexible enough to handle many different specifications. Usually the question of the appropriate specification comes down to the extent of our empirical knowledge of the relevant economic behavior.

11.5 FOREIGN TRADE ACTIVITIES

Thus far, foreign trade activities have been discussed very little except to note that they require, at minimum, entries in the commodity balance rows and the objective function. Typically, exports are portrayed in sector models as facing either perfectly elastic demands, or demands that are perfectly elastic up to a bound that represents a quota in the importing country or some other market limitation. However, export demands may in fact be somewhat inelastic, and in that event the export market displays many of the characteristics of a domestic market, and it may be modeled much as another domestic market would be (Chapter 8). Pomareda and Simmons (1983) have built a model of Mexican vegetable production and exports that includes downward-sloping export demand functions in the U.S. market. Multiple foreign markets for the same product may be handled in the same way: all points on all demand functions (for the same product) have entries in a common supply-demand balance, and also in the objective function, but each market has its own set of demand variables and hence its own convex combination constraint.

Analogous treatments apply in the case of import supply functions, in the rare cases that they are not perfectly elastic. The applicable specification is that which is used for domestic factor supply functions (Chapter 9).

In a sector model, exports and imports are not linked by a balance of payments constraint, because it applies only to the economy as a whole. Similarly, the exchange rate is not a variable in a sector model, and all foreign prices can be converted to domestic currency before entering them into the model.

Regarding the exchange rate, a natural question that arises is whether to use the official exchange or a calculated shadow exchange rate for converting foreign prices. This is an important issue that arises in the context of other components of the model as well. To answer the question, it is necessary to review the purposes of the model. The models described in this text are, as noted previously, optimization models in the mathematical sense but simulation models in the economic sense. They attempt to simulate approximately how the decision makers of the sector would react to a given exogenous change. Thus, while the phrase "optimal solution" is used throughout the text, it means the solution that simulates behavior under the parameters of the

Table 11.8   Mini-Tableau for Foreign Trade Activities

	E	M	Y	RHS
Consumption level commodity balance	1	-1		≤ 0
Farm income row	$P_e^w(1 - t_e)e$		-1	$= 0$
Objective function	$P_e^w(1 - t_e)e$	$-P_m^w(1 + t_m)e$		Maximize
Export bound	1			$\leq \bar{E}$

Notes: E = exports, M = imports, Y = farm income
        P_e^w = FOB world price of exports
        P_m^w = CIF world price of imports
         e = exchange rate
        t_e = net export taxes (+) or subsidies (−)
       t_m = import tariffs
       $\bar{E}$ = upper limit on exports.

model. Since farmers do not react to a shadow exchange rate but rather to the official rate,[10] it is the latter which should be used for the model. Use of a shadow rate makes sense only if an experiment is being designed to explore the sector's potential reactions in the event that the shadow rate were made the official rate. Similar observations may be made regarding the use of shadow wages for hired labor and shadow prices for factors and products in general.

By the same reasoning, the model's specification needs to include tariffs, export taxes, and subsidies, or else the sector's policy environment is not being described completely (see Section 7.1). Any kind of tax or subsidy constitutes a modification to a price, and therefore it needs to enter the objective function. If there is an accounting row for farm income, then export prices, adjusted for taxes and subsidies, also enter that row, because they are part of the calculation of gross farm revenue from sales. However, there is an asymmetry in treatment here, for import prices do not enter the farm income row. Farmers do not pay the cost of imports. Of course, import prices influence farm-gate prices, and in the model this linkage occurs through incorporation of import prices in the objective function. For the case of horizontal export demand and import supply functions, Table 11.8 shows a typical specification of foreign trade activities for a single product. The farm income row is a purely accounting row (hence the exact equality), and it may be preferred to incorporate it into a report writing routine rather than into the model itself. In either event, the specification is the same.

The export bounds can be useful elements of the model even if demands appear to be truly infinitely elastic. First, the use of bounds, and the associated shadow prices, allows *ex post* computation of coefficients indicating comparative advantage, such as domestic resource cost ratios. Chapter 12 discusses this point. Second, by parameterizing the export bounds it is possible to explore the consequences for the sector of achieving greater export volumes. In reality, export sales almost always encounter marketing limitations of one kind or another at any moment in time. For imports the issue is somewhat different. In most countries, agricultural imports tend to respond rather quickly to shortages in domestic supply, and the restraint on imports, if any, comes in the form of policy intervention. It may be useful to include import bounds in the model, and vary them over different solutions, in order to measure the consequences of different policies toward imports, but otherwise import bounds usually are not included.

If foreign trade activities are important, some attention should be paid to the marketing costs for exports and imports. In Table 11.8, exports and imports enter the supply-demand balance at the level of the consumer rather than the producer. Marketing costs are roughly similar for exports and domestic products, and if the export entries were in the producer-level commodity balances, those costs would not be registered. If anything, export marketing costs may be higher, and if so the incremental costs should be included in the objective function and the farm income row in Table 11.8. The same reasoning applies to imports. If their total handling and marketing costs differ, on average, from those for domestic products, then a term ($\pm$) to reflect that difference would have to be added to the parameter $[-p_m^w(1 + t_m)e]$ in Table 11.8. In actuality, there are cases in which an imported product can serve some domestic markets more cheaply than domestic products can, and vice versa for other markets. Spatial disaggregation of markets in the model can help in situations like this, but otherwise some care should be taken in compiling average marketing costs for imports.

For cases of common market arrangements or other close trading relationships between countries, a sector model can be made multicountry. The MOCA model for Central America is an example (Cappi et al. 1978). The objective function in that model is the sum of producer and consumer surplus in all markets of all the concerned countries, and international trade activities look very much like interregional shipment activities within a country—they subtract a unit of supply from the commodity balance in the shipping country and add it to the corresponding commodity balance in the receiving country, at a cost to the objective function. Tariffs were added to the cost coefficients in the trading activities, and trade barriers were modeled as bounds on those activities.

11.6 LIVESTOCK AND CROPPING RELATIONSHIPS

In almost every country the livestock sector is an important part of agriculture and therefore the feedgrains sector is as well. Many models have been constructed for the livestock sector alone and many for the cropping sector alone, and a few for integrated livestock and cropping sectors. But even the models of individual sectors need some kind of treatment of the livestock-cropping linkages. There are cases in which cultivable land is suitable for either crops or livestock, so the possibility of reallocations of land forms one linkage. A more common linkage arises out of the possibility of allocating cropland to feedgrains or other crops. A third kind of linkage is observed mostly in middle- and lower-income developing countries, and that is the use of draft power for field operations, for farm transportation, and, in some cases, for pumping irrigation water. (Not long ago in Egypt, most of the irrigation water was pumped out of canals and onto fields via ancient water wheels powered by draft animals.)

The feedgrain linkage is the most complex one, and it may be handled in a variety of ways. Starting from the cropping sector, there are three basic approaches, listed in increasing order of generality: (1) simply specifying price-elastic demand functions for livestock feeds, allowing in some form for the cross-price effects (Chapter 9), (2) specifying an exogenous "national herd" of each species and the associated requirements for each type of feed or nutrient, and (3) making both the herd size and the technology of herd maintenance endogenous, in the stationary equilibrium approach described in Chapter 4.

In either approach 2 or 3 an issue is how to make the model simulate the variety of animal feeds that are used in reality, and to make it change the feed composition in response to relative price changes. Some models define the herd's feed requirements in terms of nutrients, usually calories, proteins, and total dry matter (TDM). Each feed has a known content of each nutrient that can be entered into the model. The feeding problem then becomes a kind of diet problem of cost minimization (implicitly) subject to the endogenous prices of the feed, and subject to other factors which may influence herd compostion and size. Table 11.9 illustrates this specification.

The approach of Table 11.9 ensures that the national herd will receive the requisite nutrients, and in an economical way. The problem is that it will not bring more than three different kinds of feed into the optimal solution, because there are at most three binding constraints for feeds (see the Appendix on the theory of linear programming). In reality the number of feed products

Table 11.9   Mini-Tableau for Livestock Nutrient Requirements

	Corn	Sorghum	Oats	Soybeans	Cattle	Sheep	RHS
Commodity balances							
Corn	1						≤ 0
Sorghum		1					≤ 0
Oats			1				≤ 0
Soybeans				1			≤ 0
Nutrient balances							
Calories	$-n_{11}$	$-n_{12}$	$-n_{13}$	$-n_{14}$	$+r_{11}$	$+r_{12}$	≤ 0
Proteins	$-n_{21}$	$-n_{22}$	$-n_{23}$	$-n_{24}$	$+r_{21}$	$+r_{22}$	≤ 0
TDM	$-n_{31}$	$-n_{32}$	$-n_{33}$	$-n_{34}$	$+r_{31}$	$+r_{32}$	≤ 0

Note: The n_{ij} are the unit nutrient contents of each feed; the r_{ij} are the nutrient requirements.

may be very large, as witnessed by the following partial list:

> Pasture hay (possibly more than one kind)
> Alfalfa
> Barley
> Sorghum
> Corn
> Oats
> Wheat
> Bran
> Straw from the above grains and rice
> Soybean meal
> Cottonseed cake and oil
> Sesame cake and oil
> Safflower and sunflower cake and oil
> Cow vetch
> Leaves and stalks of pulses
> Sugar beet leaves
> Sugarbeet paste
> Molasses

(The economic problem is complicated by the fact that several of these feeds are by-products.)

The only way to induce the model to include a greater variety of feeds in the solution is to define the different feed mixtures (or rations) that are commonly used and to define a different herd maintenance activity for each mixture. An illustration is found in the recent model for Turkey of Norton and Gencaga (1985). They define 33 alternative rations for cattle, sheep, goats, poultry, and horses, donkeys, and mules. Each ration is a vector of annual coefficients (in metric tons) of inputs of 2 to 6 feeds. Examples are as follows, from that study:

Ration 1

Pasture hay	0.730
Barley	0.183
Bran	0.183
Oilseed cake	0.073
Straw	0.730

Ration 2

Sugar beet paste	1.825
Barley	0.183
Pulse by-products	0.365
Oilseed cake	0.183
Molasses	0.183
Straw	0.730

Ration 4
  Alfalfa   0.365
  Barley   0.365
  Oilseed cake   0.183
  Straw   1.460
Ration 31
  Oilseed cake   0.0073
  Corn   0.00365

The first three rations listed here are more suitable for one cow (per year) and the last one for a chicken. Accordingly, 33 alternative ways of maintaining the five groups of animals were defined, each alternative utilizing one of the unique rations. The maintenance vectors also differed in other inputs and in productivity, so a typical solution had ten or more different vectors, that is, ten or more different rations. This approach ensured diversity and flexibility in the feed composition. While the example concerns a model of the stationary equilibrium type, it can be adapted as well to multiperiod programming models.

11.7 DATA RECONCILIATION AND MODEL VALIDATION

A programming model usually has a large number of equations and variables, often in the hundreds and sometimes in the thousands, so it is not always obvious how the model can be validated. The profession has not yet reached a consensus on procedures for validating a sector programming model. Nevertheless validation tests can and should be carried out for each applied model, and they are not necessarily complicated or time consuming.

Many of the difficulties in validating a model arise from the data it is being validated against. In the first place, in most countries data corresponding to some of the programming model's variables simply do not exist. A prime example is agricultural employment, as a measure of man-days or man-months actually worked on the farm. And even total net farm income for, say, the cropping sector is not known in most countries. In the second place, many of the data series are not very reliable and sometimes are mutually inconsistent. These difficulties tend to be greater in developing countries and in particular they affect time series on total production by product, and estimates of product prices.

Data difficulties do not necessarily imply that models should not be built. After all, as a colleague has observed, it is better to use good logic (embodied in the model) for policy analysis than to compound the problem of poor data with poor logic! Also, the attempt to construct a model can help give impetus and priorities to data collection efforts. But the frequency of problems with data does suggest that careful reconciliation of data must precede validation of the model, to the extent possible.

There are four principal dimensions in which consistency is required in the data set:

- The product-product dimension
- The product-input dimension
- The product-price dimension
- The technological coefficients dimension

The product-product dimension refers to the supply-demand balances, taking into account all sources of supply, including imports, and all sources of demand, including industrial uses, livestock feed uses, and wastage. The UN Food and Agriculture Organization (FAO) has taken a leading role on a world-wide basis in reconciling data on supply and demand, through their Supply Utilization Accounts for each country. However, those accounts do not cover all products, and the FAO's reconciled production figures may differ from those which the national agricultural analysts prefer to use, so the reconciliation may have to be done independently. The reconciliation process can be facilitated by the presence of household budget data on per capita consumption levels of food products. In bringing the supply and demand estimates into mutual consistency, it may be necessary to take into account unusual amounts of inventory accumulation or decumulation. One way of handling the inventory problem is to use a three-year average of yields for the "base year," thus creating a synthetic base year as regards production. Consumption levels tend to be more stable than production levels, with the variations in production being taken up by changes in inventories.

The product-input dimension introduces technical coefficients for production into the reconciliation process. The most basic example concerns land use. The sum over all crops of production divided by yield should be equal to the reported total cultivated area. This is a reconciliation on the supply side of production, yields, and cultivated area. In some situations it may be appropriate to carry it out by region as well as nationally. Another example would be the reconciliation of area cultivated by crop, fertilizer input coefficients, and reported total fertilizer use. The needed equality may be written

$$\sum_j \sum_h a_{fjh} X_{jh} = F \qquad (11.8)$$

where a_{fjh} = the fertilizer input coefficient for product j, in farm class h
   X_{jh} = the total area sown in product j in farm class h
   F = total fertilizer used[11]

If desired, the reconciliation can be performed by type of fertilizer product (urea, superphosphates, etc.) or by fertilizer nutrient (nitrogen, phosphorus, and potassium).

The product-price dimension refers to costs of production vs. market prices, and the associated quantities produced and sold. If processing and marketing costs are taken into account, and if markets are competitive, then marginal cost should be equal to price. An inconsistency may be caused by three kinds of error:

- An error in the calculated marginal cost of production
- An error in the reported price
- An error in the reported quantities produced and sold

An error in the quantity estimates can cause an inconsistency in the price-cost relationship if the price or cost estimate were based in part on quantities. For example, in evaluating shaky data from a survey of rural market prices, the compiler of statistics may be influenced by the fact that a bumper crop has been harvested, and hence he or she may choose a price in the lower end of the range of raw estimates.

Of course there are no official statistics on the marginal costs of production, but the analyst can (and should) compute them from the vectors of production coefficients and the data on input prices. Again, estimates of quantities produced may effect the calculation. *Ceteris paribus*, larger harvests of a given crop may mean its cultivation was extended into more marginal areas, as would be expected under a rising supply curve. Hence marginal costs would be calculated on the basis of the less efficient production vectors.

In either of these cases, reconciliation of the price and cost estimates is achieved by adjustment of the quantity estimates, with prices and costs moving in reaction to the quantity change, according to the demand and supply functions, respectively. Figure 11.3 shows the initial inconsistency (quantity produced and quantity sold both equal to 1000; marginal cost equal to 100; price equal to 80), and the reconciliation (lower quantities; lower marginal cost; higher price).

Other possible procedures for data reconciliation in the product-price dimension include (1) adjusting the price estimate alone, (2) adjusting the coefficients of the production vector; and (3) adjusting the estimates of input prices. The step(s) taken depend upon the particular situation and the judgment of the specialists who are involved.

The final dimension of data reconciliation involves the technology coefficients of production. The production set needs to be consistent in a technological sense. For example, if one vector has more fertilization than another, *ceteris paribus* it should have a higher yield. Also, because of the higher yield it should have a higher labor input. Another example concerns planting dates. The vector for the later planting date also should have some field tasks

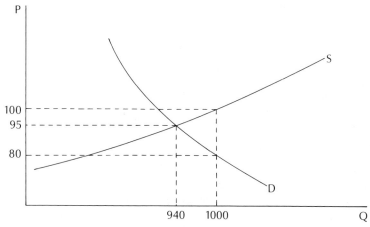

Figure 11.3 Data reconciliation in the product-price dimension.

occurring later, and this difference should be reflected in the calendar of inputs. It is a bit tedious to check the production vectors for problems of this sort, but it is worthwhile to do so, for it is surprising how often inconsistencies inadvertently creep in.

A consistent data set is of course not necessarily an accurate data set, but logical consistency is indispensable if the data are to be used. Also, the judgments that influence the data set during the reconciliation process may be as valid as, or more valid than, the raw quantitative estimates. Numerical data constitute much of our "picture of the world" in economic analysis and even without models, policy analysts and decision makers are accustomed to thinking in terms of the values of key parameters, that is, in terms of simplified models.

Once the data have been made consistent, the next step is to eliminate coding errors (debug the model). It is not uncommon for the first one or several solutions to be infeasible, owing to an inadvertent error in the RHS, an error in the sign of an equation, or, more usually, coding errors in the names of the rows and columns. Use of matrix generator programs reduces the incidence of these kinds of errors, but it does not eliminate them.

Validation of the model is a process that leads to (1) a numerical report of the model's fidelity to the historical data set, (2) improvements of the model as a consequence of imperfect validation, (3) a qualitative judgment on how reliable the model is for its stated purposes, and (4) a conclusion (preferably explicit) for the kinds of uses that it should not be used for. Validation begins with a series of comparisons of model results with the reported actual values of the variables. Most often, simple comparisons are made and measures of deviations are calculated, and production variables are given the most emphasis. (Some of the outcomes of those comparisons are discussed below.) However, more complete tests are possible and have been done. The following six tests are useful:

1 The capacity test
2 The marginal cost test
3 The land rental test
4 Tests on levels of input use
5 Production tests
6 Price tests

These tests are discussed in order.

The capacity test was first proposed and used by Kutcher (1972, 1983). It is a very basic test and is perhaps not as important as some of the others, but if there are any doubts about whether the model would pass the test, then it should be imposed. It consists of verifying whether the constraints of the model allow at least the observed output levels for all products. As a by-product, the test yields estimates of the amount of excess productive capacity in the model's structure. It is implemented by adding constraints that require the model to sell (or sell plus retain for home consumption, in the event that the latter option is included) at least as much as the observed base-year output of each product. Kutcher recommends conducting the test under fixed-price selling activities, but in fact it can be conducted under downward-sloping demand functions as well. The specification of the objective function is irrelevant, for the selling constraints will reveal if the model's capacity is sufficient. An insufficiency of capacity will result in an infeasible solution. Excess capacity will show up as slack in the selling constraints.

The marginal cost test also was proposed by Kutcher (1972, 1983). It is designed to compare price with marginal cost for all outputs, in a context where marginal costs include the implicit opportunity costs of fixed resources and also depend on which technology vectors are in the solution, by farm class. To carry out this test, all demand (selling) activities are deleted from the model, and the production of each commodity is constrained to be at least as great as in the base period. The objective function is then re-defined to be the minimization of the total costs of production. In the corresponding solution, the shadow prices on the minimum production constraints are the desired marginal costs of production.

When the results of the test are interpreted, it should be noted that cases in which the marginal cost is significantly less than price usually are caused by one of three factors: (1) omission of some important element of the cost structure, such as specialized management skills in growing high-value vegetables; (2) failure to reflect noncompetitive market forms, such as agreements to restrict production on the part of producers' associations; or (3) inadequate specification of the crops' riskiness and farmers' risk aversion. To capture this last factor adequately, the total costs in the objective function should include the risk cost, à la MOTAD, as explained in Chapters 5 and 10. Alternatively, if actuarially fair crop insurance is in effect, for this test the risk specification can be replaced by the insurance premiums.[12]

The land rental test consists of comparing the dual solution's land rents with actual annual rents. If the primal model contains an explicit rent coefficient for land, then the dual rent must be added to the primal rent before the comparison is made. The dual rent is the shadow price on the land constraints; the annual rent is the sum of seasonal rents. This test was first carried out by Bassoco et al. (1973, p. 412). They converted the model's time streams of uniform land rents to purchase prices, at alternative discount rates close to the interest rates on the informal credit market. The comparison was then made with actual purchase prices for land . Since land is one of the most basic inputs to agricultural production, the land rental test is a good indication of the model's accuracy in valuing agricultural production and its associated inputs. In turn, this means that it is a test of the accuracy of the model's structure for transforming inputs into outputs.

The tests on levels of input use consist of comparing the model's outcomes with actual input use. The advantage of these tests is that there usually are a few inputs for which base-year observations are fairly reliable, such as fertilizer, other agrochemicals, and irrigation in special irrigation districts. Poor results on the input tests can mean problems with the input coefficients, but they also can mean problems with output levels, and therefore the tests on input levels should be evaluated jointly with the tests on production levels.

Production is the variable most commonly used in validation tests, and for a number of agricultural models there are reported validation results for it. Typically, there is considerable variation over products in the closeness of the fit to the historical data, and the model builder may be willing to accept greater deviations in minor products if the predictions are good for the major products. There is no consensus on the statistic to be used in evaluating the fit, but in most cases simple measures such as the mean absolute deviation (MAD) or the percentage absolute deviation (PAD) have been used. (The MAD also is called the mean absolute error.) The Theil index has been suggested as well.[13]

Table 11.10 shows the production PADs for a sample of models. There does not exist a threshold value of the PAD which clearly determines acceptance or rejection of the model. On the basis of current practice as reflected in Table 11.10 perhaps the following rough guidelines can be given: a PAD below 10% is good, a PAD of 5% would be exceptional, and a PAD of 15% or more indicates the model may need improvement before it can be used.

Production tests may be carried out also within multiple regions of a sector, although normally the fit is better at the aggregate level. Within a sector model, at the level of a region (or farm class) the tendency is toward overspecialization in the dominant crops, although the inclusion of risk-averse behavior in the model specification greatly reduces that tendency.

The price test is identical to the production test except that it is performed on product prices. Recall (Chapter 8) that the product prices are the shadow prices on the commodity balance constraints. If there are separate

Table 11.10   Validation Measures for Agricultural Sector Models

Model name	Country	References	Concept	PAD
CHAC	Mexico	Bassoco and Norton (1983)	Production	13.4%
MAAGAP	Philippines	Kunkel et al. (1978)	Acreage	9.1%
TASM	Turkey	Le-Si, Scandizzo, and Kasnakoglu (1982)	Production	7.2%
—	N.E. Brazil	Kutcher and Scandizzo (1981)	Production	8.2%
	Costa Rica			7.0%
	El Salvador			12.0%
MOCA	Guatemala	Cappi et al. (1978)	Production	7.1%
	Honduras			9.3%
	Nicaragua			8.7%
TOLLAN	Region of Mexico	Howell (1983)	Acreage	13.9%

balances at the producer level and the consumer level, then the corresponding shadow prices indicate producer and consumer prices, respectively. Consumer prices also may be calculated from the primal solution *ex post* by applying the demand functions to the quantities sold. In carrying out the price test, it should be borne in mind that the price deviations from reality are, in most cases, greater than the quantity deviations. This result occurs because most of the price elasticities of demand are less than unity in absolute value.

Through validating the model, information is obtained about its structure, and one of the main questions is what to do with that information. While judgments on the model's adequacy must be made, it also is important to continue to improve the model. Building an applied model is a process, and the most successful models evolve through time to take into account new findings. There never is a definitive version, but rather at any moment in time the model represents a kind of orderly data bank that reflects both the strengths and limitations of the available quantitative information.

With these considerations in mind the validation tests can be used to indicate areas where the model most needs improvement, and then further information can be sought in those areas. As in the case of data reconcillation, it may not be obvious which parameters are the cause of a poor fit. Overproduction of a crop may be caused by (1) overestimates of yields, (2) underestimates of input requirements, (3) underestimates of input prices, (4) yield and input errors for competing crops, (5) misspecification of the market forms or farmer decision rules, or (6) overestimates of resource availability. The last factor, however, is likely to be the cause only if there is a systematic overstatement of production across all products. Each of these factors may be worth investigating.

An important rule in the process of validating and improving the model is to document carefully each step and the reasons behind it. Arbitrary adjustments in parameter values, with the aim of improving the model's fit, are to be strictly avoided.[14] The initial version of the model has to be documented, if nothing else in carefully labeled computer listings, and then each subsequent change should be recorded (with a date!) and the reason for the change. It is essential that the model-building team impose this kind of discipline on themselves, for no one else can. It is an unfortunate fact that there are models whose coefficients have become a mishmash of adjusted values with no clear justification other than a better fit. It is far preferable to have an unsatisfactory fit, but a clear documentation of the model's development, rather than a better fit but arbitrary parameter values. Among other things, a model with arbitrary adjustments does not provide a basis for future work and extensions. This aspect of the work is stressed because it is an area where slips frequently occur with large models, if only because the model builders are under time pressure. The rules for altering the model after the initial validation attempt should be (1) to change the model only if further investigation yields new information, and (2) to document all changes. If done in this spirit, the validation process can lead to a better model. In all respects, the more a model's origins and limitations are documented, the more credible it becomes from a viewpoint of scientific inquiry, and the greater its potential for usefulness.

As noted earlier, the model builders also need to make a list of topics for which the model cannot be used. In the static equilibrium models, a common example concerns adjustment paths over time. In the comparative statics mode, the model can indicate a new equilibrium situation toward which the sector is likely to move, but it cannot indicate the time or path required to make that move. Likewise, a model that has fixed input-output ratios for fertilizer for each crop—that is, no fertilizer response functions—cannot be used for experiments concerning variations in fertilizer prices.

Some writers (e.g., Paris 1981) have raised the issue of the existence of alternative, near-optimal solutions, or degeneracy in the terminology of mathematical programming. This always is a concern in programming models, but in the experience of the authors it can be very much diminished by improving the economic specification of the model. For example, in a sector model with no risk specification and fixed-price demand functions, the solution is apt to set some products equal to zero and to exaggerate the production of others. However, once risk and downward-sloping demand functions are introduced, that is, the specification is made more complete, the possibilities of such solutions are substantially reduced and even reasonable perturbations of parameter values are not likely to induce them.

An example also can be given of the opposite kind, where the specification of a subset of the model is certain to bring about degeneracy and hence arbitrariness in the selection of vectors in the optimal basis. In one of the present authors' modeling efforts, two forms of agricultural credit were specified, institutional and noninstitutional. The cost of the former was lower but it also faced a restrictive bound. The amount of institutional credit was sufficient to cover only about 20% of total credit needs. The model contained five farm classes, but their technologies of production did not differ as regards the productivity of credit, and the model contained no rules for allocating credit over types of farms. Hence in the solution the institutional credit was allocated arbitrarily over the farm classes, and it tended to be assigned all to one class. This example illustrates well the problem of degeneracy, but it also illustrates the fact that the specification can cause (and cure) degeneracy.

11.8 DATA ISSUES

Data requirements have been discussed in passing throughout the book, so here we offer a brief summary. As regards data, the distinguishing feature of agricultural sector models is that they are based largely on cross-section data rather than on time series. And with the exception of recursive programming models (see Chapter 12), they are validated against a single base year rather than against a time series. The production vectors are compiled from cross-sectional data on farm budgets, and the base-year data set on prices and quantities is another kind of cross section. Time series are needed, however, for the risk submatrix, and in many cases this is one of the more difficult data requirements to fulfill. When projections (comparative statics solutions) are made, it is helpful to have available a time series on yield growth rates and other parameters in order to be able to define the projections.

In establishing the resource endowments, it is necessary to subtract the resources dedicated to production activities which are excluded from the model, such as minor crops. For land and irrigation supplies, usually estimates are available of the amount used by crop. For labor involved in minor crops, the information is more difficult to obtain. Two approaches have been used. One is to make the best estimates possible of the labor inputs to these crops, with the aid of field experts, and then subtract that labor from the endowments of family labor. The effects of errors on the model's structure are likely to be small, because those crops use a small proportion of the sector's total resources. The other approach is to form an aggregate vector for all other crops (called "garden vegetables" or "other crops") and include it in the production set. This also is a reasonable practical option, provided that acceptable estimates can be made of the weighted average price for other crops and of the input/output coefficients.

Some family labor may be involved in on-farm nonagricultural activities or local off-farm activities. Those demands for labor may be reflected in the reservation wage. It may be appropriate to add a further specification in the form of a wage earning activity for the nonagricultural occupations. In that case, an upper bound is needed to reflect the limited (short-run) opportunities for that kind of work. The additional labor activities then may cause the shadow wage for family labor to rise above the reservation wage in some seasons.

The demand parameters usually are among the more difficult to obtain or estimate. The weakness of time series data makes estimates via that route problematical. Usually only income elasticities can be estimated and price elasticities have to be obtained via other means. For the MOCA model (Cappi et al., 1978), own-price and cross-price elasticities were obtained from previously estimated income elasticities and application of the Frisch procedure (1959). A necessary intermediate step was calculation of Frisch's money flexibility parameter by use of internationally estimated equations from other studies (de Janvry et al., 1972; Lluch and Williams 1973). The Frisch equations are as follows, for any pair of goods i, k:

$$e_{ii} = -E_i\left(\alpha_i - \frac{1 - \alpha_i E_i}{w}\right) \qquad (11.9)$$

$$e_{ik} = -E_i\alpha_k\left(1 + \frac{E_k}{w}\right) \qquad (11.10)$$

where e_{ii}, e_{ik} = own- and cross-price elasticities, respectively
  E_i, E_k = income elasticities of demand
  α_i, α_k = budget shares in consumption
  w = money flexibility coefficient

Equations (11.9) and (11.10) will generate a complete matrix of own- and cross-price elasticities. If u is the marginal utility of money (income),

$$u = \frac{\partial U}{\partial Y} \qquad (11.11)$$

then w is defined as

$$w = \frac{\partial u}{\partial Y}\frac{Y}{u} \qquad (11.12)$$

or the elasticity of the marginal utility of money, with respect to changes in money. See the studies cited above for further discussion.

This procedure is appealing but it does have theoretical and practical limitations. In theory, the Frisch equations require "want independence" in the consumers' utility function; that is, that the utility obtained from the consumption of one good is independent of the quantity consumed of other goods. The more disaggregated the analysis, the less likely it is that this assumption holds. For example, it may not hold for coffee and sugar, or even for corn and beans or chili peppers. The practical limitation is that the own-price elasticities so derived appear to be quite low in absolute value, and so considerable weight is placed on the role of the cross elasticities.

Estimation of demand systems also has been attempted on the basis of cross-sectional surveys about household income and expenditures, with the extended linear expenditure system (Powell 1966, Lluch et al. 1977). While this approach appears to give useful estimates for relatively aggregate (single-digit) commodity groups, it sometimes breaks down as the commodities become more disaggregated—the incidence of incorrect signs on the parameters increases noticeably. An interesting example of estimating demand system via the linear expenditure system is given by Sasaki (1982) for Japan. Sasaki estimates complete matrices of demand coefficients for 21 commodities, ten of which are agricultural. Unfortunately, some of the key parameters appear to be unstable, varying with the period over which sample means were calculated. For example, the income elasticity for rice is $+0.328$ when 1951–1960 means are used and -1.231 when 1961–1970 means are used. Similarly, the income elasticity for other cereals is -1.160 for 1951–1960 and $+0.382$ for 1961–1970. And the signs on the price elasticities switch as well.

The model builder is usually left with more traditional approaches: estimation of single equation demand functions or of subsystems of demand functions for agricultural commodities (Brandow 1961, George and King 1971). Often elasticities are "borrowed" from studies of other countries. There is no particular defense of this bit of pragmatism, but two points may be made in its favor. One is that demand elasticities do not vary greatly over countries for principal products or product groups (grains, oilseeds, legumes, vegetables, etc.). The other is that sector models do not appear to be very sensitive to moderate variations in price elasticities of demand. They are much more sensitive to variations in wage rates and export and import prices.

As of this writing, the model-building community is awaiting a breakthrough that will yield better information on demand elasticities or alternative kinds of demand structures.

Two other common parameters that present difficulties in estimation are the risk aversion parameter (Φ) and the reservation wage for family labor. As discussed in Chapter 10, there are methods for estimating Φ (Dillon and Scandizzo, 1978), but they are time consuming. An alternative approach is to vary the value of Φ over alternative solutions and to calculate *ex post* which value leads to the best fit of cropping patterns (see, e.g., Hazell et al. 1983). The same procedure is applicable for the reservation wage, and ideally it should be parametrically varied jointly with Φ. In principle, as noted above, estimation of production functions that distinguish family and hired labor would yield estimates of the marginal productivities of the two kinds of labor and hence give a basis for setting the reservation wage.

Fortunately, the vast majority of the parameters in the model are relatively easy to quantify, and if necessary field visits or small surveys can be arranged to check their values. A listing of the standard kinds of data needed for a typical model would include the following items:

1 Input/output coefficients for production by product, technology, region, and farm type
2 Resource endowments

3 Base-period quantities produced and marketed
4 Quantities and prices, and tariffs, taxes, and subsidies, for imports and exports
5 Input prices
6 Processing and marketing margins and physical input/output coefficients for processing and marketing
7 Demand elasticities
8 A time series on price and quantity by product and region, for the risk matrix
9 The risk aversion parameter

The first six categories of data often are available from existing studies, and sometimes some of the items in categories 7 and 8 are also.

11.9 MODEL MANAGEMENT

Model management embraces the organization of the work and the institutional linkages, the documentation of the model, and its computer management. Building an applied model does not require a large team, nor does it necessarily require a long period of time. In the proper setting, comprehensive sector models have been constructed in as little as three months (Norton and Gencaga 1985), but four to six months might be a more reasonable expectation if secondary data sources can be used. Some published sector models have taken much longer, but that is because they were part of a more broadly oriented research project, or because they were done on a part-time basis, or because new surveys for data collection were carried out as the first phase of the study. A farm-level or regional model can be developed more quickly than a sector model can, unless the model presents difficult research issues.

The main skills required on a sector model team are (1) economic model building, preferably with some experience in policy-related issues; (2) agricultural economics, with a detailed understanding of agriculture in the country being modeled; and (3) computer management of models. In several cases, these skills have been embodied in three individuals, and the team has been complemented by some research assistance. While the team itself can be small, working communication is required with other specialists, chiefly field experts who are familiar with production conditions and costs, and also a "policy maker" or person who is in a position to review the model's results from the viewpoint of economic policy.

In structuring the work flow with an applied model, it should be borne in mind that the sponsors of the effort are likely to lose interest if they have to wait one to two years for the first results. This is especially true if sponsors are in decision-making positions. There are ways to schedule the work so that early outputs can be provided. For example, in building a sector model it is possible to use farm-level and regional components before the complete model is finished. It also is possible to distribute the production coefficients themselves, along with estimates of input prices (including the land rental and the implicit wage for family labor), as a contribution to discussions about the cost of production by product and farm type. In the same spirit, reconciled data sets for the base year, in the product-product dimension and otherwise, are useful early outputs of the model-building process.

Documentation of the model includes not only technical reports on the model's structure and applied reports on its results, but also reports on the data inputs and the changes in the model that are made over time. A convenient way to organize the working documentation is to maintain a loose-leaf binder with sections for nomenclature and units, parameter values and data sources, mini-tableaus on special aspects of the model, and decisions on changes in structure or data. An applied model can have a fairly long lifetime and different people can be involved in it at various stages, so documentation of this type helps provide continuity to the work. It is helpful to date all the pages in the binder.

On a conceptual level, the two main tools for ensuring the integrity of the model structure while it is being developed are tableaus and algebraic statements. Both are used extensively in this book, as they are complementary ways of viewing the model. Tableaus organize the information of the model in reasonably self-contained blocks, with emphasis on the columns. The algebraic treatments go equation by equation and therefore emphasize the rows. To visualize some aspects of the model, such as supply-demand balances, algebra is more convenient. Tableaus are better for other aspects, such as technological variations in production and input supplying activities.

As discussed in Chapter 6, the coefficients are entered into the computer by columns. A statement of the model by equations can be transformed into columns in computer-readable format by means of a matrix generator program. As well as performing this task, a matrix generator also reduces substantially the number of data entries that must be keypunched and, accordingly, reduces the incidence of error in generating the model in the computer. It can be a very helpful device in managing a model. Perhaps the best example of matrix generators for economic models is the sophisticated GAMS[15] package developed recently in the World Bank.

In the absence of a full generator, or someone with the time and skills to write one, either a partial generator can be written quickly or the model can be entered manually into the computer. A partial generator can be quite useful, for example, to speed up the tedious calculations of demand coefficients by segment in the case of linear models. While entering coefficients manually may seem like a medieval procedure, it does have some positive points. The more the modeler reviews the data, the more he or she learns about them and the greater the chances of eliminating inconsistencies or improving the model in other ways. Procedures that are too automated serve to separate the modeler from the data and weaken his or her understanding of them. In the last analysis, a model is a data set, and the process of coding or punching the numbers and names of the model always brings to mind relationships to explore further and ways to improve the model. Probably the ideal procedure for moving the data into the computer would be to use a good matrix generator but then to spend considerable time reviewing the column listing (BCDOUT in IBM lingo) created by the computer and organizing the columns into a series of tableaus. The tableaus can then be used in reviewing the model with other specialists.

If multiple uses of the model are planned, another very helpful tool is a report generator. This tool creates computer-generated tables that are much easier to analyze than the raw output of the solution algorithm. While there are some advantages in handling the data inputs to the computer manually, there are no benefits whatever in manually multiplying, dividing, adding, and subtracting the model's results! Inevitably it will be necessary to go back to the raw output and pull out the odd result that is not contained in the generated tables, but still a standard set of tables can be quite helpful.

Styles of model management will vary with individuals and with models, but the observations in this section suggest that it is an important subject for a successful model-building project, and accordingly it merits some thought at the beginning of the exercise.

NOTES

1 An exception to this rule is the MOCA model for Central America, which contains farm size distinctions for each country but not regions within countries. See Cappi et al. (1978).

2 An exception here is the TIGER model for the Muda River Basin of Malaysia, which is a monoculture rice zone. See Bell, Hazell, and Slade, 1982.

3 The model builder may prefer in some instances to specify processing and marketing at a more local level.

4 The term "local" is understood as embracing all subregional distinctions, such as districts, farm size classes, zones based on soils, etc. In some applications, there is not much spatial disaggregation, and the regional level is also the local level.

5 From the beginning, the nomenclature for CHAC has been a mixture of Spanish and English abbreviations. The Honduran model (García, 1984) is all in Spanish.

6 The initial values used to construct the wheat demand function were: flour consumption, 5250 thousand tons; flour price, 170 dollars/ton; price elasticity of demand for flour, -0.3. The reader may wish to verify that the procedures of Chapter 8, when applied to these initial values, yield the coefficients in the demand columns of Table 11.1.

7 In using this procedure for developing parts of the production side of the model, provision would have to be made for distributing the labor and machinery inputs over seasons. The seasonal pattern of labor and draft animals in the original vector X_0 might given some guide, but supplementary information may be needed in this regard.

8 Sometimes the input supply functions are introduced after the first version of the model is developed, and in such cases the prior separation of input supplies from production greatly facilitates the work of model revision.

9 A common practice is to express physical units in, say, 60 hp tractor equivalents.

10   If a parallel market in foreign exchange is present, adjustments may have to be made to take that market into account.

11   In most cases, the fertilizer data will refer to the amount sold to farmers, but that amount is not likely to differ much from the fertilizer used, as there is little interyear on-farm storage of fertilizer.

12   Using the insurance premiums leaves out the covariance side of risk, which can be important in determining cropping patterns and therefore opportunity costs of resources.

13   The Theil index is

$$\frac{\left[\frac{1}{n}\sum_{i}(\hat{X}_i - X_i)\right]^{1/2}}{\left(\left[\frac{1}{n}\sum_{i}(\hat{X}_i)^2\right]^{1/2} + \left[\frac{1}{n}\sum_{i}(X_i)^2\right]^{1/2}\right)}$$

where X_i is the observed value and $\hat{X}_i$ is the simulated value.

14   The same injunction applies to bounding production variables to force them to be equal to the base-year values.

15   GAMS stands for Generalized Algebraic Modeling System.

Part Three

Applications and Extensions for Policy Analysis

Chapter 12

Methods of Policy Analysis

12.1 POLICY INSTRUMENTS AND GOALS IN SECTOR MODELS

This chapter, and the one following, discuss ways in which programming models can be applied to questions of economic policy for agriculture. The emphasis is on sector-wide models, for it is at the sector level that most policy issues arise, but references also are made to the use of farm models and regional models where appropriate. Examples are given of applications made with existing models, and especially for Mexico, Turkey, Egypt, Peru, and Central America. To introduce those examples, some background information is provided on the key models used. The examples cover static and comparative statics analysis, and they include issues of pricing policy, evaluation of investment projects, dynamic analysis, and, in Chapter 13, analysis of public risk management policies.

It is not possible to make hard and fast rules for policy analysis; there is a bit of art to it. The main difficulty is in translating policy concerns, which may be rather broad, into specific analytic questions that can be addressed by the model. Sometimes, of course, that cannot be done, and even when it can the model analysis may deal with only a part of the policy concerns. Nevertheless, the model can provide relevant information for the decision process which could not be obtained otherwise, and this chapter suggests, with the aid of examples, some of the circumstances in which that is possible. We also discuss how to set up the appropriate model experiments needed to obtain the relevant solutions.

In Chapter 7 it was pointed out that the policy problem is inherently a two-level planning problem in its mathematical structure. The two-level planning problem is difficult to solve, so most of this chapter deals with the more practical one-level approach of simulating the sector's response to possible policy changes, that is, using the positive model rather than a normative model. However, in Section 12.9 we provide a feasible way of handling the two-level planning problem under some circumstances.

Given that the positive model is to be used, the objective function will typically be the sum of producer and consumer surplus. Policy goals will not appear explicitly in the objective function. They are variables in the model, or simple transforms of model variables which can be calculated *ex post* by hand or via a report generator. After a "base solution" is obtained, the essential procedure is to alter the model in a way that reflects a new policy, or new values of policy instruments, and then to solve the model again, recording the new values of the goal variables. By proceeding in this manner through a series of policy changes, a table can be built up that shows the relationship between policy options and their effects on different goals. (Such a table is discussed more fully in Section 12.6 below.)

The agricultural sector frequently is expected to fulfill multiple, and conflicting, roles. Some common examples are creating more employment, earning foreign exchange, helping to make (or keep) the country self-sufficient in food, increasing farm incomes, and keeping food prices low to consumers. Since these goals are not always mutually consistent, the analyst can be constructive by showing just which goals are advanced by particular policies, and which are not. It is not realistic to expect a policy maker to be able to quantify the policy preferences ("policy weights") among goals in advance, but by showing the multiple consequences of each policy with the aid of a model, the decision process can be facilitated.

Policy variables are represented in the model's structure by coefficients in the matrix, the right-hand side, and/or the objective function. Thus a policy variable is fixed in value for a given solution. One example would be the endowment of irrigated land, which is represented by the right-hand side coefficient in the constraint on the availability of irrigated land. More investment in irrigation would be reflected in an increase in that coefficient's value (or those coefficients' values, in the case of seasonal or monthly constraints).

Another example is the price of an input, such as irrigation water or fertilizer. A change in the pricing policy for irrigation would be reflected in a change in the coefficient c in Table 11.5. At the macroeconomic level, a change in exchange rate policy would be reflected in a change in the value of the coefficient e which appears in three places in Table 11.8. Successful introduction of new technologies of production can be modeled by adding new column vectors of production coefficients with, for example, new values of the index t in Table 7.1. A program that leads to reduction of marketing and storage costs can be represented by reducing the absolute value of the coefficients Δ_{jr} in Table 7.3.

Many of the policy-related experiments with a programming model are carried out by making changes of this kind and solving the model again. Usually it is preferable to make only one change at a time, and then obtain a new solution before making further changes. This permits identification of the effects of each individual policy change. However, occasionally it is useful to make several changes before a new solution is obtained, when it is desired to simulate the effects of a package of policies. The joint effect of several policy changes is likely to be different than the sum of effects of individual changes, owing to interaction terms and to the inherent nonlinearity of the supply response functions and of other aspects of the model's structure.

Clearly this procedure involves prior specification of policy changes which may be considered desirable and reasonable by at least some persons in policy making positions. Thus the model work requires close coordination with decision makers, or with someone representing them. Simulation of the consequences of prespecified new policies may not seem as elegant as an attempt to derive an "optimal policy," but the latter is fraught with difficulties. First, there are the aforementioned computational difficulties associated with multilevel solutions. Second, notwithstanding the concept of Pareto optimality, opinions regarding what is optimal in an economic sense (as opposed to a mathematical sense) will differ from person to person. Some individuals may prefer a package of policies that generates more employment, others may prefer to emphasize foreign exchange earnings, and so forth. By simulating the multiple consequences of policy changes, the analyst can provide an objective basis on which these preferences can be debated.

In carrying out such procedures for policy analysis, it is important that goal variables *not* be entered into the model's objective function, and that their levels not be constrained. To include goal variables in the objective function would be to override its simulating (positive) role. The model's solution no longer would have a market-clearing character, and its interpretation would be unclear. The same comments apply to constraining the levels of goal variables. At the margin, constraints dominate the solution; only after they are met does the objective function have scope for improvement.

As discussed in Chapter 7, when the model includes farm-level output and input choices the inclusion of goal variables in the objective function is equivalent to simulating the institutional framework of centralized planning, in which cropping decisions are made by government fiat. The same interpretation would apply to placing a constraint on the level of goal variables. Therefore such procedures are inappropriate for analysis of market economies and mixed economies. However, maximizing a goal variable directly can serve one analytic purpose, and that is to find the frontier, or maximum level of the goal that is conceivably attainable.

But even this frontier may not be very useful, because it bears little relationship to the points that are attainable under the market system and under the budgetary limitations on government policy. For example, suppose that in a country like Mexico cotton and sugar cane are the most labor-intensive crops. A solution that maximized employment would correspond to planting much of the country in those two crops (supposing it were agronomically feasible); to do so would cause domestic market prices for those goods to collapse and so farmers would suffer large financial losses. In such a hypothetical case, it would be out of the question to compensate the losses with subsidies, for lack of sufficient budgetary funds, and so the employment-maximizing cropping pattern could not even be approximated in reality. These considerations reinforce the arguments for using the positive model via a sequence of experiments involving changes in policy parameters, rather than using frontiers, to address policy issues.

12.2   SELECTED APPLIED MODELS[1]

This section discusses three sector-wide programming models which have been applied to questions of policy either by a government or by an international agency. The three were designed for the agricultural economies of Mexico, Egypt, and Turkey. Each model has some special characteristic not found in other models, and together they provide unique insights into the power and scope of mathematical programming models for policy analysis.

12.2.1   The Mexican Model CHAC

CHAC[2] was the earliest positive programming model constructed for a developing country. As of this writing it has been used for more than ten years by the Mexican government to produce a number of policy documents for agriculture (examples are found in Secretaría de la Presidencia 1973 and 1983, and Bassoco et al. 1983). It was developed as part of a collaborative research project carried out jointly by the World Bank and the Mexican government, and it has been documented in several publications over the years (principally Goreux and Manne 1973, Bassoco and Norton 1975 and 1983, and Norton and Solís 1983).

The initial research project included economy-wide studies and studies of the energy and agriculture sectors (Goreux and Manne 1973), and then the agricultural work was carried on independently. It always has had an institutional sponsor in Mexico, and it has been applied to specific questions arising from that sponsor's concerns. The first home for CHAC was the Central Bank of Mexico (Banco de México). As key personnel involved in the model changed agencies CHAC moved in turn to the Ministry of the Presidency (Secretaría de la Presidencia); the office of Presidential Advisors, under the framework of the Mexican Food System (Sistema Alimentario Mexicano); and back to the Ministry of the Presidency, which now is called the Ministry of Programming and Budgeting (Secretaría de Programación y Presupuesto).

In structure, the model follows the general outlines presented in Chapters 7 through 10, although the earliest versions did not contain the risk specifications. It was the first sector-wide programming model to use downward-sloping demand functions and to use efficient linearizations of those functions. The CHAC project sponsored the work on risk which led to the seminal paper by Hazell and Scandizzo (1974) and the material in Chapter 10 of this volume.

The model contains supply and demand specifications for about 33 crops (that number has varied slightly from version to version), organized spatially in four major regions and 20 subregions. (This last number also varied over different versions.) The major regions were used mainly to define possibilities for labor migration, and the subregions were used for defining basic variations in available crops and technologies. For some of the subregions, further subdivisions were made on the basis of farm size and differences in irrigation facilities. The nonirrigated subregions were defined in terms of altitude and annual rainfall, and therefore they are noncontiguous entities.

All together the model contains over 2300 alternative production vectors, including over 200 for corn. Inputs are monthly in the case of land, labor, and water, and they are annual otherwise. The annual inputs are draft animal services, machinery services, chemical inputs, improved seeds, short-term credit, and a residual category of other inputs. On the supply side, family labor is distinguished from hired labor, and the former has a reservation wage that is lower than the market wage. The initial version of the model contained some 1500 equations, and later versions about 2200 equations.

The main data sources for the production coefficients were the regular cost-of-production studies of the agricultural banks and the national crop insurance company, supplemented by some special surveys.

Apart from formal questions of model design, the work with CHAC has been distinctive in two other respects. First, considerable emphasis was placed on flexibility in model structure, in order to facilitate subsequent changes in the model's structure. The reasoning was that to be useful, the model would have to be solved a large number of times under many variations of structure and data. This meant a larger model in number of rows and columns, but the practical advantages were felt to outweigh the implied increase in computational cost. The other distinctive feature of the CHAC was the emphasis placed on design of meaningful policy experiments with a model that simulated market equilibrium, subject to specified policy interventions. Many of the discussions in this chapter had their origin in that work.

12.2.2 The Egyptian Model HĀPY[3]

The Egyptian model was the outgrowth of another collaborative project, this time involving the World Bank and the Egyptian Ministry of Irrigation, with the support of the United Nations Development Program. The motivation behind the model study and other related studies was the concern that the availability of water from the Nile could become a constraint on national growth by 1990. As agriculture consumes about 95% of the Nile waters, it is an obvious focus of this concern. The immediate goals of the analysis were to estimate agriculture's needs for water under different scenarios, to estimate the marginal productivity of water in agriculture, and to evaluate alternative investments in irrigation. Later, the analyses were expanded to include the effects of agricultural pricing policies. The initial version of the model is described in Kutcher (1980), and the investment version is discussed in Norton (1982).

HĀPY contains 25 crops and their production is specified for 15 canal command groupings, which are aggregations of the 50 canal commands used in operating the Nile irrigation system. Farm surveys by the national extension service provided the bulk of the data in the model. The initial version was based on 1978 data, and a revised version for investment analysis was developed on the basis of 1980 data. The model contains about 1000 equations.

Whereas CHAC contains downward-sloping demand functions for livestock feed, but no explicit livestock activities, HĀPY contains livestock herds and their associated demands for feed. The herds, however, are exogenous in numbers of animals, so their purpose in the model is to account for feed requirements. Those requirements are expressed in nutrient terms.

In its initial applications the model provided, among other things, results regarding the economic benefits of spreading water more thinly over all irrigated areas, in order to be able to irrigate the "new lands," and compared this with irrigating existing lands more intensively. In its second version it was used to jointly evaluate a large number of proposed irrigation investments. Taken together, the proposed investments are large enough in scale that they would have nonmarginal effects on sector production levels. Also, the increments in production would vary over crops, and hence relative prices would change as a consequence of the investments. For this reason, a joint evaluation of the investments using the model with endogenous prices yields different conclusions than does a traditional project-by-project evaluation under the assumption of fixed prices. This investment work with HĀPY contributed to the development of the material presented in Section 12.8 below. As of 1985, the third round of analyses and reports with HĀPY was being developed in Cairo.

12.2.3 The Turkish Model TASM[4]

TASM was developed primarily to address issues of comparative advantage and pricing policy in Turkish agriculture, in a context of concern about the sector's future possibilities for expansion through increased export competitiveness. There have been two Turkish models, TASM I and TASM II. TASM I is similar to CHAC in the essentials of its structure but departs from both

CHAC and HĀPY in including endogenous sizes of livestock herds. TASM II, which has a new data set, departs further in including marketing-processing activities (as per Chapter 8), regional product demand functions, fertilizer response functions, and explicit alternative feed rations (as per Section 11.6). The inclusion of regional supply, demand, and processing activities necessitated the addition of interregional shipment activities for many products. TASM II contains five regions which are aggregations of Turkish provinces. There are about 1000 equations, with some 70 agricultural products, quarterly inputs for land and labor, and annual inputs otherwise. The basic references are, for TASM I, Le-Si, Scandizzo, and Kasnakoglu (1982), and for TASM II, Norton and Gencaḡa (1985).

Both TASMs were used in developing analyses for World Bank reports on Turkish agriculture, and as of this writing TASM II is operational in the Turkish Ministry of Agriculture. The models have been used to estimate growth prospects for the sector, to estimate regional differences in the degree to which arable land is a binding constraint on growth, to estimate input requirements, to explore the effects of changes in fertilizer pricing policy, and to measure Turkey's international comparative advantage by crop. The discussion in Section 12.4 is based primarily on the work with TASM II, and to a lesser extent on the CHAC work.

12.2.4 Other Relevant Models

A number of other sector models have been built; five can be singled out as good illustrations of key points in the text. They are the Philippine model (MAAGAP) of Kunkel et al. (1978), the Tunisian model of Condos and Cappi (1976), the Brazilian model of Kutcher and Scandizzo (1981), the Central American model (MOCA) of Cappi et al. (1978), and the Malaysian model (TIGER) of Bell, Hazell, and Slade (1982, Chapters 3 and 4). MAAGAP is especially good in the treatment of processing activities, the Tunisian model on livestock choices, the Brazilian model on crop consortiums, MOCA on intercountry trade linkages, and TIGER on mechanization and draft power choices in the context of fortnightly resource balances and constraints. Interesting programming models of investment choices at the local level are found in Husain and Inman (1977), Willis and Hanlon (1976), and Bassoco, Mutsaers, Norton, and Silos (1983). Several regional models for Mexico, by Kutcher, Pomareda and Simmons, Howell, Benito, and Candler, are found in Norton and Solís (1983).

12.3 AVERAGE AND MARGINAL COSTS OF PRODUCTION

Many prescriptions for economic policy are based on marginal equivalences. A well-known example is the recommendation to implement marginal-cost pricing in public enterprises. However, as noted in Chapter 11, published agricultural data do not include marginal costs of production. At most average costs are reported, but even that is rare and such estimates usually are based on very few observations.

A programming model can be used to compute both average and marginal costs. The greater the disaggregation of farm types in the model, the more representative these costs will be. For a given crop, average costs can be computed on the basis of a model solution as follows:

$$C_a = \sum_i \sum_h \sum_r \sum_t \theta_{hrt} a_{ihrt} P_i / y_{hrt} \qquad (12.1)$$

where the indexes are i = input
$\qquad\qquad\qquad$ h = farm type
$\qquad\qquad\qquad$ r = region
$\qquad\qquad\qquad$ t = technique of production

and where

θ_{hrt} = the shares of acreage in the given crop, by indexes h, r, and t, in the validated base solution
a_{ihrt} = input/output coefficients (including land and other fixed resources)
P_i = input prices, including shadow prices for fixed resources
y_{hrt} = yield per hectare.

The input prices may be either exogenous or endogenous, or both, as the cost calculation is made after the model's solution is obtained.

Average costs calculated in this way differ somewhat in concept from those which are based on field surveys. The terms in equation (12.1) include the opportunity cost of fixed resources and, as appropriate, they may allow for seasonal variation in those opportunity costs. Thus from the viewpoint of economic theory estimates from equation (12.1) are preferable to those which are based on records of farmers' cash outlays. The latter usually exclude costs associated with fixed resources, or rely on arbitrary methods for accounting for those costs.

Marginal costs may be derived from a model's solution in a number of ways. In a model structured so that price equals marginal cost, it is necessary only to look for the price in the case of products that are sold on the domestic market. The simplest way to find the price is to look up the dual variable on the commodity balance. As shown in Chapter 8, that dual variable is in fact the product price. If there are two commodity balances, one at the producer level and one at the consumer level (Chapters 7 and 8), then the corresponding dual variables represent the farm-gate and consumer prices, respectively.

An alternative, but equivalent way to obtain the product price is via the primal solution. In a linear programming model, the prices on all segments of the demand curves are prespecified, and so for a given product the price is the sum of segment prices times segment values in the solution. (No more than

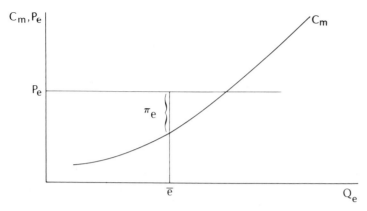

Figure 12.1 Measuring the marginal cost of production for an exported good.

two segments will appear in the solution.) These two procedures for calculating price (marginal cost) will give the same figure, except for possibly minor discrepancies arising from the discontinuities involved in the segmentation of the demand curve. Any discrepancies can be reduced by increasing the number of demand segments in a given range of quantity (or price) variation. Thus, a comparison of the primal and dual values of a product price can be a useful indicator of whether a finer demand segmentation is needed in a linear model.

Yet another approach, which is relevant for a linear or quadratic model, is to calculate the product price *ex post* by solving the inverse demand function on the basis of the quantity sold in the solution.

For products that are exported against a bound, the marginal cost of production can be found from the information provided in the shadow price on the export bound. The relation is

$$C_m = P_e - \pi_e \tag{12.2}$$

where P_e is the export price and π_e is the shadow price on the export bound. The latter represents the economic rent accruing to those who produce for export. Figure 12.1 shows π_e graphically; $\bar{e}$ in the figure is the bound on exports.

If a product is both exported against a bound and sold on the domestic market, then the two marginal costs should be the same. The cost of obtaining a marginal unit for either market should be the same, unless access to the limited export market effectively is rationed. In that case, producers who enjoy access may have different production costs than those who sell on the domestic market. If in reality only certain producers export, the modeler may wish to specify a separate commodity balance for export, with the provision that only certain farm types have entries in that balance. Those farm types also would, of course, have access to the domestic market.

Table 12.1 shows the tableau for the case in which some farms (type 1) can sell only to the domestic market while others (type 2) can sell either to the

Table 12.1   Mini-Tableau for Export Allocation over Farm Types

	X_1	X_2	M_2^e	M_2^d	M_1	
Production balance, farm type 1	$-y_1$				$+1$	≤ 0
Production balance, farm type 2		$-y_2$	$+1$	$+1$		≤ 0
Export balance			-1			≤ 0
Consumption balance				-1	-1	≤ 0

domestic or the export market. Activities X_1 and X_2 represent production for the two farm types, and y_1, y_2 are the corresponding unit yields. The variables M_2^e and M_2^d represent the export and domestic marketing activities for farms of type 2, and M_1 represents the (domestic) marketing activity for farms of type 1.

Average and marginal costs of production can and do differ significantly in most countries. That is, both more and less efficient producers coexist in the sector. Many less efficient producers are not driven out for a variety of factors. For one thing, a producer may be relatively efficient in producing his principal crop but less efficient in producing his secondary crop. Yet the secondary crop's revenues may cover its variable costs, so he is willing to continue producing it, even though others do so at lower cost. Also, a higher income, or preferable lifestyle, may not be guaranteed in nonagricultural occupations, so poorer producers may prefer to stay in agriculture rather than endure the disruption of a change.

12.4   COMPARATIVE ADVANTAGE

It is often useful to develop measures of comparative advantage on the basis of both average and marginal costs of production. A commonly used measure of comparative advantage is the domestic resource cost (DRC) of earning, or saving, a unit of foreign exchange. Algebraically, the DRC is written, for a single good,

$$\text{DRC} = \frac{C - eC^i}{eP^w - eC^i} \tag{12.3}$$

where C is the cost of production
   e is the exchange rate
   P^w is the border price of the good
   C^i is the cost of imported inputs

The cost C may be either average or marginal, and it is suggested that the DRC calculation be performed for each concept. The border price P^w should not be the international price but rather the actual CIF import price or FOB export price. For the cost of imported inputs, two approaches are possible.

One is to include the costs of all inputs that are imported at least in part. The other is to include only the imported shares of those inputs, e.g., only 25% of fertilizer inputs if in fact only 25% of fertilizers are imported. The latter is probably preferable on grounds of accuracy, but the choice may depend upon the evolution of imported inputs over time and the prospects for new domestic production capacity in the input industry.

For the average cost case, the imported inputs can be identified readily from the model's input/output coefficients used in equation (12.1). For the marginal cost case, such identification is not quite as easy. There are two fairly simple ways of finding the marginal use of imported inputs, or any particular inputs. The first way is to identify the particular production vectors that are associated with the marginal points on the cost curve. This can be done by varying the product price (or rotating the demand curve as described in Section 12.6 below) slightly, and seeing which production vectors come into the solution or drop out of it. Those are the marginal vectors on the cost curve. (The designation of which vectors are marginal will be conditional on the prices of other products, for they will influence the opportunity cost of fixed resources.) The input coefficients in those vectors will give the marginal requirements for particular inputs, per ton of output.

An alternative and simpler approach is to make use of accounting balances for use of inputs. When the price of the output is changed marginally, both the output level and the levels of input use will change. Those changes are, by definition, at the margin, and so the ratios of input changes to output changes are the marginal input/output coefficients.

Another commonly used measure of comparative advantage is the effective rate of protection, or EPC. For the average cost case, it can be expressed as

$$
\text{EPC} = \frac{P^d - \left[\sum_i \sum_h \sum_r \sum_t \theta_{hrt} a_{ihrt} P_i^d / y_{hrt} \right]}{P^w - \left[\sum_i \sum_h \sum_r \sum_t \theta_{hrt} a_{ihrt} P_i^w / y_{hrt} \right]}
\tag{12.4}
$$

where the symbols are as defined for equation (12.1) above; P with no subscript is the product price, and the superscripts d and w represent domestic and border (world) prices respectively. For the marginal cost case, computation of the EPC requires identification of the marginal production vectors via solutions in the way described above. (A useful discussion of measures of comparative advantage for agriculture is found in Scandizzo and Bruce 1980.)

Comparative advantage measures can be helpful in designing export marketing strategies and trade incentives. One of the first applications of a programming model to trade questions was made with the Mexican model CHAC. DRC calculations were made for 33 crops with the model, and the crops were ranked according to those calculations. Those crops that had a DRC lower than the exchange rate (in pesos/dollar) were deemed candidates for export promotion, especially those crops with very low DRCs. For those with higher DRCs, significant improvements in productivity would have to be achieved before export or import substitution could be expected to take place. The first set of DRC calculations with CHAC was made on the basis of 1968 data; subsequently it turned out that the 1968–1980 export and import growth rates by crop were closely correlated with those original DRC rankings. The rankings later were recalculated on the basis of 1976 data and were found not to differ very much from the earlier calculations. Discussions of these applications and others are found in Duloy and Norton (1973b) and Bassoco and Norton (1983).

Interregional comparative advantage also may be explored with programming models. One indicator of a region's relative efficiency in production is provided by an experiment consisting of raising a product's price and recording the regional shares of the resulting incremental output. In cases in which regional production is tied to local processing capacity, running the model without processing activities (or without regional limits on processing capacity) may lead to a solution in which the regional cropping patterns differ significantly from the actual ones. This procedure was followed with CHAC: it was found that the model allocations for sugar cane indicated relatively more cane in the tropical regions and relatively less in the northwestern irrigated districts, as compared with the actual patterns, even though cane yields in the northwest were about twice as high as in the tropics. This was a clear indication that cane had a comparative advantage in the tropics. The reason was the high opportunity cost of irrigated land in the northwest, for the production of fruit, vegetables, and other high-value crops. On the basis of this analysis, a decision was made by the Mexican government not to finance expansion of sugar milling capacity in the northwest (Bassoco and Norton, 1983, p. 151).

A quantification of interregional comparative advantage can be obtained by computing regional average costs of production on the basis of the model's coefficients and the vectors which appear in the solution. It is important that regionally fixed resources and their shadow prices be included in the computations. The relevant equation is the regional variant of (12.1), where the summation is not taken over the regional index r:

$$C_a^r = \sum_i \sum_h \sum_t \theta_{hrt} a_{ihrt} P_i / y_{hrt} \qquad (12.5)$$

Again, the values of C_a^r will be conditional upon the particular resource endowments and other elements of the solution. Changes in the model's parameters can be expected to lead to changes in the C_a^r.

12.5 INPUT USE AND INPUT PRICING

A major concern of agricultural policy makers is the future rate of input use in agriculture. One aspect of this concern is how the level of gainful agricultural employment may respond to agricultural growth and to relative price changes.

The requirements for modern inputs such as agrochemicals, machinery, improved seeds, and credit may also change in response to sector growth and price changes.

By virtue of its detail on the input side, a sector programming model is a useful instrument for calculating the input requirements associated with different cropping patterns and policy strategies. In this regard, one of the most common applications of such models is the simple one of tabulating input use levels in the base solution and then in alternative solutions. Sometimes it is helpful to record the input requirements by region, farm size class, or crop group. These measures help identify the major sources of demand for modern inputs and give guidance for programs of supplying those inputs. Of particular interest is the projected growth of input demand. It can be expressed in terms of simple growth rates or in terms of elasticities with respect to output growth. (For an example of the latter see the CHAC model, Bassoco and Norton 1983, p. 142.)

Special interest resides in seasonal labor patterns, which often are highly peaked. The model generates seasonal agricultural employment, which is something that is not easily measured by direct surveys in developing countries. Figure 12.2 shows the seasonal employment patterns in Mexican agriculture as they were calculated with the CHAC model. CHAC also was used to quantify the employment-creation effects of various trends and policy measures such as yield growth, irrigation investment, and a proposed tax on imports of agricultural machinery, in an effort to determine whether total employment creation in agriculture would match the net annual increase in the rural labor force, allowing for expected rates of rural-urban migration (Secretaría de la Presidencia 1983, pp. 189–193).

Input demands vary with prices. Chapter 7, Section 7.5, discusses the use of a sector model to trace out relationships which show input demands as functions of input prices. TASM II was used to derive national demands for fertilizers, and to calculate the effects of higher fertilizer prices on agricultural production levels. Those effects were calculated from model solutions under different fertilizer prices (see Norton and Gencağa 1985, pp. 6–7). It turned out that, for Turkish agriculture as a whole, raising the fertilizer price by reducing its subsidy did not have much effect on output levels owing to the shape of the fertilizer response function at prevailing levels of output. Other experts concurred in that finding; in general it is a useful rule to solicit the reactions of field experts or other specialists to the principal findings of a model-based study. If they do not agree, the model structure may (but not necessarily!) need revision. At minimum, a dialogue should develop regarding the reasons behind the model's results.

Another way of expressing input relationships is through isoquants, which link pairs of inputs. Isoquants are especially useful for inputs that are close substitutes, as in the case of labor and farm machinery. Once the isoquant is known, then direct calculations of the effects of changes in relative input prices on input use can be made. As with supply functions, isoquant-like

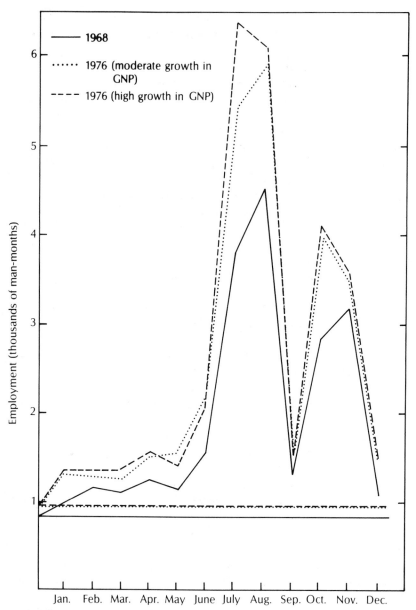

Figure 12.2 Seasonal employment projections in CHAC. Source: Bassoco and Norton (1983, p. 140). These solutions were made in 1973.

constructs are implicit in the model, and can be traced out numerically via appropriate solutions of the model.

As traditionally defined, an isoquant is a conditional concept: it shows input substitution possibilities when output is held constant. But in actuality, when relative input prices are altered output levels also change. Output will increase for some products and decrease for others, and the aggregate index of output will change. Similar effects will occur in a sector model. The input-substitution surface that can be traced out with the model is not therefore a true isoquant but rather a general locus of input substitution, or GLIS. For policy purposes, the GLIS is of more interest than the isoquant, for if input prices are changed there is no mechanism for holding output constant. The procedure for tracing out the GLIS is simply to calculate solutions under different pairs of values of input prices, e.g., under a sequence of values of the wage rate and the cost of agricultural machinery. In general, different levels of input prices will produce different solutions, even if the same ratio of input prices is maintained. This happens because of other inputs to the production process, whose relative prices to the price of the inputs under consideration are changed.

It is possible to use the model to trace out an approximate isoquant, and also an approximate isoprofits curve, by imposing a constraint on an index of output or profits. However, the presence of such a constraint will distort the

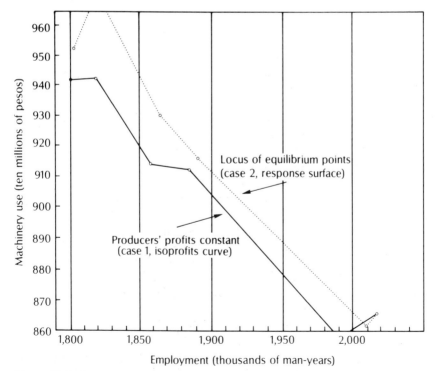

Figure 12.3 Sector isoquants for capital and labor in CHAC. Source: Bassoco and Norton (1983, p. 132).

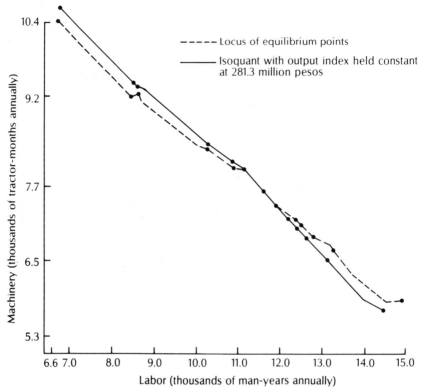

Figure 12.4 Machinery-labor substitution on all farms induced by variations in the wage rate. Source: Howell (1983, p. 397).

shadow prices on the commodity balances so that they will no longer equal the corresponding primal prices, that is, a competitive market solution is no longer obtained. The size of this error is an empirical matter, and there may be cases in which it remains within acceptable bounds for purposes of generating the approximate isoquant.

The studies in Mexico provide examples of the GLIS and the approximate isoquant (Bassoco and Norton 1983, Howell 1983). Figures 12.3 and 12.4 show those examples. For both kinds of surfaces, the arc elasticities differ from point to point. Also, the first derivative is not continuous, and in some range of values the surfaces may not even be convex from below. These effects arise because of the discrete nature of the production functions and because movements along the surface affect first one product and then another.

12.6 SUPPLY RESPONSE AND OUTPUT PRICING POLICIES

Supply response functions can be traced out numerically by varying the price of fixed-price selling activities (as in Chapter 7). When the model contains downward-sloping demand functions, a more convenient method is to rotate those functions in successive solutions. The rotation is accomplished by

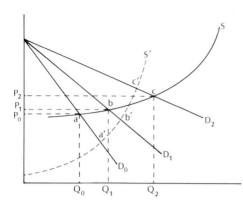

Figure 12.5 Tracing out a supply response function.

changing one coefficient, the right-hand side of the convex combination constraint. For example, three points on the supply function for a given crop can be found with right-hand side values of 1.0, 1.2, and 1.4 in the convexity constraint for that crop. Those values will generate the demand functions D_0, D_1, and D_2 in Figure 12.5. If the implicit supply response function is S, the corresponding supply-demand intersections will be points a, b, and c. If the supply response function is S', the intersections will be points a', b', and c'. For the case of function S, the modeler will observe the price-quantity pairs (P_0, Q_0), (P_1, Q_1), and (P_2, Q_2) in the successive solutions. These points and others may be connected *ex post* to create the supply response function shown in the figure. The arc elasticity of supply may then be calculated. For the arc defined by points a and b, it is

$$\eta_{ab}^s = \frac{(Q_1 - Q_0)}{(P_1 - P_0)} \cdot \frac{(Q_0 + Q_1)}{(P_0 + P_1)} \tag{12.6}$$

A priori, it is impossible to know the magnitude of price and quantity responses associated with a given increase in the right-hand side of a convexity constraint. Responses depend on the shape of the unknown supply response function. Experience with programming models indicates that supply response elasticities may be quite variable as quantities increase, although they generally tend to diminish in value. Some early segments of the function may even be flat. The modeler should be prepared to experiment with a range of values of the convexity RHS before finding solutions that give significant increases in quantity along the supply response function.

Suppose it is desired to know the supply response functions for a particular region without changing the price in other regions. In this case, the marketing-processing activities may be used to set up the appropriate experiments. To move outward along a regional supply response function, the coefficient $-\Delta_{jr}$ found in Table 7.3 can be altered by the algebraic addition of a term Δ^* (shown on the vertical axis in Figure 12.6). This change corresponds to a regional price subsidy of amount $P_1 - P_0 < \Delta^*$, referring to Figure 12.6. In terms of the demand function facing the region's producers, it constitutes a

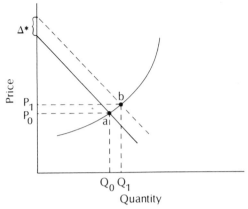

Figure 12.6   The procedure for finding a regional supply function.

parallel shift. The elasticity of supply response is then calculated *ex post*, as before.

Some points of interpretation may be in order regarding the supply response functions obtained from a sector model. First, following the distinction made in Chapter 7, they are not conventional supply functions since prices of fixed resources and other outputs are not held constant. For purposes of policy analysis, the supply response concept is the more relevant, for in general other prices will not remain constant when one good's price is changed. That good will substitute for others in production and consumption, at least to some extent, and hence the market equilibrium prices of other goods will change.

Second, it may be asked whether the measured elasticity is a short-run or long-run concept. In one sense it is a long-run elasticity, because it refers to change in behavior between two equilibrium points after all adjustment processes have been completed. However, the static model does not allow for fixed capital formation, so in that respect the elasticity is a short-run concept. In measurements of short-run supply response based on historical time series, full responses to the price change often have not been worked out before another exogenous change intervenes to alter the response. To distinguish the elasticities derived from a programming model from other kinds of elasticities, they may be called "equilibrium short-run elasticities."

Because the programming model describes a situation of full adjustment, it is likely to give elasticities that are greater in value than corresponding econometric estimates. This need not always be the case, however. The CHAC model gave an elasticity of about 0.5 for maize, identical with an estimated elasticity based on historical time series data reported in Cartas and Cifuentes (1982). Also, at the farm level, Shumway and Chang (1977) found econometrically estimated elasticities and programming model elasticities to be comparable in value. The greater the differentiation of farm types in the programming model, the smaller the supply response elasticity is likely to be for modest price increases. Also, inclusion of the risk-aversion specifications discussed in Chapters 5 and 10 results in lower elasticities for the riskier crops (see Chapter 13).

For purposes of applied work, it is best to regard the programming and econometric elasticities as different constructs, each with its own uses. For purely forecasting questions about the supply effects of price changes on a single commodity, the econometric elasticities are usually preferable. The programming simulations of supply response are particularly useful in three areas of analysis:

1 Comparative simulations of supply response. For example, whether greater supply responses are likely to come from changes in output or input prices, or whether, say, farm income is likely to be increased more by a subsidy applied to the maize price, to the sorghum price, or to the wheat price.
2 Simulations of cross-supply effects and other derived effects from price changes. It can be helpful to project not only the supply response to own-price changes but also the associated crop substitution effects. An additional ton of maize may be gained at the cost of 0.30 tons of sorghum, 0.10 tons of soybeans, etc. Also, owing to the complexities of crop rotations and competition for resources on the supply side, some crops will be complements rather than substitutes, and the model's solutions will indicate the strength of these complementarity relationships. The model also provides simulations of the net effect ($\pm$) of output price changes on employment, foreign exchange earnings, and other aggregate goal variables.
3 Simulations of the structure of supply response. Sometimes it is of interest to know which regions and farm size classes respond most to a change in price incentives and, consequently, to calculate the net income effects for each type of farm. Another aspect of the structure of supply response is its disaggregation into net expansion of cultivated area, substitution for other crops, and yield increases. The programming model is well suited for investigating these kinds of questions.

These points are quite relevant to the formation of pricing policy, for policy usually does not seek to promote the production of a given crop for its own sake, but rather as a means to greater levels of farm income, increased incomes for certain classes of farmers, more agricultural foreign exchange earnings, and so on. In this perspective, a model is most useful when comparing the effectiveness of different policy instruments in achieving given ends; for example, when the consequences of changes in prices of different outputs and inputs are simulated.

Tables 12.2 and 12.3 provide an example of comparative evaluations of different instruments of pricing policy taken from one of the CHAC studies carried out by the Mexican government in 1982. To construct the tables, it was

Table 12.2 Mexico: Changes in Sector Objectives per 10 Million Pesos Spent on Alternative Price Support Instruments

Objective \ Instrument	Maize	Beans	Sorghum	Wheat	Rice	Barley	Soybeans	Sesame	Safflower
Producer profits	1.024	0.123	0.569	0.048	0.229	0.233	0.396	0.378	0.589
Sector income	0.820	0.156	0.525	0.054	0.343	0.224	0.516	0.420	0.685
Irrigated areas	0.325	-0.088	0.290	0.006	0.074	0.075	0.247	0.140	0.411
Northwest	0.084	-0.098	0.113	0.006	0.049	0.037	0.022	0.070	0.068
North	0.044	0.010	0.059	0.006	0.025	0	0.022	0	0.205
Center	0.193	-0.010	0.196	-0.012	0	0	0.202	0	0.103
South	0.004	0	0	0	0	0	0	0	0
Rainfed areas	0.495	0.234	0.236	0.048	0.270	0.112	0.280	0.280	0.274
Northwest	0.008	0.010	0.010	0.006	0.025	0.037	0.011	0.070	0.034
North	0.048	0.020	0.039	0	0	0	0	0	0.103
Center	0.294	0.068	0.020	0.012	0.025	0.037	-0.045	0.280	-0.034
South	0.143	0.137	0.162	0.030	0.196	0.075	0.291	0	0.103
Employment	0.172	0.082	-0.148	0.011	0.160	0.032	0.252	0.110	0.291

Note: Units are in 10 millions of pesos, except for employment, which is expressed in thousands of man-years. Sector income includes the income of hired labor.

Source: Calculated from solutions of the model CHAC and reported in Bassoco and Norton (1982).

Table 12.3 Mexico: Changes in Sector Objectives per 10 Million Pesos Spent on Alternative Input Subsidies

Instrument / Objective	Subsidies at a rate of 30% of input prices			
	Agrochemicals	Seeds	Surface irrigation water	Machinery
Producer profits	0.550	0.325	1.180	1.470
Sector income	0.450	0.316	1.160	0.574
Irrigated areas	0.243	0.162	1.260	0.115
Northwest	−0.033	0.044	0.696	0.013
North	0.037	0.007	0.435	0.040
Center	0.224	0.103	0.130	0.135
South	0.007	0.007	0.043	−0.072
Rainfed areas	0.202	0.154	−0.010	0.457
Northwest	0	0.007	0.043	0.013
North	0	−0.029	0	0.031
Center	−0.018	0.096	−0.174	0.233
South	0.210	0.074	0	0.175
Employment	0.118	0.022	−0.043	−0.269
Foreign exchange savings	0.163	0	0	0.761
Maize production	0.875	−0.007	0.043	n.a.

Note: Units are in 10 millions of pesos except for employment, which is expressed in thousands of man-years, and maize production, which is in thousand tons.

Source: Calculated from solutions of the model CHAC and reported in Bassoco and Norton (1982).

**Table 12.4   Supply Response and Cross-Price Effects Arising from Changes
in the Price of Corn, Costa Rica, 1976[a]**

Corn		Rice		Sorghum		Beans	
Price	Quantity	Price	Quantity	Price	Quantity	Price	Quanti
0.080	62.69	0.074	107.90	0.051	14.51	0.026	11.67
0.093	75.12	0.085	107.00	0.058	14.50	0.023	8.62
0.133	95.83	0.119	104.31	0.079	14.42	0.355	6.89
0.258	115.79	0.225	86.91	0.153	14.19	0.811	6.88

Note: Prices are in Central American pesos per kilo and quantities are in thousand tons. The prices are produc
prices.
[a] The corn price was changed exogenously by rotating the domestic demand curve. All other values in the tab
are determined endogenously to the model.
Source: Calculated from solutions of the model MOCA.

necessary to work out the implications for the government budget of each
price support instrument. To develop measures of the effectiveness of policies
per unit of government expenditures, the model's simulated effects of the
instruments were divided by the associated budgetary requirements. The
instruments are price supports for different crops and subsidies on certain
inputs. It can be seen that the instruments vary in their effects, but that the
maize price support appears to be the most efficient instrument for generating
employment and additional net farm income.

Table 12.4 provides an example of the analysis of supply response for
Costa Rica, carried out with a submodel of the multicountry model MOCA
(Cappi et al., 1978).[5] The demand function for corn was rotated rightward
through increases in the right-hand side of its convex combination constraint.
The results show the price and quantity effects for four basic crops. It can be
seen that the substitution effects are strongest with respect to beans and are
weakest with respect to sorghum. For the entire range of corn prices shown in
Table 12.4, the own-price (arc) elasticity for corn is 0.589, and the cross-price
elasticities are: rice-corn, -0.213; sorghum-corn, -0.022; and beans-corn,
-0.411.

Table 12.5 shows the net effects of the corn price change on Costa Rica's
foreign trade in corn. It can be seen that it would take an unrealistically large

Table 12.5   Foreign Trade Effects of Different Levels of the Corn Price, Costa Rica

Producer price	Total production	Net production	Imports (−) Exports (+)	Domestic consumption	Degree of national self-sufficiency
0.080	62.69	59.55	− 41.65	101.2	58.8
0.093	75.12	72.03	− 29.17	101.2	71.2
0.133	95.83	91.04	− 10.16	101.2	90.0
0.258	115.79	110.00	8.80	101.2	108.7

Note: Prices are in Central American pesos per kilo and quantities are in thousand tons. The prices are
producer prices.
Source: Calculated from solutions to the model MOCA.

Table 12.6 Effects of the Corn Price on Selected Macroeconomic Variables, Costa Rica

Producer price	Producers' gross margin	Cost of imports	Total cost of supply	Average cost of supply	Consumer expenditures	Gross export earnings	Implicit subsidy (−) or tax (+) on consumers	Implicit subsidy (−) on exports	Fiscal income (+) or outlays (−)	Tariff income	Net effect on the balance of payments
0.080	5.02	3.33	14.84	0.147	16.19	—	+ 1.35	—	1.35	1.35	− 3.35
0.093	7.00	2.33	15.86	0.157	16.19	—	+ 0.33	—	0.33	0.33	− 2.33
0.133	12.79	0.81	20.19	0.199	16.19	—	4.00	—	− 4.00	0.18	− 0.81
0.258	29.91	—	37.11	0.337	16.19	0.71	− 17.95	− 2.26	− 20.21	—	+ 0.71

Note: Prices are in Central American pesos per kilo and all other figures are in millions of Central American pesos.
Source: Calculated from solutions to the model MOCA.

price increase to convert Costa Rica from an importer to an exporter of corn. The budgetary consequences of attempting to promote corn self-sufficiency for Costa Rica were also calculated, as shown in Table 12.6. For those calculations, it was assumed that the consumer price would remain unchanged and that the higher producer price would be attained through subsidies to producers. The budgetary consequences of a policy of corn self-sufficiency are considerable.

12.7 ANALYSIS OF STRUCTURAL CHANGE

Programming models are especially well suited for the analysis of structural change. In dealing with structural change, it should be borne in mind that the line between structural change and mere parametric changes is a blurred one. For example, if a new export market is opened up for a particular product, it may be possible to represent that change in the model simply by raising the RHS upper bound on exports. Is that a case of structural change or merely parametric change within the given structure? Another example could be the removal of a long-standing subsidy on an input, which is represented in the model by raising the exogenous price of the input. Again, this may be viewed as a structural change or a parametric variation.

For specifying the model experiments, however, the definition of structural change may not be so important. The basic point is that the model is a helpful tool for understanding the consequences that follow when a parameter, or set of parameters, takes on values not experienced historically.

For agriculture, two especially relevant examples concern technological change in production and land reform. Technological change often occurs through the introduction of a new plant variety, and its associated package of inputs. Such a change would be modeled by enlarging the model's set of column vectors to include one or more additional vectors that represent the new production possibilities. (Of course, care has to be taken to be sure that the new coefficients are realistic at the farm level, and not only based on data from experiment stations.)

Depending on the intensity of inputs, and their associated costs, the new technology might or might not be adopted in the model solution. Sensitivity tests could be conducted to determine the wage rate, or the prices of other inputs, at which the new technology enters or leaves the optimal basis. The model solutions would also show the effects of the new technology on farm incomes, employment, output price levels, and other target variables. Procedures like these were utilized in the TIGER model for the *ex post* analysis of an investment project in Malaysia (Bell, Hazell, and Slade 1982).

When land reform experiments are conducted with a programming model, it is a simple matter to explore alternative assumptions about the productivity of inputs on the reformed land. The reallocation of resources that is attendant on land reform is modeled by changing the RHS values for land endowments for the different farm classes, while leaving the labor endowments unchanged. If it is assumed that the smallholders who are beneficiaries of the reform will apply their previous production practices to the reformed lands, then no change need be made in the production coefficients matrix of the model. If, on the other hand, agricultural extension, credit, etc., will be provided along with the reform, then it may be useful to conduct another experiment with higher yields, and possibly with greater intensities of modern inputs, in the production coefficients for the smallholders. Land reform experiments were conducted with the model for northeast Brazil (Kutcher and Scandizzo 1981) and with a revised version of the MOCA model for Central America (SIECA, 1981).

12.8 EVALUATION OF ALTERNATIVE INVESTMENT PROJECTS

12.8.1 Programming Models and Project Evaluation

Although the benefits of investment activities extend over several years, investments often can be evaluated with a static model. The procedure is applicable not only when benefit streams are uniform over time, but also when they vary in the initial years after completion of the investment project.

What are the advantages of using a model, as opposed to the traditional procedures for evaluating projects? Principally they are three:

1 A model like the ones discussed in this book will simulate producers' changes in cropping and input use in response to the additional resources made available through the investment. This can help avoid the observed tendency in many traditional project evaluations to overestimate the extent to which the high-value crops will be successfully promoted by the project, especially in the case of irrigation projects.

2 Because the model simulates producer responses to the project, it can provide information in addition to the economic efficiency of the project on its probable performance in contributing to such goals as employment creation and foreign exchange earnings.

3 In cases of programs of investments that are nonmarginal in magnitude, relative prices are likely to be affected, and hence traditional, micro-level evaluation procedures will be biased by their assumption of constant prices. A programming model can give a joint evaluation of a package of investments and rankings of the components of the package, in an environment in which prices will be determined in part by the level and composition of investment.

A programming model may be used in different ways to address issues of investment. One way is to use it to attempt to quantify only the benefits of the project(s). A second way is to use it to compute internal rates of return for the projects, using information on project costs as well as on factors that influence benefits. Both these procedures involve use of the positive (simulating) model. A third way is to use a two-stage planning procedure which also involves a normative model defined in terms of explicit goals of investment policy. These three procedures are discussed in turn.

12.8.2 Evaluating Project Benefits

Using a model to quantify only the benefit side of a project is most useful in the prefeasibility stage of work, when considering whether or not to make the expenditures necessary to conduct a formal feasibility study. That kind of study provides detailed estimates of the project's costs, but a decision on whether the study is needed can be made on the basis of a very rough project costing plus estimates of project benefits, and the model is a useful tool for supplying the latter.

The first step in indirect project evaluation is to specify the types of resources that will be expanded by the investment: irrigable land, irrigation water supplies, rainfed land, livestock herds, stocks of trees, etc. The next step is to specify some hypothetical increases in those resources as changes in right-hand side parameters of the project region in the model. By solving the model both with and without these changes, comparison of the solutions will show the changes in farm income, production, employment, and other variables that would arise from the project.

The model also provides estimates of the shadow prices of the affected resources. These shadow prices measure the economic welfare benefits (change in producer and consumer surplus) deriving from unit increases in the resource endowments. As such, they constitute upper bounds on the unit costs of expanding the resources if the project's benefit-cost ratio is to remain at or above 1.0.

Table 12.7 shows the results of such a procedure carried out with a submodel of CHAC representing the Río Colorado irrigation district in northwestern Mexico (Bassoco, Norton, and Silos 1983). It can be seen from the table that there is a general (although not universal) tendency for all categories of benefits to increase at a decreasing rate as irrigation water continues to be expanded. The table also shows that the cutoff point for project scale will vary with the types of benefits emphasized. For example, in this case, employment creation encounters sharply diminishing returns after the irrigation supplies are increased by 15%, whereas farm incomes continue to increase substantially even when irrigation is expanded beyond 20%.

A somewhat different example was provided by Bassoco, Norton, and Silos (1983) using the El Bajío submodel of CHAC. From solutions of that model the shadow prices of rainfed and irrigated land were computed, and the difference between the two figures was interpreted as the upper limit, according to criteria of economic efficiency, on the cost of creating new irrigated land, if the benefit-cost ratio of the project is to remain above 1.0. An implicit assumption in this procedure was that cropping patterns in newly irrigated areas within El Bajío would be similar to those on existing irrigated areas in that region.

Using a model to evaluate a project is also helpful in determining how much the project's financial benefits are affected by changes in pricing policy, and in answering questions about how complementary investments would

Table 12.7 Effects of Making More Irrigation Water Available in the Río Colorado District, Mexico

Item	Base-solution value	Percentage increase in water				
		10	15	20	25	30
Farmers' incomes (millions of pesos)	305.0	335.4 (+ 10.0)	341.4 (+ 11.9)	362.5 (+ 18.9)	374.2 (+ 22.7)	385.8 (+ 26.5)
District income (millions of pesos)	388.0	425.4 (+9.6)	434.7 (+ 12.0)	458.5 (+ 18.2)	471.6 (+ 21.5)	484.7 (+ 24.9)
Employment (thousands of man-years)	31.60	34.14 (+8.0)	35.59 (+ 12.6)	36.21 (+ 14.6)	36.55 (+ 15.7)	36.89 (+ 16.7)
Shadow price of gravity-fed water (pesos per 10,000 cubic meters)	1077	1052 (−2.3)	937 (− 13.0)	937 (− 13.0)	737 (− 31.6)	737 (− 31.6)

Note: Figures in parentheses denote percentage change over base solution value.
Source: Bassoco, Norton, and Silos (1983), p. 473.

affect the project's viability. The Río Colorado model was also used to review the question of changes in yields and project benefits. At the time of the study, cotton yields in the project area were declining owing to increases in soil salinity, so explorations were made of the effects of those declining yields. An additional solution was carried out under the assumption that cotton yields were 13% lower, a decline that appeared likely to occur over a period of four or five years on the basis of past trends. This reduction lowered the shadow price of irrigation water by 26%, that is, it reduced the returns to investments, in terms of economic efficiency, by that amount.

Given the uncertainty attached to the outcome of agricultural research and extension (R & E), it is impossible to say what kinds of R & E efforts could avoid the projected decrease in yields. However, the following conclusion was drawn: if in the judgment of experts the allocation of less than 26% of the investment budget, say 10–15% to be safe, would be likely to halt the decline in yields, then such an allocation would be justified by the increase in returns to the total investment package in the district. A 10–15% allocation of the total investment budget would in fact have increased the prevailing R & E effort in that district several-fold, and specialists felt it would have been very likely to arrest the decline in cotton yields.

12.8.3 Explicit Project Choices in the Model[6]

Explicit project choices can be analyzed with a model when it incorporates both the benefits and costs of projects. An investment project is specified as a column vector of numbers that represent the costs and physical consequences of the project. The model translates these consequences into economic benefits via its simulation of producers' reactions to the increased resource endowments. But in this case the increase in the resource endowments is endogenous, depending on which projects are in the optimal solution, and at what levels.

The programming model utilizes additional resources only as long as their marginal contribution to the objective function is at least as great as their marginal cost. In the optimal solution these two measures will be equalized. Given this characteristic, the model can be used as a tool for project appraisal. To show this, first the way of entering investment activities in the model is presented, and then the interpretation of the solution is discussed.

Suppose the following technical data are given for three irrigation investment projects in a certain region:

	I_1	I_2	I_3
Investment cost per hectare ($000)	5.52	6.10	7.49
Annual operating cost per hectare ($)	100	92	112
Maximal size of the project (000 ha)	34.4	15.7	28.3

Suppose also that the average annual operating costs per hectare for the existing irrigation facilities in the region are $80. Then the incremental operating costs for the three projects are $20, $12, and $32, respectively. It is these incremental costs which need to be entered as part of the investment activities, for the model already will be charged the base cost of $80 per hectare through the activities that currently supply irrigation water. The investment activities do not supply water directly but rather raise the upper bound on irrigation water or irrigable land. If the bound is expressed in terms of land, the mini-tableau for these investment activities is as shown in Table 12.8.

In the tableau, the initial endowment of irrigable land is L_0, and the investment activities release that constraint. If all three projects were imple-

Table 12.8 Mini-Tableau for Irrigation Investment Activities

	Irrigation activities				
Row	I_1	I_2	I_3	I_{TOT}	RHS
January irrigable land	−1.0	−1.0	−1.0		$\leq L_0$
⋮	⋮	⋮	⋮		⋮
December irrigable land	−1.0	−1.0	−1.0		$\leq L_0$
Investment cost	5.52	6.10	7.49	−1	≤ 0
Limit, I_1	1.0				≤ 34.4
Limit, I_2		1.0			≤ 15.7
Limit, I_3			1.0		≤ 28.3
Objective function	−0.020	−0.012	−0.032	−r	Maximize

mented fully, the amount of irrigable land available would be $L_0 + 34.4 + 15.7 + 28.3$. The activity I_{TOT}, for total investment, registers the total cost of the selected projects, in thousand dollars. The real interest rate times that cost is charged to the objective function, as are the incremental operating costs. When an investment activity enters the optimal solution, it expands the resource endowment or makes other, specific physical improvements (such as permitting the use of more efficient technologies). Its cost is the exogenous annualized cost of capital, or the real interest rate plus depreciation.

The model results refer to a representative year t in some period in the future. For that year, investments are undertaken up to the level at which the annual flow of net benefits equals the annualized investment cost. For the moment, the flows of benefits are assumed to be uniform over time; that assumption is relaxed later. The benefits are simply the increment in the objective function's value that occurs through use of the additional resource endowments provided by the investment. That increment is created via production, sales, and other activities, and hence it cannot be computed before knowing the model solution.

The nature of the interest rate in the model can be explored by assuming that the time stream of benefits associated with the project could be simulated by a sequence of identical solutions of the model—one for each year subsequent to completion of the project—and by doing some *ex post* discounting. Each solution is subscripted t, and the benefits at time t are defined as the increment in the objective function value, with respect to the value it would have taken in the absence of the investment project. The following demonstration shows that the interest rate in the model is equivalent to an internal rate of return.

In the optimal solution projects are chosen so that, for the last unit of investment,

$$B_t = rI, \tag{12.7}$$

where B_t is the net benefit at time t associated with the marginal amount of investment in the solution, r is the real interest rate, and I is the marginal amount of investment in dollars.[7]

For the total amount of investment, the relation is

$$B_t \geq rI^* \tag{12.8}$$

where $I^* = I_{TOT}$ in Table 12.8.

The present value of the stream of benefits in the model associated with I^* is

$$B_p = \sum_{t=1}^{T} \frac{B_t}{(1+r)^t} \geq rI^* \sum_{t=1}^{T} \frac{1}{(1+r)^t} \tag{12.9}$$

and as $T \to \infty$, B_p approaches its limiting value:

$$\lim_{T \to \infty} B_p \geq rI^* \frac{1}{r} = I^* \qquad (12.10)$$

In the limit, the present value of the benefits is greater than or equal to the present value of the investment, which is the defining characteristic of the internal rate of return (IRR). Thus the model chooses the amount I, and its composition, so that every component project has an IRR at least as great as r. If no projects have an IRR as great as r, then there will be no investment in the optimal solution.

The normal procedure for working with an investment model of this sort is to vary r over different solutions and record the amounts of investment, by project, in the solution. This procedure will show the minimum IRR for different packages of investment and will trace out a marginal efficiency-of-investment (MEI) schedule.

When the benefit streams are nonuniform, a conversion factor may be applied in the model to account for the nonuniformities. The most likely case is that of a project start-up period, when it may take several years before the benefits attain their level at full development. For that case, the conversion factor is of the form

$$k = \frac{\bar{B}}{B} \qquad (12.11)$$

where $\bar{B}$ is the average benefit over the life of the project, and B is the annual benefit at full development. Now since the benefits are endogenous in the model and derive from diverse activities, the factor k cannot be applied directly to the benefits. But it can be applied in an equivalent way to the investment costs, which are exogenous parameters in the model.

Let us rewrite the fundamental equality (12.7)

$$kB = rI \qquad (12.12)$$

equivalently,

$$B = r\left(\frac{I}{k}\right) = r\hat{I} \qquad (12.13)$$

so that I/k may be entered into the model instead of the original investment cost I. That is, once k is known, the figures 5.52, 6.10, and 7.49 in Table 12.8 would be divided by k before being entered into the table. (If k differed by project, each figure would be divided by its own k.)

The starting point for the calculation of k for a given project is to decompose the benefit stream into its components for the start-up period and for the period of full development:

$$\bar{B} \sum_{t=1}^{p} \frac{1}{(1+r)^t} = \sum_{t=1}^{g} B_t \frac{1}{(1+r)^t} + B \sum_{t=g+1}^{p} \frac{1}{(1+r)^t} \qquad (12.14)$$

where p is the number of years in the project's lifetime and g is the number of years in the start-up period.

To substitute (12.11) into (12.14), it is easier to normalize the benefits so that $B = 1$, yielding

$$k = \frac{\displaystyle\sum_{t=1}^{g} B_t^f \frac{1}{(1+r)^t} + \sum_{t=g+1}^{p} \frac{1}{(1+r)^t}}{\displaystyle\sum_{t=1}^{p} \frac{1}{(1+r)^t}} \tag{12.15}$$

where B_t^f represents the year t benefits expressed as a fraction of the full-development benefits B. The parameter B_t^f usually is known by project engineers, along with g and p, and thus (12.15) can be calculated for a given level of r.

The application of (12.15) is illustrated below for a project with a 40-year lifetime, a seven-year start-up period, and with benefits beginning at 50% of their full-development level. The calculation of k is made twice, once for $r = .04$ and once for $r = .06$. The time stream of benefits is assumed to be as follows:

Year	1	2	3	4	5	6	7	8	...	40
B_t^f	0.5	0.5714	0.6428	0.7142	0.7856	0.8570	0.9284	1.0	...	1.0

Then at $r = .04$,

$$k = \frac{4.2195 + 13.7907}{19.7928} = 0.9099$$

and at $r = .06$,

$$k = \frac{3.8943 + 9.4639}{15.0463} = 0.8878$$

For the case of $r = .04$ in Table 12.8, the entries 5.52, 6.10, and 7.49 all are divided by 0.9099.

When investment activities are entered explicitly into the model, the IRR resulting from the analysis is a financial rate of return, not an economic rate of return. Inputs such as labor and foreign exchange (imported inputs) are not "shadow priced" in the primal, but rather are costed at prevailing market prices, or true opportunity costs in the case of family labor. This is in keeping with the descriptive nature of the model. If it is felt that, say, the exchange rate is out of equilibrium, then in order for the analysis to yield an economic rate of return the exchange rate would have to be shadow priced at the estimated equilibrium rate, and the prices of imports and exports would have to be revised accordingly.

The programming model could be used to simulate what would happen if the exchange rate were moved to an equilibrium level. Similarly, it could be used to simulate different wage levels. But it must be borne in mind that these kinds of solutions are in fact simulations of hypothetical policy changes.

The Egyptian model H$\overline{A}$PY was modified in the ways described in this section to include investment activities like those shown in Table 12.8. Some 69 investment activities were included for possible projects involving expansion of the land area irrigable with the Nile waters (via installation of canals, drains, and other infrastructure). In the aggregate, these investment projects were sufficient to increase total production significantly and to alter relative prices. Hence the ranking of projects that resulted from the model, in terms of their IRRs, was different than the ranking that had been obtained with traditional project-by-project evaluations.

Another example of a model with endogenous investment activities is found in the farm-level study of Husain and Inman (1977). The area under study was a proposed cooperatively managed farm of some 1600 hectares in a World Bank project area in the Middle East. The model contains six alternative crops, alternative planting dates for each crop, inputs specified in 24 bimonthly periods, and 28 alternative types of agricultural machinery which could be purchased and utilized. Product prices were fixed since the study was carried out at the farm level. The specification of machinery purchase options was as in Chapter 11, but it was more complex owing to the complementarities between some pieces of machinery. The model, called SARF, also includes crop-specific irrigation response functions.

The main purpose of the model was to analyze the effects of different interest rates on the composition of machinery purchases. But it was also used as a normative model to explore the consequences of the farm's adoption of different objective functions. The alternative objectives explored were (1) maximization of profits, and (2) maximization of wages plus profits. These two alternatives were designed to express the tradeoffs between incomes of shareholders in the cooperatives and nonshareholders. The latter supplied labor but received no share of the profits. The model quantified the extent to which low interest rates, and hence large purchases of machinery, benefited shareholders at the expense of nonshareholders, via displacement of labor. In terms of project design, the SARF model indicated appropriate combinations of machinery purchases and associated cropping patterns, under different interest rates and wage rates.

In their conclusions, Husain and Inman pointed out that models like SARF can be used for farm budget analysis, cropping pattern planning, the planning of machinery stock acquisition and usage, and planning the timing and amounts of irrigation releases. They made some interesting general observations:

> The underlying premise of this model is that project design could be improved and project appraisal facilitated if analysts could explore a larger set of alterna-

tives than they are presently able to do (by manual procedures). This premise has two parts: (i) the specification of technical and behavioral relationships, which is the art and science of the analyst and (ii) given a specified set of relationships, the evaluation of the effect of alternative policy instruments, which is essentially a question of technology (existence of algorithms like linear programming and easy access to computers). The first part of the premise is the more difficult; it could be aided by theory as well as feedback from selective empirical adventures but it requires sensitive judgments from analysts. The second part is simpler. ... At this stage, however, [lack of modeling skills] is the binding constraint on improving project designs/appraisals (Husain and Inman, 1977, p. 36).

12.8.4 A Normative Investment Model

The project rankings calculated in the manner of the $\overline{\text{HA}}$PY and Mexican regional models reflect only one policy objective: to maximize the efficiency of the investments in generating financial returns to farmers, as expressed in the IRR criterion. Farm-level studies can explore different objective functions, but at the sector level incorporation of other policy objectives in the analysis has to be done in a somewhat roundabout way. Different combinations of investment projects can be defined *a priori* and then each combination can be put in the model and its corresponding solution obtained. By comparing the solutions, it then is possible to compare the different combinations in terms of their effects on farm income, employment, foreign exchange, and other goal variables. The final decision could be made on the basis of these comparisons, if appropriate.

A more direct procedure would involve exploration of the Euclidean space of policy goals and investment projects. Such an exploration could be conducted with a model whose detached coefficients tableau looked like Table 12.9. The tableau shows each project's effects on the goals via the coefficients e_1 through x_n, and the goal variables E through X represent the effect on each goal of the total investment package. Each project is limited in the extent to which it may be implemented, and the total package is bounded by the amount of available investment financing, FL. The objective function weights z_1 through z_5 are measures of the hypothetical policy preferences with respect to the goals, and one application of the model would consist of varying those weights over different solutions to see the consequences for the investment program. The question is how to generate the model in the tableau.

If a descriptive programming model is available, then a two-stage procedure can be devised. In the first stage, the descriptive model is solved n times, once with each project included in the model as per Table 12.8 above. This procedure yields n simulations of the effects of the projects, though there will be fewer than n if some of the solutions result in the project not being undertaken. Assume that m of the solutions contain an investment at a positive level. The information from those m solutions is then arranged in the form of the column vectors in the left part of the matrix in Table 12.9, that is, the column vectors I_j. The right-hand side information is added, plus the

Table 12.9   A Normative Investment Model

Item	Irrigation activities						Goal variables					RHS
	I_1	I_2	I_3	$\cdots$	I_n	I_{TOT}	E	F	Y	YS	X	
Employment (E)	e_1	e_2	e_3	$\cdots$	e_n		-1					$= 0$
Foreign exchange (F)	f_1	f_2	f_3	$\cdots$	f_n			-1				$= 0$
Farm income (Y)	y_1	y_2	y_3	$\cdots$	y_n				-1			$= 0$
Income on small farms (YS)	ys_1	ys_2	ys_3	$\cdots$	ys_n					-1		$= 0$
Food production (X)	x_1	x_2	x_3	$\cdots$	x_n						-1	$= 0$
Bound, I_1	1											$\leq B_1$
Bound, I_2		1										$\leq B_2$
Bound, I_3			1									$\leq B_3$
$\vdots$				$\ddots$								$\vdots$
Bound, I_n					1							$\leq B_n$
Total investment	c_1	c_2	c_3	$\cdots$	c_n	-1						$= 0$
Financial limit						1						$\leq FL$
Objective function							z_1	z_2	z_3	z_4	z_5	Maximize

identity matrices, and the normative model is ready for use except for the z_j coefficients, which are discussed later.

Thus far, the main drawback to this procedure is the implicit assumption of fixed prices, if the investment program is large relative to the sector's existing resource endowment. To relax this assumption, the first-stage solutions can be conducted somewhat differently. Instead of putting one investment activity in the model for each solution, combinations of investment activities can be used. Each alternative combination should fully utilize the available financing. The combinations should represent a sufficient expansion of the resource base that product prices are affected. The creation of the table in Table 12.9 then proceeds as before, except that now each I_j represents a combination of projects. The right-hand side values B_j of the bounds on projects can be changed to be 1.0 in each case, that is, each combination can be funded fully or at any lower value.

A procedure similar to this was followed in the case of an investment programming model for Peru (Norton, Santaniello, and Echevarría, 1983). That study also addressed issues related to funding an aggregate, multiyear investment program before all the individual projects of the program were known. A decision was made to identify representative projects, past or present, for each line of investment, and to conduct the analysis of choices in terms of the amount of funding for each line. Information on the representative projects was used as a basis for calculating the benefits of each line of investment, and so with this direct approach it was possible to skip the first stage of solving the descriptive model and go directly to the normative model shown in Table 12.9. In this case, all of the principal agricultural products were traded goods, so the working assumption was made that the investment program would not be likely to affect product prices.

The selected investments were to be made in the first period and the benefits would accrue over a horizon as long as 40 years. Some summation and discounting equations were added to create variables representing the discounted 40-year stream of benefits. Five categories of benefits were included: sector income, income in the poorer regions, production of basic foods, employment creation, and foreign exchange earnings.

In highly simplified form, the equations of the model (called TICLIO) were as follows:

$$\max \hat{Z} = \sum_i w_i Z_i \tag{12.16}$$

subject to

$$Z_i = \sum_j \sum_t \left[\frac{z_{ijt}}{(1+d)^t} \right] \sum_p I_{pj} \tag{12.17}$$

$$\sum_p \sum_j c_{pj} I_{pj} \leq F \tag{12.18}$$

$$\sum_{j \in J_m} \sum_p I_{pj} \leq R_m \tag{12.19}$$

where $\hat{Z}$ = policy objective function
       Z_i = policy goal variables
       I_{pj} = investment activities by project p and line j

and the parameters are

   z_{ijt} = benefit in terms of goal i arising from investment activity j at time t
   c_{pj} = investment cost coefficients
   F = aggregate financial limit on the investment program
   R_m = other bounds on components of the investment program

In basic structure the model was simple, but a number of interesting details were incorporated via equations (12.19). One of the equations (12.19) was an administrative capacity limit for irrigation investments; that is, an expression of the fact that public agencies have limits on their capacity to implement projects. Another set of equations in (12.19) referred to physical limits in each region on the volume of projects, that is, the number of hectares susceptible to irrigation, reforestation, and so forth. Yet another set constituted "representativeness" constraints on the projects which exemplified each line of investment. For each line of investment there were several illustrative projects, and if a project was typical of, say, only 25% of the investments in its line, then the representativeness constraints prevented that project from representing in the solution more than 25% (or a somewhat higher share) of the investment in that line.

The model was applied in a variety of ways. First, it was found that the proportionate increase in all goal variables was higher for a relaxation of the

Table 12.10   Policy Tradeoffs as Measured with the Investment Model for Peru

	Objective function				
	1	2	3	4	5
Item	Sector income	Income in poor regions	Employment	Foreign exchange	Basic food production
Increments in					
Sector income	651.90	619.60	534.05	604.07	586.67
Income in poor regions	540.29	619.60	519.87	474.75	534.61
Employment	2656.15	2881.55	3044.16	2529.31	2678.11
Foreign exchange	486.72	399.02	298.10	586.70	455.65
Basic food production	449.49	453.21	249.38	383.47	518.37
Irrigation investment	42.74	30.79	12.72	50.99*	50.99*
(coast)	(22.29)	(—)	(—)	(33.31)	(9.62)
(mountains)	(20.46)	(21.51)	(12.72)	(17.68)	(20.65)
(jungle)	(—)	(9.28)	(—)	(—)	(20.72)
Forestry investment	26.12*	26.12*	26.12*	17.19	—
(coast)	(—)	(—)	(4.35)	(—)	(—)
(mountains)	(17.08)	(17.08)	(12.73)	(8.14)	(—)
(jungle)	(9.05*)	(9.05*)	(9.05*)	(9.05*)	(—)
R & E investment	29.41*	26.85	29.41*	29.41*	29.41*
(coast)	(2.56*)	(—)	(2.56*)	(2.56*)	(2.56*)
(mountains)	(13.68*)	(13.68*)	(13.68*)	(13.68*)	(13.68*)
(jungle)	(13.18*)	(13.18*)	(13.18*)	(13.18*)	(13.18*)
Marketing investment	(—)	17.00*	17.00*	(—)	17.00*

Notes: An asterisk denotes that the line of investment is at its financial upper limit. R & E refers to research and extension.
Source: Norton, Santaniello, and Echevarría (1983), p. 167.

administrative capacity constraint than for a relaxation of the financing constraint. In other words, the model indicated the program would have benefited more from improvements in the staff's implementation capacity than from more project funding, and in fact after the program was approved implementation capacity turned out to be very much the limiting factor.

A set of solutions was designed to explore the consequences for composition of the investments of different policy goals. Table 12.10 shows the solutions for each case in which one $w_i = 1.0$ and the others are equal to zero. Through a series of additional solutions and discussions with officials of the government and the funding agency (The Interamerican Development Bank), it was determined that the preferred program had policy weights (w_i) of 0.75 for sector income and 0.25 for employment creation. This set of weights was then adopted for officially measuring the progress of the program as individual projects were implemented.

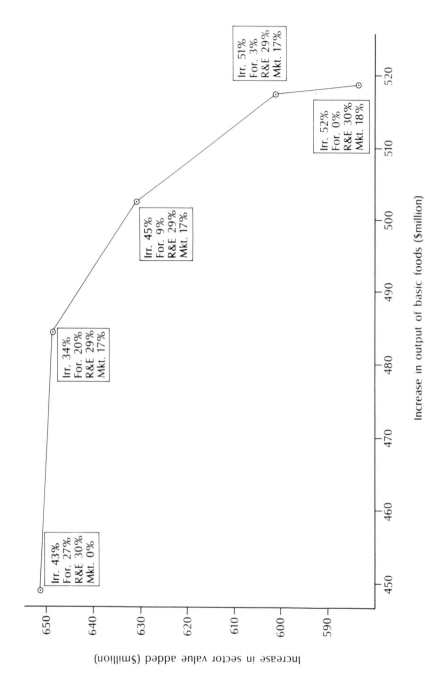

Figure 12.7 Program choices between value added and output of basic foods.
Source: adapted from Norton, Santaniello, and Echevarria (1983, p. 170).

319

Another set of experiments was addressed to tracing out the tradeoffs, or frontiers, among pairs of policy goals. Figure 12.7 shows the frontier for sector income vs. output of basic foods, and the associated composition of the investment program for each node on the frontier. The composition is expressed in terms of shares of each of the four major lines of investment: irrigation, reforestation, research and extension, and marketing. In general, these frontiers revealed that the tradeoffs (slopes) were quite extreme as the axes were approached. The implication of this finding was that the preferred program was not likely to lie along an axis, that is, it would not correspond to giving one policy goal a weight of 1.0 and the others zero weights.

Finally, the study pointed out that historical data can provide bounds on the relative values of the policy weights, as starting points in a dialogue about their values. For two policy goals, let their increments over the past, say, ten years be $\hat{w}_1$ and $\hat{w}_2$. Suppose that policy makers are unhappy with past trends and that they want to place more emphasis on increasing goal 2 (perhaps employment). Then for the weights in the policy model it can be inferred that

$$\frac{w_2}{w_1} > \frac{\hat{w}_2}{\hat{w}_1} \tag{12.20}$$

12.9 OTHER MULTILEVEL PROCEDURES

Multilevel procedures involve more than one model, and the models are linked in the sense that the solution to one model provides inputs into another model. Although in principle these procedures can involve many models, almost all practical experiences are limited to two models. Multilevel procedures are required under the following kinds of circumstances:

1 One large model that includes all the relevant considerations in a single set of equations may be too large to solve in a practicable way. Therefore it has to be broken into component models which are solved individually in an iterative fashion, with solutions from each model providing information for revising coefficients in another model. The outcome of such an iterative process (eventually) provides a joint solution of the set of models which is equivalent to a solution of the original large model. Dantzig and Wolfe (1961) devised the first procedure like this, which was called decomposition.

2 The objective functions that are appropriate to different levels of decision models may differ, and therefore no single model can encompass them. This is the multilevel programming problem discussed in Chapter 7.

3 There may be an informational problem in the sense that one model cannot be specified completely without information that is obtained from solutions of another model.

Decomposition procedures are not used much in practice, because today's computing power usually is sufficient to solve even very large models and direct solution is more rapid than solutions via decomposition. However, the literature on decomposition techniques has provided added insights into the structure of optimization models and also has helped further to understand the nature of actual multilevel decision processes in an institutional sense. Some of the seminal works in this area are by Malinvaud (1967), Kornai (1967, 1969), and Heal (1973).

The information problem, which also has institutional analogs, was explored in Kornai (1969), Duloy and Norton (1973c), and Manne (1973b). For the sake of illustration, let us suppose that the two levels are the economy-wide (macro) level and the sector level. They are sometimes called the upper and lower levels, respectively, the center and the periphery, or the inner and outer problems.

To model the choices in the entire economy, it is necessary to know the production functions—or activity analysis vectors—at the level of each sector. In many circumstances it is not possible to obtain that information without effectively constructing a sector model. But once a sector model is constructed, it may not be efficient to combine it with a macro model—because of model size and differences in objective functions, and also because the sector model contains a lot of information that is irrelevant to macro considerations. A macro model builder does not want to be bothered with monthly land and labor constraints in each of many different localities or with the consequences for crop rotations of planting corn in March or May.

In these circumstances, a workable two-level procedure involves solving the sector model several times under variations in macro parameters, e.g., wage rates, interest rates, and the exchange rate. Each solution is then summarized in aggregate form as a vector of numbers representing total sector production, employment, exports and imports, use of capital, use of chemical inputs, energy, other industrial inputs, and so forth. A set of vectors like this describes the sector's feasible space from a macro viewpoint—that is, the alternative vectors that are achievable under reasonable variations in macro parameters.

This description of the feasible space then is inserted into the macro model as a set of column vectors of the input/output type. Clearly, this is possible only if the macro model is of the activity analysis type, as in Manne (1973a). This procedure eliminates the need to iterate with the sector model as in a decomposition approach, but note that multiple solutions of the sector model are required in order to specify the macro model.

In most cases of policy planning in market economies, macro and sector policy deliberations are not closely enough linked to benefit from such procedures. But at the sector level itself there is a two-level problem, as discussed in Chapter 7 and briefly above in connection with the Peruvian investment model. The two levels are (1) the decentralized level of producer and consumer decisions, which is the topic of most of this book, and (2) the policy choice level, at which decisions are made on policy instruments.

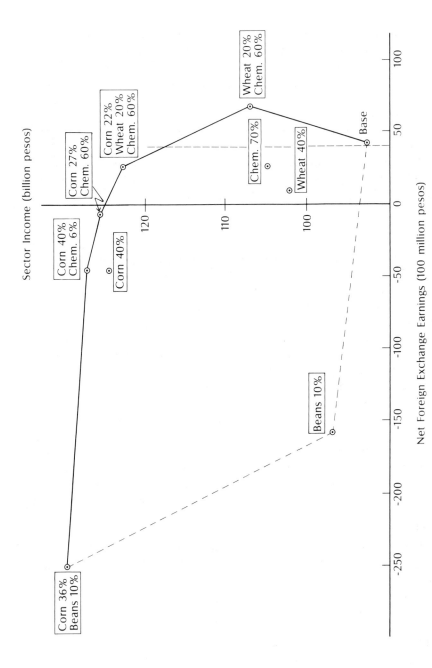

Figure 12.8 A policy feasible space. The percent figures are subsidy rates by product.
Source: Ballenger (1984, p. 135).

In general, this two-level procedure can be modeled in much the same way as the multilevel informational problem. The descriptive sector model can be solved several times under different values of the policy instruments, and then each of those solutions can be summarized in the form of a vector of target variables (employment, export earnings, etc.) and instruments (price support levels, input prices, investment amounts by type, etc.). The policy model then looks somewhat like Table 12.9. The budgetary consequence of each instrument can also be evaluated from the sector model's solutions and entered into a budget constraint row in the policy model.

Proceeding in this way permits formal exploration of the policy options under different weights in a policy objective function. It also provides a tool for defining the "policy feasible space," that is, the set of values of the target variables which could be attained under acceptable variations in the value of policy instruments. The policy feasible space is necessarily convex, as shown in the illustration in Figure 12.8, which is taken from Ballenger (1984).

Tracing out the policy feasible space also reveals the policy feasible frontier. Based on the few studies conducted along these lines so far, it is likely that the actual policy configuration will be found to lie inside the frontier, that is, with existing budgetary limitations, a new combination of policies can be found that will increase at least one target variable without decreasing any others (Candler and Norton 1977, Ballenger 1984). Furthermore, each of the policies in such a combination would have been deemed acceptable beforehand, or else they would not have been included in the analysis to begin with.

The policy feasible space shown in Figure 12.8 was constructed from a policy model which in turn was derived from a truncated version of the CHAC model for Mexico. Each of the circled points on the solid frontier was obtained as a solution to the policy model under different weights in the policy objective function. The circled points below and to the left of the solid frontier correspond to individual solutions of the truncated CHAC model. The base point corresponds to the CHAC solution with no subsidies. That part of the policy feasible space which lies to the right of the vertical dashed line is the complementary subset of the space; it is the area in which either target variable may be increased without decreasing the other target variable. In this case, it can be seen that most of the points on the frontier imply tradeoffs between the two policy goals. Conceptually, the main drawback of this procedure is that there is no guarantee that the true frontier (of the policy feasible space) actually has been found. However, in practice, with enough exploration via solutions of the policy model under different objective function weights, the analyst can be reasonably confident that the frontier has in fact been found.

This kind of policy analysis is generalizable to many different types of government intervention in the agricultural sector. It would appear to be among the more practicable of the various multilevel methods that have been proposed and tried.

12.10 COMPARATIVE STATICS AND DYNAMICS

12.10.1 Comparative Statics

As the previous sections in this chapter demonstrate, much of the applied analysis with programming models is carried out via simulation of alternative static equilibria. The simulations represent hypothetical outcomes toward which the sector would tend if only one parameter, or selected parameters, were changed. But there is no time period associated with them.

Comparative statics solutions can be conducted in a time-dated fashion. The appropriate parameters of the model are adjusted to their presumed values for some year in the future, and then the model is solved. In interpreting the solution, the implicit assumption is that a new equilibrium is established by the designated year, that is, that markets will have adjusted. Experience in projecting sector growth rates with programming models suggests that this is not an unreasonable assumption.

Projections of growth prospects are in fact the most common kind of comparative statics analysis. Usually, several alternative projections are made in order to explore the possible effects of external factors, such as growth in export markets, and of domestic policies, such as investment in irrigation and other kinds of land improvement. As in the other analyses, much of the interest lies in examining the different effects of alternative policies.

A comparative statics analysis requires at least two solutions: a base solution and a projection solution, the latter referring to a particular year in the future. To set up the projection solution, the following kinds of changes need to be made in the model's coefficients:

1   Rotate the demand function
2   Change export and import bounds and prices, as appropriate
3   Change the resource endowments in the right-hand side vector
4   Change input prices and supply functions, as appropriate
5   Change the technology coefficients for production and processing, particularly the crop and livestock yields in production

It should be noted that projections are carried out in constant prices, so changes in the prices of exports, imports, and production inputs should reflect expected changes in real prices, that is, prices deflated by a general price index. Clearly, these prices are an example in which considerable uncertainty may be associated with the projections of parameter values, and so it may be desirable to perform sensitivity analysis in the form of alternative projections.

Demand functions are rotated via changes in the right-hand side values of the convex combination constraints. Suppose that aggregate real income is expected to increase by 30% over the projection period, and that the income elasticity of demand for a product is 0.5. In that case, the domestic demand function needs to be rotated rightward by 15%. This rotation is accomplished by increasing the right-hand side of the convex combination constraint from a value of 1.0 to a value of 1.15.

Resource endowment changes can represent important allocations of public funds, as in the case of investment programs for irrigation and expanding the amount of nonirrigated cultivable land. Some attention has to be paid to endowments of agricultural labor, which are increasing in some countries and decreasing in others.

Part of the changes in technology over time can be captured by endogenous shifts along the production function in the static model. However, typically the entire production function will be shifting outward over time, and this effect can be best represented simply by increasing unit yields. The rate of increase selected normally is the historical rate, unless there are specific reasons for projecting a different rate. As with other parameters in the model, the technological parameters can be used to conduct interesting sensitivity tests. The consequences for incomes, employment, and the like can be traced out for different rates of yield growth.

12.10.2 Dynamics

The procedures for comparative statics analysis are the same at the farm level and the sector level, but in the case of dynamic analysis the procedures may differ. At the farm level, the dynamic linkages are of three kinds: (1) the farmer's income in a given year will affect his savings and therefore may affect his possibilities for investments; (2) investments affect the capacity for production in later years; and (3) there exist biological intertemporal linkages, such as the yield curve over time in tree crops and other perennials, and reproduction and growth rates for livestock. Also, a farmer may reasonably be expected to have a subjective discount rate, and his objective function will include, among other variables, some transformation of his discounted income stream. Hence it often is important to make farm models multiperiod, as discussed in Section 4.3.

In a sector model, not all these dynamic linkages are present. Savings are not endogenous to the model. They could be, but many investments in the sector require public funding, so there is no point in specifying a savings-investment relationship in the model. Also, the objective function does not admit of discounted income streams, since it has a market-simulating function. Hence, in procedural terms, a multiperiod analysis with a sector model usually is carried out as a sequence of comparative statics solutions.

In the event that some investments are endogenous in the manner discussed in Section 12.8.3, then *ex post* linkages can be made among the time sequence of static solutions. The endogenous level of investment in the period t model could be used to calculate the right-hand side parameters that represent resource endowments in the model for period $t + 1$.

Other linkages of this type can be envisaged. For example, if a rural-urban migration function were available (outside the model), then the endogenous agricultural income in the solution for period t could be applied, via a side calculation, to determining the endowments of rural labor in the right-hand side of the model for period $t + 1$. The extent to which these kinds of linkages are desirable or practicable depends on the situation being modeled. A special form of intertemporal linkage has been developed, called recursive programming, and it is reviewed below.

12.10.3 Recursive Programming

In its most general form, a recursive programming model can be defined as "a sequence of optimization problems in which one or more parameters or coefficients in any problem in the sequence are functionally dependent on the optimal variables of preceding members of the sequence" (Day 1963b). A simple example would be a sequence of comparative static solutions in each of which the resource constraints were updated on the basis of the investment decisions of the optimal solution for the previous period.

A more specific form of recursive programming was developed by Henderson (1959) and Day (1961, 1963b) in an attempt to incorporate behavioral dynamics into programming models. Even when a model is well specified in terms of incorporating farmers' price expectations and their behavior towards risk, consumption, leisure, and investment decisions, it is often the case that time sequences of comparative static solutions only track history poorly in simulating actual adjustments from year to year in cropping patterns and resource use. Discrepancies may arise from incorrect model specification and from data errors. But they may also arise if key factors affecting farmers' decisions over time are not incorporated in the model. The latter may include lags in the dissemination of knowledge about new technologies or market conditions, changes in farmers' perceptions about the profitability and riskiness of new technologies, or simply farmers' reluctance to change from established cropping and technology practices.

These kinds of considerations are inherently difficult to measure and incorporate in a model in an explicit way, particularly in a dynamic setting in which markets and technologies, and hence perceived information, change frequently. Henderson (1959) and Day (1963b) argued that such information difficulties lead farmers to react cautiously in adjusting their cropping patterns from one period to the next, and they proposed modeling such cautious behavior through a set of flexibility constraints. These constraints are imposed on individual cropping activities, and take the form

$$\left(1 - \beta_{j,\,\min}\right) X_{jt-1} \le X_{jt} \le \left(1 + \beta_{j,\,\max}\right) X_{jt-1}. \tag{12.21}$$

Here X_{jt} denotes the level of the jth cropping activity in the model solution for period t, and this level is constrained to lie within a range determined in part by the activity's level in the model solution for the previous period. The coefficients $\beta_{j,\,\min}$ and $\beta_{j,\,\max}$ are, respectively, the minimum and maximum proportions by which farmers are assumed to be willing to deviate from the cropping level of the previous period.

Recursive programming models have to be initialized to some base period or year. For example, in period $t = 1$, the values of $X_{jt-1} = X_{j0}$, all j, would need to be initialized. Thereafter, sequences of solutions are obtained, each solution of which relates to a specific period or year. Given a fixed set of model coefficients, a sequence of solutions will typically converge to an equilibrium solution in which none of the flexibility constraints will be binding. If the model is then perturbed by changing a coefficient, such as a commodity price, then a new sequence of solutions will follow. The flexibility constraints may initially restrict the speed with which the optimal cropping pattern can adjust to the price change, but eventually the sequence of solutions should converge to a new equilibrium solution in which the flexibility constraints are again no longer binding.

Since the flexibility constraints play a key role in controlling a model's solutions when in a disequilibrium state, the estimated values of $\beta_{j,\min}$ and $\beta_{j,\max}$ are crucial to the model's ability to track or predict actual adjustment paths. Unfortunately, there are no really satisfactory ways of estimating the β coefficients.

In practice, the β coefficients are assumed to be constant over time, and they may simply be based on the largest upward and downward adjustments observed in the area of a crop over some historical period. Another approach is to sort pairs of adjacent observations from time series data on X_j into two groups, those in which $X_{jt} > X_{jt-1}$ and those in which $X_{jt} < X_{jt-1}$. (Note that one can form as many pairs as the original number of observations less one, since, for example, the series X_{j1}, X_{j2}, and X_{j3} leads to the pairs X_{j1}, X_{j2} and X_{j2}, X_{j3}). Within each group a regression equation of the form $X_{jt} = b_j X_{jt-1}$ can then be run to provide estimates of β_j. The estimated b_j for the group satisfying $X_{jt} > X_{jt-1}$ is an estimate of $1 + \beta_{j,\max}$, and the estimated b_j for the remaining group is an estimate of $1 - \beta_{j,\min}$. Estimated values of the β coefficients are usually adjusted during model validation tests to enable the model to best track some historical period.

For a particularly interesting application of recursive linear programming in which an attempt is made to track the impact of the green revolution on the farm economy of the Indian Punjab, see Day and Singh (1977).

NOTES

1 Portions of this section are adapted from Kutcher and Norton (1982).
2 CHAC is named after the Mayan rain god.
3 HAPY is an early Egyptian god of the harvest.
4 TASM is the acronym for Turkish Agricultural Sector Model.
5 These calculations were made by Carlos Pomareda.
6 This section is adapted in part from Bassoco, Mutsaers, Norton, and Silos (1983).
7 For simplicity, we ignore depreciation of the project's capital assets.

Chapter 13

Applied Studies of the Role of Risk

13.1 INTRODUCTION

In Chapter 10 we argued that neglect of risk and risk-averse behavior could lead to important biases in the results from agricultural sector models. In particular, the supply of risky crops and the valuation of important resources are likely to be overestimated. We shall review empirical evidence on the size of these biases in this chapter, as well as compare model results obtained for expected price and unit revenue forecasting behavior.

Incorporating risk in a model not only helps eliminate biases but it also provides a means for evaluating some public policies aimed at reducing or spreading risks for farmers. Such policies include crop insurance and price stabilization schemes. A key element in evaluating such policies is to allow for the effect of risk reduction on aggregate supply response. That is, if a crop becomes less risky as a result of policy interventions, then total production may increase. This risk response effect can be usefully simulated in mathematical programming models.

13.2 IMPACT OF RISK ON CROPPING PATTERNS AND PRICES

Hazell et al. (1983) explored the empirical importance of incorporating risk and risk-averse behavior in part of the Mexican model CHAC. They selected eight irrigated district models from CHAC which, in aggregate, account for significant shares of the national production of cotton, tomatoes, dry alfalfa, rice, soybeans, and safflower. The selected districts also produce a wide range of cereal crops and vegetables, and some sugar cane. The districts, which are not contiguous geographically, are Culiacán, Comisión del Fuerte, Guasave, Rio Mayo, and Santo Domingo in the Pacific Northwest; Ciudad Delicias and La Laguna in the North Central region; and Bajo Rio San Juan in the Northeast.

Each of the eight districts was modeled as a large farm, and included seasonal constraints for land, labor, and water, and a range of technology options to permit flexibility in the choice of mechanization level, the date of planting, and the combination of family and hired labor (see Chapter 12). Crop returns were specified as risky, and farmers were assumed to adhere to an $E[u] = E - \Phi\sigma$ utility specification. Risk in activity returns was estimated from a 10-year time series on prices and yields, and a MOTAD approximation was used assuming farmers act on the basis of expected price forecasts (see Chapter 10).

The district models were linked in block diagonal form and integrated into an aggregate market structure similar to that in CHAC. That is, the market comprised linear domestic demand functions for groups of commodities, and these groups were assumed to be demand independent. Substitution was allowed between products within groups at rates fixed by base-year relative prices. The domestic demand curves were given the same price elasticities as in CHAC but were located at mean output levels appropriate for

Table 13.1   Price Solutions by Commodity Group for Different Values of Φ, Model of Irrigated Districts, Mexico

Demand Group	Commodity	Values of Φ[a]						Base-year price
		0	0.5	1.0	1.5	2.0	2.5	
		(pesos per metric ton)						
1	Sugar cane	68	70	72	68	68	68	70
2	Tomatoes	321	703	988	1200	1494	1772	1150
3	Chilies	1031	1125	1124	1352	1330	1547	1500
4	Cotton fiber	5770	5770	5770	5770	5770	5770	5770
5	Forage crops	499	475	445	449	444	443	446
6	Food crops	1373	1316	1241	1233	1227	1217	1285
7	Cereals	1044	1043	992	970	958	989	817
8	Melons	446	416	420	468	476	416	741
9	Vegetable oils	1014	1004	1022	1058	1133	1200	1164
10	Cucumbers	516	436	284	148	148	148	590
	MAD[b]	219	175	153	123	146	172	

Note: Prices are reported as group indexes, using base-year quantity weights.
[a]Larger Φ values indicate greater risk aversion; $\Phi = 0$ corresponds to risk-neutral behavior.
[b]The MAD is the mean absolute deviation of the solution values from the base-period values.
Source: Hazell et al. (1983), p. 237.

Table 13.2 Quantities Produced for Domestic Market for Different Φ Values, Model of Irrigated Districts, Mexico

Crop	Values of Φ^a						Base-year quantities
	0	0.5	1.0	1.5	2.0	2.5	
			(metric tons)				
Dry alfalfa	137,323	139,120	140,916	140,916	140,916	140,916	170,019
Cotton	484,488	476,111	445,869	358,485	285,965	268,476	243,454
Green alfalfa	173,445	175,714	177,983	177,983	177,983	177,983	226,109
Rice	115,369	115,784	118,774	118,774	141,885	143,695	126,197
Sugar cane	2,659,859	2,659,859	2,659,859	2,659,859	2,659,859	2,659,859	2,627,020
Safflower	75,777	74,467	72,752	67,437	86,449	70,914	72,490
Barley	510	517	523	523	523	523	665
Chilies	15,409	15,161	15,161	14,789	14,789	14,294	14,459
Beans	30,278	30,278	31,060	31,060	26,428	26,765	33,001
Chickpeas	1,239	1,264	1,272	1,272	1,250	1,251	1,585
Tomatoes	223,682	202,712	185,237	171,257	153,781	136,241	174,752
Sesame	9,643	9,475	9,258	8,581	8,161	7,662	9,224
Maize	194,989	200,993	198,093	163,852	163,851	163,406	210,801
Cantaloupe	9,966	10,589	10,589	9,967	9,966	10,589	6,935
Cucumbers	20	33	35	359	2,195	2,301	19
Watermelons	22,213	23,601	23,601	22,213	22,213	23,601	10,850
Sorghum	336,856	341,263	345,670	345,669	345,670	345,669	285,818
Soybeans	59,815	58,781	63,359	75,595	63,982	68,706	57,220
Wheat	326,064	320,453	328,585	369,565	369,566	367,959	343,979
Potatoes	45,065	45,065	46,228	46,228	21,734	22,010	27,139

[a]Larger Φ values indicate greater risk aversion; Φ = 0 corresponds to risk-neutral behavior.
Source: Hazell et al. (1983), p. 238.

the eight district aggregates. Exports and imports were also permitted at fixed prices, and constraints on these possibilities were taken from CHAC but prorated according to the ratio of output from the eight districts to national output for each product.

Pertinent results from the model are presented in Tables 13.1 and 13.2. Table 13.1 shows the effect of different Φ values on the domestic equilibrium prices by commodity groups. On the one hand, the prices of groups 2 (tomatoes), 3 (chili), and 9 (vegetable oils) all increase with Φ, indicating corresponding reductions in the quantities produced for the domestic market. On the other hand, the prices of groups 5 (forage crops), 6 (food crops), 7 (cereals), 8 (melons), and 10 (cucumbers) decrease as Φ increases, indicating that production of these crops for the domestic market increases as producers become more risk averse. The quantity effects are shown in detail in Table 13.2 at the individual commodity level. The prices of groups 1 (sugar cane) and 4 (cotton fiber) show no response to the risk-aversion parameter.

These results demonstrate the ambiguities involved in predicting the effect of risk-averse behavior on the supplies of individual crops. Such ambiguities arise because, as shown in Chapter 10, the contribution of a crop to the total risk of a cropping plan depends not only on the variance of its own returns, but also on the covariances between its returns and the returns of all the other crops. Thus, crops whose output declines as Φ increases either have large variances and/or large covariances with other crops. The opposite holds for crops whose output increases with Φ.

The last columns in Tables 13.1 and 13.2 contain base-year values (three-year averages) of prices and quantities. By comparing these values with the model solution corresponding to risk neutrality ($\Phi = 0$) some indication of the biases inherent in ignoring risk are obtained.

The risk-neutral solution predicts unrealistically high levels of production of cotton, tomatoes, cantaloupes, potatoes, watermelons, and sorghum, and particularly low prices for groups 2, 3, and 8. Once risk-averse behavior is assumed ($\Phi > 0$), there is a definite improvement between the model's predictions and the base-year values. In fact, the solution corresponding to $\Phi = 1.5$ provides a surprisingly good fit. A simple measure of "goodness of fit" is the mean absolute deviation (MAD) of the solution values from their base-period counterparts. The MAD of the price fits are shown in the last row of Table 13.1, and they clearly demonstrate the superiority of the solution for $\Phi = 1.5$.

13.3 RISK AND THE VALUATION OF RESOURCES

One of the benefits of constructing aggregate linear programming models is that they may provide shadow prices for scarce resources that can be useful in guiding investment decisions. For example, in the Mexican irrigated districts model described above, the shadow prices for irrigation water could be particularly useful in guiding additional public investments in irrigation. But how are these values affected by risk and risk-averse behavior?

**Table 13.3 Shadow Prices for Water with Different Values of Φ,
Model of Irrigated Districts, Mexico**

District	Values of Φ[a]					
	0	0.5	1.0	1.5	2.0	2.5
	(Pesos / 1000 m³)					
El Fuerte	313	0	0	0	0	0
Culiacán	0	0	0	0	0	0
Rio Mayo	1516	1248	1123	1033	851	845
Guasave	782	355	0	0	0	0
Ciudad Delicias	719	714	523	346	182	115
Bajo Rio San Juan	842	598	172	0	0	0
Santo Domingo	2380	1934	1672	1285	943	656
La Laguna	816	620	487	478	418	352

[a]Large Φ values indicate greater risk aversion; Φ = 0 corresponds to risk-neutral behavior.
Source: Hazell et al. (1983).

Table 13.3 contains the shadow prices by district for different values of Φ. These values were taken from the annual water constraints in the model, and they measure the annual return from an additional unit of water when it is used in an optimal seasonal pattern determined by the model.

The shadow prices consistently decline as Φ increases. Thus, if risk neutrality were assumed in the model specification, this would lead to an upward bias in the marginal valuation of irrigation water. In fact, if the true value of Φ is around 1.5, then neglect of risk-averse behavior would lead to valuing irrigation water at more than twice its true social value in most districts.

13.4 RISK AND SUPPLY RESPONSE BEHAVIOR

In a study of milk production in West Germany, Hanf and Mueller (1979) constructed an aggregate linear programming model based on representative farms. They specified risky prices and yields for the major farming activities, and as in the Mexican model, used a MOTAD formulation to approximate $E[u] = E - \Phi\sigma$ utility maximizing behavior. Unlike the Mexican model though, prices were fixed exogenously in their model, so it was not necessary to make any assumptions about farmers' price forecasting behavior. A fixed price specification is justifiable since prices are largely controlled by the Common Market.

To obtain aggregate supply functions for milk, Hanf and Mueller used parametric linear programming to solve the model for different milk prices. They then fitted linear regressions to the resultant price-quantity pairs to obtain smooth supply functions. Functions were obtained for different values of Φ, and the results are summarized in Figure 13.1.

The milk supply function corresponding to risk-neutral behavior (Φ = 0) is flatter and has a higher intercept on the price axis. As Φ increases, the supply function becomes steeper indicating a more inelastic response to price

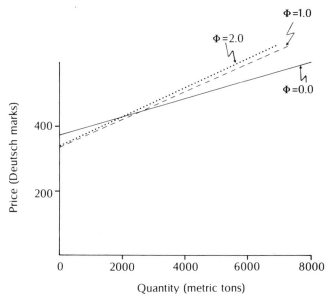

Figure 13.1 Supply functions of milk for different values of Φ, dairy model, West Germany. Source: Hanf and Mueller (1979).

increases. In this case, neglect of risk-averse behavior in model specification would lead to an overestimate of the supply elasticity of milk.

Hazell et al. (1983) also report commodity supply functions for different levels of risk-averse behavior. Figures 13.2 and 13.3 contain results from an aggregate model of the important vegetable growing districts of Mexico.[1] This model also has an $E[u] = E - \Phi\sigma$ risk specification, and a linear market

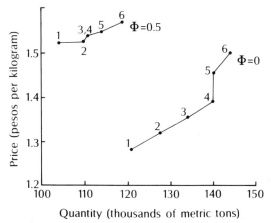

Figure 13.2 Domestic supply response for safflower, model of vegetable districts, Mexico. Solutions are numbered as follows: 1, base period; 2, with 5% quantity shift in relevant demand; 3, with 10% quantity shift; 4, with 15% quantity shift; and so on. Source: Hazell et al. (1983).

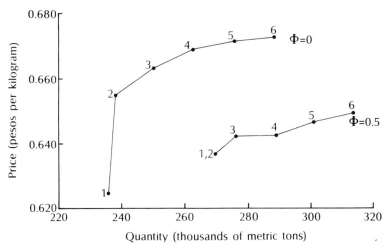

Figure 13.3 Domestic supply response for sorghum, model of vegetable districts, Mexico. Solutions are numbered as follows: 1, base period; 2, with 5% quantity shift in relevant demand; 3, with 10% quantity shift; 4, with 15% quantity shift; and so on. Source: Hazell et al. (1983).

structure similar to that in CHAC. Farmers are assumed to act on the basis of expected price forecasts.

Since domestic prices are endogenous to the model, it was not possible to derive directly the effects of price changes on domestic supplies. Rather, the domestic demand curves had to be rotated, and the model allowed to determine the new equilibrium values of both prices and the quantities supplied (see Chapter 12). Supply response functions derived in this way also allow for price and quantity adjustments in all other markets; they are not, therefore, the partial supply functions described in economic textbooks but must be considered as total supply response relations.

Figure 13.2 shows the shift in the supply function of safflower when Φ is increased from 0.0 to 0.5 (A Φ value of 0.5 had the lowest price MAD in the base year for this model). The supply function corresponding to $\Phi = 0.5$ lies above and to the left of the risk-neutral supply function, indicating that safflower is a relatively risky crop. In contrast, the supply function for sorghum in Figure 13.3 depicts a case where supply increases when risk averse behavior is introduced. Sorghum is therefore a relatively low-risk crop which replaces other more risky crops as Φ increases.

13.5 CONTRASTS BETWEEN ALTERNATIVE PRICE FORECASTING RULES

Hazell and Scandizzo (1977) compared expected price and unit revenue forecasting behavior for different values of Φ. For this purpose they used the model of selected irrigation districts in Mexico described in Section 13.2. The relevant model objective functions are developed in Chapter 10.

Table 13.4 Price Solutions for the Expected Price Forecasting Model with Various Φ Values, Model of Irrigated Districts, Mexico

Demand group	Commodity	Values of Φ[a]					Actual base period prices
		0	0.5	1.0	1.5	2.0	
		(Pesos / ton)					
1	Sugar cane	68	68	70	68	69	70
2	Tomatoes	330	705	1071	1319	1636	1150
3	Chilies	700	741	748	828	965	1500
4	Cotton fiber	5770[b]	5770[b]	5770[b]	5770[b]	5770[b]	5770[b]
5	Dry alfalfa	308	347	442	485	498	400
	Green alfalfa	75	69	64	63	62	100
	Barley	848	787	793	806	801	930
	Chickpeas	1725	1673	1631	1818	1987	990
	Maize	1044	981	1023	1106	1128	860
	Sorghum	557	568	549	533	549	630
6	Rice	1195	1101	1047	1035	1038	1220
	Beans	2334	2179	2091	2053	2040	1830
	Chickpeas	1725	1673	1631	1818	1987	990
	Potatoes	391	468	537	699	882	930
7	Maize	1044	981	1023	1106	1128	860
	Wheat	971	912	905	935	959	800
8	Cantaloupe	329	488	705	935	928	680
	Watermelons	297	291	260	299	280	780
9	Safflower	1550	1401	1391	1484	1509	1550
	Sesame	3444	3384	3151	3000	2989	2410
	Cotton oil	651	690	796	1047	1206	830
	Soybeans	1382	1364	1356	1422	1466	1600
10	Cucumbers	569	681	838	790	317	590
Price MAD		315	279	245	265	298	0
Social welfare (billions of pesos)		4.21	4.04	3.97	3.83	3.83	n.a.[c]

[a]Large Φ values indicate greater risk aversion; Φ = 0 corresponds to risk-neutral behavior.
[b]Export price.
[c]n.a. means not available.
Source: Hazell and Scandizzo (1977).

Tables 13.4 and 13.5 show the domestic price solutions obtained for the two types of price forecasting behavior. These values are the expected market clearing prices in equilibrium. Since there is obviously a one-to-one relationship between the market prices and the total production of each crop sold in the domestic market, differences in solution prices also reflect differences in production.

In general, unit revenue expectations (Table 13.5) lead to higher domestic prices and lower production for the domestic market than with expected prices (Table 13.4). This affect is particularly pronounced in the case of chilies, while wheat and maize provide the only significant exceptions. These results indicate that the price-yield covariances are generally negative in Mexico, and hence

Table 13.5 Price Solutions for the Unit Revenue Forecasting Model with Various Φ Values, Model of Irrigated Districts, Mexico

Demand group	Commodity	Values of Φ (pesos / ton)[a]					Actual base period prices
		0	0.5	1.0	1.5	2.0	
1	Sugar cane	75	73	74	73	74	70
2	Tomatoes	428	756	1150	1387	1729	1150
3	Chilies	2927	2980	3071	3233	3380	1500
4	Cotton fiber	5770[b]	5770[b]	5770[b]	5770[b]	5770[b]	5770[b]
5	Dry alfalfa	492	465	467	459	472	400
	Green alfalfa	139	103	90	88	90	100
	Barley	860	791	776	742	761	930
	Chickpeas	1725	1595	1535	1588	1720	990
	Maize	1011	957	1016	1000	1036	860
	Sorghum	605	546	505	515	542	630
6	Rice	1424	1377	1322	1247	1256	1220
	Beans	2259	2082	2023	1929	1992	1830
	Chickpeas	2063	2106	2068	2105	2218	990
	Potatoes	1900	2341	2241	2216	2296	930
7	Maize	1027	1011	1045	1079	1132	860
	Wheat	955	899	899	896	909	800
8	Cantaloupe	528	749	454	743	734	680
	Watermelons	521	499	520	490	463	780
9	Safflower	1567	1494	1489	3048	1451	1550
	Sesame	3548	3360	3043	3048	3093	2410
	Cotton Oil	747	761	818	1003	1171	830
	Soybeans	1495	1466	1437	1477	1467	1600
10	Cucumbers	579	702	291	108	6	590
Price MAD		349	342	315	339	395	0
Social welfare (billions of pesos)		4.48	4.27	4.10	3.96	3.85	n.a.[c]

[a]Larger Φ values indicate greater risk aversion; Φ = 0 corresponds to risk-neutral behavior.
[b]Export price.
[c]n.a. means not available.
Source: Hazell and Scandizzo (1977).

the expected revenue per cropped hectare is less than expected price times average yield (see Chapter 10).

The MADs between the prices obtained from models and their base year counterparts are also reported in Tables 13.4 and 13.5. These MADs are consistently lower for the expected price forecasting model, implying that the behavior of farmers in the selected irrigated districts of Mexico is more accurately approximated by expected price than per unit revenue forecasts. This is inconsistent with the notion that farmers are always rational. It also suggests, as argued in Chapter 10, that there must be a corresponding loss in social welfare.

Hazell and Scandizzo (1977) calculated the expected sum of the realized, or *ex post*, producer and consumer surplus over all markets for the model solutions (see Chapter 10 for a justification of this measure of social welfare). These values were obtained directly from the objective function of the unit revenue model, and from the same equation carried as a nonconstraining row in the expected price model. The values are reported in the last row of Tables 13.4 and 13.5.

The results demonstrate that per unit revenue forecasts do lead to higher values of social welfare, sometimes significantly so. For $\Phi = 0$, for example, welfare is 270 million pesos greater when farmers plan on the basis of unit revenue rather than expected price. The difference in welfare between the two sets of solutions diminishes as Φ increases, suggesting that private risk-averse behavior on the part of farmers can offset, to some extent, the shortcomings of expected price forecasting behavior. Indeed, when $\Phi = 2.0$, the two model formulations have almost identical welfare outcomes.

13.6 EVALUATION OF CROP INSURANCE CONTRACTS FOR FARMERS

Crop insurance has often been proposed as a way of assisting farmers in coping more effectively with production risks. Proponents argue that insurance enables farmers to use resources more efficiently, encourages the use of improved technologies, and helps to ensure that the farm family has an adequate income each year to meet essential living expenses and repay debt.

In practice, crop insurance has rarely proved attractive to farmers in the sense that they are willing to pay the full cost of providing it. As a result, most crop insurance has had to be provided by the public sector, and it is often heavily subsidized or even compulsory (Hazell and Valdes 1984).

The design or evaluation of a crop insurance scheme should begin with an evaluation of the economic benefits for farmers. Such an analysis provides a basis for calculating the subsidy that will be required if the insurance is to be purchased on a voluntary basis. It also provides a basis for estimating the likely impact of the insurance on farm production and incomes.

Hazell, Bassoco, and Arcia (1986) recently developed a whole-farm planning model for evaluating crop insurance contracts. They assumed that farmers maximize E, σ utility, and specifically, that the relevant model objective function is to maximize $E[u] = E - \phi\sigma$. Within this framework, crop insurance will have desired effects for a farmer if it reduces σ, the standard deviation of farm income. However, to be economically viable to the farmer, the premium to be charged for the insurance should not exceed the gross gain in expected utility resulting from its adoption.

In addition to improving expected utility, crop insurance may also reduce the risk of financial catastrophe—that is, the risk that income in any one year may fall below financial requirements to meet debt obligations and essential family living expenses. Hazell, Bassoco, and Arcia modeled this consideration with a chance constraint. Specifically, they added the requirement that

$$Pr\{Y_t \geq S\} \geq 1 - \alpha \qquad (13.1)$$

where Y_t denotes the tth possible outcome for income net of all production costs (including interest charges on borrowed credit), S denotes the minimum amount of income required by the farm family to meet essential living costs, and α is a preassigned level of risk. Since a positive income implies that the value of all inputs financed with seasonal credit are recovered, the criterion requires that a farm plan be chosen so that income is adequate to cover seasonal debt repayment and essential family living costs, at least $1 - \alpha$ proportion of the time.[2]

Since the farmer is likely to give greater priority to the economic survival of himself and his family than to the repayment of seasonal debt, Hazell, Bassoco, and Arcia assumed that when (13.1) is not satisfied the farmer defaults on all or part of his loan. On this basis, (13.1) can be interpreted as the probability of default, and α specifies the acceptable default rate. The farmer and the lender may have rather different views about what is an acceptable default risk. Since the lender's views are probably the more stringent, Hazell, Bassoco, and Norton interpreted α as the default rate acceptable to the lender. This interpretation also solves the problem of having to choose values of ϕ and α which are behaviorally consistent (see Chapter 5). If these parameters represent the risk tolerance of different individuals then there is no reason for them to bear any relation to each other.

If Y is normally distributed, (13.1) can be reformulated as a legitimate linear programming constraint.[3] Specifically, (13.1) is equivalent to $Pr\{Z_t \geq S^*\} \geq 1 - \alpha$, where $Z_t = (Y_t - E[Y])/\sigma$ and $S^* = (S - E[Y])/\sigma$. Here Z_t is a normal random variable with mean zero and standard deviation one, and S^* is the value of Z at which α percent of the distribution lies in the tail to the left of Z, (S^* is the α percentile). Consequently, by using tables of the cumulative function of the standard normal distribution, one can find a value of K_α (which will be negative for $\alpha < 0.5$) such that

$$E[Y] + K_\alpha\sigma \geq S \tag{13.2}$$

is exactly equivalent to the requirement in (13.1).

If this constraint is binding in the solution to a farm model, then crop insurance contracts that act to reduce σ will, by easing the constraint, enable higher values of the objective function (expected utility) to be attained. This will enhance the value of the insurance contracts to the farmer beyond its direct impact on expected utility.

The full structure of the Hazell-Bassoco-Arcia model can be summarized as follows:

$$\max E[u] = E[Y] - \phi\sigma \tag{13.3}$$

such that

$$Y = c'X - ir \tag{13.4}$$

and

$$\sigma = (X'\Omega X)^{1/2} \qquad (13.5)$$
$$w'X - r \le h \qquad (13.6)$$
$$E[Y] + K_\alpha\sigma \ge S \qquad (13.7)$$
$$AX \le b \qquad (13.8)$$

where X = a vector of activity levels
c = a vector of expected activity gross margins
Ω = a matrix of covariances of activity gross margins
r = the amount of seasonal credit borrowed
i = the interest charge on seasonal credit
w = a vector of activity seasonal credit requirements
h = the amount of funds available from the farm family for on-farm seasonal investment
A = a matrix of activity resource requirements
b = a vector of fixed resource supplies.

Equation (13.6) requires that any credit requirements $w'X$ in excess of h must be met by borrowing credit r, and that such credit has an interest charge i which is deducted from income. Equation (13.7) limits the amount of credit that can be borrowed to the amount at which the probability of default is equal to or less than α, the default risk acceptable to the lender.

Crop insurance contracts affect this model through changes in the gross margin covariances of the insured crops (the effect of the indemnity payments), and through changes in expected gross margins (because of the insurance premiums to be paid). These changes in Ω and c affect the optimal choice of X and r, and hence the optimal values of $E[Y]$ and σ.

To calculate the changes in Ω that must be made for a specific crop insurance experiment, it is assumed that time series of gross margin data exist for each crop corresponding to the various insurance options. Where these data series do not already exist, as for example, when designing a new crop insurance contract, then they must be calculated from existing time series of uninsured revenues. Table 13.6 contains an illustrative set of calculations.

In this example, indemnities are assumed to be paid in those years in which the yield is less than 85% of the mean yield. Further, the indemnity paid is calculated as the difference between the mean uninsured revenue (1158.6 pesos) and actual revenue. On this basis, indemnities are paid in years 3 and 5, and these act to reduce the standard deviation of the revenue series from 268.0 pesos to 112.6 pesos.

Given the revenue series for all relevant insured and uninsured options for each crop, then, after detrending, these provide the basis for calculating the relevant elements of Ω (or for calculating the revenue deviations if a MOTAD approximation is used). If it is desired to simulate the effects of a compulsory

Table 13.6 Example of Insurance Calculations

Year	Price (pesos / ton)	Yield (tons / ha)	Uninsured revenue (pesos / ha)	Insured revenue (pesos / ha)
1	5164	0.273	1410	1410
2	5119	0.252	1290	1290
3[a]	5104	0.159	812	1159
4	5049	0.267	1348	1348
5[a]	5014	0.186	933	1159
Mean	5090	0.227	1158.6	1273.2
Standard deviation	59.1	0.054	268.0	112.6

[a] Years in which indemnities are paid.
Source: Hazell, Bassoco, and Arcia (1986).

crop insurance scheme, then only insured options are introduced in the model. Note that separate crop activities must be added for each insurance option to be considered, including an uninsured activity if crop insurance is voluntary.

In addition to the above, the cost of insurance must be subtracted from the expected gross margin of each insured activity. This cost is the annual premium paid per hectare minus the average indemnity received—the net premium. The net premium should equal the average administrative costs per hectare of providing the insurance. It will be less than this though if the insurance is subsidized, and the net premium will be zero if the administrative costs are fully subsidized.

Hazell, Bassoco, and Arcia applied their approach to an aggregate model of agriculture in the rainfed areas of Mexico. They obtained their model from CHAC, made the necessary modifications to the objective function, and added a probabilistic debt repayment constraint. The model was solved assuming fixed product prices and using a MOTAD approximation in estimating σ.

There is already a national crop insurance scheme in Mexico operated by Aseguradora Nacional Agrícola y Ganadera, S.A. (ANAGSA). This is a credit insurance scheme which assists farmers in repaying bank credit for insured crops in the event of certain natural disasters (for example, hail, flood, or drought). The scheme has not been very effective in the rainfed areas, and the purpose of the analysis was to evaluate alternative crop insurance contracts for corn and beans, with a view to increasing farm incomes and the aggregate production of corn and beans in the rainfed areas.

Activities for producing corn and beans without insurance as well as with each of three insurance options were included in the model. The model was, therefore, free to choose between insuring or not insuring these crops, as well as choosing among the three insurance policies, or to choose any linear combination thereof.

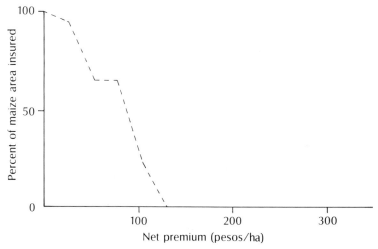

Figure 13.4 Share of maize area insured for different net premiums, model of rainfed areas, Mexico. Source: Hazell, Bassoco, and Arcia (1986).

Assuming an aggregate risk parameter of $\Phi = 1.0$, and a bank-imposed maximum debt default risk (α) of 0.1%, Hazell, Bassoco, and Arcia solved their model for different levels of the insurance subsidy. This was done by varying the expected gross margins in the income row. When the administrative costs of insurance were fully subsidized (that is, when the net premium was zero), all the maize planted was voluntarily insured in the optimal solution. Maize production was also 23.6% higher than when the insured activities were removed from the model, and average farm income was 8.9% higher. Beans insurance proved not to be attractive even when fully subsidized.

Comparing solutions for no insurance with voluntary and fully subsidized insurance, the gain in expected utility worked out at 91 pesos per hectare of insured corn. This is a direct measure of the maximum premium that farmers should be willing to pay in order to purchase insurance without being any worse off. The full costs of providing the proposed insurance were not known, but they would probably be about 300 to 400 pesos per hectare in base year prices. Clearly, the economic benefits to farmers are inadequate in relation to the cost of providing the proposed insurance contracts.

Figure 13.4 shows the result of reducing the insurance subsidy. The percentage of the maize area insured declines rapidly as the net premium increases, and no maize is insured at all if farmers have to pay a net premium of 125 or more pesos per hectare.

13.7 EVALUATION OF CROP INSURANCE PROGRAMS AT THE SECTOR LEVEL

Crop insurance programs may lead to substantial changes in the aggregate supplies of both insured and uninsured commodities. Some of these changes may be deemed desirable in themselves, for example, increased maize supplies

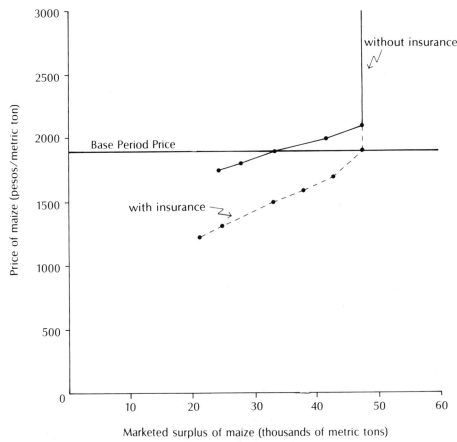

Figure 13.5   Supply functions for maize with and without crop insurance, model of rainfed areas, Mexico. Source: Hazell, Bassoco, and Arcia (1986).

in Mexico. Changes in production may sometimes lead to increased employment in agriculture, or to a reduction in food prices that is beneficial to consumers. These kinds of ramifications need to be considered in any social cost-benefit analysis of public subsidies for crop insurance schemes. Mathematical programming models can be a useful aid in such analyses.

As a simple example of the effect of crop insurance on aggregate commodity supplies, we return to the Hazell, Bassoco, and Arcia study. They used their model to derive aggregate maize supply functions for the rainfed areas of Mexico, with and without crop insurance. Since the model had fixed prices, the experiments simply involved parameterizing the maize price. The results are portrayed in Figure 13.5.

The supply function corresponding to no insurance is quite elastic over the price range 1750 and 2100 pesos/ton, but becomes perfectly inelastic at the latter price. At the model base year (1976) price of 1900 pesos/ton, a total maize surplus of 33,370 tons is marketed. If the price were increased to 2100 pesos/ton, the surplus would jump to 47,640 tons.

When insurance is introduced, a marketed surplus of 47,640 tons is produced at the base year price, and the supply function is totally inelastic at that point. This means that price increases above the base year price would not increase the supply of maize when crop insurance is available. It is also clear that a price increase of only 200 pesos per ton without any insurance schemes would provide the same level of maize surplus as would the introduction of the crop insurance options considered. A price increase might therefore be a simpler way to increase maize production. It would also serve to increase the welfare and incomes of farmers. In the absence of any insurance, Hazell, Bassoco, and Arcia found that a 200 pesos per ton increase in the base year price of maize would increase expected utility and average income by 530 and 682 pesos per farm. These amounts are larger than the gains obtained with crop insurance at the base year price.

In another study of crop insurance in Mexico, Bassoco, Cartas, and Norton (1986) used the CHAC model to analyze the sector-wide economic benefits attributable to the ANAGSA program. They used a revised version of CHAC which included risk and $E[u] = E - \phi\sigma$ utility maximizing behavior. The latter was incorporated using a MOTAD approximation and assuming expected price forecasting behavior. The aggregate risk-aversion parameter Φ was set at 1.0; a value deemed to be "reasonable" as well as providing a good fit to the base year.

The model was first solved without any crop insurance. Then, using simulated time-series data for ANAGSA insurance, the model was resolved assuming that insurance was compulsory for all farmers. The insurance experiment was repeated with and without the public subsidy. The results are summarized in Table 13.7.

Measuring social welfare as the *ex ante* sum of the producer and consumer surplus, the subsidized insurance program leads to an increase of 1190 million pesos in aggregate welfare. This increase is gross of the cost of the subsidy. In 1980 (the model's base year), the cost of the subsidy amounted to 5225 million pesos. This estimate is lower than the cost implicit in the model solution because in reality the insurance is only compulsory for farmers who borrow official credit. Even so, it is clear that there is a sizeable net social loss as a result of the subsidized insurance. On the other hand, the subsidized insurance does have a beneficial impact on farmers; both producer surplus and sector income are larger than in the no-insurance situation. There is also a favorable impact on employment because of changes in the mix of crops grown. However, because commercial farmers receive a disproportionate share of the subsidy, the distribution of income within agriculture worsens somewhat, as shown by the increase in the Gini coefficient.

If the crop insurance program were not subsidized, there would still be a loss in net social welfare compared to the no-insurance situation. This loss

Table 13.7 Welfare Effects of the Mexican Crop Yield Insurance Program, Mexican Agricultural Model CHAC

		Yield insurance	
Variable	No insurance	No subsidy	With subsidy
Objective function[a] (10 million pesos)	17,962.2	17,269.0	18,081.0
Producer surplus (10 million pesos)	2,798.8	3,100.2	3,194.9
Consumer surplus (10 million pesos)	15,163.4	14,168.8	14,886.1
Sector income (10 million pesos)	3,674.9	4,079.8	4,136.6
Gini coefficient (index)	0.3386	0.3327	0.3449
Employment (thousand man-years)	1,561.9	1,607.2	1,636.6
Production (index)	100.0	98.7	100.5
Maize (thousand tons)	8,180.0	7,948.0	8,179.0
Imports (10 million pesos)	182.0	183.5	182.5

[a]Defined as the *ex ante* sum of the producer and consumer surplus.
Source: Bassoco, Cartas, and Norton (1986).

arises because the insurance is compulsory and, in aggregate, the administration costs exceed the value of the risk reduction benefits conferred by the program. In fact, farmer's costs are sufficiently increased by the unsubsidized insurance that aggregate production declines by 1.3%. However, because of the generally inelastic nature of the demand for agricultural products, the decline in output leads to price increases that raise producer surplus and sector income beyond the levels attained if crop insurance were not introduced.

13.8 EVALUATION OF PRICE STABILIZATION SCHEMES WITH MATHEMATICAL PROGRAMMING

Price stabilization is one form of intervention in risky markets that has been widely analyzed in the literature. The main focus has been on the welfare gains or losses to producers, consumers, and the aggregate of the two, in models of single commodity markets; see Turnovsky (1978) and Newbery and Stiglitz (1981) for comprehensive reviews.

A limitation of these analyses is that stabilization interventions in any one market may have important spillover effects in other markets. These spillover effects may arise from commodity substitution in demand, and/or from competition for scarce resources in production between the stabilized crop and other commodities. In addition, even though the importance of producers' aversion to price and yield risks has been recognized as a determinant of supply (Just 1974), the implied changes in average supply following price stabilization typically are ignored.[4] Also, nearly all the analytical work on price stabilization has focused on a very narrow set of policy objectives, particularly the changes in producer and consumer surplus, producers' income, and storage costs. However, price stabilization may affect a wider range of policy variables when allowance is made for risk response and multimarket interactions.

Price-endogenous mathematical programming models can take account of multiproduct relationships in supply and demand, and can simulate the effects of risk-averse behavior at the farm level. They also can provide a wealth of detailed information about production, resource use, consumption, prices, and trade, at both the micro (farm or regional) and sector-wide levels. Hazell and Pomareda (1981) have shown how these advantages can be utilized to provide a comprehensive analysis of price stabilization.

Their approach is suitable for analyzing stabilization schemes in which the domestic price of one (or more) commodities is fixed at its expected market equilibrium value. Such price stabilization would be achieved through the establishment of buffer stocks. To assure a self-liquidating stock on average, the price at which a market is to be stabilized is the expected market clearing price in equilibrium. This price can be obtained from the model. The problem is to modify the model to obtain the market equilibrium solution corresponding to the stabilized situation.

Hazell and Pomareda presume a sector model with linear demand functions and in which farmers maximize $E[u] = E - \phi\sigma$ utility. Using the notation of Chapter 10, the relevant model objective function is then:

$$\max Z_1 = X'E[N](\alpha - 0.5BE[N]X) - c'X - \Phi(X'\Omega X)^{1/2} \quad (13.9)$$

when farmers hold expected price forecasts, and

$$\max Z_2 = E[X'N(\alpha - 0.5BNX)] - c'X - \Phi(X'\Omega X)^{1/2}$$
$$= \text{Equation}(13.9) - 0.5\sum_i \sum_j X_i X_j \sigma_{ij}\beta_{ij} \quad (13.10)$$

when farmers hold unit revenue expectations.

Within this framework, stabilizing the price of the jth crop changes the variance and the covariance terms in Ω involving that crop. An important part of the method of experimenting with price stabilization therefore follows: one must recalculate all the relevant elements of Ω using the stabilized price $\bar{P}_j = E[\bar{P}_j]$ and then resolve the model for a new equilibrium.

However, producers will adjust their cropping patterns to arrive at a new optimal plan given their assumed E, σ utility functions. This is the risk-response effect induced by stabilization, and the expected market-clearing price for the stabilized crop no longer will be the same. The stabilized price, $\bar{P}_j = E[P_j]$, now will have to be revised to retain a self-liquidating buffer stock, the elements of Ω recalculated, and the solution process repeated. This iterative procedure is repeated until Ω converges.[5]

As will later become clear, a small modification is also required in the demand specification for the stabilized crop in Equation (13.10). This is because the marketed quantity is no longer stochastic when the stabilizing agency sells a fixed amount $\bar{Q}_j$ to consumers each year, and Equation (13.10) must be revised so that $E[Q_j^2] = \bar{Q}_j^2$ for the stabilized commodity. This can be done by setting $\sigma_{ij} = 0$, all i, in Equation (13.10).

The poststabilized solution provides the expected values of all activities in the new market equilibrium. Any changes from the prestabilized solution stem from supply adjustments following changes in farm-level risks, or from the disappearance of the covariance between price and yield leading to identical unit revenue and price expectations for the stabilized crop. Assuming producers were risk-neutral ($\Phi = 0$) and that they plan on the basis of price expectations [objective function (13.9)] then the pre- and poststabilized solutions would, in fact, be identical, with $\bar{P}_j$ remaining constant. Even though the model activity levels would not change under these conditions, the removal of price and market supply variations still leads to changes in the expected values of the consumer surplus, producer surplus, and income.

The surplus and income changes can be calculated in the model. Given the assumed market structure, prices in the tth year are given by $P_t = \alpha - \beta Q_t$. Expected consumer surplus in the prestabilized situation is

$$E[W_{ct}] = E[Q_t'(\alpha - 0.5BQ_t) - P'Q_t]$$

$$= 0.5E[Q_t'BQ_t] \qquad (13.11)$$

and expected *ex post* producer surplus is

$$E[W_{pt}] = E[Q_t'(\alpha - BQ_t)] - c'X - \Phi(X'\Omega X)^{1/2} \qquad (13.12)$$

The producer surplus is defined net of the risk term $\Phi(X'\Omega X)^{1/2}$, which is the income compensation that producers require for accepting the risk associated with X. By deleting this term in Equation (13.12), the expected value of producers' income in the prestabilized markets is obtained.

Aggregate social welfare is measured as the sum of the expected producer and consumer surpluses. In the prestabilized market this is the sum of Equations (13.11) and (13.12) and is equal to model objective function (13.10).

The establishment of a buffer stock agency stabilizes the prices of a subset of the vector P_t. By partitioning the relevant matrices, the price and quantity vectors are

$$\begin{bmatrix} P_{1t} \\ P_{2t} \end{bmatrix} = \begin{bmatrix} \alpha_1 \\ \alpha_2 \end{bmatrix} + \begin{bmatrix} B_{11} & B_{12} \\ B_{21} & B_{22} \end{bmatrix} \begin{bmatrix} Q_{1t} \\ Q_{2t} \end{bmatrix} \tag{13.13}$$

and

$$\begin{bmatrix} Q_{1t} \\ Q_{2t} \end{bmatrix} = \begin{bmatrix} N_{1t} & 0 \\ 0 & N_{2t} \end{bmatrix} \begin{bmatrix} X_1 \\ X_2 \end{bmatrix} \tag{13.14}$$

If the buffer stock agency wishes to stabilize prices P_1 at $\overline{P}_1$, where $\overline{P}_1$ is the vector of prices that ensure self-liquidating stocks on average, the agency would plan to buy all the production of Q_1 each year and to release the quantities of Q_1 to the domestic market each year that are required to maintain prices at $\overline{P}_1$. If Q_1 and Q_2 are demand-independent groups (that is, $B_{21} = B_{12} = 0$), the agency sells constant amounts $\overline{Q}_1 = E[N_1]X_1$ to the domestic market. When Q_1 and Q_2 are not demand independent, P_1 is subject to random variations arising from Q_2 as well as from variations in Q_1. Since the agency would not carry stocks of Q_2, the actual quantities of Q_1 sold would have to be varied from year to year to compensate for variations in Q_2. $\overline{Q}_1$ would then denote only the expected value of the amount sold by the agency to maintain prices at $\overline{P}_1$.

To simplify the analysis we assume $B_{12} = B_{21} = 0$ so that $\overline{Q}_1$ is constant. The expected consumer and producer surpluses in the stabilized situation are then

$$E[W_c] = 0.5\overline{Q}_1'B_{11}\overline{Q}_1 + 0.5E[Q_2'B_{22}Q_2] \tag{13.15}$$

and

$$E[W_p] = \overline{Q}_1'(\alpha_1 - B_{11}\overline{Q}_1) + E[Q_2'(\alpha_2 - B_{22}Q_2)] \\ - c'X - \Phi(X'\Omega X)^{1/2} \tag{13.16}$$

Expected producers' income is then Equation (13.16) with the risk term $\Phi(X'\Omega X)^{1/2}$ omitted.

Taking the sum of Equations (13.15) and (13.16), expected social welfare in the stabilized situation is

$$E[W] = \overline{Q}_1'(\alpha_1 - 0.5B_{11}\overline{Q}_1) \\ + E[Q_2'(\alpha_2 - 0.5B_{22}Q_2)] - c'X - \Phi(X'\Omega X)^{1/2} \tag{13.17}$$

Equation (13.17) is a modified version of (13.10) in which $E[Q_j^2]$ is replaced by $\overline{Q}_j^2$ for all stabilized commodities. It is also the relevant model maximand for obtaining the market equilibria corresponding to unit revenue forecasting behavior in the stabilized situation. Because prices and yields are no longer correlated for the stabilized commodities, producers act as price forecasters when planning X_1 and as unit revenue forecasters when planning X_2.

The gain in expected social welfare from stabilizing P_1 is the value of Equation (13.17) minus Equation (13.10). If producers are risk neutral and plan on the basis of expected price forecasts, the value of X remains constant, $\overline{Q}_1$ equals $E[Q_1]$ of the prestabilized situation, and the welfare gain is

$$
\begin{aligned}
E[\Delta W] &= 0.5\left(E[Q_1' B_{11} Q_1] - \overline{Q}_1' B_{11} \overline{Q}_1 \right) \\
&= 0.5 \sum_i \sum_j X_{1i} X_{1j} \sigma_{1ij} \beta_{1ij}
\end{aligned}
\tag{13.18}
$$

To obtain the values of the surpluses and income measures defined above, it is only necessary to incorporate Equations (13.9), (13.10), and (13.12) into the model and to have access to the value of $\Phi(X'\Omega X)^{1/2}$ from the solution. Since either (13.9) or (13.10) would be the model maximand, only two additional accounting rows are required. These are quadratic equations, but they can be linearized concurrently with the objective functions using the techniques described in Chapter 8.

An assumption underlying the derivation of these welfare measures is that the activity levels X are nonstochastic. Since X (the crop areas planted) depends in part on producers' forecasts about prices, it is implied that producers hold constant forecasts over time.

If the assumption of nonstochastic activities is relaxed, the surplus and income measures used in the model will be incorrect. It is possible to derive the correct measures (see Hazell and Pomareda 1981), but they involve additional terms that cannot be calculated in a mathematical programming model. The approach to evaluating price stabilization schemes outlined here is therefore limited to situations where one can assume that producers anticipate either expected price or unit revenue every period.

Hazell and Pomareda illustrated their approach with the aid of a price-endogenous model of the agricultural sector of Guatemala. Mathematically, this model has a similar structure to the Mexican CHAC model, except that producers are assumed to maximize $E[u] = E - \phi\sigma$ utility. The model is fully described in Pomareda (1980).

Hazell and Pomareda used the model to evaluate a hypothetical price stabilization scheme for beans. Model solutions were obtained for expected price and unit revenue forecasting behavior. The results corresponding to an aggregate risk-aversion parameter of $\Phi = 1.65$ are summarized in Table 13.8.

Price stabilization for beans leads to a gain in social welfare of 1.3% (or $12.75 million) when producers hold expected price forecasts. This is equivalent to a gain of $135/ton of beans produced which, while sizeable, is probably too small to justify the costs of a buffer stock. If producers hold unit revenue forecasts instead, the social gain is $12.0 million, or 5.9% smaller. This smaller gain is to be expected since unit revenue forecasts are superior, and social welfare is necessarily larger in the prestabilized market (see Chapter 10).

There are other effects from stabilizing bean prices. Bean production increases by 4.3% and 9% for expected price and unit revenue forecasts, respectively. This additional output is produced with resources that otherwise would be idle. There is also a sizeable decline in the standard deviation of

Table 13.8   Results for Various Price Stabilization Experiments, Guatemala

	Prestabilized price model	% Change with bean price stabilized	Prestabilized revenue model	% Change with bean price stabilized
Income and welfare measures (millions US$)				
Social welfare	980.9	1.30	981.6	1.22
Consumer surplus	906.3	0.02	891.6	0.87
Producers' income	275.3	2.36	288.9	−0.12
Standard deviation of producers' income[a]	53.7	−7.60	53.1	−6.54
Agricultural trade balance (millions US$)	281.1	0	282.2	0
Agricultural employment (thousands full-time jobs)	5083.0	0.33	5059.5	0.65
Production (10^3 tons)				
Maize	1031.6	0	1031.6	0
Rice	27.9	0	26.7	0
Sorghum	50.2	0	48.2	0
Beans	90.2	4.32	86.3	9.04
Wheat	67.1	0	67.1	0
Retail Prices (US$ / ton)				
Maize	179	0	179	0
Rice flour	322	0	387	0
Sorghum	171	0	199	0
Beans	516	−14.15	590	−24.92
Wheat flour	510	0	510	0

[a]Sum of standard deviations over all farm groups.
Source: Hazell and Pomareda (1981).

producers' income. In both cases, the domestic bean price declines substantially, and there is an increase in agricultural employment of 17,000 jobs in the case of price expectations, and of 33,000 jobs with revenue expectations.

The results in Table 13.8 show some ambiguity in the gains to producers and consumers. Consumers gain from bean price stabilization when producers hold unit revenue forecasts, but they lose when expected price forecasts prevail. The opposite happens to producers' interests as measured by their average income.

NOTES

1 The districts are Culiacán, Humaya, El Fuerte, and Guasave which are in the State of Sinaloa.
2 Repayment of longer term debt obligations can easily be incorporated by including the required annual payment in S.
3 See the section on chance constraints in Chapter 5.
4 Newbery and Stiglitz (1981) are an important exception.
5 The procedure is similar to the one described in Section 10.7 of Chapter 10.

The Theory of Linear Programming

The purpose of this appendix is to provide a self-contained and reasonably comprehensive exposition of the essentials of linear programming theory. It covers the principal equilibrium theorems and basis theory, with proofs. It is written to serve both as a review for practitioners and as a principal reference for students. The formal results given here are available in other texts, but they are not elsewhere drawn together in a unified way. Several sources have been used in the writing of this material; the main guides have been Lancaster's *Mathematical Economics* and Hadley's *Linear Programming*. Other useful references are Allen (1962), Dantzig (1963), Almon (1967), Baumol (1961), Intriligator (1971), Gale (1960), Dorfman, Samuelson, and Solow (1958), and Gass (1985).

This appendix is designed to be read with little mathematical background in optimization theory. The mathematical prerequisities are calculus and linear algebra.

A.1 CLASSICAL BACKGROUND

Optimization problems may be divided into unconstrained and constrained varieties, and the latter into problems with equality constraints and problems with inequality constraints. Thus there are three broad categories, and the corresponding solution methods were worked out at points very far apart in time. Unconstrained optimization problems were first solved with the methods of calculus, developed in the seventeenth century by Sir Isaac Newton (1642–1727) and Gottfried Wilhelm Leibniz (1646–1716). The solution to optimization problems constrained by equalities was found a century later by the inventor of the calculus of variations, Joseph-Louis Lagrange (1736–1813). For inequality-constrained problems, the solution procedures were not found until the 1940s, by John von Neumann and George Dantzig. Two good reasons may be adduced for the long time lapse before these last procedures were discovered: they require an electronic computer if the problem contains more than about four variables, and it probably never occurred to earlier mathematicians to *pose* the problem of maximization or minimization subject to inequality constraints. World War II and its immense logistical planning difficulties provided impetus to the problem which von Neumann and Dantzig solved.[1] Mathematics is indeed the handmaiden of its times! Newton's calculus, after all, was a way of answering questions about the shape of the orbit of Halley's comet.

Optimization with inequality constraints differs in one fundamental respect from the earlier problems: there does not exist a closed, analytic expression which describes the solution. For that, it is necessary to know the "optimal basis," or the list of names of the variables that appear in the optimal solution. For that reason, a considerable portion of this appendix is given over to the topic of basis theory.

A.1.1 The General Optimization Problem

The general optimization problem (*Problem 1*) may be written

$$\max Z = f(X) \tag{A.1}$$

such that

$$g^i(X) \le 0, \quad \text{all } i \tag{A.2}$$
$$X_j \ge 0, \quad \text{all } j \tag{A.3}$$

where X = a vector of real variables with jth element X_j
  f = a single-valued function
  g^i = the ith constraint

The function $Z = f(X)$ is called the objective function.

A maximum is defined by X^* such that

$$f(X^*) \ge f(X), \quad \text{all } X \in R \tag{A.4}$$

where R denotes the relevant set of real numbers for the problem at hand, and

$X \in R$ means that only X whose elements are members of R are to be considered. Similarly, a minimum is defined by X^{**} such that

$$f(X^{**}) \leq f(X), \quad \text{all } X \in R \tag{A.5}$$

Maxima and minima are called extrema, or extreme points.

A more useful concept is that of a local maximum: X^* such that

$$f(X^*) \geq f(X), \quad \text{all } X \in N \tag{A.6}$$

where N is a neighborhood of X^* and a subset of R. When a local maximum is invoked, then the concept defined in (A.4) is a global maximum. Some authors use the terms relative and absolute maxima, respectively.

There are two theorems that ensure the existence of an extreme point under certain conditions: Weierstrass's theorem and Rolle's theorem. However, these theorems do not guarantee that any optimization problem put into the computer will have an answer. It is likely that at least a third of the first 50 optimization problems a student-practitioner puts into the computer will violate one or more of the conditions of Weierstrass's theorem, and hence will not have an optimum.

Weierstrass's Theorem[2]   A continuous function defined over a closed, bounded, nonempty set attains a maximum at least once over the set.

Rolle's Theorem[3]   If f is a continuous function in the closed interval $[a, b]$, and if $f(a) = f(b)$, then f has at least one extreme point in the open interval (a, b).

The theorems are slightly different: Rolle's version guarantees the existence of an interior extreme point, whereas Weierstrass's version guarantees the existence of a maximum anywhere in the set, including possibly on the boundary. Nevertheless, their conditions are similar. Both require that f be continuous and the set over which it is defined be closed, that is, that it contain its own boundary. Both also require—Weierstrass explicitly, Rolle implicitly—that the set be nonempty and bounded.

As will be seen subsequently, in mathematical programming the counterpart of the requirement of a nonempty set is that there exist a feasible solution. The closedness of the set is guaranteed by the use of weak inequality constraints (e.g., less than or equal to); in numerical solution procedures it is impossible to specify strict inequalities (strictly less than). There is no guarantee that a problem is bounded, nor that it has a feasible solution. Fulfillment of these conditions depends on the particular model specification, and the inevitable errors of coding or translation in numerical work frequently lead to violation of one of these conditions. Continuity of f is assured in the specification of the function to be maximized or minimized; in numerical work, these functions normally take on a rather simple form, and so continuity is not usually an issue.

A.1.2 Conditions for Optimality

Consider first the specialized problem of maximizing (A.1), without conditions (A.2) and (A.3). If X is a scalar, sufficient conditions for a local maximum are

$$\frac{\partial Z}{\partial X} = 0, \qquad \frac{\partial^2 Z}{\partial X^2} < 0 \qquad\qquad\qquad (A.7)$$

For a local minimum, the direction of the inequality is reversed. The condition that the first derivative vanish is a necessary condition.

When X is a vector, the conditions refer to partial derivatives:

$$\frac{\partial Z}{\partial X_j} = 0, \quad \text{all } j \qquad\qquad\qquad (A.8a)$$

$$\sum_i \sum_j \left(\frac{\partial^2 Z}{\partial X_i \partial X_j} \right) dX_i \, dX_j < 0 \qquad\qquad (A.8b)$$

in the case of a maximum. Another way of stating requirement (A.8b) is that the quadratic form $(dX)'(\partial^2 Z/\partial X^2)(dX)$ must be negative definite.[4] Again, (A.8a) is a necessary condition and (A.8b) is sufficient.

If (A.8a) is fulfilled for a given set of values of the X_j, it is possible that the point describes neither a maximum nor a minimum, but rather a saddle point. A saddle point occurs when (A.8a) is satisfied and when

$$\frac{\partial^2 Z}{\partial X_j^2} < 0, \quad \text{at least one } j \qquad\qquad (A.9a)$$

$$\frac{\partial^2 Z}{\partial X_k^2} > 0, \quad \text{at least one } k \qquad\qquad (A.9b)$$

At such a point, the function $Z = f(X)$ is rising along some axes j and falling along other axes k. Saddle points have considerable importance in the theory of mathematical programming, as will be discussed subsequently. Maxima, minima, and saddle points collectively are called stationary points. The three kinds of stationary points are illustrated in Figure A.1 for a two-dimensional vector X. In the figure, the stationary points are denoted e_1, e_2 and e_3, for a maximum, minimum, and saddle point, respectively.

When constraints are introduced into the optimization problem, characterizing an extreme point requires different methods. For the case when the

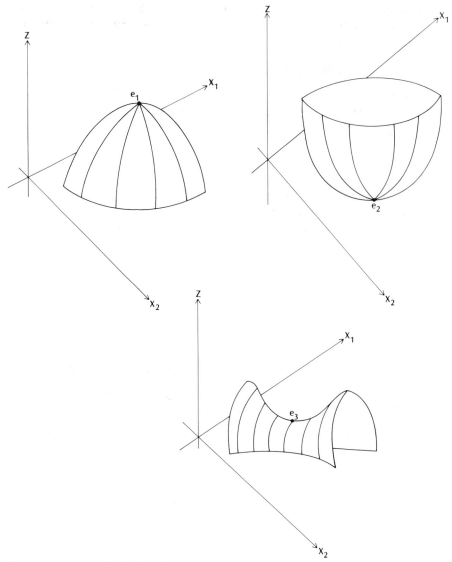

Figure A.1 Three kinds of stationary points. Adapted with permission of the publisher from R. G. D. Allen (1962, p. 353).

constraints (A.2) are strict equalities and the nonnegativity requirements (A.3) can be ignored, Lagrange provided the fundamental insight. He proved that the maximum value of the objective function $f(X)$ subject to $g^i(X) = 0$, all i, may be found by solving for the maximum of a new unconstrained function

$$\mathscr{L} = f(X) + \sum_i \lambda_i g^i(X) \qquad (A.10)$$

In his honor, $\mathcal{L}$ is called the Lagrangean function. Applying basic calculus, the maximum of (A.10) may be found from

$$\frac{\partial \mathcal{L}}{\partial X_j} = 0, \quad \text{all } j = 1, \ldots, n \tag{A.11a}$$

$$\frac{\partial \mathcal{L}}{\partial \lambda_i} = g^i(X) = 0, \quad \text{all } i = 1, \ldots, m \tag{A.11b}$$

$$\sum_i \sum_j \left(\frac{\partial^2 \mathcal{L}}{\partial X_i \partial X_j} \right) dX_i \, dX_j < 0 \tag{1.11c}$$

In practice, frequently only conditions (A.11a) and (A.11b) are used, along with heuristic information which helps determine what kind of stationary point is present. These conditions give $n + m$ equations for the n variables X_j and the m new variables λ_i. The latter are called Lagrange multipliers. The counterpart concepts in mathematical programming are the dual variables, or shadow prices.

The multiplicity of names appears to conceal the true nature of these mysterious variables λ_i. What are they? Courant reminds us that mathematically they simply are constants of proportionality between the derivatives of the objective function and of the constraint functions.[5] In the case of a single constraint, this may be seen in Figure A.2. The approximately parallel lines represent successively higher values of $f(X)$, and the points (such as d_i) along the line $g(X)$ represent points where the constraint is satisfied. In this case, it is clear that the maximal value of $f(X)$ will be attained at d_5 where $f(X)$ is tangent to $g(X)$, that is, where their derivatives are identical. In other words,

$$\left.\begin{array}{c} \dfrac{\partial f}{\partial X_1} = \lambda \dfrac{\partial g}{\partial X_1} \\[2ex] \dfrac{\partial f}{\partial X_2} = \lambda \dfrac{\partial g}{\partial X_2} \\[2ex] \vdots \qquad \vdots \\[2ex] \dfrac{\partial f}{\partial X_n} = \lambda \dfrac{\partial g}{\partial X_n} \end{array}\right\} \tag{A.12}$$

These conditions follow from the equation of a tangent plane with slope m:

$$m\frac{\partial f}{\partial X} + \frac{\partial g}{\partial X} = 0$$

and the fact that the functions f and g have the same tangent plane

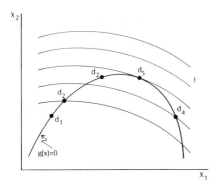

Figure A.2 Lagrange's solution.

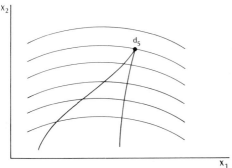

Figure A.3 Lagrange's solution when the derivatives of $g(X)$ are not continuous.

(hyperplane in n-dimensional space) at the point of optimality. Conditions (A.12) are in fact conditions (A.11a), and, together with (A.11b) they serve to determine the n optimal X_j and also the Lagrange multiplier λ (for the case of one constraint). While the geometry doesn't easily extend to the case of multiple constraints, the algebra does, and (A.11a) and (A.11b) remain adequate to determine the stationary values of vectors X and λ.

The graphical reasoning fails if the derivatives $\partial g / \partial X_j$ are not continuous, as in Figure A.3. In that case, $\partial g / \partial X_j = 0$ at optimality and we have what is called a degenerate solution in mathematical programming terminology.

The general mathematical programming Problem 1 does not meet the requirements for Lagrange's method. The constraints in (A.2) are typically inequality constraints rather than strict equalities, and (A.3) requires that all the activities be nonnegative.

The inequality constraints (Figure A.2) can be converted to equalities by introducing slack variables. Let

$$S_i = g^i(X)$$

then Problem 1 can be reformulated as

$$\max Z = f(X) \tag{A.13}$$

such that

$$g^i(X) - S_i = 0, \quad \text{all } i \qquad\qquad (A.14)$$

$$X_j \geq 0, \quad \text{all } j \qquad\qquad (A.15)$$

Model (A.13) through (A.15) is sometimes called the canonical form of the problem.

But for (A.15), the canonical form of the problem could be solved by the method of Lagrange. However, the nonnegativity requirements require a modified approach which is due to Kuhn and Tucker (1951).

Kuhn and Tucker derived a set of necessary and sufficient conditions that X must satisfy if it is to be an optimal solution to Problem 1. As before, form the Lagrangean function

$$\mathscr{L} = f(X) + \sum_i \lambda_i g^i(X)$$

where λ_i are Lagrangean multipliers. Then the Kuhn-Tucker conditions for an optimal solution are

$$\frac{\partial \mathscr{L}}{\partial X_j} \leq 0, \quad \text{all } j \qquad\qquad (A.16)$$

$$\frac{\partial \mathscr{L}}{\partial \lambda_i} \geq 0, \quad \text{all } i \qquad\qquad (A.17)$$

$$X_j \cdot \frac{\partial \mathscr{L}}{\partial X_j} = 0, \quad \text{all } j \qquad\qquad (A.18)$$

$$\lambda_i \cdot \frac{\partial \mathscr{L}}{\partial \lambda_i} = 0, \quad \text{all } i \qquad\qquad (A.19)$$

$$X_j, \lambda_i \geq 0, \quad \text{all } i, j \qquad\qquad (A.20)$$

Of these, the requirements in (A.18) and (A.19) are known as the complementary slackness conditions. They require that an activity cannot be active and at the same time have a nonzero opportunity cost (A.18), and a resource cannot be slack and at the same time have a nonzero dual value (A.19). We shall have more to say about this in Section A.3.

The Kuhn-Tucker conditions do not provide an analytical procedure for deriving the optimal solution; equations (A.16) through (A.20) cannot be solved as a simultaneous system of equations for the unknown values of X_j and λ_i. As such, special algorithms have had to be developed for solving mathematical programming problems. The Kuhn-Tucker conditions do, however, establish the conditions that X must satisfy if it is to be identified as the optimal solution.

A.2   LINEAR PROGRAMMING PROBLEMS

A.2.1   Characteristics of Linear Programming Problems

A mathematical programming problem has two components:

1   A feasible set R defined by the set of constraints and by the nonnegativity conditions; for the vector of linear programming variables X, it is required that $X \in R$.

2   A single-valued continuous objective function $Z(X)$.

In linear programming, $Z(X)$ and the constraints which define R are linear functions. This does not significantly restrict a model builder's freedom of expression, for most well-behaved nonlinear problems are readily converted to a linearized form. Usually there is no loss of computational efficiency in such a conversion, and there may even be a gain in some instances.

The typical mathematical programming problem may be stated succinctly as

$$\text{find } X^* \in R$$

such that

$$Z(X^*) \geq Z(X) \quad \text{for all } X \in R$$

Most numerical algorithms, however, do not solve this problem, but rather they solve the following problem:

$$\text{find } X^* \in R$$

such that

$$Z(X^*) \geq Z(X) \quad \text{for all } X \in (E \cap R)$$

where E is a neighborhood of X^*. In other words, most algorithms find a local optimum and not a global optimum. (The expression $E \cap R$ indicates those points which are found both in set E and in set R.)

By far the largest share of the work involved in building a mathematical programming model goes into constructing the feasible set. Following Weierstrass, the important requirements of a feasible set are that it be bounded and closed. The property of closedness is ensured in any numerical optimization procedure; it is impossible to solve a problem with an open feasible set, such as

$$\max Z(X), \, X \in \tilde{R}, \, \tilde{R} = \{ X | 0 < X < \overline{X} \}$$

For any value of $X \in \tilde{R}$, however close it may be to $\overline{X}$, there always exists another $\hat{X}$, $\hat{X} > X$. The practical implication of the requirement of closedness is that we cannot, for example, ask the computer to find a profit-maximizing

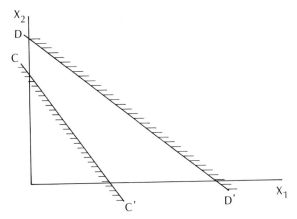

Figure A.4 An infeasible problem.

output mix for a steel plant, subject to the constraint that total steel production be less than 0.5 million tons. If there are technical reasons why this plant's steel production cannot reach 0.5 million tons, then the analyst is required to find a production level that may serve as a weak upper bound. The problem's constraint has to be restated as, say, total steel production must be less than or equal to 0.48 million tons.

Boundedness has to be imposed on the problem with the appropriate constraints, so that the objective function is restricted to finite values. In many cases though, the objective function takes the form $Z(\hat{X})$, where $\hat{X}$ is a subset of X. When this occurs, there may not be a set of constraints that directly bound the $\hat{X}_i$, but rather the bounding occurs through constraints on the X_i that are not in $\hat{X}_i$, and through the relations between those X_i and the $\hat{X}_i$. In such cases, whether or not the problem is bounded may not be immediately obvious, especially if the model contains a large number of constraints and variables. Anyone who works extensively with mathematical programming models will experience cases in which a problem turns out, inadvertently, to be unbounded.

Figures A.4 and A.5 illustrate an infeasible problem and an unbounded problem, respectively. In Figure A.4, there are two constraints, labeled CC' and DD'. The shading on each line represents the direction of feasibility. Thus, constraint CC' would be of the general form

$$a_{11}X_1 + a_{12}X_2 \leq b_1$$

and constraint DD' would be of the general form

$$a_{21}X_1 + a_{22}X_2 \geq b_2$$

Algebraically, these constraints are not necessarily inconsistent, but with particular numbers they could be inconsistent, leading to the two incompatible

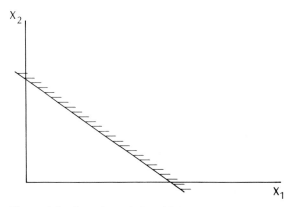

Figure A.5 An unbounded problem.

subsets of the feasible area that are pictured in Figure A.4. In Figure A.5 the constraint takes the form

$$a_{11}X_1 + a_{12}X_2 \geq b_1$$

This imposes a lower bound on the X_i, but in the absence of any upper bound a finite solution to the problem does not exist.

Figure A.6 illustrates the not-uncommon circumstance in which there are more constraints than variables. The lines a through e are constraints and the axes are nonnegativity conditions. If the objective function is such that the optimum is found at point h, then constraints c, d, and e are redundant. Frequently, however, it is important to leave those constraints in the numerical specification of the problem, for two reasons. First, it is not necessarily obvious beforehand which constraints are indeed redundant, and one of the analyst's tasks in specifying and solving the problem may be to identify which constraints have no bearing on the solution. Second, most applied models are solved many times under variations in the numerical specification, and changes in the model's coefficients may make relevant some of the previously redundant constraints. For example, a change in the slope parameter(s) of the objective function could make point j or k optimal, making constraints c or d and e binding. Alternatively, with an unchanged objective function an outward shift of constraint b could make point m optimal, thus making constraint c relevant to the determination of the optimum.

The important point to remember is that in linear programming it is not required that the number of variables be equal to the number of constraints. Usually the number of variables is greater, but the number of constraints may be greater as long as they are not mutually inconsistent (which would lead to the outcome illustrated in Figure A.4). As will be seen later, the number of nonredundant constraints in the solution generally will turn out to be equal to

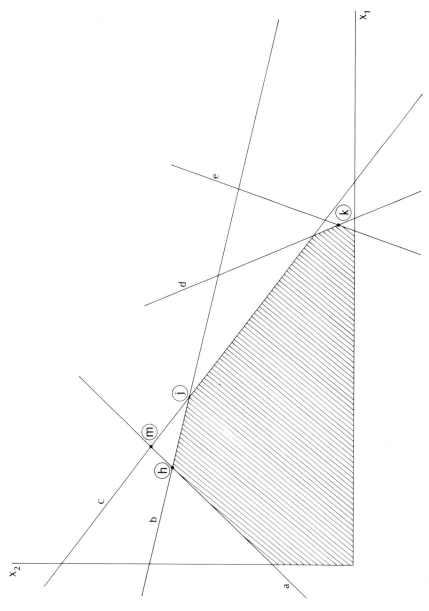

Figure A.6 A problem with more constraints than variables (feasible area is shaded).

361

the number of nonzero variables. But, as the foregoing examples have illustrated, it usually is not desirable to try to detect redundant constraints *a priori* and eliminate them from the statement of the problem.

Linear programming problems may contain equality constraints. In economic applications, inequality constraints are more common, but there are occasional instances when the specification of economic behavior requires that a relation be observed exactly. Many relations that would seem to be equalities from the viewpoint of economic theory are in fact more conveniently expressed as inequalities. An example is the supply-demand equilibrium condition, which normally is written in programming models in the form that the quantity demanded may not exceed the quantity supplied. Under proper specification, the model's solution usually will not contain excess supplies; if it does, that is an indication to the model builder that either there is an error in the set of coefficients or there is something unusual about the model's structure.[6]

Equality constraints sharply narrow the extent of the feasible space. For example, in Euclidean 2-space the imposition of an equality constraint requires that the solution be confined to a single line passing through the space. If nothing else, the presence of such constraints raises the required solution time and cost, and therefore one should reflect carefully before deciding that an exact equality statement really is necessary to define the feasible space.

It is a general characteristic of a linear programming problem that its solution will occur at a boundary point of the feasible set, because the objective function is linear. In the case of a nonlinear objective function, the optimum may (but not necessarily) occur at an interior point of the feasible set.

A.2.2 Primal and Dual Formulations

In algebraic form, the primal form of the general linear programming problem (*Problem 2*) may be written as

$$\max Z = \sum_{j=1}^{n} c_j X_j \tag{A.21a}$$

such that

$$\sum_{j=1}^{n} a_{ij} X_j \le b_i, \quad i = 1, \ldots, m \tag{A.22a}$$

$$X_j \ge 0, \quad j = 1, \ldots, n \tag{A.23a}$$

or, alternatively, in matrix and vector notation (*Problem 2A*) as

$$\max Z = c'X \tag{A.21b}$$

such that

$$AX \leq b \qquad \text{(A.22b)}$$
$$X \geq 0 \qquad \text{(A.23b)}$$

where a prime superscript indicates a row vector. Both forms will be used interchangeably in this exposition.

To each primal problem there corresponds a dual problem. The dual problem to Problem 2 is written as *Problem 3*[7]:

$$\min Y = \sum_i b_i \lambda_i \qquad \text{(A.24)}$$

such that

$$\sum_i a_{ij}\lambda_i \geq c_j, \quad j = 1,\ldots,n \qquad \text{(A.25)}$$
$$\lambda_i \geq 0, \quad i = 1,\ldots,m \qquad \text{(A.26)}$$

Every linear programming problem has its dual, and the theorems below develop the primal-dual relationships. For the moment, it should be noted that the dual variables λ_i play the same role, conceptually, that Lagrange's multipliers do in the case of an equality-constrained problem. It is proven below that the optimal value Z^* of the primal objective function is always equal to the optimal value Y^* of the dual objective function.

The following example illustrates a primal problem and its dual, both in numbers and in the graph in Figure A.7.

Problem 4 primal

$$\max Z = 3X_1 + 2X_2 - 6X_3$$

such that

$$
\begin{aligned}
-2X_1 + X_2 - X_3 &\leq 2 && [\lambda_1] \\
X_1 + 2X_2 - X_3 &\leq 8 && [\lambda_2] \\
X_1, X_2, X_3 &\geq 0
\end{aligned}
$$

Problem 4, dual

$$\min Y = 2\lambda_1 + 8\lambda_2$$

such that

$$
\begin{aligned}
-2\lambda_1 + \lambda_2 &\geq 3 && [X_1] \\
\lambda_1 + 2\lambda_2 &\geq 2 && [X_2] \\
\lambda_1 + \lambda_2 &\leq 6 && [X_3] \\
\lambda_1, \lambda_2 &\geq 0
\end{aligned}
$$

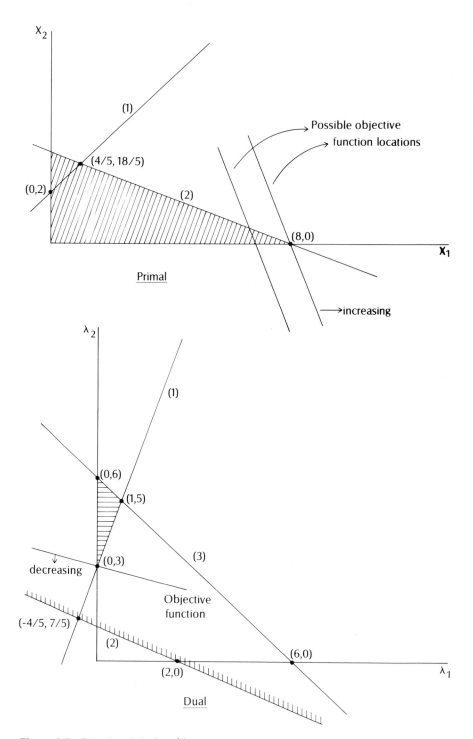

Figure A.7 Primal and dual problems.

Notice that the coefficients of the dual constraints (rows) are the vertical columns of coefficients in the primal. This is always the case in linear programming. The right-hand side values of the dual constraints are the objective function coefficients in the primal, and vice versa. To facilitate reading the problems this way, in the primal problem the dual variables are written in brackets beside their corresponding primal equations, and vice versa in the dual problem. Note the dimensionality: if the coefficient matrix A in the primal is $m \times n$, its counterpart in the dual is $n \times m$. The symmetry of the problems enables us to write the dual in the following matrix and vector notation:

Problem 3A

$$\min Y = b'\lambda \qquad (A.27)$$

such that

$$A'\lambda \geq c \qquad (A.28)$$
$$\lambda \geq 0 \qquad (A.29)$$

A comparison of Problem 2A and Problem 3A shows that the coefficients used in the primal and dual are identical. The variables are different, as are the relationships among the coefficients. The solution may be expressed in terms of either or both problems.

Figure A.7 presents Problem 4 in graphical terms ($X_3 = 0$ in the optimal solution to this example). The constraints are labeled in the order in which they appear in the algebraic statements of both the primal and dual. The optimum is reached at the point $(8, 0)$ in the primal and the point $(0, 3)$ in the dual. Note that there is one redundant constraint in the dual (constraint no. 2). As is shown in the following section, this outcome is expected when there is one more constraint than variables.

We turn now to development of the formal relationships between the primal and dual problems.

A.3 SOME THEOREMS

This section develops in a self-contained manner the principal theorems concerning the nature of linear programming solutions. Only Weierstrass's theorem has to be accepted without proof. We start with the fundamental lemma.

Fundamental Lemma of Linear Programming If X and λ are feasible vectors for the primal and dual problems, respectively, then the following relationship holds:

$$c'X \leq \lambda'AX \leq \lambda'b$$

Proof Note that the primal constraints give the relationship

$$AX - b \leq 0 \tag{A.30}$$

Since λ is feasible by hypothesis, it follows that

$$\lambda \geq 0 \tag{A.31}$$

Therefore,

$$\lambda'(AX - b) \leq 0 \tag{A.32}$$

and so

$$\lambda'AX \leq \lambda'b \tag{A.33}$$

The dual constraints give

$$\lambda'A - c \geq 0 \tag{A.34}$$

and, since $X \geq 0$ by the hypothesis of feasibility,

$$c'X \leq \lambda'AX \tag{A.35}$$

Inequalities (A.33) and (A.35) together yield the desired result. The fundamental lemma is employed frequently in the subsequent results. Taken on its own, the fundamental lemma separates the spaces of feasible values for the primal and dual objective functions. All values in the latter are greater than those in the former, for all values of λ and X except at the points defined by $\lambda'AX$.

The next theorem ensures that, under certain conditions, an optimal solution exists.

Existence Theorem of Linear Programming The primal and dual problems have optimal solutions if and only if both have feasible vectors.

(As a corollary, it may be noted that if the primal has a feasible vector, then so does the dual, and vice versa. Sometimes it is easier to check for feasibility via the primal, and sometimes via the dual.)

Proof Let $\hat{\lambda}$ be any feasible vector from the dual. Then, from the fundamental lemma,

$$c'X \leq \hat{\lambda}'b \text{ for all feasible } X \tag{A.36}$$

Then the set

$$\{U = c'X, X \text{ feasible}\}$$

is bounded from above by $\hat{\lambda}'b$. It also is bounded from below by the nonnegativity conditions, and both bounding inequalities are weak, and so the set U is closed. Therefore the conditions of Weierstrass's theorem are met: the set U is closed, bounded, and nonempty (the feasibility of X guarantees that U is nonempty), and $c'X$ is a continuous function. Hence $c'X$ reaches a maximum at least once, that is, an optimal solution exists. Similar reasoning proves that $V = \lambda'b$ attains a minimum.

An example illustrates an application of the existence theorem. Does the following problem have an optimal solution?

$$\max Z = X_1 + X_2$$

such that

$$-2X_1 - X_2 \leq 2$$
$$- X_1 - X_2 \leq 1$$
$$X_1, X_2 \geq 0$$

To answer the question, the existence theorem requires that we check for feasibility of the dual:

$$\min Y = 2\lambda_1 + \lambda_2$$

such that

$$-2\lambda_1 - \lambda_2 \geq 1$$
$$- \lambda_1 - \lambda_2 \geq 1$$
$$\lambda_1, \lambda_2 \geq 0$$

Clearly, no positive values of λ_1, λ_2 will allow the dual constraints to have positive left-hand sides, and so those constraints cannot be satisfied. Thus the dual is infeasible, and so the primal has no solution. The reason the primal has no solution is that it is unbounded from above: its constraints do not prohibit X_1, X_2 from taking arbitrarily large values.

We turn now to the important theorem which states that the primal and dual objective functions are equal at optimality.

The Duality Theorem A feasible vector X^* of the primal problem is optimal if and only if the dual has a feasible vector λ^* such that $c'X^* = \lambda^{*\prime}b$. Then the vector λ^* is optimal for the dual.

Only the sufficiency part of the theorem is proven here.

Proof of Sufficiency Let X^*, λ^* be feasible solutions such that $c'X^* = \lambda^{*\prime}b$, and let X be any other vector which is feasible for the primal. Then from the fundamental lemma

$$c'X \leq \lambda^{*\prime}b \tag{A.37}$$

and thus, from (A.37) and the hypothesis of the theorem,

$$c'X \leq c'X^* \tag{A.38}$$

which implies that X^* is optimal for the primal problem. Optimality of λ^* in the dual follows from similar reasoning.

The final theorem of this section describes the relationships between slack constraints and values of the primal and dual variables. It has considerable practical usefulness.

The Equilibrium Theorem of Linear Programming[8] (1) If X^*, λ^* are feasible for the primal and dual problems, respectively, they are optimal if and only if

(a) $\lambda_i^* = 0$ whenever $\sum_j a_{ij} X_j^* < b_i$

(b) $X_j^* = 0$ whenever $\sum_i a_{ij} \lambda_i^* > c_j$

(2) The optimal point always will be such that the number of nonzero variables (excluding slack and surplus variables) in each of the primal and dual problems will be no greater than the number of constraints in that problem.

Only the first part is proven here. A variant of the second part is proven in the section below on basis theory.

Proof Part 1: For proving necessity, if X^* and λ^* are optimal, then by the fundamental lemma and the duality theorem,

$$c'X^* = \lambda^{*\prime}AX^* = \lambda^{*\prime}b \tag{A.39}$$

From the left-hand equality in (A.39),

$$\lambda^{*\prime}AX^* - c'X^* = 0 \tag{A.40}$$

and so

$$(\lambda^{*\prime}A - c')X^* = 0 \tag{A.41}$$

Since λ^* is feasible, from the dual constraints we have

$$\lambda^{*\prime}A - c \geq 0 \tag{A.42}$$

and since X^* is feasible we know that

$$X^* \geq 0 \tag{A.43}$$

Therefore every term must be zero in

$$(\lambda^{*\prime}A - c')X^* = \sum_j \left(\sum_i a_{ij} \lambda_j^* - c_j \right) X_j^*$$

[because, by (A.42) and (A.43), no term j may be negative]. Hence it must be the case that either

or

$$\left.\begin{aligned} \left(\sum_j a_{ij}\lambda_i^* - c_j\right) &= 0 \\ X_j^* &= 0 \end{aligned}\right\} \tag{A.44}$$

which proves part (1b) of the theorem. For part (1a), we may use the right-hand inequality in (A.39) and argue analogously.

To prove sufficiency for part (1), suppose X^* and λ^* are feasible and satisfy conditions (1a) and (1b). Then every term j is zero in

$$\sum_j \left(\sum_i a_{ij}\lambda_i^* - c_j\right) X_j^* = (\lambda^{*\prime}A - c')X^*$$

and the same is true for every term i in

$$\sum_i \left(\sum_j a_{ij}X_j^* - b_i\right)\lambda_i^* = (AX^* - b)'\lambda^*$$

Therefore $c'X^* = \lambda^{*\prime}AX^* = \lambda^{*\prime}b$, so that, by the duality theorem, X^*, λ^* are optimal. This completes the proof of part (1).

The equilibrium theorem has several important implications. One is that it is possible to verify the optimality of a program's primal solution without knowing the value of the dual objective function. This can be done by checking for correspondence between nonbinding (primal and dual) constraints and zero values of the corresponding variables.

For applications in economics, the following implications of the theorem are useful:

1 Any resource not fully used up has a zero shadow price, i.e., at the margin, its optimal valuation is zero.
2 If the programming problem formulated is an economic sector model, then no product whose unit production cost exceeds its price will be produced at the optimum.
3 The value of the primal objective function equals the sum of resource values, when those resources are valued at the optimum. This is Euler's theorem, or the exhaustion-of-product condition.
4 The number of nonzero variables in the primal will not exceed the number of primal constraints.

The second implication follows from the interpretation of the λ_i as input and output prices, and the X_j as column vectors of Leontief or process analysis production coefficients. Then the following condition implies that unit costs of production exceed the product price:

$$\sum_i a_{ij}\lambda_i > P_j$$

If this occurs in the optimal solution, and the P_j are the c_j of the objective function, then by part (1) of the equilibrium theorem it follows that $X_j^* = 0$.

The equilibrium theorem also can be used to check for optimality, as illustrated in the following example.

Show that $X^* = (8,0)$ is the optimal primal solution to

$$\max Z = 3X_1 + 2X_2$$

such that

$$-2X_1 + X_2 \leq 2$$
$$X_1 + 2X_2 \leq 8$$

Procedure   The vector $(8,0)$ implies $Z = 24$. Put $(8,0)$ into the primal constraints. The first one turns out to be nonbinding $(-16 < 2)$, and hence by the theorem $\lambda_1 = 0$ if $X^* = (8,0)$ is optimal. Since $X_2 = 0$, the second dual constraint must be nonbinding if optimality holds. Since $\lambda_1 = 0$, the value $\lambda_2 = 3$ is required to achieve a dual objective function value of 24 and it also is consistent with a nonbinding second dual constraint. Since $Z = 24$ can be attained in both the primal and dual programs, then $X^* = (8,0)$ and $\lambda^* = (0,3)$ are indeed the optimal solution vectors.

A.4   BASIS THEORY

A typical linear programming problem contains more variables X_j than will appear in the optimal solution. If it were known beforehand which set of variables would constitute the optimal solution, their optimal values could be found by straightforward simultaneous equation procedures. Thus in solution algorithms a good deal of attention is given to defining the variables that are nonzero in the optimal solution. This issue is the central concern of basis theory. Basis theory also provides important results on the number of nonzero variables in an optimal solution.

To prepare the way, let us restate Problem 1 in scalar form as *Problem 5*:

$$\max Z = c_1 X_1 + \cdots + c_n X_n$$

such that

$$a_{11} X_1 + \cdots + a_{1n} X_n \leq b_1$$

$$\vdots \qquad\qquad \vdots \qquad \vdots$$

$$a_{m1} X_1 + \cdots + a_{mn} X_n \leq b_m$$
$$X_1, \ldots, X_n \geq 0$$

Recall from the discussion of slack variables that the kth slack variable may be defined by the kth constraint:

$$a_{k1}X_1 + \cdots + a_{kn}X_n + S_k = b_k \qquad (A.45)$$

(where the slack variable S_k is preceded by a minus sign in the case of greater-than constraints).

Note that the coefficients matrix associated with the slack variables has a diagonal structure and, in fact, is the identity matrix. This property permits Problem 5 to be rewritten in equivalent canonical form as Problem 6:

$$\max Z = c'X$$

such that

$$(A|I)\tilde{X} = \hat{A}\tilde{X} = b$$
$$\tilde{X} \geq 0$$

where $\tilde{X} = (X_1, \ldots, X_n; X_{n+1}, \ldots, X_{n+m})$ and the last m components of $\tilde{X}$ are slack variables, and $\hat{A}$ is the augmented matrix $(A|I)$.

When the problem is written in canonical form, it can be seen that in order for a solution to exist it is required that, when $m < n$,

$$\text{rank}(\hat{A}) = \text{rank}(\hat{A}, b) = m \qquad (A.46)$$

The rank (or "column rank") of the matrix $\hat{A}$ is the maximum number of linearly independent columns in $\hat{A}$.[9] Thus, condition (A.46) says that the set of column vectors $\hat{A}, b$ is linearly dependent, that is, there exist values of $\tilde{X}_j$ such that

$$\sum_j \hat{A}^j \tilde{X}_j = b \qquad (A.47)$$

where $\hat{A}^j$ denotes a column vector of $\hat{A}$.

Definitions A basis is a set of m column names of the matrix $\hat{A}$ or, equivalently, the set of names (not values) of m activities $\tilde{X}_j$ such that (A.47) holds. Hereafter, the basis is referred to simply as a set of columns of $\hat{A}$, but it is understood to include the columns corresponding to slack variables as needed. The set of columns in $\hat{A}$ corresponding to the basis may be called the basic matrix, and will be denoted by A_B. It follows that

$$A_B \in \hat{A} \qquad (A.48)$$

and

$$\text{rank}(A_B) = m \qquad (A.49)$$

A basic solution is any solution $\tilde{X}$ to (A.47), $\tilde{X} \lessgtr 0$. A basic feasible solution is a basic solution which has the additional property that $\tilde{X} \geq 0$. We are now in a position to develop the principal theorems of basis theory.

Basis Theorem No. 1 If the canonical problem

$$\hat{A}\tilde{X} = b, \ \tilde{X} \geq 0$$

has a feasible solution, it has a basic feasible solution.

Proof (inductive) Following Lancaster (1968), suppose there exists a nonbasic feasible solution X, that is, $X \geq 0$ and X has $k > m$ nonzero variables. Again letting $\hat{A}^j$ denote the jth column of $\hat{A}$, then

$$\hat{A}X = \sum_{j=1}^{n} \hat{A}^j X_j \qquad \text{(A.50)}$$

(i.e., each element of $\hat{A}^j$ is multiplied by X_j). Without loss of generality, we can take the first k variables to be the k nonzero variables. Since the remaining $n - k$ variables are zero,

$$\sum_{j=1}^{k} \hat{A}^j X_j = \hat{A}X = b \qquad \text{(A.51)}$$

But the columns of $\hat{A}^j$ are vectors of order m, so for $k > m$ the set of vectors $\hat{A}^j$ must be linearly dependent.

Since the vectors $\hat{A}^j$ are linearly dependent, we can find a set of weights V_j, which are not all zero, such that

$$\sum_{j=1}^{k} V_j \hat{A}^j = 0 \qquad \text{(A.52)}$$

Now the relationship between the X_j and the V_j will be examined. Choose the maximum of the ratios V_j/X_j and call it θ. From equations (A.51) and (A.52) the following linear combination can be formed:

$$\sum_{j=1}^{k} \hat{A}^j X_j - \frac{1}{\theta} \sum_{j=1}^{k} V_j \hat{A}^j = b \qquad \text{(A.53)}$$

(since the second left-hand term is zero).

By rearrangement,

$$\frac{1}{\theta} \sum_{j=1}^{k} \hat{A}^j \left(\theta - \frac{V_j}{X_j} \right) X_j = b \qquad \text{(A.54)}$$

But from the definition of θ, $[\theta - (V_j/X_j)] = 0$ for one value of j and it is positive for all other values of j, if $\theta \geq 0$. Consider the vector

$$\frac{1}{\theta}\left[\theta - \frac{V_j}{X_j}\right]X_j = W \qquad (A.55)$$

This vector W constitutes a nonnegative solution to $\hat{A}X = b$, that is, $\hat{A}W = b$. But, importantly, it has only $k - 1$ nonzero components.

This procedure can be continued, each time finding a new vector W which is a solution to $\hat{A}W = b$ and each time W having a smaller rank, as long as $k > m$. When the point is reached at which $k = m$, the vectors X_j become linearly independent and the process stops.

Hence X can be reduced to a vector (still feasible) of dimension m, that is, to a basic solution. Q.E.D.

Note the relationship of this theorem to part (2) of the equilibrium theorem of linear programming, that the optimal solution will have no more nonzero variables than the number of constraints.

Definition An extreme point of the feasible set is a point that cannot be expressed as a convex combination of other points in the set, but any other point can be expressed as a convex combination of extreme points.

Intuitively, an extreme point is a "corner" in the boundary of the feasible space. The origin is an example of an extreme point. In n-space, an extreme point (as any point) has n coordinates, and therefore it is written as an n-dimensional vector when the model has n variables. There are always at least $m + n$ extreme points in a model's feasible space, and sometimes many more (where, as before, m indicates the number of constraints).

Basis Theorem No. 2 Any extreme point of the set of feasible solutions also is a basic feasible solution.

Proof Following Hadley (1962), the proof consists of showing that the vectors in the matrix $\hat{A}$ that are associated with the nonzero components of the extreme point are linearly independent. This in turn is demonstrated by showing that linear dependence among those vectors leads to a contradiction of the extreme point assumption.

Since an extreme point has n components (or coordinates), it may be written $X^e = (X_1^e, \ldots, X_n^e)$. It is assumed that k components of X^e are nonzero, and that they are numbered so that they are the first k components. Therefore the solution to the model represented by the extreme point can be written

$$\sum_{j=1}^{k} X_j^e \hat{A}^j = b, \; X_j^e > 0 \qquad (A.56)$$

Now we make the contrary assumption that the columns in $\hat{A}$ corresponding to the positive components of X^e are linearly dependent. If this were the case, then there must exist u_j not all zero such that

$$\sum_{j=i}^{k} u_j \hat{A}^j = 0 \tag{A.57}$$

For a sufficiently small ε, the following scalars can be formed:

$$X_j^e + \varepsilon u_j > 0, \; X_j^e - \varepsilon u_j < 0$$

Defining an n-dimensional vector U which has u_j in the first k positions and zero in the last $n - k$ positions, it is possible to write two vectors

$$\left. \begin{aligned} X_1 &= X^e + \varepsilon U \geq 0 \\ X_2 &= X^e - \varepsilon U \geq 0 \end{aligned} \right\} \tag{A.58}$$

From (A.57)

$$\hat{A} U = 0 \tag{A.59}$$

so

$$\hat{A} X_1 = b, \; \hat{A} X_2 = b \tag{A.60}$$

Hence X_1, X_2 are feasible solutions to the model, and they differ from X^e. Furthermore it is possible to write

$$X^e = \tfrac{1}{2} X_1 + \tfrac{1}{2} X_2 \tag{A.61}$$

Equation (A.61) contradicts the assumption that X^e is an extreme point, and therefore it cannot be true that the columns of A corresponding to the positive components of X^e are linearly dependent. They must be linearly independent. But there are only m independent columns in A, and m independent columns constitute a basis. Therefore X^e must be a basic solution. This completes the proof.

Theorem on Optimal Solutions   The optimum of a linear programming problem is reached either at an extreme point or at a set of extreme points.

Proof   Consider any boundary point X that is not an extreme point. The point X can be expressed as a linear combination of extreme points X^k. Choose the minimum number of extreme points necessary to define X so that no extreme point has a zero weight. There must be at least two of these nonzero extreme points. Then X can be expressed as

$$X = \sum_k d_k X^k, \; d_k > 0, \; \sum d_k = 1 \tag{A.62}$$

where d_k are constants.

Now consider the Cartesian product of vectors $c'X$, for the vector c of objective function weights:

$$c'X = c'\left(\sum_k d_k X^k\right) = \sum_k d_k(c'X^k) \qquad (A.63)$$

Over all extreme points X^k, choose the one for which $c'X^k$ is maximized. (If several have the same value, choose one of them.) Denote this maximum value by the letter V. Now if V is substituted for every $c'X^k$ in (A.63), then the right-hand side of that equation cannot be reduced, and it might be increased. Thus

$$c'X \leq V \qquad (A.64)$$

There are two possible outcomes in (A.64):

1 The maximum V of the expression $c'X^k$ is not reached at all extreme points that are used to define X, so $c'X^k < V$ for some k, and hence $c'X < V$. This means that X is *not* a maximum (i.e., X is a boundary point which is not a linear combination of optimal extreme points).
2 The maximum V of the expression $c'X^k$ is reached at all extreme points so that $c'X = V$. Then if X is optimal, so are all the extreme points (and all linear combinations of them).

Therefore no point in the feasible set, except an extreme point, can be optimal unless it is a convex combination of extreme points.   Q.E.D.

The theorem on optimal solutions, taken together with basis theorem no. 2, has given us a very important result: *an optimal solution to a linear programming problem does not need to have more than* m *nonzero variables, when the model has* m *constraints.* This result follows from equating an optimal solution with an extreme point, and the latter with a basic feasible solution.

For the model builder, this result provides a reminder of the importance of the row dimension in the model. If a model has 50 constraints and 500 variables, then 450 of those variables will be irrelevant to any given solution. In agricultural models, this result indicates why it usually is necessary to have monthly or seasonal resource constraints, and perhaps a MOTAD risk matrix as well, in order to obtain a solution with a sufficient variety of crops and/or technologies at nonzero levels.

NOTES

1 The Russian mathematician L. V. Kantorovich is generally credited with first having posed the linear programming problem in 1939 in the context of practical concerns about organizing production, but he did not provide solution procedures.
2 Karl Theodor Wilhelm Weierstrass (1815–1897) was one of the founders of the modern theory of functions.

3 Michel Rolle (1652–1719) was known principally for his work on algebra.

4 Let A denote the Hessian matrix of second-order partial derivatives, (ie. $a_{ij} = \partial^2 Z/\partial X_i \, \partial X_j$), then $(dX)'A(dX)$ will be negative definite if

$$a_{11} < 0, \quad \begin{vmatrix} a_{11} & a_{12} \\ a_{21} & a_{22} \end{vmatrix} > 0, \quad \begin{vmatrix} a_{11} & a_{12} & a_{13} \\ a_{21} & a_{22} & a_{23} \\ a_{31} & a_{32} & a_{33} \end{vmatrix} < 0, \dots, (-1)^n |A| > 0,$$

where vertical bars denote a determinant and n is the dimension of A. In other words, the principal minors of $|A|$ must alternate in sign. For a useful discussion of these conditions when X is a two-dimensional vector, see Silberberg (1978), pp. 102–107.

5 See Courant (1936), pp. 188–191.

6 If the quantities demanded are fixed, the presence of joint products in the production functions may lead to one or more products in excess supply. In such a case, writing the supply-demand equilibrium conditions as equalities may lead to an infeasible solution.

7 It is a nearly universal convention that primal variables are subscripted j and primal constraints i. The reverse convention holds on dual subscripts.

8 This theorem is the linear counterpart of the Kuhn-Tucker theorem of nonlinear programming.

9 Recall that linearly independent vectors Y_i cannot be expressed as linear combinations of each other. For a good review of this topic and related topics, see Hadley's *Linear Algebra* (1961).

Bibliography

Ahn, C. Y., Singh, I., and Squire, L. 1981. A model of an agricultural household in a multicrop economy: The case of Korea. *Review of Economics and Statistics* 4:520–25.

Allen, R. G. D. 1962. *Mathematical Analysis for Economists*. London: Macmillan.

Almon, C. 1967. *Matrix Methods in Economics*. Reading, MA: Addison-Wesley.

Anderson, J. R. 1974. Simulation methodology and application in agricultural economics. *Review Marketing and Agricultural Economics* 42:3–55.

_____, Dillon, J. L., and Hardaker, J. B. 1977. *Agricultural Decision Analysis*. Ames, IA: Iowa State University Press.

Ballenger, N. S. 1984. *Agricultural Policy Analysis for Mexico: Sectoral and Macro Impacts*. Ph.D. dissertation, University of California at Davis.

Barnum, H. N., and Squire, L. 1979. *A Model of an Agricultural Household*, World Bank Staff Occasional Paper No. 27, Baltimore: The Johns Hopkins University Press.

Bassoco, L. M., and Norton, R. D., 1982. *Análisis de las Interrelaciones del Sector Agrícola en un Horizonte de Corto y Mediano Plazo*. Sistema Alimentario Mexicano, Mexico, D.F. (October).

_____, and Norton, R. D. 1983. A quantitative framework for agricultural policies. In: *The Book of CHAC: Programming Studies for Mexican Agriculture* (R. D.

Norton and L. Solís, eds.), pp. 113–61. Baltimore: The Johns Hopkins University Press.

_____, and Rendón, T. 1973. The technology set and data base for CHAC. In: *Multi-level Planning: Case Studies in Mexico* (A. S. Manne and L. M. Goreux, eds.), pp. 339–72. Amsterdam: North-Holland.

_____, Cartas, C., and Norton, R. D. 1986. Sectoral analysis of the benefits of subsidized insurance in Mexico. In: *Crop Insurance for Agricultural Development*: *Issue and Experience* (P. Hazell, C. Pomareda, and A. Valdes, eds.), pp. 126–42, Baltimore: Johns Hopkins University Press.

_____, Duloy, J. H., Norton, R. D., and Winkelmann, D. 1973. A programming model of an agricultural district. In: *Multi-Level Planning: Case Studies in Mexico* (A. S. Manne and L. M. Goreux, eds.), pp. 401–16. Amsterdam: North-Holland.

_____, Mutsaers, A., Norton, R. D., and Silos, J. S. 1983. Incorporating policy guidelines in the design of agricultural investment projects. In: *The Book of CHAC: Programming Studies for Mexican Agriculture* (R. D. Norton and L. Solís, eds.), pp. 480–510. Baltimore: The Johns Hopkins University Press.

_____, Norton, R. D., and Silos, J. S. 1983. Procedures for treating interdependence in the appraisal of irrigation projects. In: *The Book of CHAC: Programming Studies for Mexican Agriculture* (R. D. Norton and L. Solís, eds.), pp. 458–479. Baltimore: The Johns Hopkins University Press.

Baumol, W. J. 1961. *Economic Theory and Operations Analysis*. Englewood Cliffs, NJ: Prentice-Hall.

_____. 1963. An expected gain–confidence limit criterion for portfolio selection. *Management Science* **10**:174–82.

Bell, C., Hazell, P. B. R., and Slade, R. 1982. *Project Evaluation in Regional Perspective: A Study of an Irrigation Project in Northwest Malaysia*. Baltimore: The Johns Hopkins University Press.

Bergendorff, H. G., Hazell, P. B. R., and Scandizzo, P. L. 1974. On the equilibrium of a competitive market when production is risky. World Bank Development Research Center, Washington, DC, mimeographed.

Binswanger, H. P. 1980. Attitudes toward risk: Experimental measurement in rural India. *American Journal of Agricultural Economics* **62**:395–407.

Boussard, J-M. 1971. Time horizon, objective function, and uncertainty in a multi-period model of farm growth. *American Journal of Agricultural Economics* **53**:467–77.

_____, and Petit, M. 1967. Representation of farmers' behavior under uncertainty with a focus-loss constraint. *Journal of Farm Economics* **49**:869–80.

Brandow, C. E. 1961. *Interrelation Among Demands for Farm Products and Implications for Control of Market Supply*. Bulletin 680, Pennsylvania State University, Agriculture Experiment Station, University Park, Pennsylvania (August).

Brink, L., and McCarl, B. 1978. The trade-off between expected return and risk among corn belt farmers. *American Journal of Agricultural Economics* **60**:259–63.

Buckwell, A. E., and Hazell, P. B. R. 1972. Implications of aggregation bias for the construction of static and dynamic linear programming supply models. *Journal of Agricultural Economics* **23**:119–34.

Candler, W., and Norton, R. D. 1977. *Multi-Level Programming and Development Policy*. World Bank Staff Working Paper No. 258, Washington, DC (May).

_____, Fortuny-Amat, J., and McCarl, B. 1981. The potential role of multi-level programming in agricultural economics. *American Journal of Agricultural Economics* **63**:521–31.

Cappi, C., Fletcher, L., Norton, R. D., Pomareda, C., and Waiver, M. 1978. A model of agricultural production and trade in Central America. In: *Economic Integration in Central America* (W. R. Cline and E. Delgado, eds.), p. 317–70 and appendix G. Washington, DC: The Brookings Institution.

Cartas, C., and Cifuentes, E. 1982. Relaciones de Precios Intersectoriales, Sistema Alimentario Mexicano, Mexico, DF.

Charnes, A., and Cooper, W. W. 1959. Chance constrained programming. *Management Science* **6**:73–79.

Chen, J. T., and Baker, C. B. 1974. Marginal risk constraint linear program for activity analysis. *American Journal of Agricultural Economics* **56**:622–27.

Cocks, K. D. 1968. Discrete stochastic programming. *Management Science* **15**:72–79.

Condos, A. and Cappi, C. 1976. Agricultural sector analysis: A linear programming model for Tunisia. Rome: Food and Agriculture Organization of the United Nations, Policy Analysis Division.

Courant, R. 1936. *Differential and Integral Calculus*, Vol. 2. New York: Interscience.

Dantzig, G. B. 1963. *Linear Programming and Extensions*. Princeton, NJ: Princeton University Press.

_____, and Wolfe, P. 1961. The decomposition principle for linear programs. *Econometrica* **29**:101–11.

Day, R. H. 1961. Recursive programming and supply prediction. In: *Agricultural Supply Functions—Estimating Techniques and Interpretations* (E. O. Heady, C. B. Baker, H. G. Diesslin, et al., eds.). Ames, IA: Iowa State University Press, reprinted in (K. A. Fox and D. G. Johnson, eds.) 1969, *Readings in the Economics of Agriculture*, American Economic Association, London: George Allen & Unwin Ltd.

_____ 1963a. On aggregating linear programming models of production. *Journal of Farm Economics* **45**:797–813.

_____ 1963b. *Recursive Programming and Production Response*. Amsterdam: North-Holland.

_____, and Singh, I. 1977. *Economic Development as an Adaptive Process: The Green Revolution in the Indian Punjab*. Cambridge: Cambridge University Press.

Dean, G. W., and de Benedicitis, M. 1964. A model of economic development for research farms in southern Italy, *Journal of Farm Economics* **46**:295–312.

de Janvry, A., Bieri, J., and Nuñez, A. 1972. Estimation of demand parameters under consumer budgeting: An application to Argentina. *American Journal of Agricultural Economics* **54**:422–30.

Dillon, J. L., and Heady, E. O. 1961. A model for entrepreneurial decisions under free competition. *Metroeconomica* **13**:20–28.

_____, and Scandizzo, P. L. 1978. Risk attitudes of subsistence farms in northeast Brazil: A sampling approach. *American Journal of Agricultural Economics* **60**:425–35.

Dorfman, R., Samuelson, P. A., and Solow, R. 1958. *Linear Programming and Economic Analysis*. New York: McGraw-Hill.

Duloy, J. H., and Hazell, P. B. R. 1975. Substitution and nonlinearities in planning models. In: *Economy-wide Models and Development Planning* (C. R. Blitzer, P. B. Clark, and L. Taylor, eds.), pp. 307–25, London: Oxford University Press.

_____, and Norton, R. D. 1973a. CHAC: A programming model of Mexican agriculture. In: *Multi-Level Planning: Case Studies in Mexico* (A. S. Manne and L. M. Goreux, eds.), pp. 291–338. Amsterdam: North-Holland.

_____, and Norton, R. D. 1973b. CHAC results: Economic alternatives for Mexican agriculture. In: *Multi-Level Planning*: *Case Studies in Mexico* (A. S. Manne and L. M. Goreux, eds.), pp. 373–99. Amsterdam: North-Holland.

_____, and Norton, R. D. 1973c. Linking the agricultural model and the economy-wide model. In: *Multi-Level Planning*: *Case Studies in Mexico* (A. S. Manne and L. M. Goreux, eds.), pp. 435–62, Amsterdam: North-Holland.

_____, and Norton, R. D. 1975. Prices and incomes in linear programming models. *American Journal of Agricultural Economics* **57**:591–600.

Enke, S. 1951. Equilibrium among spatially separated markets: Solution by electric analogue. *Econometrica* **19**:40–47.

Farhi, L., and Vercueil, J. 1969. *Recherche pour une Planification Coherente*: *Le Model de Prevision du Ministere de L'Agriculture*, Paris: Editions du Centre National de la Recherche Scientifique.

Fisher, R. A. 1920. A mathematical estimation of the methods of determining the accuracy of an observation by the mean error, and by the mean square error. *Royal Astronomical Society* (Monthly Notes) **80**:758–69.

Fletcher, L. B., Graber, E., Merrill, W. C., and Thorbecke, E. 1970. *Guatemala's Economic Development*: *The Role of Agriculture*. Ames, IA: The Iowa State University Press.

Fox, K. A. 1953. A spatial equilibrium model of the livestock feed economy in the U.S. *Econometrica* **21**:547–66.

Freund, R. J. 1956. The introduction of risk into a programming model. *Econometrica* **24**:253–63.

Frisch, R. 1959. A complete scheme for computing all direct and cross demand elasticities in a model with many sectors. *Econometrica* **27**:177–96.

Gale, D. 1960. *The Theory of Linear Economic Models*. New York: McGraw-Hill.

García, M. 1984. *Modelo Sectorial de Programación Lineal para la Producción Nacional de Granos Básicos*, Estudio de los Efectos de Políticas de Desarrollo Agrícola para el Consumo de Alimentos de la Población Centroamericana, Secretaría Permanente del Tratado General de Integración Centroamericana (SIECA), Tegucigalpa, Honduras.

Gass, S. I. 1985. *Linear Programming*: *Methods and Applications*, 5th ed., New York: McGraw-Hill.

George, P. S., and King, G. A. 1971. *Consumer Demand for Food Commodities in the U.S. with Projections for 1980*. Monograph 26, Giannini Foundation, California Experiment Station (March).

Georgescu-Roegen, N. 1969. Process in farming vs. process in manufacturing: A problem of balanced development. In: *Economic Problems of Agriculture in Industrial Societies* (U. Papi and C. Nunn, eds.), New York: Macmillan.

_____. 1972. Process analysis and the neoclassical theory of the production function. *American Journal of Agricultural Economics* **54**:279–94.

Ginsburgh, V. and Waelbroeck, J. 1975. A general equilibrium model of world trade, part I. Cowles Foundation Discussion Paper No. 412, Yale University.

Goreux, L. M., and Manne, A. S. 1973. *Multi-Level Planning*: *Case Studies in Mexico*. Amsterdam: North-Holland.

Guise, J. W. B., and Flinn, J. C. 1970. The allocation and pricing of water in a river basin. *American Journal of Agricultural Economics* **52**:411–21.

Hadley, G. 1961. *Linear Algebra*, Reading, MA: Addison-Wesley.

_____. 1962. *Linear Programming*. Reading, MA: Addison-Wesley.

Hall, H. H., Heady, E. O., and Plessner, Y. 1968. Quadratic programming solution of competitive equilibrium for U.S. agriculture. *American Journal of Agricultural Economics* **50**:536–55.

Hanf, C. H. and Mueller, R. A. E. 1979. Linear risk programming in supply response analysis. *European Review of Agricultural Economics* **6**:435–52.

Hardaker, J. B., and Troncoso, J. L. 1979. The formulation of MOTAD programming models for farm planning using subjectively elicited activity net revenue distributions. *European Review of Agricultural Economics* **6**:47–60.

Hazell, P. B. R. 1970. Game theory—an extension of its application to farm planning under uncertainty. *Journal of Agricultural Economics* **21**:239–52.

———. 1971. A linear alternative to quadratic and semivariance programming for farm planning under uncertainty. *American Journal of Agricultural Economics* **53**:53–62.

———. 1979. Endogenous input prices in linear programming models. *American Journal of Agricultural Economics* **61**:476–81.

———, and Pomareda, C. 1981. Evaluating price stabilization schemes with mathematical programming. *American Journal of Agricultural Economics* **63**: 550–56.

———, and Scandizzo, P. L. 1974. Competitive demand structures under risk in agricultural linear programming models. *American Journal of Agricultural Economics* **56**:235–44.

———, and Scandizzo, P. L. 1975. Market intervention policies when production is risky. *American Journal of Agricultural Economics* **57**:641–49.

———, and Scandizzo, P. L. 1977. Farmers' expectations, risk aversion, and market equilibrium under risk, *American Journal of Agricultural Economics* **59**:204–19.

———, and Valdes, A. 1984. Choosing the right role for crop insurance. *CERES*, **17**:17–20. (May–June).

———, Bassoco, L. M., and Arcia, G. 1986. A model for evaluating farmers' demand for insurance: Applications in Mexico and Panama. In: *Crop Insurance for Agricultural Development: Issues and Experience*, (P. Hazell, C. Pomareda, and A. Valdes, eds.), pp. 35–66, Baltimore: Johns Hopkins University Press.

———, Norton, R. D., Parthasarathy, M., and Pomareda, C. 1983. The importance of risk in agricultural planning models. In: *The Book of CHAC: Programming Studies for Mexican Agriculture* (R. D. Norton and L. Solís, eds.), pp. 225–49. Baltimore: The Johns Hopkins University Press.

Heady, E. O. 1952. *Economics of Agricultural Production and Resource Use*. Englewood Cliffs, NJ: Prentice-Hall.

———. 1954. Simplified presentation and logical aspects of linear programming technique. *Journal of Farm Economics* **24**:1035–48.

———, and Candler, W. 1958. *Linear Programming Methods*. Ames, IA: Iowa State University Press.

———, and Egbert, A. C. 1959. Programming regional adjustments in grain production to eliminate surpluses. *Journal of Farm Economics* **41**:718–33.

Heal, C. M. 1973. *Theory of Economic Planning*. Amsterdam: North-Holland.

Henderson, J. M. 1959. The utilization of agricultural land: A theoretical and empirical inquiry. *Review of Economic Statistics*, **41** (3):242–59.

Ho, F-S., and King, R. A. 1972. A low-cost spatial equilibrium solution procedure. *American Journal of Agricultural Economics* **54**:373–74.

Hogan, A. J., Morris, J. G., and Thompson, H. E. 1981. Decision problems under risk and chance constrained programming: Dilemmas in the transition. *Management Science* **27**:698–716.

Hong, S. H. 1980. *General Equilibrium Analysis of Korean Taxation Policy*. Ph.D. dissertation, Stanford University.

Howell, H. 1983. Machinery-labor substitution in Mexico's central plateau. In: *The Book of CHAC: Programming Studies for Mexican Agriculture* (R. D. Norton and L. Solís, eds.), pp. 375–411. Baltimore: The Johns Hopkins University Press.

Husain, T., and Inman, R. 1977. *A Model for Estimating the Effects of Credit Pricing on Farm-Level Employment and Income Distribution*. World Bank Staff Working Paper No. 261, Washington, DC.

Intriligator, M. D. 1971. *Mathematical Optimization and Economic Theory*. Englewood Cliffs, NJ: Prentice-Hall.

Jones, R. W. 1965. The structure of simple general equilibrium models. *Journal of Political Economy* **73**:557–72.

Judge, G. G., and Wallace, T. D. 1958. Estimation of spatial price equilibrium models. *Journal of Farm Economics* **40**:801–820.

Just, R. H. 1974. *Econometric Analysis of Production Decisions with Government Intervention: The Case of the California Field Crops*, Berkeley: University of California, Giannini Foundation, Monograph No. 33.

Kataoka, S. 1963. A stochastic programming model. *Econometrica* **31**:181–96.

Kawaguchi, T., and Maruyama, Y. 1972. Generalized constrained games in farm planning. *American Journal of Agricultural Economics* **54**:591–602.

Kennedy, J. O. S. 1975. Using regression analysis to reduce aggregation bias in linear programming supply models, *Australian Journal of Agricultural Economics* **19**:1–11.

King, R. A. 1953. Some applications of activity analysis in agricultural economics, *Journal of Farm Economics* **25**:823–33.

Knight, F. H. 1921. *Risk, Uncertainty and Profit*. Boston, MA: Houghton Mifflin.

Koopmans, T. C. (ed.), 1951. *Activity Analysis of Production and Allocation*, Cowles Commission Monograph 13. New York: Wiley.

Kornai, J. 1967. *Mathematical Planning of Structural Decisions*. Amsterdam: North-Holland.

——. 1969. Man-machine planning. *Economics of Planning* **9**:209–34.

Kuhn, H. W., and Tucker, A. W. 1951. Nonlinear programming. In: *Proceedings of the Second Berkeley Symposium on Mathematical Statistics and Probability* (J. Neyman, ed.). Berkeley, CA: University of California Press. pp. 481–92.

Kunkel, D. E., Rodriguez, G. R., Jr., Gonzalez, L. A., and Alix, J. C. 1978. Theory, structure and validated empirical performance of MAAGAP: A programming model of the agricultural sector of the Philippines. *Journal of Agricultural Economic Development* **8**:1–25.

Kutcher, G. P. 1972. *Agricultural Planning at the Regional Level: A Programming Model of Mexico's Pacific Northwest*. Ph.D. dissertation, University of Maryland.

——. 1980. *The Agro-Economic Model*. Technical Report No. 16, Master Plan for Water Resources Development and Use, Egyptian Ministry of Irrigation, Cairo (May).

——. 1983. A regional agricultural programming model for Mexico's Pacific Northwest. In: *The Book of CHAC: Programming Studies for Mexican Agriculture*, (R. D. Norton and L. Solís, eds.), pp. 317–51, Baltimore: The Johns Hopkins University Press.

——, and Norton, R. D. 1982. Operations research methods in agricultural policy analysis. *European Journal of Operational Research*. **10**:333–45.

——, and Scandizzo, P. L. 1981. *The Agricultural Economy of Northeast Brazil*. Baltimore: The Johns Hopkins University Press.

Lancaster, K. 1968. *Mathematical Economics*, New York: Macmillan.

Lau, L. J., Yotopoulos, P. A., Chou, E. C., and Lin, W. L. 1981. The microeconomics of distribution: A simulation of the farm economy. *Journal of Policy Modeling* 3:175–206.

Lee, J. E. 1966. Exact aggregation: A discussion of Miller's theorem. *Agricultural Economics Research* 18:58–61.

Le-Si, V., Scandizzo, P. L., and Kasnakoglu, H. 1982. Turkey agricultural sector model (mimeographed). The World Bank, Washington, DC.

Levy, H., and Markowitz, H. M. 1979. Approximating expected utility by a function of mean and variance. *American Economic Review* 69:308–17.

Lluch, C., and Williams, R. 1973. Cross-country patterns in Frisch's money flexibility coefficient. Development Research Center. The World Bank, Washington, DC (unpublished draft).

Lluch, C., Powell, A. A., and Williams, R. A. 1977. *Patterns in Household Demand and Savings*. Oxford: Oxford University Press.

Loftsgard, L. D. and Heady, E. O. 1959. Application of dynamic programming models for optimum farm and home plans, *Journal of Farm Economics* 41:51–67.

Loucks, D. P. 1975. Planning for multiple goals. In: *Economy-wide Models and Development Planning* (C. Blitzer, P. Clark, and L. Taylor, eds.), London: Oxford University Press, pp. 213–33.

Low, A. R. C. 1974. Decision taking under uncertainty: A linear programming model of peasant farmer behavior. *Journal of Agricultural Economics* 25:311–20.

McCarl, B. A., and Spreen, T. H. 1980. Price endogenous mathematical programming as a tool for sector analysis. *American Journal of Agricultural Economics* 62:87–102.

McInerney, J. P. 1969. Linear programming and game theory—some extensions. *Journal of Agricultural Economics* 20:269–78.

Malinvaud, E., 1967. Decentralized procedures for planning. In: *Activity Analysis in the Theory of Growth and Planning* (E. Malinvaud and M. O. L. Bacharach, eds.), Ch. 7, London: Macmillan.

Manne, A. S. 1973a. DINAMICO: A dynamic multi-sector, multi-skill model. In: *Multi-Level Planning: Case Studies in Mexico* (A. S. Manne and L. M. Goreux, eds.), pp. 107–50, Amsterdam: North-Holland.

_____. 1973b. On linking ENERGETICOS to DINAMICO. In: *Multi-level Planning: Case Studies in Mexico* (A. S. Manne and L. M. Goreux, eds.), pp. 277–89, Amsterdam: North-Holland.

_____, Chao, H. P., and Wilson, R. 1978. Computation of competitive equilibrium by a sequence of linear programs. Department of Operations Research, Stanford University, January.

Markowitz, H. M. 1959. *Portfolio Selection: Efficient Diversification of Investments*. New York: Wiley.

Martin, N. R., Jr. 1972. Stepped product demand and factor supply functions in linear programming analyses. *American Journal of Agricultural Economics* 54:116–20.

Maruyama, Y., and Kawaguchi, T. 1971. An approach to farm planning under 'ambiguity'. In: *Policies, Planning and Management for Agricultural Development*. Papers and Reports for the XIVth International Conference of Agricultural Economists, Oxford: Institute of Agrarian Affairs.

Mash, V. A., and Kiselev, V. I. 1971. Optimization of agricultural development of a region in relation to food processing and consumption. In: *Economic Models and Quantitative Methods for Decisions and Planning in Agriculture*. Proceedings of an East-West Seminar (E. O. Heady, ed.), Ames, IA: Iowa State University Press.

Miller, C. 1963. The simplex method for local separable programming. In: *Recent Advances in Mathematical Programming* (R. L. Graves and P. Wolfe, eds.), pp. 88–100, New York: Wiley.

Miller, T. A. 1966. Sufficient conditions for exact aggregation in linear programming models. *Agricultural Economics Research* **18**:52–57.

Moscardi, E., and de Janvry, A. 1977. Attitudes toward risk among peasants: An econometric approach. *American Journal of Agricultural Economics* **59**:710–16.

Nakajima, C. 1970. Subsistence and commercial family farms: Some theoretical models of subjective equilibrium. In: *Subsistence Agriculture and Economic Development* (C. R. Wharton, Jr., ed.), Chicago: Aldine.

Nelson, C. H., and McCarl, B. A. 1984. Including imperfect competition in spatial equilibrium models. *Canadian Journal of Agricultural Economics* **32**:55–69.

Newbery, D. M. G., and Stiglitz, J. E. 1981. *The Theory of Commodity Price Stabilization.* New York: Clarendon Press/Oxford University Press.

Norton, R. D. 1982. The Egyptian agro-economic model and Egypt's irrigation investment choices. Report for the EMENA Projects Office, The World Bank, Washington, DC.

———, and Gencağa, H. 1985. Turkey: Agricultural sector performance possibilities. Working Papers 7a–7c, EMENA Agricultural Projects Office, The World Bank, Washington, DC.

———, and Scandizzo, P. L. 1981. Market equilibrium computations in activity analysis models. *Operations Research* **29**:243–62.

———, and Schiefer, G. W. 1980. Agricultural sector programming models: A review. *European Review of Agricultural Economics* **7**:229–64.

———, and Solís, L. 1983. *The Book of CHAC: Programming Studies for Mexican Agriculture.* Baltimore: The Johns Hopkins University Press.

———, Santaniello, V., and Echevarría, J. A. 1983. Economic evaluation of a sector investment program: A case study for Peru. *Journal of Policy Modeling* **2**:149–77.

Norton, R. D., P. L. Scandizzo, and L. Zimmerman, 1986. Foreign trade and factor incomes in Portugal: An application of a general equilibrium model. *Journal of Policy Modeling,* forthcoming.

Officer, R. R., and Halter, A. N. 1968. Utility analysis in a practical setting. *American Journal Agricultural Economics* **50**:257–77.

Paris, Q. 1981. Multiple optimal solutions in linear programming models. *American Journal of Agricultural Economics* **63**:724–27.

———, and Rausser, G. C. 1973. Sufficient conditions for aggregation of linear programming models. *American Journal of Agricultural Economics* **55**:659–66.

Piñeiro, M. E., and McCalla, A. F. 1971. Programming for Argentine price policy analysis. *Review of Economics and Statistics* **53**:59–66.

Plessner, Y. 1957. Activity analysis, quadratic programming, and general equilibrium. *International Economic Review* **42**:283–303.

Pomareda, C., 1980. *Estudio de Desarrollo Agrícola de Centroamerica,* vol. 1. Guatemala: ECID., Secretaría Permanente del Tratado General de Integración Económica Centroamericana, January.

———, and Simmons, R. L. 1983. A risk programming model for Mexican vegetable exports. In: *The Book of CHAC: Programming Studies for Mexican Agriculture* (R. D. Norton and L. Solís, eds.), pp. 352–74 Baltimore: The Johns Hopkins University Press.

Powell, A. A. 1966. A complete system of consumer demand equations for the Australian economy fitted by a model of additive preferences. *Econometrica* **34**:661–675.

Pratt, J. W. 1964. Risk aversion in the small and in the large. *Econometrica* **32**:122–36.

Rae, A. N. 1970. Capital budgeting, intertemporal programming models with particular reference to agriculture, *Australian Journal of Agricultural Economics* **14**:39–52.

———. 1971a. Stochastic programming, utility, and sequential decision problems in farm management. *American Journal of Agricultural Economics* **53**:448–60.

———. 1971b. An empirical application and evaluation of discrete stochastic programming in farm management. *American Journal of Agricultural Economics* **53**:625–38.

Romero, C. and Rehman, T. 1984. Goal programming and multiple criteria decision-making in farm planning: An expository analysis. *Journal of Agricultural Economics* **35**:177–90.

Roy, A. D. 1952. Safety-first and the holding of assets. *Econometrica* **20**:431–49.

Samuelson, P. A. 1952. Spatial price equilibrium and linear programming. *American Economic Review* **42**:283–303.

Sasaki, K. 1982. Estimation of the consumer demand system in postwar Japan. Collaborative paper no. CP-82-14, International Institute for Applied Systems Analysis, Laxenburg, Austria.

Scandizzo, P. L., and C. Bruce, 1980. "Methodology for Estimating Agricultural Price Incentive Effects." Washington, DC: World Bank Staff Work. Pap. No. 344.

———, Hazell, P. B. R., and Anderson, J. 1984. *Risky Agricultural Markets: Price Forecasting and the Need for Intervention Policies*, Boulder, CO: Westview Press.

Schrader, L. F., and King, G. A. 1962. Regional location of beef cattle feeding. *Journal of Farm Economics* **44**:64–81.

Secretaría de la Presidencia, Mexico. 1973. *Lineamientos de la Política Económica y Social del Sector Agropecuario*, Mexico, DF (December).

Secretaría de la Presidencia (Ministry of the Presidency), Mexico. 1983. A program for Mexican agriculture. In: *The Book of CHAC: Programming Studies for Mexican Agriculture* (R. D. Norton and L. Solís, eds.) pp. 162–99. Baltimore: The Johns Hopkins University Press.

Sengupta, J. K., and Portillo-Campbell, J. H. 1970. A fractile approach to linear programming under risk. *Management Science* **16**:298–308.

Shackle, G. L. S. 1961. *Decision, Order and Time in Human Affairs*. Cambridge: Cambridge University Press.

———. 1949. *Expectations in Economics*, Cambridge: Cambridge University Press.

Sheehy, S. J., and McAlexander, R. H. 1965. Selection of representative bench mark farms for supply estimation. *Journal of Farm Economics* **47**:681–95.

Shubik, M. 1977. Competitive and controlled-price economies: The Arrow-Debreu model revisited. In: *Equilibrium and Disequilibrium in Economic Theory* (G. Schwodiner, ed.), pp. 213–24 (Cowles Foundation Paper No. 461). Dordrecht, Holland: D. Reidel.

Shumway, C. R., and Chang, A. A. 1977. Linear programming vs. positively estimated supply functions: An empirical and methodological critique. *American Journal of Agricultural Economics* **59**:344–57.

SIECA. 1981. *Un Marco Cuantitativo para Planificación Agrícola: Proyecto Estudio de Desarrollo Agrícola con el Modelo Agrícola Centroamericano*. Centro de Estudios Centroamericanos de Integracion y Desarrollo, SIECA, Guatemala.

Silberberg, E. 1978. *The Structure of Economics: A Mathematical Analysis.* New York: McGraw-Hill.

Simmons, R. L., and Pomareda, C. 1975. Equilibrium quantities and timing of Mexican vegetable exports. *American Journal of Agricultural Economics* **57**:472–79.

Smith, V. L. 1963. Minimization of economic rent in spatial price equilibrium. *Review of Economic Studies* **30**:24–31.

Spreen, T. H., and Takayama, T. 1980. A theoretical note on aggregation of linear programming models of production. *American Journal of Agricultural Economics* **62**:146–51.

Stanton, B. F. 1977. Notes on the use of the IBM MPSX linear programming package. A.E. Res. 77-14, Dept. of Agricultural Economics, Cornell University, September.

Swanson, E. R. 1959. Selection of crop varieties: An illustration of game theoretic technique. *Revista Internazionale di Scienze Economiche e Commercialli* **6**:3–14.

Takayama, T., and Judge, G. G. 1964a. Equilibrium among spatially separated markets: A reformulation. *Econometrica* **32**:510–24.

———, and Judge, G. G. 1964b. Spatial equilibrium and quadratic programming. *Journal of Farm Economics* **46**:67–93.

———, and Judge, G. G. 1971. *Spatial and Temporal Price and Allocation Models.* Amsterdam: North-Holland.

Tauer, L. W. 1983. Target MOTAD. *American Journal of Agricultural Economics* **65**:606–10.

Thomas, W., Blakeslee, L., Rogers, L., and Whittlesey, N. 1972. Separable programming for considering risk in farm planning. *American Journal of Agricultural Economics* **54**:260–66.

Thompson, S. C. 1967. An Approach to Monte-Carlo Programming, Study No. 3., Dept. of Agriculture, Farm Management Section, University of Reading, Reading, England.

Thomson, K. J., and Hazell, P. B. R. 1972. Reliability of using the mean absolute deviation to derive efficient E, V farm plans. *American Journal of Agricultural Economics* **54**:503–6.

Throsby, C. D. 1967. Stationary-state solutions in multi-period linear programming problems, *Australian Journal of Agricultural Economics* **11**:192–98.

Tirel, J. C. 1971. General design of French model. In: *Economic Models and Quantitative Methods* (E. O. Heady, ed.). Ames, IA: Iowa State University Press.

Tramel, T. E., and Seale, A. D., Jr. 1959. Reactive programming of supply and demand relations—applications to fresh vegetables. *Journal of Farm Economics* **41**:1012–22.

Tsiang, S. C. 1972. The rationale of the mean-standard deviation analysis, skewness preference, and the demand for money. *American Economic Review* **62**:354–71.

Turnovsky, S. J. 1968. Stochastic stability of short-run market equilibrium under variations in supply. *Quarterly Journal of Economics* **82**:162–67.

———. 1978. The distribution of welfare gains from price stabilization: A survey of some theoretical issues. In: *Stabilizing World Commodity Markets*, (F. G. Adams and S. A. Klein, eds.), pp. 119–48. Heath: Lexington.

Von Neuman, J., and Morgenstern, O. 1944. *Theory of Games and Economic Behavior.* Princeton, NJ: Princeton University Press.

Walker, O. L., Heady, E. O., Tweeten, L. G., and Pesek, J. T. 1960. *Application of Game Theory Models to Decisions on Farm Practices and Resource Use.* Iowa State University Agriculture Experiment Station, Research Bulletin No. 488, Ames, IA.

Wicks, J. A., and Guise, J. W. B. 1978. An alternative solution to linear programming problems with stochastic input-output coefficients. *Australian Journal of Agricultural Economics* **22**:22–40.

Willett, K. D. 1982. *A General Equilibrium Analysis of the Economic Effects of Pollution Control Policies*. Ph.D. dissertation, University of New Mexico.

Willig, R. D. 1976. Consumer's surplus without apology. *American Economic Review* **66**:589–97.

_____. 1979. Consumer's surplus without apology: Reply. *American Economic Review* **69**:469–474.

Willis, C., and Hanlon, W. 1976. Temporal model for long-run orchard decisions. *Canadian Journal of Agricultural Economics* **24**:17–28.

Yaron, D. 1967. Incorporation of income effects into mathematical programming models. *Metroeconomica* **19**:141–64.

_____, Plessner, Y., and Heady, E. O. 1965. Competitive equilibrium and application of mathematical programming. *Canadian Journal of Agricultural Economics* **13**:65–79.

Zusman, P. 1969. The stability of interregional competition and the programming approach to the analysis of spatial trade equilibria. *Metroeconomica* **11**:45–57.

Index